Family Bonds

Family Bonds

Free Blacks and Re-enslavement Law

in Antebellum Virginia

TED MARIS-WOLF

The University of North Carolina Press Chapel Hill

To Rachel and Micah,
loves of my life

Contents

Illustrations

Family Bonds

Though the ideas, relationships, and situations I explore in the following pages will likely interest those who follow debates over law, race, and citizenship today, this is the exploration of what it meant to live as a free African American in one section of the upper South from the American Revolution through the Civil War. It is the story of free blacks' collective efforts to be accepted as Americans, to pursue life, liberty, and happiness by protecting family bonds, navigating local courts, and securing their hard-earned property.

Sometimes, the best way to see the Big Picture is by examining little ones. I have thus chosen to tell this story as much as possible from the perspective of free African Americans, through interwoven and overlapping minibiographies of those who were threatened with expulsion and hired white attorneys to help them petition local and state authorities for options, even for enslavement to a white owner of their choosing if necessary. I am especially interested in such individuals' relationships to the laws of their land, as well as to those individuals responsible for the law's creation and enforcement. In this respect, this is a study of interracial Virginia neighborhoods before the Civil War and the fault lines that found their way onto papers preserved in county courthouses throughout the state. How these documents were made reveals the context of their content and provides a window into their makers' minds, leading us past the hands of white lawyers to shared goals of African American clients, acquaintances, and neighbors. Though little known in our day, Henry Champ, Araminta Frances, Mary Elizabeth Roland, and others became well known in their communities. Something had gone terribly wrong in their efforts to belong in their neighborhoods, and as a result the machinery of the law had been set in motion against them. As free people, however, they courageously engaged with the very legal system that threatened them, and they did so in ways they believed they might succeed. For these individuals, their claim to belonging largely hinged on their resourcefulness and longstanding reputation in their neighborhoods.

Law mattered to free African Americans in the nineteenth century, as it does to undocumented workers today, but what mattered more than one's residency status was the degree to which a free black person was known and valued as an upright individual and reliable worker in his or her community. To be seen as "a man of good habits & correct deportment" or a woman "of exemplary moral worth" or a "usefull and an excellent citizen" by one's white neighbors was to be considered exempt from at least a portion of race-based laws intended for more "dangerous & troublesome neighbours" of color.[2] In how they conducted their lives locally, many free black individuals who lived in violation of the expulsion law overcame demeaning racial stereotypes they inherited from contemporary white society at large to earn their neighbors' respect, or at least good words, when required.[3] In this way, even white Virginians who believed in the abstract that free blacks should be removed en masse from the state were frequently willing to overlook the letter of the law in order to vouch for an individual they saw as belonging, who, as one neighbor said of another, "has lived in our neighborhood from infancy without reproach."[4] Many of the relatively few free blacks who found themselves threatened by expulsion countered by mobilizing the circles of whites who knew them well, who worshipped in the same congregation, drank in the same tavern, or labored or lived alongside them. At such times, sympathetic white neighbors were willing to stake their good names on those of free black residents—even in a racial climate where calling another white man "a damned rogue—worse than a free negro" could invite a $1,000 lawsuit for damages.[5] The significance of law—now as then—lies in its application, and the law of nineteenth-century Virginia mattered to free blacks to the degree that it was applied by neighbors and local courts or by themselves to advance their interests. For some, it dictated the limits and possibilities of freedom. For others, it seems not to have mattered much at all, until the day a white acquaintance decided to use his position on a grand jury to label them or other black neighbors as illegals. In these cases, many free African Americans employed attorneys to prevent, slow, stop, or undo the actions of such whites and the legal processes they initiated to a far greater degree than we have assumed.

Sporadic roundups of illegal free black residents demonstrated just how much race could matter in the nineteenth-century Upper South. Some free blacks were targeted by their local court because they were successful property holders or businesspeople. Jealous white neighbors were often the ones who directed authorities to apply the expulsion law to those next door or down the road. For others, an illicit interracial affair or desperate economic circumstances had the same effect. African Americans knew that the enforcement of the expulsion law (like that of all laws) was neither consistent nor predictable. They also knew that not all freedoms were equal. If legal freedom ultimately required their removal from home and separation from loved ones, then for some African Americans, legal enslavement became preferable. Upon reaching safe haven in Canada in 1853, Isaac Forman, a twenty-three-year-old man who had fled Richmond by steamship, confessed that freedom without family lost much of its meaning. Forman wrote to Underground Railroad operative William Still, "What is freedom to me, when I know that my wife is in slavery?"[6] Following this logic, free blacks helped create what mistakenly has been considered to be the most restrictive race-based Southern law of the antebellum period, Virginia's "voluntary enslavement" law of 1856; a protective measure of last resort, urged by those who faced the reality of removal and the separation from families who straddled freedom and slavery. Not only did African Americans help shape the legal culture of their communities, but they advanced their interests by influencing the creation and use of antebellum state law, an achievement that has been overlooked.

In the story that unfolds below, we are again reminded of a tragedy of United States history. Not only did the South's legal system before 1865 keep millions of Americans unfree and treat them unequally; certain black people who did achieve their liberty before the Civil War faced a threat to one of the most important liberties of all—the freedom to remain in one's lifetime home among family and friends. Free African Americans were creative and resilient and could petition for a right to residency, even self-enslavement, to protect themselves and those liberties they held most dear. In the process, these everyday men and women used the law and the services of white lawyers to claim certain basic rights they believed were due all free Americans.

INTRODUCTION

As autumn approached in 1859, Henry Champ, along with his wife and five young children, absconded from Frederick County, Virginia, leaving home and loved ones behind for new lives in the verdant hills near Barnesville, Ohio. Like a fictional fugitive in the recently published *Uncle Tom's Cabin*, Henry Champ undertook his epic journey to secure liberty for himself and his family on Ohio's free soil. Champ was unusual, however, in that he had been free—by birth—in Virginia, and his story reminds us that the iconic crossing of the Ohio River not only symbolized the perilous attainment of freedom for enslaved individuals escaping the antebellum South, but for some free blacks as well.[1]

Up until their flight from Virginia, Henry and Anna Champ had led lives typical of the state's nearly sixty thousand free blacks.[2] They had begun a family, secured livelihoods, and chose to selectively follow state law, according to their changing needs and circumstances. Annual tax lists compiled by the local Commissioner of the Revenue testify that Henry and Anna Champ consistently increased their personal property, from nil in 1851 to $30 in household and kitchen furniture in 1857.[3] Entries in the federal census tell us how: through hard work in their community—Henry as a blacksmith and Anna as a "washer."[4] Like other hardworking folks then (and now), Henry Champ avoided paying his taxes on at least one occasion. In February 1854 the assessor listed him among other delinquent free black residents in the county, and the local court ordered him "to be hired out" by the sheriff until his levy had been paid, as the law directed. Local custom typically muted the law in Frederick as it did in other counties, however, and Champ simply went about his business, a few pennies richer. He and most of the others listed "were not hired for want of bidder."[5] Despite his periodic unwillingness to pay state taxes, Henry made sure to comply with other state laws. Upon turning twenty-one in 1847, he followed the letter of the registration law by visiting the county court clerk to obtain his "certificate" (or so-called free papers). Through the eyes of the clerk, we have our only glimpses of Henry Champ, "a black or dark tawny coloured man twenty one years old," who stood "five feet five and a quarter inches" with "a scar on the forehead above the left eye." Most importantly, the clerk had scribbled that Champ "was free born[,] his mother being a free woman."[6] As inaccurate and insulting as their contents could be, one's freedom papers were cherished as tangible though paper-thin proofs of one's liberty, when needed.[7]

In Virginia, as elsewhere in the South, children inherited the legal status of their mothers, so one's race, even that of "a black or dark" man like Champ, did not necessarily denote one's legal status.[8] In Frederick, as in other Virginia counties, color lines ran crooked, despite the long-standing efforts of the state's legislators to create a biracial society, at least on paper, in which whiteness equated a person with freedom and blackness slavery. Virginia's laws—and authorities' willingness or ability to enforce them— had lagged behind the messiness of lived reality since the first days of the colony, as men and women of European, Native American, and African descent had mixed and given birth to children whose appearance and complex identities defied simple labels.[9] The elite white men who drafted the laws of early Virginia nonetheless sought to invent and maintain racial categories that served as legal ideals, in which whites were innately entitled to liberty, blacks belonged as property, and Natives existed as free noncitizens.[10] One's race, as a social construction, could be a boon or a severe disability, and individuals throughout the eighteenth and nineteenth centuries attempted to use Virginia's race-based law to their advantage when possible. White men claimed the social and political privileges provided by law, as did white women to a lesser extent, while enslaved individuals petitioned their courts to be considered white or Native American when such an action offered a plausible route to freedom. Race mattered, but the weight of its reality in day-to-day life was determined by one's acquaintances and neighbors in ways that were never as clear-cut as Virginia law suggested.[11]

By Champ's day, racial hostility and discrimination were facts of life for African Americans, but for those who had won their freedom or had been born free, their status entitled them to certain legal rights denied those who remained enslaved. Free African Americans in Virginia could own property, file suits, write wills, and hire white attorneys to represent them and file petitions on their behalf in local courts or the state legislature in

Richmond. Though not citizens, free blacks often lived their lives as if they were. By participating in the everyday affairs of their neighborhood—by cultivating white acquaintances, attending mixed-race congregations, working alongside white tradespeople, even boarding in white families' homes—free blacks performed the roles of respectable citizens denied them by Virginia law.[12]

I have chosen to begin this book with Henry Champ's story because it echoes our commonly held understandings of the challenges and tragedies that accompanied the lives of blacks in a society governed by racial prejudice—something many of my African American students still sadly relate to today. They are unsurprised by the circumstances of Henry Champ's life in antebellum Virginia and understand and sympathize with his family's decision to flee to Ohio. In fact, many of my students can relate stories from their own family histories of relatives who left the South in the twentieth century for new yet uncertain lives in the North. Like their relatives who fled racial terror, mass incarceration, and countless indignities in twentieth-century Virginia, Champ and his family were pushed from their home as much as they were pulled by the promise of life in the North.

Henry Champ lived in violation of a state expulsion law that made him (and as many as twenty thousand other free African Americans) illegal residents by the late 1850s.[13] The law stipulated that no black person freed after 1 May 1806 could remain in Virginia longer than one year after reaching the age of twenty-one without gaining permission.[14] In this, the law could not have been more clear; Virginia was to be a land for whites (who were by definition free) and blacks (who would always be enslaved). Those in between (newly freed blacks) had to find another state or country in which to take up residence. Champ had violated the expulsion law on three accounts: First, though he had been born free, his mother (who had been free at the time of his birth) had won her freedom *after* 1 May 1806, the cutoff date for a free person's (and her children's) exemption from prosecution under the expulsion law. Second, Champ was thirty-one years old by 1857, exceeding by a decade the limit to his legal residency in the state. Finally, though Champ had diligently registered himself at his first opportunity, demonstrating his upright character to local authorities, he had neither sought nor attained "lawful permission" to remain in Virginia after his twenty-first birthday, which was required by the law.

In an unusual flurry of activity, in Frederick County from November 1857 to June 1858 circuit court grand juries had indicted eighteen free blacks in addition to Henry Champ—eight women and ten men—for re maining in the state without lawful permission. Located in Virginia's northern tip, Frederick County was home to more than twelve hundred free blacks, who comprised 7.3 percent of the county's population, more than twice the state average. Of those charged with living in the county illegally, nine were convicted, including Henry Champ. By state law, these nine faced the prospect of permanent enslavement through public auction by the county sheriff.[15] How had Champ managed to live and work ten years in Frederick County illegally? Had anyone noticed? If they had, why hadn't they reported him to the sheriff or some other authority? We also wonder why Champ himself felt comfortable living as an "illegal" for all of those years, at least comfortable enough to seek out the county clerk to register himself during that time. Had he known about the 1806 law?

According to local custom and community norms, it would be extraordinary for a free person to actually be re-enslaved as the result of conviction for remaining in the state illegally (which almost never happened), though his indictment must have jarred Champ's sense of what was normal or customary in the county. Indeed, the law's potential to overrule or negate longstanding local custom prompted Champ to earnestly fight to prevent his conviction by hiring a white lawyer, which fellow free blacks routinely did to conduct business in the courthouse.[16] First, he pleaded not guilty to the charges brought against him, and when that did not work, pleaded guilty—to no avail.[17] Thus, having been swept up in one of the state's rare roundups of illegal black residents, Champ found himself a convicted criminal for continuing to live in the land in which he had been born free and faced the prospect of becoming a slave.

This picture of Champ is a familiar one, resembling that drawn by most scholars of free black life in the South before the Civil War. His story seems to confirm our understandings of the powerful role of race in our nation. Indeed, freedom—even for a free-born man of color—was fragile and could be taken away with the stroke of a judge's pen. According to law, judge Richard Parker, a wealthy slaveholder who traveled Virginia's thirteenth circuit, had the power to make Champ an absolute slave, to condemn him to a life of toil that would likely have led him to a cotton or sugar plantation in the Deep South. Unwilling to leave his fate to the court, however, Champ resisted his conviction and devised a way to escape the threat of enslavement by employing his social connections and standing in the community in ways that might not have been possible fifty or one hundred years later in a southern court of law.[18] On the same day he received his conviction in court, Champ engaged his lawyer to draft a petition for self-enslavement to William Strother Jones, a prosperous farmer who owned sixteen slaves, whom he apparently knew. Already one of the few free blacks in Virginia ever to be indicted then convicted by his county court for violating the expulsion law, Champ became one of an even smaller group who took advantage of the state's 1856 so-called voluntary enslavement law, which allowed free blacks to enslave themselves in a complicated process that involved selecting their own master.

With the assistance of white allies—his attorney and Jones—Champ used one Virginia law to counter another, or at least to stall its further enforcement. Champ filed the petition, it seems, with little intention of following through with it.[19] Instead, Judge Parker allowed Champ's petition to delay his sentencing until the following term of court, in November, five months away.[20] When the Frederick County Circuit Court met again that fall, Henry Champ had vanished and so had his family. Parker dismissed Champ's fraudulent petition for self-enslavement and perfunctorily issued an order to bring him to judgment.[21] Champ never saw Parker's order nor faced judgment in a Frederick County courtroom. By then, he, Anna, and their children—Sarah, Harriet, Charles, Francis, and Mary—had settled in Barnesville, Ohio, where they began life anew among other free blacks who had left Virginia and North Carolina in recent years.[22]

■ This is a book about thousands of free African Americans like Henry Champ who attempted to forge meaningful lives in their neighborhoods while residing there illegally. Neither aliens nor citizens, free blacks claimed their liberty and a right to residency among those they loved and knew well, and pursued their lives, their liberty, and their family happiness in places where they had roots. Some, like Champ, were ultimately unsuccessful and left home for uncertain futures in Ohio, Pennsylvania, Liberia, or on other "free soil" where they found equally complicated laws and societies that were neither kind nor welcoming to free people of color. On the other extreme, a small group of those who stayed found themselves singled out, threatened with re-enslavement, and as a last resort, sought new owners of their choosing. However, many managed by the force of their humanity and through hard work to claim a right to residency they believed they were due, and convinced white acquaintances to make room for them in their homes, on their land, in the church, or in the broader community.

This is also a book about law, in the broadest sense, and the people who made it, broke it, or used it to improve their lives or attempt to ruin those of others in Virginia through the Civil War.[23] As it does today, law in Henry Champ's Virginia reflected and shaped the culture, society, and behavior it presumed to regulate. Even if Champ had been unaware of the expulsion law prior to his indictment in 1857 (highly unlikely indeed), it was the law, or rather its enforcement, that shaped the course of his and his family's life forever after. Champ's experience in Frederick County demonstrates the degree to which the law mattered when it was applied and the willingness of free blacks to use the law to challenge enforcement and the legal processes it unleashed. The stories of Champ and others also show how African Americans constructed their lives before their indictments, by employing state law selectively and visiting their courthouses when necessary, in an attempt to avoid the kind of harassment that Champ ultimately experienced. Below, I examine instances in which the expulsion law mattered and when it did not to free blacks and their white neighbors. I explore the logic of its creation, enforcement, and nonenforcement as well as its role in reflecting and shaping the neighborhood life it was designed to regulate.

Tracing the workings of the law-in-the-books in the past reveals important aspects of everyday life for individuals like Henry Champ, but the informal, unwritten, and unspoken laws forged and enforced at the individual, group, or neighborhood levels mattered too, especially to free blacks who lived as illegal residents. Where formal, written law could not protect them, they followed informal codes of behavior in household relationships, church gatherings, or neighborhood associations in which hard-earned reputations could command enough reciprocity from those who saw themselves as honorable to counter the threat or weight of formal law's enforcement. In the following pages, I show that these informal, almost invisible forms of law existed not only outside, alongside, or in opposition to formal law, but often *within* formal law and its operation in local courthouses. One's demonstration of community norms could trump the letter of the law and one's reputation (that is, one's perceived commitment to community norms over time) hovered like a halo or hung like a dark cloud over one when he or she entered the courthouse to indict a neighbor, file a petition, or plead for innocence. In expanding our lens on local law to include the reputation forged by free African Americans, as well as those of neighboring whites, I build upon a vast and expanding literature by historians who have pushed the study of law far beyond an examination of statutes and the men who passed them.[24] Not only am I interested in the everyday people who used and shaped formal law (as I believe free blacks did as well as their white counterparts), I seek to show that the forces that governed everyday life encompassed a wide range of competing formal and informal codes, norms, and customs. In this way, the laws of the land include those laws-in-the-books as well as less formal laws that could affect one's life as much as a formal statute.[25]

When viewed in the light of the laws of the land and not simply the formal law of government, the logic behind the actions of Henry Champ and other illegal residents of Virginia enters into focus more clearly than before. We begin to understand why individuals made the choices they did within a broad range of constraints that confronted them—from those of conscience, knowledge, or moral principles to those of household, neighborhood, or community norms. Champ's indictment, conviction, petition for self-enslavement, and then dramatic flight from Virginia to Ohio were extraordinary, but the process through which Champ sought to safeguard his and his family's freedom—at every step—was not. Prior to Henry's indictment, he and Anna Champ had woven themselves and their loved ones into the social and economic worlds of their Frederick County neighborhood in ways that free African Americans, especially those who lived in the state illegally, forged, maintained, and respected customary rights within their communities. Champ's case stands out as an exception to the general success of Virginia's illegal free black population in asserting their claims to residency in ways that whites and fellow free blacks recognized. Though state law theoretically denied them the right to remain in their home communities after more than one year of freedom, thousands of African Americans forged the necessary social and economic bonds within their neighborhoods and lived according to the letter of those less formal neighborhood laws to help counter statutes that could at any time be used against them.

Following the less formal laws of local churches, taverns, and workplaces, free blacks who lived in Virginia illegally commonly behaved as if they were truly legal residents, an extralegal fiction that most neighboring whites, including local officials, tacitly accepted. Because many free blacks sought to appear as respectable and worthy residents in their communities, white neighbors often supported African Americans' claims to legal residency, even when such claims clearly violated state law and perhaps even their own personal racial prejudices.[26] Though free blacks had no legal rights as citizens before the Civil War, the laws of Virginia and of other states recognized certain rights of free residents, which allowed free African Americans to buy and sell land, challenge their black and white neighbors in civil suits, and employ white lawyers on their behalf to file motions, petitions, and other actions in their local courts. Beyond state law, free blacks asserted (and white neighbors largely accepted) their right to residency in their home communities, where they were well known and had established reputations, often first while enslaved, then as free people. As it turns out, formal written law was just one aspect of the laws of the land that free blacks had at their disposal.

In a surprising number of instances, attorneys and judges viewed residency in Virginia by free blacks of "good character" as a kind of right of freedom, even to a greater degree than state law allowed.[27] The steadfast and long-standing contributions of African Americans in their communities and neighborhoods in spite of enduring legal, social, and racial restrictions made it difficult for many republican-minded judges and white neighbors who knew them well to sanction their forced removal in county courts, where abstract principles of the law met real people and the other laws they brought with them to court.[28] Beyond a general unwillingness to sanction the removal of free blacks (as they had the removal of Native Americans at various points in the nineteenth century), white Virginians exhibited a tolerance of free black neighbors that is surprising, especially in light of what followed—Reconstruction's demise and a century-long wave of horrific violence against African Americans in Virginia and throughout the South.

With the institution of slavery intact before the Civil War, white slaveholders and poorer whites made room in their communities for African Americans who were born free or had become free after the American Revolution. Some localities exhibited a greater tolerance than others, and a survey of free black communities across the state shows that the parameters of one's liberty were defined by personal circumstances and the degree to which one could successfully weave oneself into the local worlds of neighborhood, work, church, and household, each with its own set of ever-shifting rules and expectations. By doing so, African Americans asserted themselves as rightful residents, and in their everyday lives confronted their white neighbors with personalities, skills, and familiar faces that made certain rights of freedom difficult to deny.[29]

Like Champ, some of Virginia's free blacks were ultimately unable to demonstrate a right to residency to their white neighbors and found themselves singled out for prosecution. In fact, repressive statutes remained on Virginia's books and were sporadically used to target individual African Americans through the Civil War, sometimes with tragic results. On at least seventeen occasions from 1856 to 1865, Virginia county or circuit courts convicted free blacks of remaining in the state in violation of the law and ordered them sold into absolute slavery, as permitted by the Virginia constitution. Perhaps many more were enslaved in the preceding period. The machinery of the law and those driving it could be harsh, calculating, and brutal, as could a white person, whose words to a grand jury could initiate prosecution against a free black neighbor who had lived illegally nearby for years. In at least one case, a Norfolk City woman, Mary Dunmore, was sold into bondage for $100 in 1859 for remaining in the state contrary to law.[30]

Most free blacks who lived in Virginia illegally after 1806, however, never found themselves re-enslaved or prosecuted for violating state law. Instead, those who chose to remain leaned upon an intricate, interracial social fabric they and their families had woven over the years to recognize and affirm their illicit freedom if needed. Even in the city of Richmond, which was among the most repressive localities for free blacks, only 124 individuals were charged with remaining in the state illegally from 1830 to 1860 and of those, only 12 were convicted.[31] The relationships cultivated by African Americans in their daily lives could supply legal assistance if ever the ire, angst, or jealousy of white neighbors crystallized into formal legal action. Such associations could yield competent (if not sympathetic) legal counsel, character witnesses in court, or petitioners willing to stake their good names in support of individual free blacks. Legal cases became contests of social strength and credibility, in which the reputations of free African Americans and their contacts were weighed against those of whites who had offered evidence against them and against the letter of the law, which in the case of expulsion allowed local courts to issue exemptions based upon the perceived character of individual free blacks. Legal cases like Champ's and Dunmore's were relatively rare because contests between the enforcement of state law and whites' acceptance of free blacks were often waged outside the courtroom, in the private arenas of everyday interactions among neighbors, workers, and churchgoers. As a result, it was the rare individual who found himself or herself in the predicament that Champ and Dunmore experienced.

It is hard to prove a negative, but a central argument of this book is that because so few free blacks were re-enslaved under the 1806 law or sought self-enslavement after 1856, the thousands of illegal free black residents whose names surface in census rolls, tax lists, and court books managed to belong in their neighborhood by living lives according to the laws of the land, in direct violation of Virginia statutes. By finding the limits in nineteenth-century Virginia society, we can begin to define the norms of those who lived within them. And so I have sought to identify the most desperate cases of individuals who, rather than leaving their home communities, chose to renounce their legal freedom in return for legal residency as slaves. Through an examination of self-enslavement cases, we encounter other limits present in society, in addition to the limits to freedom felt by free blacks through the Civil War. We can identify the limits of formal law and what its enforcement could—and could not—do. We see the limits to what white Virginians felt they could do in order to protect slavery and maintain racial social hierarchies, even if it meant a less racially "pure" society. We see the reluctance of government officials (at various levels) to overstep the will of the governed, and the limits of individuals to act outside society's norms. Finally, we explore the limits faced by historians who seek to cobble together fragmentary evidence into meaningful narratives of past lives. Below, I have attempted to reconstruct incomplete portraits of African American lives from records created by white authorities like the court clerk who registered Henry Champ, men who had little concern for documenting or preserving the memory of the African American experience. I am painfully aware of the missing pieces which, if discovered, might illuminate an individual's circumstances far better than I have been able to do in the following pages. As a result, I have chosen to point out the gaps in my research with the occasional "perhaps" or "maybe," rather than mask my uncertainty and inability to make further conclusions.[32]

This book examines a collection of petitions for self-enslavement that, despite their rarity, involved rather ordinary folks. In seeking to illuminate the everyday worlds of Virginia's illegal free black residents, I have chosen to examine the cases of those for whom nearly everything went awry. The legal system they employed created the documents, now moldy and often barely legible, that frame their lives and make such a study possible. The extraordinary circumstances they faced in navigating from slavery to freedom and sometimes back again to slavery tell us a great deal about how Virginia's free blacks, in general, used their liberty to claim a right to lives in their home communities in the pursuit of happiness—sometimes successfully, sometimes not. Take, for example, the life map of Judy Cullins, whose story is just recoverable enough so as to raise critical questions about the meaning of freedom to those who had once found themselves enslaved to their white neighbors. In August 1858, thirty-year-old Judy Cullins stood before the Circuit Court in Powhatan County, Virginia, as a newly enslaved woman, with incidents from her life in bondage and freedom inscribed on her body. The court clerk described her as five feet tall, "dark brown," and bearing "a scar on the Nose and one over the right eye," and a third made more recently "on the left arm just above the Wrist."[33] Judy had been born the property of John Cullins; along with her mother, Nancy, and her four sisters, Jane, Ann, Sally, and America, she had been promised freedom in Cullins's will in 1833. It had been a long, uncertain road to liberty, however, as the women were first given to Cullins's two un-married daughters, Henley and Polly, for as long as those white women should live.[34] Polly died first. In 1846, an aged and failing Henley Cullins sought "to provide for her own happiness" and to become "free from the harassment of debts and the management of property," by trading her life-time interest in the surviving women and their children to a neighbor, Creed Taylor, in exchange for "an ample supply of food and raiment, and a comfortable home" for "the remainder of my life."[35]

Henley Cullins died the next year, in 1847, and, as John Cullins had di-rected in his will, Judy, Nancy, Ann, Sally, and America were finally eman-cipated.[36] As for all blacks liberated in Virginia after May 1806, their long-awaited liberty had come with a condition: they had to leave the state within a year. But like so many other African Americans freed in the mid-nineteenth century, Judy Cullins and her family counted on the fact that the state's expulsion law was rarely applied to those who had woven them-selves into the economic, social, or religious life of the community. Like other free blacks who had cultivated reputations as useful, reliable, and integral members of their neighborhoods, they chose to remain where they were and to navigate their way through the legal system, if necessary, rather than to relocate outside Virginia as the law directed.[37]

Judy Cullins wasted little time in exercising her newly acquired legal rights as a free woman. In 1848, she lawfully married a free black man, William Brooks.[38] Less than two years later, she joined her mother and sisters in a lawsuit, demanding that her niece, Martha, who was still held in bondage by Creed Taylor, be released. Likely in retaliation for their par-ticipation in this court action, Judy and her sisters soon found themselves charged with remaining illegally in the state by a grand jury of the county court, on which sat Creed Taylor, the very object of their suit.[39] Judy Cul-lins's case might have ended with her conviction and sale as a slave, which the law allowed, but instead the court dropped her charges in 1851, after a deputy sheriff attested that she was no longer a resident of the county.[40] Despite her supposed departure, however, Cullins visited the same court only two months later to obtain official certification of her legal freedom (her "free papers") as a resident of Powhatan County, an act she repeated in 1854.[41] Though our understanding of Cullins's life circumstances is far from complete, it is clear in this case that local authorities overlooked as-pects of state law to allow a free black woman they knew well to remain a part of her community.

As was so often the case, however, Cullins's circumstances changed, as did the attitudes of at least some neighboring whites. Though officials had been unwilling to fully apply Virginia residency laws to Cullins earlier in the decade, she remained an illegal resident in the state of her birth—a fact neither she nor her white neighbors would forget. By 1858 Cullins must have felt the weight of the law to such a degree that eleven years after first obtaining her liberty, she took her final legal action as a free woman—by renouncing that very liberty. She "desires to choose an owner," her petition to the Powhatan County Circuit Court stated, offering no explanation for her wish. On 25 August 1858, Cullins became the legal slave of William C. Scott, the forty-three-year-old white lawyer who had represented Cullins and her family in the lawsuit they had filed earlier.[42] Thereafter, Cullins all but disappeared from official records, except for a possible appearance in the 1860 census as the unnamed thirty-six-year-old female among Scott's six slaves.[43] Cullins maintained the longstanding community bonds she had worked so hard to forge, at the expense of her legal liberty.

Cullins's journey from slavery to freedom and to slavery again pulls us through time and a scattered heap of historical records in unconventional ways, allowing us to view law and society from the perspective of free blacks who initiated legal processes, pushed for legislation, and used laws they helped create to claim liberties that became all the more meaningful in the face of hostile authorities, restrictive codes, and widespread discrimination. Like the story of Judy Cullins, that of self-enslavement in Virginia is not fully one of individual triumph over a harsh legal system, any more than it is completely one of defeat. To a greater extent than we have recognized, Cullins and other free blacks had a voice in their courts, and through hired attorneys they constructed and communicated narratives (through motions, petitions, or testimony) according to the logic of their situations and designed to help them beat the odds, or to at least come close.[44] Cullins ultimately failed but her legal renunciation of freedom was, as we will see in the cases of others, anything but a clear indication of what her life would look like as a slave for the second time. As with all of the minibiographies presented here, Cullins's raises critical questions about the nature of nineteenth-century southern society, law, and everyday life. For example, how was Cullins able to participate in Powhatan County's formal legal system while remaining there illegally? Why wasn't she indicted by the court for violating the expulsion law in 1848, twelve months after her emancipation as the law directed, rather than in 1850? After some white person or people had gone to the trouble of charging Cullins with violating the state's expulsion law, why were the local sheriff and court officials willing to declare her a nonresident and dismiss the case against

Petition of Judy Cullins for enslavement, 1858. Judy Cullins's petition for enslavement in 1858 contains some biographical information but few details regarding her life circumstances, hopes, and dreams as a woman legally entering slavery for a second time. (Courtesy Library of Virginia, Richmond)

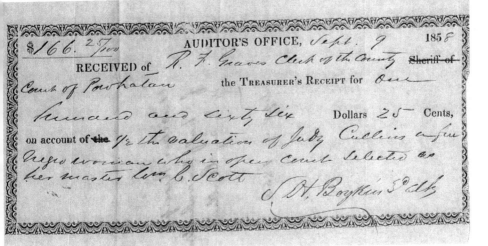

Auditor's Office receipt for enslavement of Judy Cullins, 1858. As directed by law, the Powhatan County court assessed the value of Judy Cullins at the conclusion of her enslavement proceedings in 1858 and collected half the amount from her new owner, William C. Scott. (Courtesy Library of Virginia, Richmond)

her, even though she was still living openly in her home county? Moreover, why was Cullins then permitted to register as a free woman—twice—afterwards, as she continued to remain in Powhatan County contrary to law? Why, at long last, would Cullins choose to give up everything she had obtained during eleven years of liberty, as well as her coveted legal status itself, to become enslaved again in 1858? And finally, what was life like for Cullins during her second stint as a slave? The story of Judy Cullins allows us to better answer questions that apply to the everyday experiences of thousands of those African Americans who lived in the state illegally—not simply those who sought self-enslavement—and to many aspects of the daily lives of the state's legal free black population as well.

From the stories of those who found themselves in lawyers' offices and local courtrooms to defend their interests, we begin to understand more generally the experiences of many individuals who crafted lives in ways to *avoid* direct engagement with the law, who operated instead within alternative moral and legal spheres that bound them to their communities as free people. Whereas historians have analyzed the idea and role of honor in shaping the lives of southern whites to a great extent, less well known are the roles played by reputation and community perception in forging and limiting African American freedom in Virginia communities where white residents never viewed their black neighbors as a monolithic class of people. For those African Americans facing expulsion, reputation became their primary legal instrument, especially for those who then petitioned for self-enslavement to avoid prosecution and remain among loved ones.

This study probes the complicated, ambiguous nature of self-enslavement by examining the phenomenon in Virginia, where the first self-enslavement law appeared in the 1850s, from the perspectives of those who participated in the process. This investigation into the formation and application of Virginia's self-enslavement laws challenges most previous interpretations of self-enslavement legislation and suggests new answers to questions of how and why such laws were created. Moreover, several individual cases highlighted in this work show that free blacks in Virginia were not only knowledgeable about state laws, but actively sought to manipulate them to their own benefit with the aid of local white lawyers. More surprisingly, African Americans were the driving force behind the creation of at least one law—the Voluntary Enslavement Law of 1856—which is commonly referred to as one of the most repressive southern laws passed in the antebellum period.

The life-altering decisions made by self-enslaving free blacks further complicate scholars' understandings of freedom and its meanings to those who struggled to achieve or preserve it in mid-nineteenth-century Virginia. Free African Americans defined their liberty not only in terms of the future—the educational, economic, and social opportunities freedom promised—but also in terms of their individual pasts and their desire to enhance the lives they had already forged in slavery.[45] If in the abstract the goal of newly freed people was to expand their possibilities and maximize their liberty in all respects, for many freedom lost much of its meaning without at least some continuity with their past. Newly freed men and women sought to maintain relations with family and friends, to build upon the personal reputations they had established while enslaved, and to live in the communities to which they had belonged before their emancipation. In this respect, newly freed blacks in Virginia were frequently torn between pursuing opportunities and activities elsewhere and remaining at home among blacks and whites who knew them well. This study is as much about African Americans' notions of freedom in an age of slavery as it is about their dedication to family and home in a society bent on their dislocation and separation.

It was primarily this difficult choice between freedom outside the South and the enjoyment of family and community life at home under the legal constraints affecting free blacks that prompted African Americans in at least forty-three Virginia counties to petition the General Assembly or their county courts for the right to enslave themselves, during a ten-year period beginning in 1854 and extending nearly until the end of the Civil War.[46] Petitioners came from all regions of what is now Virginia—from Accomack and Norfolk counties in the east to Washington, Bland, and Giles counties in the southwest, to Frederick, Loudoun, and Fairfax counties in the north. The phenomenon of self-enslavement in Virginia did not stem from the actions of pro-slavery legislators attempting categorically to enslave the state's free black population—such an interpretation of the law in Virginia is a misreading not only of most white lawmakers' intentions but also of the ways African Americans used the law. To enslave oneself in Virginia, even during the politically tense 1850s (under the law of 1856) or during the Civil War (under a more flexible revised law passed in 1861) was not an easy task. Safeguards in the laws ensured that neither the state nor individual slaveholders could coerce free blacks into servitude.[47] Both that fact and the small number of individuals who sought to enslave themselves indicate that free blacks were not enslaved under either law without their consent—albeit consent that people might feel pressed to offer when they were concerned about the possibility of expulsion from the state. In fact, when the state did play any part in self-enslavement proceedings, it was in an attempt to stymie them. Thus, the number of free blacks who *petitioned* to enslave themselves to a master of choice (more than 110 Virginians) was markedly greater than the number of those who *succeeded* in doing so (65, or about 60 percent). Nor was self-enslavement in Virginia the province of a group of "paupers decrepit with age" who sought support from benevolent whites. Petitioners were mostly healthy, younger men and women, many of whom had spouses and children, either free or enslaved; only a small fraction of self-enslavement cases involved people who were elderly and unable to care for themselves.[48] Of those individuals whose age could be identified, men averaged thirty-six and women thirty-two years old at the time of their petition.[49]

Petitioners for self-enslavement often chose masters whom they knew well, who lived in their neighborhood, or who owned a spouse or family members. And in at least some cases it is clear that legal enslavement to a friendly white master allowed the new slave to enjoy certain rights and privileges usually unavailable to others in bondage. One petitioner transferred his real estate and personal property to his new owner, an acquaintance since childhood, who then deeded it back to the black man's wife after the Civil War. In another instance, a petitioner continued as an entrepreneur during the period after he became re-enslaved: he purchased land, saved money, and expanded his profitable bartending and carriage rental businesses, all while he was the legal property of another. In defining "the boundaries of American liberty," historian Sean Wilentz concludes that "each intervening generation of Americans has worked out its own answers and its own compromises, always within material and ideological constraints, and always in light of how Americans have understood their own history."[50] This study is an examination of the boundaries of American liberty, both for free blacks in Virginia during the 1850s and 1860s and for their white neighbors. For certain free African Americans, the boundary of freedom appeared starkly as that line they would cross should they be forced to leave the state forever without their loved ones and their connections to home. Whatever the benefits of legal freedom, individuals could renounce them in exchange for the freedom to partake of life within their cherished families and communities.

This study reveals an unexpected and equally important boundary of liberty for white Virginians, many of whom portrayed themselves (and are readily depicted by historians today) as people willing to make slaves of free people and to deport free black residents of the state in order to protect the institution of slavery. This study makes clear, however, that the intellectual inheritance of the American Revolution—and the body of republican notions that grew out of that period—still helped to define liberty for most white Virginians, even in the 1850s. However willing some whites were to craft repressive laws against the state's free black population and to discriminate against certain individuals in their communities, the overwhelming majority were unwilling to sacrifice those principles they held most dear to expel or enslave freedpeople *en masse*, even if they thought that doing so might help to save the very economic and social institution that maintained their way of life.

Instances of self-enslavement and the individuals involved in such cases also offer the scholar rare opportunities to examine less well-known aspects of African American life in bondage and freedom. This study attempts to illuminate interludes and events in the lives of free and enslaved African Americans not typically examined, including the period between the death of one's owner and one's emancipation, as well as the journey taken by hundreds of newly emancipated men and women from rural plantations to coastal Virginia and on to new lives in Liberia. It also allows us to reflect in new ways upon the meanings of citizenship and residency to free blacks and to whites through the Civil War, and the degree to which questions regarding both were resolved not through law or in the state legislature but informally in the neighborhood.

The story of Virginia's self-enslavement law, from its creation to its application and revision, is an unexpected one, in which African Americans played a surprising central role. By examining the actions of free black individuals and their personal circumstances, law and society—the Big Picture—in Virginia and elsewhere in the Old South come into view. Men and women in the mid-nineteenth century were indeed influenced by the large forces of their day, but through their actions, relationships, and commitments to community and family, they also shaped the evolution of those forces, and to some extent their own destinies.

CHAPTER ONE

FREEDOM BOUND IN A
NEW REPUBLIC

Daniel Hickman was born enslaved, likely in Accomack County on Virginia's Eastern Shore, in 1787, the same year James Madison and other slaveholding Virginians helped to draft the United States Constitution in Philadelphia.[1] Hickman, like others born after him, entered a society of contradictions in a new nation whose founding principles professed to "secure the blessings of liberty" to Americans and their posterity, yet which denied his personhood and promised to hold him forever as the property of others. If the Revolution had transformed Americans' notions of freedom, the foundations of the peculiar institution in Virginia and other southern states proved strong enough to withstand the tremors created by Revolutionary rhetoric and sporadic calls for general emancipation.[2] Virginia's legislature did embrace the Revolutionary spirit in at least a limited way by prohibiting the importation of African slaves into the state and by passing a law that allowed slaveholders to manumit slaves without having to seek special permission from the General Assembly.[3] Despite the actions of a few Quakers, Methodists, and other individuals who liberated themselves from their human chattel, however, most Virginians remained committed to the notion of a slaveholding commonwealth and republic.[4] In fact, Virginia's reputedly liberal manumission law of 1782 failed to recognize the inalienable right to freedom, which Thomas Jefferson had so eloquently claimed for himself and his white peers, for the state's enslaved population. Rather, the manumission law implicitly defined liberty as a privilege that might be bestowed upon slaves by their owners, and it encumbered the legal freedom some black individuals might now receive with a set of social controls designed to maintain white dominance.[5] Free blacks traveling outside their home county would be required to carry court-certified proof of their status. In addition, those free blacks who failed to keep up with their taxes could be hired out "for so long a time as will raise the said taxes and levies."[6] Such legal controls would prove difficult to enforce, and they did little to ease the concerns of whites who opposed manumission altogether. Even many emancipators or proponents of the gradual abolition of slavery agreed with Jefferson that blacks, once freed, "should be colonized to such place as the circumstances of the time should render most proper." Deportation, not restrictive legislation, would be the only way to avoid the "convulsions which will probably never end but in the extermination of the one or the other race."[7] Jefferson's views on this matter were extreme, but the laws of the new states, from Massachusetts to South Carolina, alienated African Americans—enslaved or free—from most rights due citizens of the new republic.[8] On paper they were to be foreigners of sorts, or at best native strangers.[9]

To the chagrin of Jefferson and many other founders of the nation, free and enslaved blacks in Virginia would continue to recall the Revolution as a struggle to achieve the God-given freedom of all people—and they would do so in the very terms in which patriots had framed their resistance to British authority. For many free people of color in the new nation, Revolutionary notions crystallized in claims to citizenship; either explicitly in petitions to local courts or state legislatures, or less formally in forging lives of quiet dignity in their neighborhoods. Words such as those of Patrick Henry lived on in the hearts and minds of enslaved Virginians, some of whom appropriated the rhetoric of patriots to directly seek "death or Liberty" for themselves, or at least claimed new freedoms within the bounds of bondage.[10]

The overwhelming majority of Virginia slaveholders remembered the Revolution differently. Planters and smallholders alike reconciled themselves to the American dream that had long predated their new republic; their freedom and livelihood rested upon the bondage of others and upon a political system designed to protect their interests.[11] Though the young state was home to a diverse white population of men and women of English, Welsh, German, Scotch-Irish, and French descent who represented a wide range of interests and socioeconomic levels, public opinion among whites of all classes, it had seemed to Jefferson, "would not yet bear the proposition" that their society could peaceably exist without the institution of slavery, no matter how gradually it might be abolished.[12] Virginia Quakers and Methodists who pushed state legislators in the 1780s to recognize liberty as "the birthright of mankind, the right of every rational creature" and to pass a law for general emancipation were in the minority, and the Methodists gradually accommodated themselves to slavery.[13] And from the beginning, a minority of citizens petitioned the state government to repeal the manumission law of 1782 altogether and avert the growth of a free black population that, in their view, threatened Virginia's fragile social stability, already shaken by the war.[14]

In the quarter century after 1782, an appreciable minority of slaveholding Virginians manumitted slaves under the new law, whether to abide by "the Laws of Religion" and of "Morality," to encourage discipline among the enslaved by offering emancipation as an incentive for good behavior, or to smooth the financial transition from tobacco to wheat cultivation.[15] Enslaved Virginians, too, took the initiative to make a law written by and for white slaveholders work to their own advantage. Nearly one-fifth of those manumitted from 1794 to 1806 either purchased their own freedom or had been purchased by an already-free family member.[16] By 1790, within ten years of the manumission law's passage, the free black population in Virginia had more than quadrupled, to 12,866 people, a population greater than that of any other southern state and more than one-third of all free blacks in the South.[17] As a young man, Daniel Hickman saw the population of free blacks in his own Accomack County more than double from 721 in 1790 to 1,541 in 1800, when free African Americans constituted nearly 14 percent of the county's free population.[18]

In 1793, legislators in Richmond passed a law that prohibited free blacks or mulattoes from migrating into the state and another that required those already in residence to register with local authorities—concessions to that part of the white electorate who felt most concerned by the potentially growing presence of free blacks.[19] Yet at the same time lax enforcement of the laws suggests that a more moderate majority of whites felt ambivalent or even tolerant toward free blacks with whom they worked, socialized, and lived in their neighborhoods.[20] As long as the institution of slavery went unchallenged, these whites accepted the presence of a free black minority in their counties.[21]

By the time Daniel Hickman was in his teens, Revolutionary fervor had largely run its course, and for some whites worries over the presence of free blacks in the state had become inseparable from increasing anxieties over a restive enslaved population. A successful slave revolt in Saint-Domingue (now Haiti) had kept many of Virginia's whites fearful of rebellions closer to home throughout the 1790s and beyond.[22] But it was Gabriel's failed slave rebellion near Richmond in 1800 that served as tangible proof to those who were looking for it that the state's racial order was fracturing; although Gabriel himself was a slave, some whites believed that free blacks abetted or inspired subversive activities such as his. For several years after Gabriel's plot to overthrow the state government, legislators engaged in lively debate over how best to monitor or restrain the state's free black population.[23]

A vast range of white opinion emerged. Some wanted to prohibit further manumissions of slaves outright. Others, however, continued to defend the slaveholder's right to release slaves. Finally, by 1806, the General Assembly arrived at a compromise—a law stating that no person emancipated from slavery in Virginia after that time could "after being twenty-one years of age, remain in this state more than one year without lawful permission."[24] Jefferson's vision of making deportation a condition of freedom for blacks had become a legal reality. Moreover, the law stated that any free person who claimed freedom through his or her relationship with another who had been freed since 1 May 1806, as a child might through his or her mother, also had to leave the state when he or she reached the age of twenty-one.[25] The new expulsion law denied the hard-liners their wish to abolish the right to manumit, but the threat of uprooting newly freed people from their homes, friends, and families gave pause precisely to those whites whose humane impulses might otherwise have led them to liberate slaves; thus the law of 1806 acted as a brake on further manumissions.[26] Soon after the law's passage, however, white Virginians began petitioning the Virginia state legislature for its enforcement—a clear sign that local authorities were proving reluctant to apply the law to free blacks in their neighborhoods. For every petition calling for the expulsion of free blacks from the state, another sought permission for a free man or woman of color to be exempted from the law and to be allowed to remain in Virginia. Thus, observant free blacks might well conclude that their white neighbors were anything but unified in their views toward restrictive state laws.[27] Without a systematic analysis of existing court records for all Virginia counties from the years 1807 to 1849, there is no way of knowing the extent to which authorities collectively enforced the expulsion law of 1806 during the first half of the nineteenth century.[28] Studies of several Virginia localities suggest, however, that the law, like the earlier free black registration law, was only sporadically enforced, and that its enforcement varied over time.[29] As a result, far more free people of color remained in Virginia in flagrant violation of the 1806 law than has been previously appreciated.[30] Of Virginia's free blacks in the early to mid-nineteenth century, Luther Porter Jackson seems to have accurately concluded that "despite the avalanche of laws and abuses, they stayed in the state."[31]

White opinion in Virginia had long deplored the rapid increase in the state's free black population, at least in the abstract, and the census returns for 1810 and 1820 seemed to confirm whites' worst fears; by 1820 nearly thirty-seven thousand free blacks appeared on the state's census rolls, almost twice the number of the free black population in the entire Deep South.[32] Moreover, some would-be emancipators were loath to subject such blacks as they might set free to the discrimination that would face them in a white supremacist society, including the possibility, however remote, of expulsion from the state under the law of 1806. For these reasons, some emancipators now included an important provision in their wills requiring freed people to leave the state as a condition of their liberty. More than a few whites, including then-president and former Virginia governor James Monroe, enthusiastically supported the American Colonization Society (ACS), an organization founded in 1816 with the goal of encouraging the nation's free blacks to emigrate to Africa.[33] The ACS had its own Virginia chapter, which helped fund the passage of free blacks to Liberia and provided them with limited support and land upon arrival. Historians continue to debate the intentions and goals of ACS officials, of those who manumitted blacks and sent them to Liberia, and of free black settlers themselves. What is clear is that the organization attracted various black and white Virginians and repelled others (mostly blacks). Some viewed its mission as benevolent—to establish a colony for free blacks in a place where they could thrive as free people, far from the restrictive laws and repression they experienced in Virginia. Others saw ACS objectives as pernicious—to rid Virginia of an unwanted population perceived by prejudiced whites to be unfit for freedom and dangerous to the institution of slavery. Between 1820 and 1865, the ACS succeeded in relocating about thirty-seven hundred free Virginians to Liberia, more than emigrated from any other state, many of whom later died from disease.[34] For most free blacks in Virginia, however, attachment to home and limited enforcement of the law of 1806 made a move to Liberia (or even to some free state or territory within the United States) unappealing and unnecessary.

The expulsion law of 1806, like other repressive laws on Virginia's books, did matter to free people of color, even if it was rarely enforced; the law remained at the disposal of local authorities and could be applied to free black individuals, especially during times of crisis, stress, or heightened racial tension. Ever since the expulsion law took effect, a few free blacks in Virginia had attempted to avoid the threat of expulsion not by moving to the North or to Liberia, but rather by seeking legal re-enslavement. One Lucinda in King George County in 1815 formally petitioned the state legislature for permission "to become a slave to the owner of her husband."[35] Lucy Boomer of Lunenburg County asked the state for permission to "make choice of a Master" in 1835 so that she could remain in the state.[36] Rachel Cox of Powhatan County renounced her freedom during a session of the county court in 1851 after being prosecuted for violating the 1806 law, becoming once again the property of her former mistress's estate.[37] Throughout the first half of the nineteenth century, a handful of free Virginians found creative ways to enslave themselves in order to remain at home in their communities, either by offering themselves for sale for a nominal fee (as did one seventy-year-old woman in Norfolk, who sold herself into slavery for $1 in 1837) or, in contrast, by publicly selling themselves to the highest bidder (as Peter, a resident of Fauquier County, did in 1850).[38]

By New Year's Day, 1831, Daniel Hickman, of "light Black" complexion, now forty-three years old and standing five feet nine inches tall, found himself a free man in Accomack County, his owner Elijah Hickman having emancipated him in his will.[39] Though Hickman left no known record of his feelings or expectations at the time of his liberation, the experience of the more than twenty-five hundred free blacks who lived in Accomack County—and their use of, and treatment by, local courts—suggests that freedom for Hickman held the prospect of gainful employment, the ability to participate in a limited way in the monthly county court; for a very few it meant the opportunity to become a landowner. Despite significant legal and social restrictions placed upon them by white society, many blacks in the county were determined to defend their freedom in court, become landowners, and maintain livelihoods as tradespeople. A census made in St. George's Parish in Accomack County in 1804 lists the names, residences, and occupations of seventy-six free black men and women, depicting a vibrant, industrious community which, despite the odds, worked in skilled, sustainable trades. Men worked as farmers, coopers, sailors, sawyers, shoemakers, carpenters, and ditchers. Women engaged in cooking, spinning, washing, table waiting, and cake selling.[40]

In August 1831 Nat Turner led a revolt of fellow slaves in Southampton County, Virginia, creating widespread panic among the state's white population and thus affecting how Hickman might have viewed his own newfound freedom and how whites would have perceived the presence of a newly liberated black neighbor. In many Virginia localities during the months after Turner's bloody rebellion, whites who feared similar revolts pressed their county courts to enforce some state laws concerning free blacks more stringently, at least for a short time.[41] In October, during its first meeting after Turner's rebellion, the Superior Court sitting in

Accomack County charged forty-two free blacks (seven women and thirty-five men), including Hickman, with remaining in the state contrary to the law of 1806. As unusual as this sizable crackdown on illegal black residents apparently was, what followed was fairly typical of the expulsion law's application during less tense times during the nineteenth century; a collection of unevenly pursued, drawn-out court processes with a wide range of results, indicating that even in the wake of Turner's rebellion, authorities in Accomack viewed free blacks in their community as anything but the monolithic class of indigents, thieves, and potential conspirators that many vocal whites at the time claimed they represented. It is unclear even how seriously these forty-two individuals (and other free blacks living in the county illegally who had not yet been charged) viewed this action by the court. At least two men, Levin and Arthur Custis, won formal permission from the monthly county court to continue living in the state, despite having been emancipated after 1 May 1806.[42] The remaining forty (including Hickman), however, simply ignored the charges against them and continued to lead lives in freedom, albeit a more fragile freedom than it had been before.

In December 1831 Virginia Governor John Floyd urged the General Assembly to respond to "the present crisis" with legislation that would tighten control over enslaved individuals in the short term and appropriate state funds annually to transport free blacks from the state over the longer term. With help from the ACS, Floyd believed, free black emigration would facilitate gradual abolition in Virginia, which would forever remove from the state the possibility of another Turner rebellion. Despite Floyd's privately expressed resolve not to rest "until slavery is abolished in Virginia," as well as the energetic lobbying by a large antislavery coalition of lawmakers, the General Assembly failed to pass legislation that would gradually have ended the institution in the state. Instead, those involved in the Virginia debate over slavery of 1831–32 had reinforced the state's division into various geographic and agricultural regions that differed over the issue of slavery. Delegates from the trans-Allegheny region and from counties in the Shenandoah Valley mostly supported gradual emancipation. Most representatives of counties in the Piedmont and Southside sections adamantly opposed emancipation of any kind.[43]

The slavery debate further unmasked and sharpened other sectional tensions that had plagued Virginia politics for years and had most recently surfaced during the state constitutional convention of 1829–30, in which lawmakers from nonslaveholding districts unsuccessfully sought to introduce universal white suffrage. Virginia was rapidly becoming "two slave

states" in which the eastern half would soon contain "a slave society" resembling areas of cotton cultivation in the Deep South and the area west of the Blue Ridge would constitute "a society with slavery," containing hardly any slaves at all.[44] The Turner rebellion had reignited a debate over slavery and its role in ensuring that the eastern region controlled the state's legislature and resources—an issue over which legislators had argued since the first years of Virginia statehood, when the white population began to swell in Virginia's Western Piedmont, Shenandoah Valley, and trans-Allegheny regions. In 1781, Thomas Jefferson had called unsuccessfully for a revision to the state's constitution, which maintained antiquated "freehold" voting requirements (allowing only select property-owning white males to participate in the political process) and a system of representation in the House of Delegates and Senate that disregarded differences in white population. Despite calls from Jefferson and others in the wake of the Revolution to reform Virginia's fundamentally "undemocratic government," state politics remained under the control of the conservative Tidewater and Southside regions well into the nineteenth century. In fact, sectional tension within Virginia would lead to further revision of the state constitution and increased strife in the 1850s, and eventually to the secession of trans-Allegheny counties from Virginia in 1863.[45]

Just as the issue of slavery took center stage in Richmond shortly after the Turner rebellion, so did the efforts of county courts to indict free blacks like Daniel Hickman on the local level—but vigilance subsided fairly quickly. In Accomack, after several years judge Abel P. Upshur dismissed nine of the prosecutions for violating the expulsion law that had originated in 1831, and he deemed another eight unworthy of prosecution. Some of the dismissed and unprosecuted cases may have involved blacks who had since moved away. Eleven individuals (including three women) were acquitted in separate jury trials that spanned a sixteen-year period—a further indication that, although they felt impelled in 1831 to apply the law to certain individuals, authorities did so slowly and incompletely. Two individuals died before their cases were concluded. Others were not treated as leniently. Twelve men and women were tried and convicted by separate juries, eleven in 1838 (seven years after charges had been filed against them), and were then ordered by Upshur to be sold by the sheriff at public auction on New Year's Day, 1839. At least one man, William Ewell, who had been emancipated in 1819, was auctioned by the deputy sheriff that day to Richard S. Rew, who would later complain to the state legislature that he had paid $526 for Ewell "through feelings of kindness," only to be betrayed by Ewell. In two extraordinary petitions sent to Richmond over

a five-year period, Rew demanded a refund from the state for his expenses in re-enslaving Ewell. Rew explained that his purchase of Ewell had been an act of benevolence, and he gave the impression to legislators that Ewell's bondage had been far milder than the enslavement one might experience normally. Ewell, however, clearly had seen his loss of freedom through very different eyes and soon after he had entered his "second slavery," according to Rew, he had sought the aid of "numerous friends around him, Some of whom were emancipated by the same master & at the same time," who helped him secure clandestine passage by water to New York where "his friends" there could offer "protection & concealment." Rew's petition inadvertently testifies to the bonds of freedom held by those who had first suffered enslavement then had been emancipated together. For Ewell, these community bonds were stronger than the legal status bound to him by the court. Enraged by his financial loss and, perhaps more important, by the humiliation of betrayal by one whom he had "protected" through purchase, Rew demanded that the Virginia General Assembly "refund him the sum which he paid for the negro." Rew argued that because the object of the 1806 law was "to rid the Commonwealth of a useless & burthensome population of free negroes" rather than to re-enslave the state's free black population, Ewell's escape to New York had achieved the state's goal, warranting him a refund for his expenses.[46]

By the time state legislators received Rew's second petition in 1845, the legislative docket in Richmond included measures concerning the state's obligation to provide "common education" to its people and the necessity of promoting canals, railroads, and other internal improvement projects, as well as sectional issues of representation and power between western and eastern Virginians, which had only grown more pronounced since the slavery debate of 1831–32.[47] Sectional tensions on the national level had intensified as well, as the U.S. entry into the Mexican War in 1846 spawned a debate among politicians in Washington over whether the federal government would allow slavery to exist in any territory won in the conflict.[48] Rancor in Congress between Democrats (who supported President Polk's policies in Mexico) and Whigs (who generally did not) shaped political discourse on the state level, which in turn had some effect on local debates over slavery in courthouses and grog shops throughout urban and rural Virginia. By December 1846, Daniel Hickman and the state's roughly fifty thousand free blacks once again found themselves at the center of an issue that had not dominated state or local politics since the early 1830s—the idea of their removal from Virginia.

In his first address to the legislature as governor in December 1846, William "Extra Billy" Smith made the removal of free blacks a legislative priority, infusing his call for "bold and decided treatment" against "one of our greatest evils" with rhetoric reflecting national and intrastate sectional tensions. Smith reintroduced the well-honed language of earlier colonizationists, arguing that an exploding population of free blacks posed physical, moral, and social dangers to the state. Crime rates for free blacks far exceeded those for whites, he insisted. The free black "is a moral leper," and because he occupies "here that space which separates the white man from the slave, he corrupts portions of both races." Smith's solution was to propose a law that would empower citizens in each county at the next election to vote whether or not to remove the free blacks from their midst "after six or twelve months notice." An unabashed extremist on the issue, Smith addressed his more moderate colleagues by explaining the purpose and function of such a law: "Even if the proposed law should not be adopted in a single county, its mere existence, with the power at any time to give it vitality, would materially aid us in the management of this unhappy race" by making free blacks more fearful of and obedient toward authorities.[49]

The proposed legislation embodied the central assumptions behind Virginia lawmakers' passage of restrictive state laws regarding free blacks throughout the first half of the nineteenth century—that statutes themselves, whether enforced or not, might help to restrict the behavior of free blacks and provide greater security for whites, or at least might serve as symbolic political victories to satisfy the demands of more radical constituents. The governor knew perfectly well that previous laws passed to control free blacks largely went unenforced. Those requiring free people of color to register with their respective courthouses every five years and authorizing city or county courts to hire out those who were delinquent in their taxes offered dramatic examples.[50] But for Smith and his supporters, the chief benefit of a removal law would not necessarily be in its *application* against free black individuals, but rather in the message it would send them: they must never take residency in their Virginia "home" for granted.[51]

The following day, the Democratic *Daily Richmond Enquirer* praised the governor's address, and its readers echoed many of Smith's concerns in letters to the paper. "An Eastern Virginian" wrote of the increasing numbers of free blacks in his county, declaring: "I have long been of opinion that their removal from Virginia, if practicable, would be productive of great good, not only to them, but to the white people and the slaves whom

they corrupt to an alarming extent."[52] Another reader, "H.," framed the issue with the familiar argument that free blacks posed a threat to slavery and added that their removal should be followed by efforts to curb "the degraded and unfeeling white man" who "tempt[s] our slaves to robbery." Once laws were passed expelling free blacks and controlling the poor whites, he wrote, "the honest and hard-working portion of our population would rest much more at ease than at the present time."[53]

A third reader, writing from black-majority Essex County, communicated a more mainstream view and one that took into account the perceived opinions of free blacks. He argued that "the free persons of color look to the whites for safety and good Government, and would, under no circumstances, embark in a cause apprehended by the Governor of the Commonwealth." He then invoked the spirit of the American Revolution and the power of world opinion, insisting that "to deprive them of their freedom, to transport them to distant shores, (our Bill of Rights staring us in the face,) would subject us to the derision and ridicule of the world." The same reader warned that "arbitrary proceedings, when opposed to natural rights and the fundamental principles of justice, would be more likely to incur the wrath of Deity, than to secure his commanding approval."[54] The *Richmond Daily Whig* echoed such readers' concerns and deprecated the governor's "extraordinary" proposition to deport free blacks from the state, "which will never receive, we are sure, the sanction or countenance of the Legislature or People of Virginia."[55] To empower the state government to forcibly remove free residents (as "evil" as their presence might be) would constitute an egregious abuse of state power, setting a dangerous precedent that would betray the republican system that Virginia had inherited from the Revolutionary era. Historians have frequently overlooked this view, which in fact predominated among state representatives in Richmond throughout the period from 1831 through the Civil War, when many citizens demanded greater government control of free black (and enslaved) residents.[56]

The *Whig*'s editors underestimated the extent to which some legislators and their constituents would perceive a connection between threats to slavery posed by increasingly aggressive abolitionists in the North and an ever-growing free black population at home.[57] Though in 1846–47 the overwhelming majority of lawmakers apparently found Smith's call for wholesale removal of free blacks politically untenable, legislators in the House followed the spirit of the governor's suggestion by crafting and passing a far less drastic bill; had it been enacted by the Senate, this proposal would have required free blacks to apply for legal residency from the local

court within two months of moving to a new city or county or risk being "considered and treated as free negroes going at large without a register."[58] If this bill or the legislation proposed by Smith had become law, one wonders whether it would have had any practical effect upon the everyday lives of Hickman and other free blacks living in the state, or whether it would have been mostly symbolic, as were other such laws on the books.

Calls for free black removal did not end when the legislature adjourned in spring 1847. White Virginians continued to debate the threat that some thought free blacks presented and the practicality and morality of forcibly expelling them from the state. One Essex County resident implored readers of the *Richmond Whig and Public Advertiser* in June 1847 to encourage their legislators to send free blacks, "if possible, to the remotest corner of the earth" or to "enact some peremptory law, requiring the Sargent or Sheriff of each town and county of the State, on every New Year's day, publicly to hire out, for the year, every free negro, as slaves are now hired out."[59] Such demands were again met by stiff resistance from many—perhaps most—white Virginians, who were wary of the potential cost of statewide removal or hiring-out programs, who feared the increase in state power needed to enforce such a law, or who simply saw deportation and hiring out of free people as "cruel and inhuman, and offensive to the benevolent feelings of the age."[60]

Daniel Hickman and other free black individuals living in Accomack and elsewhere in Virginia likely were aware of the discussions in Richmond and the state's newspapers, but it is difficult to gauge the extent to which the rhetoric of Governor Smith and others affected their everyday lives, if at all. In December 1847 Smith repackaged his expulsion plan in his second address to the legislature in terms he thought would appeal to his critics in the moderate majority of both the Whig and the Democratic parties. Smith dedicated a substantial portion of his remarks to the absolute necessity of combating free blacks' allegedly corrupting influence on slaves, masters, and free laborers by removing them to Liberia or Trinidad. White self-preservation, he argued, demanded immediate action. To mollify those unhappy with the idea of deporting free residents—no matter how troublesome they might be—he contended that blacks were merely *denizens*, not *citizens*, of the state; moreover, he insisted that the expulsion law of 1806 had long ago provided a legal basis for their removal. In fact, because "here the free negro is degraded by our policy—a policy which we cannot relax," he insisted, "I consider, then, that it is cruel and inhuman not to send the free negro away."[61] Reprising one of the central themes of colonizationists since the ACS's inception, Smith now presented removal as a moral imperative; it would improve the lives of whites of all classes, in all regions, he argued, but more importantly removal would allow free blacks to live in societies in which they could experience the freedom that they were incapable of achieving at home.

Free black removal again joined the construction of roads, canals, and railroads—Virginia's connections "with the great west"—as one of the "leading topics" of the day, but opponents condemned this impulse as dangerous and morally reprehensible.[62] The editors of the *Richmond Whig and Public Advertiser* captured the general white mood toward free black removal. That paper's complicated response to the governor illustrated the degree to which the controversy over expulsion was less a disagreement over the capabilities of free blacks than one over the proper limitations of republican government. The *Advertiser* wrote: "That the free negroes must, under existing circumstances, necessarily be a degraded class, and possibly a dangerous one, is admitted; but both our judgment and our feelings revolt at a proposition, which, confounding the good with the bad, looks to the legal banishment of large bodies of individuals whose residence within the limits of the Commonwealth, has been expressly sanctioned by its past policy."[63] Though a few lawmakers loyal to Smith dutifully introduced and promoted legislation "providing that the free negroes shall be removed by counties," as the governor had wanted, that proposal failed to pass either house; so did certain other efforts of extremists to restrict or expel free blacks in various localities.[64]

Exercising the passionate yet ultimately ineffective resolve that he would later bring to bear as a Confederate general at Chancellorsville and Gettysburg, Smith implored legislators the following year to "deport" blacks, who, he again insisted, were unfit to live in freedom within the United States. He now elaborated the argument he had presented in his two previous addresses. Free blacks incited slaves to discontentment, crime, and rebellion, thereby "impairing essentially the value of the slave," Smith said, and they conspired with lowly whites in criminal activity, thus "sapping seriously the character of a portion of the whites." The governor added that free blacks were employed in various jobs that whites needed and therefore had to emigrate west to get, thereby reducing the state's population and its representation in Congress—a direct threat to Southern political power and the future of American slavery. As legal and moral justification for removal, Smith offered a new argument—a comparison between the position of Native Americans and free blacks in American society. "By our law, if a slave be freed he is compelled to leave the state, no matter how strong may be his attachments, or what ties may be sundered," he explained.

"We are also familiar with the policy of removing Indian tribes by force, upon a large scale, and within a few years past; and indeed we are indebted to this policy for the homes we occupy, and the noble state of which we are so justly proud."[65]

Later proponents of colonization would seize upon the analogy between Cherokee and free black removal, justifying the latter with the former and invoking a kind of paternalist "Manifest Destiny" aimed at cleansing Virginia of its "degraded" noncitizens by doing what was supposedly best for *them*—returning them to Africa. No one was more articulate on this point than ACS representative R. W. Bailey, who petitioned the General Assembly in 1850 for an appropriation to fund large-scale colonization efforts of black Virginians to Liberia. He wrote: "The *right of the strongest*, though of dangerous interpretation, exists in nature & in equity; & its exercise is sometimes demanded by sound policy. . . . It authorized the removal of our Indian tribes to a territory west of the Mississippi. Justice is done to them when they are better provided & better protected than they could be here. Humanity is an element of this measure of justice, because their moral as well as intellectual & physical advancement is promoted by the change— as results have fully proved—while its policy is found in the more perfect integrity of our own population." Bailey went on to insist that the lawmaker's right and duty to expel free blacks from the state "for their good & our own, is as perfect in law & equity, political & moral, as that which disfranchises minors or females . . . or as that, which removed our Indian tribes to a new country for their preservation & our safety."[66]

In his *Plan of National Colonization*, published a short time later, Rev. W. S. Brown (a Kentuckian) asked, "Are there any reasons which operated in the removal of the Indian, that may not be brought to bear, with equal force, in the removal of the negro?" Answering his own question, Brown argued that there were now stronger reasons to deport the free black than there had been for the Indian, for whom "the general government furnished the means, and assumed the responsibility of removing him to territories more congenial to *his* pursuits of life, and less valuable to *her legal* citizens." In fact, Brown concluded, it was the duty of Americans to expel all free blacks from U.S. soil, out of "common feelings of humanity towards them, as an unfortunate people; whose destiny is fixed, whose name is a reproach and a by-word, who can never be allowed a voice in the administration of the government under which they live, together with the demoralizing, degenerating influence which their existence in our midst has upon society."[67] As long as removal was for free blacks' own good, banishment was not punishment but liberation. Such notions had a long history in Southern thought, especially in Virginia. In 1796, jurist Saint George Tucker offered a gradual emancipation plan, in which he insisted "that *all men* are by nature *equally free* and *independent*" and lamented the degraded state of African Americans in the United States and the "prejudices, which now form an obstacle to such incorporation" of blacks into mainstream society. Proposing gradual emancipation—but not citizenship—for African Americans, Tucker offered "some middle course" for improving the lives of African Americans and freeing white republican-minded patriots from the mind-bending hypocrisy of holding inalienably free persons in bondage. Tucker's plan would free only females born after its adoption and only once they reached the age of twenty-eight; the children of these women would be born free. In this way, Tucker boasted, "The abolition of slavery may be effected without the *emancipation* of a single slave; without depriving any man of the *property* which he *possesses*, and without defrauding a creditor who has trusted him on the faith of that property." Tucker assumed that African Americans freed by his plan would still be denied equal footing by whites in American society and therefore would choose to leave the United States.[68]

Just as Cherokees, Chickasaws, Choctaws, and other Native Americans had been made scapegoats for economic and social woes earlier in the century, free blacks were identified by Smith, Bailey, and Brown as local, tangible causes for the crises plaguing the state and the nation—the source of supposed discontent among Virginia's slaves, of class divisions, and of sectional tensions. Here and there, whites joined Smith's camp by 1848, calling for "the abolition of the Free Negro race from our limits." Free blacks not only were the cause of "contamination" among the state's slave population, but by their cheap labor they perpetuated "the frauds committed upon the honest laborer, by a system of underbidding," wrote one angry reader to the *Richmond Enquirer*, who called for the assistance of the U.S. Navy in the "shipment" from Virginia of free blacks between the ages of 25 and 45.[69]

One hundred nine citizens of Rockingham County petitioned the General Assembly "for the repeal of the law of Virginia which permits emancipated slaves to remain in the commonwealth of Virginia, twelve months after his or her right to freedom shall have accrued, and to pass in its stead a law compelling all slaves hereafter emancipated to move out of the state of Virginia within one month after his or her right to freedom shall have accrued, and not to return again." "[O]ur only object is to protect our own," the men wrote; by expelling free blacks, the insidious and ubiquitous abolitionist threat in Virginia would also be removed, thus preserving "the right to hold slaves as our private property."[70]

Ninety-three men from Augusta County, in Virginia's Shenandoah Valley, soon entered the fray, filing a printed petition to lawmakers in Richmond that sought to temper Smith's radical comments with a more moderate, practical proposal that might appeal to rational minds on both sides of the issue. Their plan would "entirely remove, with their own consent, the free people of color from Virginia and settle them in *Liberia in Africa*," not by an appropriation from the state treasury, but by allowing local courts to assess property taxes to apply toward the removal of free blacks in their districts who were "willing to emigrate to Liberia." Under this plan, free blacks would have five years to leave the state voluntarily, or face forced removal. The petitioners explained their rationale to those who feared the power of big government and who would resent paying taxes for expelling a free black population not present in their own communities: "Some counties scarcely feel [that black presence], while others are oppressed by it. . . . The measure proposed makes the burthen voluntary in each county. Its own tax is expended exclusively for its own benefit, and it is proportioned to the extent of the evil in each particular county." By 1849, in the minds of many white Virginians, such a plan was considered "mild," in that it removed at first only those willing to emigrate and allowed considerable time for those unwilling to go to Liberia to make arrangements to remove to a nonslaveholding state.[71] A group of Frederick County residents submitted an identical petition shortly thereafter.[72]

Critics of the proposals of proremoval extremists and moderates clung to past arguments, with a twist. For some, legislative attempts to single out free blacks through removal or an additional system of residence permits seemed to violate the paternalist ethos that white Virginians, including those favoring removal, claimed to embrace; in particular, expulsion would violate the rights earned by the very individuals whom benevolent masters would set free—those "poor creatures" who had been their most devoted slaves.[73] The paternalist impulse thus underlay arguments both for and against free black removal. On the one hand, free blacks were to be pitied, protected, and improved as residents in their home communities in Virginia; on the other, paternalist arguments stated that only in Liberia would the free black "acquire, possess and enjoy, of property, honor, or personal privilege—which it is impossible for us to secure to him *here*."[74] Indeed, the pros and cons of colonization to Liberia became a central issue in Virginia's popular press in the spring of 1849 in a way that they had not since the early 1830s.[75] That discussion coincided with a renewed national debate over removal and colonization, as ACS representatives lobbied the U.S. Congress for support. As the nation debated how best to absorb new territory while balancing its free soil and proslavery interests, Americans of all stripes weighed in on the removal of free blacks and the merits or injustice of colonization. Frederick Douglass perhaps spoke for Daniel Hickman and many other free blacks in Virginia who had been charged for remaining in the state illegally when he denounced removal in any form that year: "We live here—have lived here—have a right to live here, and mean to live here."[76]

Though still out of step with the mainstream of his own party and with the majority of Whigs on the issue of removal, Governor Smith had inspired intense debate over the idea that the state should move toward expulsion. In addition, his increasingly complex arguments favoring removal of free blacks likely drew some more moderate thinkers to support notions of voluntary colonization. Legislators had acted on Smith's most recent proposal by forming a special committee to consider removal, but a bill "concerning free negroes and mulattoes" went nowhere (as did a bill "to take the sense of the people on the deportation of free negroes" through popular vote and a proposed amendment to the 107th chapter of the Virginia Code, which dealt with free blacks).[77]

By 1849 Daniel Hickman, now more than sixty years old, still lived as a free man in Accomack County. If Hickman's long-standing indictment or the statewide debate on removal had limited his behavior or his expectations in the intervening years, they did not now prevent him from seeking aid from the Accomack County court. In May of that year, he asked the "Gentlemen Justices" who oversaw court activity that month, William Riley, William P. Moore, Jr., Edward O'Finney, and Edward L. Bayly, to give him an exemption from paying his taxes on account of his "age and infirmity."[78] Rather than prosecute him for contempt of eighteen years' worth of unanswered summonses from the superior court, the justices instead granted Hickman's request. Did Hickman's appearance in the lower court set off a discussion in the white community about the leniency of its law enforcement toward free blacks? Had the superior court been angered by the lower court's willingness to serve an illegal resident while ignoring the fact of his indictment many years before? (After all, the only key differences between the higher and lower court in Accomack were the presiding officials—a group of four gentleman judges in one and a professional judge in the other—and the frequency of their meetings, monthly versus biannually.) Had Hickman's appearance in court served as a concrete example to extremists in the county of how free blacks drained the public coffers and threatened social stability, as Governor Smith had alleged? Or perhaps Hickman had simply invited future court action by reminding authorities of his existence after living quietly, and otherwise lawfully, for nearly two decades. For whatever reason, five months later Commonwealth's Attorney Miers W. Fisher led the elderly Daniel Hickman before Judge George P. Scarburgh in the Superior Court of Accomack, where Hickman pleaded guilty to the offense for which he had been charged in 1831.[79] As judges before him had done with eleven others in 1838, Scarburgh now ordered Hickman to be sold as a slave "for ready cash" by Sheriff Nathaniel Topping "at the Court-House door" the following month and to be imprisoned until the day of his sale.[80] Significantly, there is no evidence that Topping ever sold Hickman in 1849 or in any following year. Instead, Hickman appears ten months later on the 1850 census living with forty-five-year-old Sukey Hickman in the household of Critty M. Warner, a white woman, and her five children.[81]

The actions of the Accomack Superior Court against forty-two free black residents in the wake of Nat Turner's rebellion in 1831, the lack of follow-up in subsequent years, Daniel Hickman's ultimate conviction, and the apparent failure to carry out his sentence mirror the complex dynamics of debate over free blacks in the General Assembly over the same period. Why was Hickman not convicted earlier and sold into absolute slavery? Why wasn't Governor Smith, trying year after year, able to persuade legislators to require or even seriously promote removal of the state's free blacks? Daniel Hickman, along with others charged with staying illegally in Virginia after their emancipation, lived not only in a society founded upon principles of freedom that rested on plantation slavery, but also in an intricate local society enmeshed in layers of additional contradictions.

By 1849, Judge Scarburgh was at last willing to prosecute Hickman's case and to convict him for violating state law. Widely admired by whites in Accomack as an able judge and skilled professor of law, the nonslaveholding Scarburgh had avoided partisan politics throughout his career but remained faithful to the South, later resigning one of the original seats in the U.S. Court of Claims when Virginia seceded from the Union in 1861. In sentencing the elderly Hickman to absolute slavery in his remaining years, had Scarburgh been driven by legal principle—the Letter of the Law—or by the principles underlying Virginia slave society? Perhaps he had been motivated by both. Even in this period of heightened debate over the role of free blacks in Virginia society, however, local officials such as the gentleman judges of the monthly court, sheriffs, and commonwealth's attorneys were nonetheless hesitant to abide by the letter of the law—even when written by a superior—and sell into absolute slavery an aged free man whom they had likely known for many years. (Apparently, they had been

Certificate of good character for Anthony Matthews, 1818. This certificate of good character written by Jonathan Clarke on behalf of Anthony Matthews of Henrico County represents the kind of logic that informed whites' complex attitudes toward free African Americans like Daniel Hickman, who could earn a degree of confidence from their neighbors through conduct perceived as "honorable." (Courtesy Library of Virginia, Richmond)

equally reluctant to reduce to bondage most of the others who had been charged along with Hickman in 1831, whether aged or not.) At the same time, a state government wary of aggrandizing its own authority or violating the liberties even of the most disadvantaged free caste refused to remove what many of its representatives alleged was the most threatening or corrupting element of the state's population.

On a neighborhood level, free people of color knew full well that their liberty could be limited, even negated, by determined local officials should they choose to enforce the state's many restrictive laws. Yet Daniel Hickman and that sprinkling of others singled out by local courts faced ambivalent neighbors on grand juries and less-than-zealous prosecuting attorneys and sheriffs, who were largely content to initiate the occasional case against them without following the law to its harsh, logical end. Here, an item from the census is suggestive. Nathaniel Topping, the sheriff charged with actually organizing the sale of Hickman, lived with John W. H. Parker, a young attorney who would successfully defend a free black family from conviction under the 1806 law not once, but twice, nearly a decade later (see chapter 5). If Topping associated himself with those who defended the rights of local free blacks, he simultaneously did so as a substantial slaveholder and one who embraced the racialist slave system on which much of his personal wealth rested.[82] Owning slaves did not necessarily prevent white Virginians from forming sympathetic views toward free African Americans; in fact it may have somehow freed them to do so. For example, William Riley, who was acting as one of the justices when Hickman had applied for an exemption to taxes, could feel certain that the wealth and power he had accumulated as a successful slaveholder and farmer would not be threatened by the presence of a small number of free blacks in the neighborhood—even one who could no longer afford to pay taxes or a young black "Laborer" like David Crippin, who lived in his household.[83] William P. Moore Jr., another justice that day, was also one of the larger slaveholders in his neighborhood and lodged two free black youths, Oscar Jubilee and Charles Ames.[84] In this way, even orders from the local courthouse faced uncertain enforcement by individuals reluctant to apply legal principles or decisions to neighbors with recognizable faces.[85] At the state level, ambivalent legislators debated the plight of free blacks and whether or not they were due any rights or privileges as residents of Virginia, at the same time that they allowed individuals exemption from prosecution under the law of 1806 and refused to pass a law mandating the removal of free blacks from the state. Did the Virginia legislature have the capacity to remove free blacks from its midst? Perhaps. Lawmakers could have passed a statute requiring forced mass removal in 1846 (or later), but they would have had to rely upon republican-minded county officials, who often looked askance at Richmond lawmakers as they did at those in Washington, to cooperate and to execute the law. But to ask whether or not the majority of Virginia lawmakers seriously entertained the idea of wholesale free black removal or its enforcement is another question entirely. It is clear that what frightened Virginia lawmakers more than an ever-growing free black population or perceived threats to the institution of slavery was an unrestrained government that, if given the power to raid farms and villages to round up free black residents, might one day return to expel or detain free white republicans.[86] In two competing Revolutionary legacies—the urge to deport free blacks en masse and the ideals of antistatist republicanism—republicanism won out. Virginia lawyers and judges proved to be staunch exponents of republican legal principles, and as a group seem to have approached free black clients and defendants they encountered as people with certain unalienable rights in their local courthouses.

CHAPTER TWO

BLACK CLIENTS,
WHITE ATTORNEYS

In December 1829 David Walker drafted a letter from his home on Boston's Brattle Street to Thomas Lewis, a free black resident of Richmond, Virginia. "I having written an Appeal to the Coloured Citizens of the World—it is now ready to be submitted for inspection," Walker declared in a note to Lewis that accompanied thirty copies of his *Appeal* for distribution "among the coloured people" of Richmond. In his self-published tract, Walker insisted that "we (coloured people of these United States) are, the most degraded, wretched and abject set of beings, that ever lived since the world began" and repeatedly mocked the "enlightened and Christian nation" that held more than two million individuals in bondage and half freedom while simultaneously professing "that all men are created equal."[1] In an unequivocal call to arms, Walker warned white Americans that "the tribunal of heaven" headed by "a God of justice" would one day soon "rise up in judgement against Christian Americans" to deliver the justice so long denied African Americans by their white oppressors.[2]

Though it was at first mistaken for yet another innocuous pamphlet "of the class of fanatical tracts upon the subject of religion, now profusely scattered through the country," it took little time for Richmond's authorities to learn that Walker's revolutionary pamphlet rejected Virginia and, more generally, southern law that empowered a "murderous government" to rule by an unjust system unbefitting of "a free republican country."[3] By New Year's Day 1830, the city's mayor had successfully seized twenty copies of the *Appeal* and joined a chorus of anxious city and state leaders in lamenting "an increasing activity in circulating amongst the people of colour insurrectionary pamphlets and speeches."[4] Later that year, Walker published two revised and even more militant editions of the *Appeal*, no doubt articulating the views of many free and enslaved African Americans in Virginia, who viewed the state's legal system merely as an instrument of white hegemony and oppression.[5]

When Walker's *Appeal* arrived in Richmond with its revolutionary message, dozens of resourceful free African Americans in the city were in the process of pursuing, securing, and retaining the services of white attorneys to represent their interests within a localized, race-based legal system overseen largely by slaveholding judges and attorneys. As repressive and downright insulting as Virginia law could be for free blacks, hundreds of free blacks nonetheless believed it worth their time, energy, and limited resources to actively participate in their local legal system rather than take up arms or leave the state—before, while, and well after Walker forcefully called upon "a God of justice" to remake American society.[6] It is true that many free African Americans had no choice in the matter; many found themselves incarcerated as suspected runaways, for failing to comply with state registration procedures, or for such serious crimes as arson, abetting fugitives, or murder. In such instances, those with the means hired attorneys, while most accepted court-appointed lawyers or represented themselves to make their cases.[7]

Thousands of southern free blacks between the Revolution and Civil War, however, actively *sought* legal action in their local courts in ways they hoped might improve their lives. While scholars of antebellum America have tended to focus on the writings of northern free blacks who decried the inherent injustice in American law, hundreds of free African Americans (many of whom were illiterate) claimed that liberty, family life, and residency in Virginia were among their inalienable rights. They made these claims not through published tracts like Walker's *Appeal*, but through their everyday use of the legal system—in motions, petitions, and civil suits they filed in their local courts.[8] County court records, state legislative petitions, and attorneys' account books attest to the fact that these individuals believed that their interests might be served if they sought the services of white lawyers to represent them. Many were incorrect; despite representation, they were defeated by a race-based legal system that complemented a repressive political system that denied them participation and protection as citizens. But historians have tended to overlook the large numbers of free blacks who succeeded in claiming a space in their neighborhoods, primarily by cultivating reputations that kept them out of local courtrooms altogether and, when necessary, by using attorneys to formally help secure that space for themselves or their loved ones. In short, white attorneys frequently engaged with Virginia law at all levels on behalf of black clients.

Scholars have written extensively on antebellum statutes governing free black behavior, and more recently on legal actions taken by free African Americans, but few have sought to examine in any depth the relationships between free black clients and their attorneys in such instances.[9] As a result, we lack a clear understanding of the attitudes of both free black individuals and their white lawyers toward race-based law, courts and legal processes, and relations within biracial communities in antebellum Virginia. Not only did free blacks tap into often-extensive interracial networks to help accomplish their various goals in local courthouses, but white attorneys were a key part of those networks and often played critical roles in legitimizing African Americans' claims to residency, family life, and liberty.[10] According to the laws of the land, free blacks were not citizens, but in their varied legal actions and those of the white attorneys who represented them, many behaved as if they were and hoped—perhaps even expected—their local courts to view them as having a set of inalienable rights as free people. Thus, many African Americans clearly saw themselves neither as "slaves without masters" nor as "almost free," but as free residents who were due a "rough equality" within their local communities. In more than a few cases, white attorneys made it difficult for those who controlled local courts to view free blacks as people without certain basic rights.[11]

■ In January 1833, with David Walker's *Appeal*, Nat Turner's revolt, and a recent state constitutional convention known for its Great Slavery Debate on the minds of many Virginians, Nelly Hoomes walked into the downtown Richmond law office of Herbert A. Claiborne and asked for assistance in "drawing [a] petition to [the] Genrl Assembly for herself & children to remain in the state," costing $10.[12] Hoomes was one of perhaps twelve thousand of Virginia's forty-seven thousand free blacks who lived in violation of the state's expulsion law, which stipulated that no adult black person manumitted after 1 May 1806 could remain in Virginia longer than one year without permission.[13] Though localities rarely enforced the expulsion law to its fullest extent, Hoomes, like many women in her situation, was certainly aware of its potential threat to her family and chose the surest way to prevent its application—by engaging the services of a well-known white lawyer. How did she find Claiborne? Why was Claiborne willing to represent a free black woman like Hoomes? More generally, under what circumstances did free blacks seek counsel, and how often did white attorneys take them on as clients? What did attorneys charge their black clients for their services, and how did this compare to the fees they charged white clients for similar services? Finally, what do relationships between black clients and white attorneys before the Civil War tell us about blacks' understandings of the legal system on the one hand and white attorneys' understandings of their roles and duties as lawyers on the other?

Of the several dozen practicing attorneys in Richmond in the 1830s, Claiborne must have appeared to be among the most responsive to the needs of potential black clients like Nelly Hoomes.[14] In fact, free African Americans comprised at least one-third of his clientele at the time. A survey of account books of Virginia lawyers, as well as information gleaned from selected Hustings Court records and legislative petitions, demonstrates that while some attorneys may have refused to take on free black clients, Claiborne and others chose to regularly represent African Americans during certain periods in their practices. The records of Claiborne are particularly instructive, as by the 1830s he had established a reliable client base among free blacks in Richmond, including those like Hoomes who lived in violation of the 1806 expulsion law. Claiborne's clients included neighbors, laborers, and craftspeople he knew and had hired, as well as individuals whom he had known (or whom his white acquaintances had known) while they had been enslaved.[15] It is clear that Claiborne's clients included individuals who were related to one another, attended church together, lived in the same neighborhood, or who socialized in the same circles. Personal relationships and word of mouth within the black community and among white acquaintances led free blacks to seek the services of Claiborne, whose long list of free black clients by 1832 resembled those of other attorneys practicing elsewhere in the state who took on a number of free black clients during the same period.[16]

Claiborne's account books, and to a lesser extent those of attorneys William Wirt Henry, Garrit Minor, J. J. Chew, James Lyons, and Charles William Dabney reveal that many free African Americans in Richmond and nearby Hanover County and Fredericksburg were aware of race-based state laws on the books, knowledgeable about legal processes, and determined to secure the assistance of white lawyers to aid acquaintances, family members, or themselves, even if it meant devising creative ways to compensate their counsel for services rendered. The account books also demonstrate that at least a few white attorneys were willing to represent black clients in a range of circumstances and apparently did so from time to time without any expectation of full monetary compensation.

Nelly Hoomes sought out Claiborne in 1833 to convert the private facts of her life into a public written narrative, a petition to the state legislature that might win her a special law allowing her to remain in the state, at least for several years. Resourceful, well connected, and proactive, Hoomes managed to convince eight prominent white Richmonders to sign her petition, which Claiborne crafted in language designed to pluck the paternalistic heartstrings of lawmakers. He portrayed Hoomes both as a helpless mother of four small children and one who had rightfully earned her freedom and a place in her community. Claiborne asserted "that Nelly has always been a most faithful and exemplary servant and if habits of industry, sobriety and good order are entitled to reward, merits the commiseration and interference of the General Assembly." Not only did Hoomes claim "her right to freedom" through years of service as a model slave, but she asserted a right to live in her neighborhood, near an enslaved man, Bartlett Hoomes, "who she has regarded as her husband," and who was the father of her four children. As Hoomes's attorney, Claiborne had agreed to advance her claims for basic rights, including those of residency, family, and liberty, but his role as Hoomes's advocate seems to have been at odds with his personal beliefs—at least those regarding notions of African Americans' rights to liberty and residency in Virginia. In his will, written in 1840, Claiborne articulated his thoughts on what, if anything, his enslaved man Dick was due upon the lawyer's death. He wrote, "It is my will and desire that my slave Dick may be indulged in the same kind of employment that he has been in . . . (either by hiring him out or keeping him in the service of the family) as long as he conducts himself with propriety, but if he should become disobedient or addicted to the intemperate use of ardent spirits I direct that he shall be sold—However as I have some reason to believe that his wife & children may hereafter be emancipated if that event should occur it is my will & desire that he may be manumitted & set free at such time as it shall be necessary to enable him to leave the state with them."[17] Apparently, neither liberty nor residency were *rights* due his longtime bondsman. Liberty, in Claiborne's formulation, could be earned through proper behavior, but once free, even Dick, whom he knew well, had to leave the state, as the law directed.

In fact, Claiborne's willingness to represent free black clients, like that of his colleagues, shows but one dimension of a complex constellation of personal and professional interactions with African Americans. As was the case with many lawyers practicing in Virginia between the Revolution and the Civil War, Claiborne's bread and butter rested on the quotidian affairs of his many white clients—deeds, wills, and the division of estates, especially those involving slaves. In addition, he augmented his legal practice with significant returns on hiring out his own slaves to neighbors.

Though by no means an abolitionist, Claiborne supported the American Colonization Society, and at times took less-than-popular positions toward African Americans' right to equal protections under the law. For example, in 1842 Claiborne and James Seddon represented Emanuel, an enslaved man sentenced to die for the murder of another slave, Isaac. Claiborne and Seddon asserted in a clemency petition, "We are confident that the prisoner would have been acquitted had the affray occured between white men."[18] Most of the attorneys secured by free blacks, however, were far less outwardly sympathetic to the plight of enslaved Virginians before the bar. In fact, in their personal and professional dealings most bought and sold slaves and profited from slave hiring at the very same time that many purchased goods from slaves (in violation of state law), defended enslaved people in court (at the behest of their owners), and represented free black clients with dutiful attention. For Claiborne, accepting free black clients appears to have stemmed from a combination of impulses, including the desire to earn a living, to offer pro bono services to poor black or white individuals deserving charity, and to perform his duty in defending the claims of free people, regardless of their color. In addition, Claiborne articulated more concern for women than most men at the time, and might have accepted proportionately more single or widowed female clients (white and black) out of a paternalistic impulse to protect the "so many meek & amiable females & helpless children" he had encountered over the years; women and children who had been "brought to want & misery by immoral and imprudent men."[19]

African Americans sought legal counsel for a variety of purposes, but among the most important was to improve their chances of being viewed by neighboring whites as belonging to their communities.[20] In residency petitions drafted by their white attorneys, free blacks like Hoomes sought permission to remain at home, first from their local courts and if unsuccessful from the state legislature. Petitions crafted for local courts differed from those submitted to the state legislature in style and substance, largely because the anticipated audience changed from one in which free black petitioners were well known by gentlemen justices in county courts to an audience of state legislators in Richmond who lacked personal knowledge of petitioners' circumstances and local reputations. For this reason, petitions submitted to the state legislature were far more likely to include language that differentiated the petitioner from other supposedly less deserving free blacks by appealing to popular racial stereotypes and rhetoric. Most often, these views were articulated in "certificates of character" that petitioners' lawyers designed to recruit the signatures of white neighbors to demonstrate support for the petitioner. In many certificates, white neighbors sought exceptions under the removal law for individual petitioners whom they knew well by appealing to the same brand of racial rhetoric legislators tended to use in their campaigns and public speeches. For example, in a series of certificates crafted by the attorney for Samuel Harris of Essex County from 1808 to 1811, white neighbors insisted "that his decent deportment, would have a favorable influence on the conduct of others of his Color"; "that his morals & deportment have been uncommonly correct for one of his description"; and that Harris was "the most correct man of Colour I have ever known," a backhanded compliment that nonetheless was intended to advance Harris's claims.[21] In order to seek permission to remain in the state from legislators in Richmond, free blacks and their lawyers employed popular racial rhetoric to show how extraordinary petitioners were and how deserving they thus were of basic rights due free people, their color notwithstanding.[22]

Certificates of character bolstered the claims contained within the petition itself, which frequently appealed to legislators' Revolutionary sensibilities of life (in one's home community), liberty, and the pursuit of family happiness. For example, Richard Gregory of Chesterfield County appealed to legislators in 1848 for the opportunity to remain in "the land of his nativity," as did others who asserted "a peculiar attachment to this their native country" and a love for "their native soil."[23] Several petitioners from Accomack County in 1815 equated residency with the right to "enjoy the blessings of freedom" for themselves and their children.[24] One year earlier, Billy from Buckingham County argued that he "became entitled to liberty the greatest of all earthly belongings," which, to be meaningful, required continued residency in his "Native State" or "Native Home."[25] The 1815 petition of Nancy from Cumberland County evoked the Declaration of Independence in claiming that "the welfare and happiness of her child & herself" would be threatened if they were compelled to leave Virginia to live "in the midst of strangers, cut off from society & aid of relations & friends, as almost to shut out from their view the prospect of freedom."[26] Others echoed an earlier draft of the Declaration by replacing a claim to happiness with proof of property ownership, as did Archie Higginbotham of Amherst County in 1833. Higginbotham's lawyer argued that "he has by honest labour acquired Real Estate in Lynchburg of Considerable Value and a Tract of Land of Considerable Value in the County of Amherst" and asked that legislators allow Higginbotham at least five more years in Virginia, so that he could "dispose of his Estate, collect the proceeds & prepare for removal."[27] If Higginbotham had to remove himself from the state, as the law directed, he nonetheless had a right as a free person to take the monetary equivalent of his hard-earned property with him. The legislature agreed and passed a special law assuring his property rights and residency for five additional years.

Other petitioners went beyond claiming a right to life, liberty, and the pursuit of happiness and property by asserting themselves as citizens. In their petitions in Accomack County in 1838, the attorneys for Isaac, John, and Patty insisted "that he is a valuable citizen," "a useful Citizen," and someone who demonstrated "every virtue which characterizes a good citizen," respectively.[28] Jane Bell of Fauquier County asserted that after manumission "she has since always conducted herself as a desired and good Citizen." A number of white male neighbors who wrote that they "have long known" Bell concurred, by signing a certificate of character that attested, "She is a woman of the most unexceptionable character and . . . respectibility of her colour—, that she is an usefull and an excellent citizen, always conducting herself in such manner as to attract the attention and . . . applause of all who know her."[29] Like free blacks who struggled for liberty and equality in northern states at the time, contemporaries like Isaac, John, Patty, and Jane Bell in Virginia also "practiced citizenship as a matter of survival."[30]

Like Bell, almost all of the petitioners justified their claims to basic rights of free people by demonstrating their usefulness and devotion to their white neighbors, as well as their upstanding character, almost always first established under slavery through many years of loyal service to a now-deceased owner. For example, Patty's 1838 petition in Accomack County claimed that "she has *ever* sustained the character of a servant distinguished for peculiar and uncommon faithfulness—*always* the *confidant*, the *intimate*, the *nurse* and *friend* of her Master, Mistress and their children—*never* maintaining the relation to them and theirs of an *ordinary menial*."[31] Certificates accompanying another petition, that of David Skurry of Amelia County, were exceptional in their detail but typical in tone. One certificate, signed by thirteen white male neighbors, including William Hudson "who was over-seer over David for 18 years," concluded that "in point of character he has no superior as a coloured man. His late Mistress (Mrs Skurry) had great confidence in him, which was manifested in many occasions. He was her body servant. She attained to a great age, & was lame from an early period of her life, being incapable of loco-motion. She was eminent for her piety, and with the assistance of David a regular attendant on Divine worship. He accompanied her on horseback, took her out of the Gigg, and carried her in his arms to a seat in the house, appropriated to the worship of God. He performed similar services to her, whenever she visited any of her numerous friends & acquaintances."[32] For Skurry, claims to freedom and residency stemmed from his exemplary service as a slave to his disabled mistress.

Those passages of petitions and certificates designed to establish one's respectable character could simultaneously appeal to racial rhetoric, which varied according to one's gender and age. For example, the 1815 petition of Mourning of Campbell County stated that she was "a woman of fair & honest character remarkable for her industry & the correctness of her conduct, and is believed to be so far advanced in life, that she will not probably have any more children."[33] A number of petitioners, especially women, sought to establish their right to residency while appealing to those fears of vocal white politicians, who deemed the increase in the state's free black population as a great "evil." In the case of Mourning, the accompanying certificate of character also appealed to slaveholding sensibilities by arguing that the passage of a law allowing Mourning to remain in the state would send a signal to the state's free blacks "and teach them as well as other slaves this useful lesson, that Honesty, Integrity and Fidelity in slaves will not be disregarded by the legislature, but will be encouraged and rewarded on all proper occasions."[34]

Most petitions to local courts and the state legislature made the case that free blacks had become an integral part of their communities, socially and economically. This is precisely the tack that Claiborne took in Nelly Hoomes's 1834 petition. Like Hoomes, many petitioners claimed legitimate family relations—that they had "intermarried" or "married" an enslaved person or had "a wife" who was enslaved—in legally recognizable terms that were not, however, sanctioned by Virginia law.[35] For example, the lawyer hired by Harry of Bath County in 1829 claimed extralegal family relations in less explicit but equally powerful terms when he wrote, "your petitioner humbly asks permission to remain with his family (who are slaves) within the Commonwealth, where all his attachments are centered."[36] The following year, Davy from Bedford County attested, "He is married to a slave the property of Doctr Thomas Wright of Franklin County and does now & for some time has lived on the land of said Wright. To be compelled to leave the place of his long residence and his wife and connections forever would be to him a most afflicting dispensation."[37] Such claims to family life that straddled slavery and freedom were by no means always successful, but they demonstrate that free African Americans believed that by securing legal representation they had both a right to challenge the expulsion law's applicability to them and a reasonable chance of succeeding in their request, if it was couched in terms that showed just how much they conformed to white social norms in the lives they forged as free people.

Much of free blacks' use of the legal system—at every level—rested upon their use of white attorneys. In many cases, lawyers agreed to represent free black clients as they did their white clients, by dutifully following legal processes in ways that would maximize their clients' chances of succeeding in their claims. For example, when blocked by recalcitrant gentlemen judges at the local level, attorneys could appeal to lawmakers in Richmond on their clients' behalf. In Pleasant Roane's 1824 petition to the legislature for residency, attorney James Hendrick vented his frustration that despite having already won a special law allowing Roane to remain in the state, "from my experience in such matters it is extremely difficult if not impossible to get a competent court in such cases" in Campbell County. He asked lawmakers to do what Roane's local court had been unwilling to do—to grant him unconditional permission to remain in Virginia, for which a vote of local justices would not be needed.[38] Richard Gregory's attorney asked for a similar special law to circumvent the justices of the Chesterfield County court in 1850, who apparently refused to hear Gregory's petition for residency.[39]

Though Virginia law did not require individuals to hire an attorney to request a motion for registration in their local courts (to obtain their "free papers"), a number of individuals nonetheless hired lawyers to do so rather than make their case themselves. This is a fact that is often overlooked by scholars because local court clerks simply failed to mention the presence or actions of attorneys in such processes concerning free blacks.[40] As a result, historians have largely ignored the role of white attorneys in free blacks' efforts to claim a right to residency in Virginia through their local courts. For example, one day in July 1835 the clerk of Richmond's Hustings Court described the court's actions toward Phoebe Kemp, a free black woman, thus: "It appearing to the court by a register issued by the clerk of the borough of Norfolk that Phoebe Kemp a woman of color is born free, it is ordered that she be registered in the office of this court."[41] Only by reading the corresponding entry in Claiborne's account book do we learn that Kemp had sought Claiborne's legal representation to transfer her registration from Norfolk to Richmond and that it was Claiborne, not Kemp, who initiated the motion for her register.[42] The nature and degree of free black involvement with the law in Virginia becomes clearer when we begin to see that free African Americans sought the assistance of white attorneys to conduct all kinds of business in their local courts and court clerks' offices. Indeed, Kemp was not alone in her desire to make the best case possible to the Richmond Hustings Court in order to win a new register. The following year, Emmanuel Pleasants also hired Claiborne to obtain a duplicate of his free papers, after having lost his original register. The court obliged, and again left no official record of Claiborne's efforts on his client's behalf.[43] Earlier, Lucy Goode and Polly, Celia, and Lewis Scott each hired Claiborne to secure their own "free papers" in local courts.[44] Other attorneys in Richmond offered similar services throughout the antebellum period, recording clients' information in their account books that helps reveal neighborhood webs into which free blacks had woven themselves. For example, James Harris hired attorney William Wirt Henry to help him obtain his free papers in Richmond in 1854, for which Henry charged his client $5. Harris paid Henry $2 of his bill and looked to J. N. Schimdt to front the remaining $3, which Harris may have repaid Schimdt later in cash or through in-kind labor or exchange.[45]

Free blacks also looked to lawyers in circumstances where a loved one's right to residency was at stake. Lawyers' accounts of such instances open another window on social networks within Richmond's free black communities and demonstrate the degree to which one's legal action could be a communal undertaking. In 1854, J. Cousins hired William Wirt Henry "to motion to register" an acquaintance, Thomas, in court. While Henry named Cousins as his client in his account book, thereby holding him responsible for the corresponding $5 fee, it was Thomas, the "bricklayer" who received his free papers, who settled the account one year later.[46] Likewise, in the 1830s, Lewis Armistead, Robert Hill, and Judith Dean engaged Herbert Claiborne to register his three sons, a sister's children, and a female acquaintance, respectively.[47] Judith Dean was the only one to pay her legal bill, which at $2.50 was roughly half the standard fee in such cases. Similarly, Sally Abrams hired Charles William Dabney in 1836 to facilitate a motion "about her daughter" in nearby Hanover County for $2.50, half of what Dabney charged William Stratton, a white man, for filing a motion on his behalf the same day.[48] Back in Richmond, Betsy Ham hired Claiborne to obtain the release of her son, Robinson, who had been "committed for want of Register" in the city jail in 1833. Claiborne arranged for James M. Moody, a white acquaintance of Ham, to testify to Robinson's free status.[49] In 1836, Minnis Hill hired Herbert Claiborne to gain a motion to register his seven children in Richmond Hustings Court, which Claiborne did, by calling upon a "Mrs. ___ Napper" to testify in court that the children were all "born free."[50] Interestingly, though the clerk recorded the court order to register the Hill children, there is no mention of Minnis Hill, who sought the children's registration in the first place, or of

Claiborne, the attorney who made it happen. Again, only by examining the attorney's account books are we able to connect Minnis Hill to Claiborne to Mrs. Napper to Minnis Hill's children—a web of relationships that crossed race, class, generational, and gender lines. Illuminating the role of attorneys in the basic processes of local courts shines a new light upon the lives and actions of free blacks, who believed they could successfully claim a right to belong in their neighborhood by simultaneously claiming a right to legal representation. Minnis Hill and others mentioned above left no written explanation of how they viewed their rights as free people in a slave society, but their actions and those of their white attorneys speak loudly. Black clients and white attorneys engaged with one another not only in civil suits, chancery suits, criminal trials, and appeals cases, but often in the more mundane processes like registration, which for many served as a claim to belonging within neighborhoods.[51] For free African Americans, to hire an attorney to secure one's motion for registration was to hedge one's bets in a localized legal system in which personal relationships and reputations (one's own and those of one's attorney) often determined the outcome of one's claim to residency.[52]

Claiborne and others also represented free African Americans who were formally charged by their local courts for remaining illegally in their communities, something Nelly Hoomes would experience several months after the petition Claiborne drafted to the state legislature was rejected in 1833.[53] In the same year, Eliza Neale hired Claiborne to combat the presentment she had received "for remaining in the state being a free person of colour."[54] In their formal claims to state and local authorities for legal residency and in their challenges to sporadic local enforcement of the state's 1806 expulsion law, free blacks sought lawyers whose connections, experience, and abilities might improve their chances of success.[55] As a result, free blacks and their attorneys overwhelmingly succeeded in overcoming charges for remaining in the state illegally. According to James M. Campbell, "between 1830 and 1860, 124 free African Americans in Richmond were charged with being illegal residents, but only 12 were convicted, 9 of whom were sentenced to be sold into slavery and 2 hired out for jail fees."[56]

In more rural localities, many free African Americans were also successful in demonstrating their right to residency among those they knew well by establishing themselves as industrious, honest, and respectable members of their neighborhoods. Relatively few were targeted by their local courts as illegal residents. When they were, many were able to hire white lawyers who played key roles in dismissing the charges.[57] For example, from 1857 to 1858 the Accomack County Circuit Court indicted thirteen free

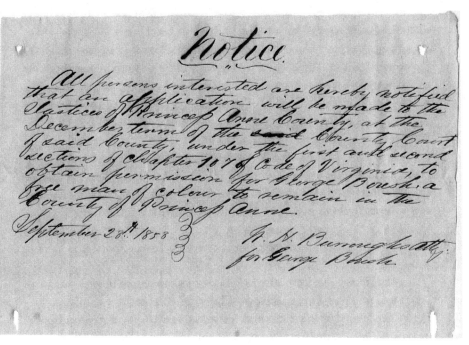

*Notice, Princess Anne County court, 1858. George Boush engaged attorney
W. H. Burroughs to draft this notice of his intent to petition the local court for
permission to remain a resident in Princess Anne County in 1858.
(Courtesy Library of Virginia, Richmond)*

blacks for violating the expulsion law—including six members of the Ewell
family (Bill, George, Bridget, Lucy, Mary, and Sarah Ewell) in November
1858 for remaining in the state "contrary to law."[58] The Ewells were among
the very few Virginians ever to be indicted *twice* for violating the state expulsion law, but their cases ended in typical outcomes—acquittal and dismissal.[59] Three years earlier, the family had been indicted along with fourteen other free blacks for the same offense. Though the Ewells had been
acquitted through the efforts of their lawyer, John W. H. Parker, three of
the others (Scipio Phillips, Nina Phillips, and Jacob Bayly) had been found
guilty and were ordered by the court to be sold as absolute slaves.[60]

Upon receiving their second round of charges in 1858, the Ewells again
hired Parker as their attorney, who called upon the judge to quash the indictments on account of legal technicalities, and most compellingly, by asserting the absurdity of the 1806 law itself. Parker insisted that the Ewells'
indictments be dismissed "because the said Indictment is not sufficient in
law" and "because all the allegations contained in said Indictment might

be true in point of fact, and still the said defendants not be guilty of any offense." Being careful not to pass judgment on the law itself, the judge nonetheless undermined its power and effectiveness in his decision. He concluded that "the Court, without deciding as to the correctness or incorrectness of all the reasons assigned by the said defendants, but being of opinion that the said Indictment does not sufficiently charge any offense, does order that the said Indictment be quashed, and that the defendants . . . go thereof without day."[61] If white Virginians were largely reluctant to implicate their free black neighbors in violating the expulsion law even in the 1850s, apparently the state's judges were also hesitant to convict those few individuals who were from time to time called before the court—even those who had been presented more than once by a local grand jury. Competent legal representation ultimately may have made the difference between dismissal and conviction for the Ewells and others in their situation.

Free African Americans also hired attorneys to secure liberty for themselves and others. Annie Lamb paid Claiborne $10 for successfully attending to her "claim of freedom" and "drawing two Deeds of manumission" in 1834.[62] One year earlier, Pharoah Sheppard hired Claiborne "for application of Habeas Corpus" on behalf of Rosella, his daughter, who was being detained against her will. Claiborne also drew up an indenture that bound out Rosella to Argyle Walker and his wife. Sheppard was likely the son of one of the two enslaved men who compromised Gabriel's planned rebellion in 1800 and had himself received permission to remain in the state after his manumission in 1808.[63] Reuben Jones also hired Claiborne to write an opinion concerning the detention of his children, only to pay the $5 cost (and other charges he had accrued for additional services) through a series of installments in the form of 394 pounds of oats, several "horse loads of wood," and "fifty bean poles" delivered to Claiborne's house.[64] Jones was one of many free black clients in the early nineteenth century who compensated his counsel through in-kind exchanges of goods or labor.

Free blacks also employed attorneys to liberate loved ones from bondage by facilitating manumission arrangements. In 1835, Reuben Mosby sought Claiborne's "opinion and advice as to contract with Saml pleasants & others for purchase" of his daughter.[65] The same year Reuben Kenny, a free man, contracted with Claiborne to draw a covenant with J. S. Debrell "to emancipate John Bunch & wife" for $5. Apparently Kenny arranged the manumission of John Bunch and his wife on credit established as a past client of Claiborne. Bunch paid Claiborne the $5 owed for the covenant three years later, in 1838.[66] In 1833, Isaac Reynolds hired Claiborne

Entry for Reuben Jones in Herbert A. Claiborne's account book. Entries in attorneys' account books often reveal the legal predicaments, social worlds, and personal networks of individual clients, as well as the nature of their relationships to their lawyers. (Courtesy Virginia Historical Society)

to draw the deed of manumission for his son, Isaac, to have it recorded in the court's deed book, and to obtain Isaac's register.[67] Such entries in Claiborne's account book not only identify connections between white and black Richmonders, but further illuminate the networks that existed among free and enslaved communities in the city. Free blacks used the legal system to liberate other free people from unlawful detention and facilitated the manumission of enslaved people to whom they were attached. Lawyers like Claiborne, regardless—or perhaps in spite—of their personal views, translated such attachments into legal action that safeguarded liberty for free people, and on occasion converted slaves into free people.

Free blacks also hired attorneys to pursue or protect private property and personal investments. In 1820, Thomas Colson, described as a "Black man," hired Fredericksburg attorney Garrit Minor to serve Samuel Washington for a $30 debt.[68] In Richmond in 1833, John Hamilton hired Herbert Claiborne to draw up a deed of trust and to facilitate the sale of land. The following year he engaged the same to devise his last will and testament.[69] In 1835, Setter Willison hired Claiborne to represent him in a chancery case, as did Daniel Lewis, who also hired Claiborne to obtain, examine, and rectify deeds and record property.[70] In 1857, Harry Clark, a shoemaker, hired William Wirt Henry to collect money owed him by the executor of an estate. Henry succeeded.[71] The brothers Minnis Hill and William Hill hired Claiborne to conduct title work on three Richmond lots in 1836 and represent them in chancery court, among other business, accruing more than $45 in attorney's fees. In lieu of cash payments, Claiborne accepted partial payment for his services in sweat equity, as Minnis Hill earned a credit of $8.50 in Claiborne's account book "for repairing [a] grate" at his house.[72] Indeed, Claiborne revealed his attitude toward the Hill brothers when he noted in their account, "Minnis Hill did some work for me he is dead & his brother poor so this may as well be considered as settled."[73] Later, in nearby Fredericksburg, Henry Young hired J. J. Chew to draw two deeds, for which he paid $5.[74] Soon after, Brener and Ellen Brooke hired Chew to devise and collect interest upon a $75 bond with Thomas B. Breton.[75]

Free blacks also sought legal representation to defend what they (and the law) viewed as their basic rights as free people—to sue, buy and sell property, and initiate various legal actions that could improve their situation. In 1833, John Booker hired Claiborne to draft a warrant against a white acquaintance, John S. Stubbs.[76] Similarly, Eaton Haynes Howel hired William Wirt Henry in 1855 "for advice & issuing [a] warrant vs. Lesters &c," accruing a $5 tab that apparently went unpaid.[77] Richard Vaugn, a free black man, hired Claiborne to represent him in Mayor's Court against an enslaved person owned by a Mr. Ritchie.[78] In the same year, Eliza Johnson hired Claiborne to release her from Mayor's Court, where she was held for an unspecified charge.[79] Lucy Ann Hoomes hired Claiborne in 1834 to defend her at Mayor's Court against charges of assault, Betsy Morris hired Claiborne to defend her daughter, Maria, in Mayor's Court, and Lucy Harris hired Claiborne to defend her in the same court against charges of receiving stolen goods.[80] In 1854, John Liggins hired William Wirt Henry "to motion release from jail" and settle $7 in associated jail fees. Three months later, two white men, Thomas Adams and Haynes Howell, paid Henry a total of $10 toward Liggins's bill, which remained unsettled nearly three years later.[81]

The account books of Henry Claiborne and his contemporaries testify to the fact that free blacks engaged with local law in ways that they hoped would advance their interests or those of loved ones. Sometimes they were successful, and at other times they were not. Free blacks hired white attorneys in antebellum Virginia to secure orders from city or county courts for their registers; to draft and submit petitions on their behalf to city or county officials and state legislators for permission to remain in the state; to secure their liberty and that of others unlawfully detained; to help arrange the manumission of enslaved individuals; to defend themselves and others who were the objects of suits initiated by the state or by white neighbors; and at other times to simply give advice on how best to proceed in formal legal processes and arenas.

Though free African Americans like Nelly Hoomes may have read David Walker's *Appeal* and in the abstract agreed with its call for the destruction and re-creation of the American justice system, in their everyday actions in their local communities many must have prayed to "a God of justice" as they used and attempted to transcend race-based, repressive state laws to win a place in their neighborhood, free a son from jail, liberate a daughter from enslavement, or devise a deed or will that would secure their hard-won property. Regardless of whether white Virginians viewed free African Americans' claims as rights, it is clear that many free blacks saw their liberty as meaningful and sought to claim certain basic rights *they* viewed as inherent in their status. However unsympathetic white attorneys in Richmond may have been toward African Americans in their private lives, at least a handful agreed to regularly represent free blacks in their claims to residency, liberty, family, and due process, all without irrevocably damaging their legal careers.

Free blacks made the antebellum Virginia legal system work in their favor more frequently than scholars have supposed, and they frequently did so by securing white counsel. Melissa Milewski has argued that African Americans' use of the legal system (and the services of white lawyers) was far more widespread in the post–Civil War South than previously assumed. She concludes that for black litigants, "the loss of legal rights was not as complete as scholars have believed," and white "lawyers aligned themselves—even if temporarily and solely for monetary reasons—with African Americans' quest for full citizenship."[82] Milewski's conclusions are persuasive and illustrate the important legacy of free black legal activity in the decades before the Civil War. Long before passage of the Civil Rights Act of 1866 or the adoption of the Fourteenth Amendment in 1868, many free African Americans successfully claimed a place in their communities and resisted radical calls for their removal or re-enslavement. Free African Americans hired attorneys who appealed to white officials' understandings of freedom, family, home, and justice, in an attempt to secure the same for their clients.

Long after Walker's *Appeal* first arrived in Virginia, but only a few months after the Accomack Superior Court had ordered Daniel Hickman to be sold as a slave, the Lunenburg County Circuit Court, located far from the Eastern Shore in south-central Virginia, initiated several removal cases of its own, among them one charging Willis and Andrew Doswell with remaining illegally in the state. After engaging a lawyer to petition their local court as well as the state legislature, the Doswells devised a solution of last resort that was as complicated and contradictory as the Virginia society and the legal system that threatened them. They enslaved themselves to a master of their choice and, in the process, unintentionally altered the debate over the future of free blacks in the state by helping to create a law that would enable other African Americans to do the same.

CHAPTER THREE

THE DOSWELL BROTHERS
DEMAND A LAW

On a spring morning in 1850, seventy-year-old planter William Arvin Sr. sat with seventeen other grand jurors in circuit court, listening to charges brought against various men of Lunenburg County in Southside Virginia.[1] Older than the nation itself, Arvin might have had the impression that the political system he had witnessed develop as a boy was now rapidly unraveling. Politicians in Washington fiercely debated how best to absorb new territory won in the Mexican War and whether to allow the institution of slavery within it. The fragile political equilibrium between North and South that lawmakers had carefully sought to preserve since the Early Republic was unraveling.[2] Local newspapers reported serious sectional tensions of another kind closer to home, as Virginians clamored for a state constitutional convention that would pit the interests of those in the nearly all-white trans-Allegheny region against easterners, many of whom lived in the booming black-majority tobacco counties like Lunenburg, where agricultural production rested firmly upon plantation slavery.[3] Daily headlines highlighted additional concerns. Ambitious public improvement projects, mostly in the western portions of the state, had created public debt and widespread anxiety among many, especially in the east. Furthermore, poorer white residents (many of whom lived west of the Blue Ridge) declared the state constitution inadequate and threatened slaveholders' influence by calling for universal white male suffrage. Moreover, critics demanded radical reforms of Virginia's county court system (in which Arvin regularly participated), which they declared an undemocratic and "self-perpetuating body" that flaunted its "distrust of popular authority and control" and was "justly obnoxious to the people at large."[4] A witness to the reigns of Jefferson, Madison, Monroe, and Tyler, Arvin may have looked upon his present-day Virginia, at least in the political realm, as a "Dominion of Memories"—its influence on the nation diminished, its own future as a united commonwealth highly uncertain.[5]

As a grand juror, Arvin could at least take comfort in the limited but real power he could exert upon his own little world in Lunenburg, which also showed signs of disorder. Most of the cases that day concerned faro, an illegal card game that had lured a number of Arvin's neighbors into back rooms of local taverns and other places for years—including, in this instance, a former constable and future jailkeeper, and a county school commissioner.[6] Other citizens were charged with "breach of peace by striking" and "selling ardent spirits," typical items on a nineteenth-century Virginia court docket.[7] Other matters, however, strongly suggested that the authority upon which Arvin's livelihood (and that of the wealthiest planters in the county) rested was in decline, and preservation of the peculiar institution was as important to local Lunenburg planters as it was to southern lawmakers in Congress.[8] Arvin and other grand jurors handed one neighbor several presentments (as such charges were called) for selling liquor to three enslaved men "without Consent in writing" of their masters, at least two of whom he had also served strong drink.[9] In all likelihood, slaves and masters had often sought libation together there—a sign that the racial order in Lunenburg was not as clear as state law asserted.[10]

Laws restricting the behavior and activities of free and enslaved blacks had been on the books for years, but time and again Arvin's white neighbors allowed their slaves to defy those laws with impunity and showed little worry when free blacks they knew well did the same. Moreover, whites themselves insisted on breaking the racial code and the law. White Virginians violated the law by selling liquor to free and enslaved blacks to such a degree, complained one contemporary, that "everybody believes that both slaves and free negroes are dealt with contrary to law at nine-tenths of the slop-shops, [or] *stores*, that are scattered over the State—and that these constitute the chief customers at such shops."[11] Whites also played cards, gambled, or hunted with slaves and frequently ignored the laws established to keep free blacks in their place.[12] Instead, some—perhaps many—socialized, kept "free and easy conversation," and even pursued romantic relations with free blacks.[13]

For years, a minority of white Virginians had complained about the dangers that free blacks posed to the state's fragile social system and had vigorously supported the idea of forcibly deporting them, only to meet considerable resistance from a more moderate majority. In December 1849 the state's new governor, John B. Floyd, had infuriated removal extremists by departing from the stance of his more radical predecessor, William Smith, and had proposed a measure supporting only the voluntary expulsion of free blacks from Virginia. Unlike Smith's earlier calls for mandatory wholesale deportation, Floyd's proposal "to give ample assistance to the Colonization Society" had quickly won favor among legislators in Richmond and their constituents, and became the first law in nearly two decades that encouraged free blacks to leave the state—by appropriating $30,000 annually for five years to support the voluntary relocation of blacks to Liberia "or other place on the western coast of Africa."[14] To help fund the initiative, the law instituted an annual tax placed on every free black male resident between the ages of twenty-one and fifty-four, to be collected by local county commissioners of the revenue.[15] Once again, removal of free blacks had become a political focal point for lawmakers otherwise preoccupied with an impending crisis of intrastate sectionalism that threatened the state's constitutional structure and the future of slaveholding influence in Virginia.[16]

The new voluntary removal law, passed just two months earlier, was likely fresh in William Arvin's mind when he offered evidence for three more presentments near the end of a long day of court (thirty-four presentments had already been handed down by the grand jury). Arvin alleged that his free black neighbors, Willis and Andrew Doswell, as well as their sister Mary, had been living in the county illegally since their emancipation in 1842. Arvin could be a stickler about Virginia's laws regarding blacks—free or enslaved. Just a few months before, he had used his seat in the same court's grand jury to help implicate Alfred H. Hunt, a white man, for "permitting many slaves . . . sixteen not belonging to him to be and remain at one time on his lot and tenement" in Lunenburg on a Sunday.[17] It is unclear which had been more offensive to Arvin—that sixteen slaves had been allowed to congregate on a neighbor's plantation in violation of the law, or that the gathering had occurred on a Sunday, perhaps in lieu of church attendance. Either way, Arvin had then found himself among those in the county who were determined to enforce the state's restrictive laws concerning free and enslaved blacks, especially against fellow whites whom they considered insufficiently vigilant.[18] Arvin may have been one of a small group of extremists in Lunenburg who believed that forced, not voluntary removal was the only practical way of ridding the county of free blacks, a view that most did not share.[19] It is also possible that William Arvin Sr. offered evidence against Willis, Andrew, and Mary Doswell because of a long-standing grudge he may have held against his white neighbor William Doswell. Thomas Arvin, a brother or nephew of

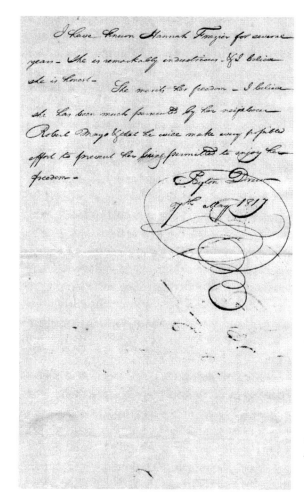

Certificate of good character for Hannah Frazier, 1817. Like Willis, Andrew, and Mary Doswell in the 1850s, Hannah Frazier of Henrico County became ensnared in a disagreement among white neighbors over whether she and other African Americans were due liberty and residency in their communities. In a contest reminiscent of that between Lunenburg's William Doswell and William Arvin Sr., Peyton Drew derided Robert Mayo, who he asserted "will make every possible effort" to prevent Frazier from "being permitted to enjoy her freedom." (Courtesy Library of Virginia, Richmond)

William Arvin Sr., had been charged in 1846 for "striking" William Doswell. In addition, a year earlier, William Arvin had been involved in a lawsuit that sought $32.32 from William Doswell.[20] It is important to note, however, that even at the family level, disagreements existed over whether free black neighbors should be held to the letter of the law, as Langston Arvin and John Arvin were among forty-seven white neighbors who would petition the state legislature the next year to allow the Doswell brothers to remain in Lunenburg. Moreover, Langston Arvin was among those summoned "to testify on behalf of Willis" Doswell in September 1854.[21]

By 1850, presentments of free blacks such as the one lodged against Willis, Andrew, and Mary Doswell were exceptional—perhaps even less common than they had been when Daniel Hickman was indicted in Accomack in 1831—but the *process* by which they were presented was not. Those free African Americans who did face charges of any kind were typically presented according to the same quotidian legal principles that applied to whites: those present at court, either as presiding officials, witnesses, or grand jurors, could accuse individuals of infractions, which the grand jury could then decide whether to pursue. Law enforcement could seem more or less restrictive, or even whimsical, depending upon who happened to be present at court or to serve as grand jurors when one's case was considered. Virginia residents—black and white—faced charges because grand jurors on a particular day decided they should.[22]

Virginians (black and white) might also find themselves presented in Virginia's courts through a kind of domino effect, where one person's presentment led to the charging of others. For example, when Josiah W. Foster was called upon by the grand jury of the Lunenburg Circuit Court to provide information on a fight involving two men at Richard A. Marshall's "Store House," Foster took the opportunity to help rid Lunenburg of other vices by reporting on nine men who had illegally played cards in Marshall's store. But Foster did not stop there. He testified that Marshall had sold "ardent spirits" to slaves on at least eight occasions during the same period. So it was that a swift, short-lived crackdown on illegal gatherings and commerce involving slaves took place in Lunenburg County in the fall of 1849—largely because of a fight between two white men at a makeshift tavern on a Saturday night.[23]

At the time of their presentments, free blacks Willis and Andrew Doswell lived in "their house," which they had built upon the plantation of William Doswell, the nephew of their former owner and an ordained minister.[24] More than seven years earlier, Andrew and Willis had been emancipated by the will of David M. Doswell, which had promised them— in addition to their freedom at age twenty-one—a horse, a five-dollar annual stipend, and the opportunity to learn and then "be put to some trade." Curiously, Doswell had insisted that the two young black men could choose their vocation—any trade, it seemed—"but not the carpenters." Until they reached legal age, they were to "remain under the absolute control" of their former master's friend and executor, Dr. Richard May, whom Doswell had admonished "to maintain and treat them humanely."[25] Willis Doswell, a thirty-two-year-old man of "bright yellow complexion," with bushy, straight hair, was the head of the house, though two years Andrew's junior. He and Andrew, "dark brown" with "short and wooly" hair, had defied the will of their deceased master and had both become carpenters since becoming free in 1842, and were supporting themselves.[26] They lived with forty-year-old Milly Ragsdale and her two young children Nilly and Alice.[27] Indeed, as many of their white neighbors would attest in a petition submitted to the Virginia legislature, Willis and Andrew had woven themselves into community life and had "conducted themselves peaceably, honestly, and industriously" since their emancipation.[28]

Unlike Willis and Andrew, their sister, Mary, had been given by David M. Doswell in his will to Richard May "during his life," and had relocated after receiving her freedom to adjacent Prince Edward County in 1843. Thirty-seven years old, five-feet-five inches tall, and described as having a "bright yellow complexion," Mary now lived with her two sons, Samuel W. Diasman and Alpheus Adolphus Gustavus, aged seven and four, respectively. She had followed Andrew and Willis's lead in registering with the Lunenburg County clerk long ago and had recently attempted to register her sons in Lunenburg in 1849, but had been denied, likely because she was no longer a resident there.[29]

There were many other free blacks who lived quiet, enterprising lives in Lunenburg, unmolested by the court despite their illegal status. More than 250 free blacks inhabited the county (about 2 percent of the population), and as many as one-third of them lived in violation of the law of 1806.[30] Free men and women of color in Lunenburg worked as farmers, painters, stonemasons, blacksmiths, bricklayers, ditchers, spinners, weavers, wheelwrights, and washers of clothes.[31] Thirty of Lunenburg's 820 households (nearly 4 percent) were composed solely of people of color—"mulattoes" or "blacks." An equal number of households was mixed—made up of whites and blacks or mulattoes living together.[32]

From 1843 to 1865, only five free blacks were formally charged by Lunenburg County officials for violating the expulsion law of 1806—four in the biannual circuit court (the three Doswells and a woman named Araminta Frances) and one in the monthly county court (Gray Winn). Winn, a free black "hireling" living on the land of a white man—probably his employer—had attracted the attention of the court in 1846, nearly a decade after he had been emancipated by the will of Priscilla Winn.[33] The case against Winn languished for almost four years, during which time other free blacks to whom the expulsion law supposedly applied continued to live in Lunenburg with either the tacit or expressed approval of authorities. Indeed, James Gray, another man freed by Priscilla Winn's will, received copies of his free papers from the county court rather than a presentment later that year.[34] Similarly, Eliza, a free woman emancipated by Tanner Shell, was granted permission by the same court to remain in the county in October 1846. The court concluded that Eliza was a woman "of good character, peaceable orderly and industrious, and not addicted to drunkeness, gaming or any other vice"—standards against which more than a few of the county's white citizens would have fallen far short.[35]

Free blacks living illegally in Lunenburg, then, were almost never prosecuted under the law of 1806, but they knew of the law because presentments, as rare as they were, were prosecuted diligently enough that eventual conviction loomed as a real possibility. But even so, relationships among individuals made for complicated, sometimes ambivalent prosecutions. William Arvin Sr. himself, the man who offered evidence against Willis, Andrew, and Mary Doswell in court, had behaved inconsistently. As determined as Arvin seems to have been to maintain racial order in his neighborhood, why hadn't he attempted to charge the Doswells with violating the expulsion law before 1850? They had, after all, been free since 1842. And when Arvin did get around to bringing charges, why didn't he complain at the same time about the dozens of other free blacks who lived around him in flagrant violation of the law? Though the Doswells stand out as clear examples of how Virginia law could constrict the lives of the state's free blacks, their case also reminds us how exceptional they were—how rare it was for their white neighbors, even those who might be most hostile, to use the law of 1806 against free black individuals.

Legislators in Richmond were aware that many of Virginia's free blacks lived in violation of state law and that a portion of their constituents—people like Arvin—demanded enforcement and removal. Most lawmakers, however, must have calculated that other than offering occasional lip service to those obsessed with deporting free blacks, it was politically expedient to ignore the Arvins in their districts and vote against the extreme proposals of a distinct minority of their colleagues that aimed to reduce the population of free blacks by removing them or by making emancipation more difficult.[36]

In the months after Willis, Andrew, and Mary Doswell were presented along with twenty-one white citizens of Lunenburg, the circuit court generally pursued the cases of whites charged with gambling more vigorously than they prosecuted the Doswells charged with violating the law of 1806. While most of the alleged gamblers were ordered to appear in court two days after their presentment, the Doswells were told to "appear here on the first day of the next term," five months later. Remaining in the commonwealth was a serious enough offense to merit their presentment—at least in this instance—but it was not so urgent a matter that it could not wait to be prosecuted until the fall. Meanwhile, the court pursued its cases against alleged gamblers in a way that reflected differences in defendants' socioeconomic standing. While many of the younger, less prominent offenders were speedily tried and convicted, others, like John A. Bishop—the former constable turned tavern operator—eluded conviction for "knowingly permitting a gaming table commonly called a Faro Bank to be established in his tavern." What perhaps tipped the verdict in his favor was the voices of three jurors, each of whom was present that day in order to answer a presentment for betting at faro in Bishop's tavern. In acquitting Bishop, perhaps they were betting on future good fortune in his tavern.[37]

On 27 June 1850, Deputy Sheriff Jonathan A. Stokes made his way to the house that Willis and Andrew Doswell had built for themselves on William Doswell's plantation. There he found only Willis, and served him a writ requiring him to appear before the circuit court on the first day of its October term.[38] Though Mary likely knew of the charges that had been filed against her in the Lunenburg County Circuit Court, she would have also known that it was extremely unlikely that she would be arrested in Prince Edward County, where she lived, and forcibly taken to Lunenburg for trial. Willis and Andrew, however, clearly felt the weight of their presentments and quickly sought the help of a local lawyer. Less than two weeks after Stokes's visit, the brothers petitioned the county court "for permission to remain in the state of Virginia and to reside in this County," a petition that the court neither formally denied nor granted, but ignored.[39] The Doswells failed to appear in court, and county officials were duty bound to act under the presentment that had been brought against them, but they did so sluggishly and perfunctorily.[40] The county court issued another round of summonses in January 1851, this time taking care to send one to the Prince Edward County sheriff as well.[41]

Willis and Andrew greeted the new year 1851 by changing their approach and acting separately from Mary, who by then might have fallen ill from complications of the birth of her third child.[42] The brothers sought the aid of William Doswell, nephew of their former master and the man who owned the land on which they lived, to petition the General Assembly in Richmond to pass a special law that would allow the brothers to remain at home in Lunenburg. The white Doswell crafted an elegant letter signed by forty-seven neighbors, which testified to the impeccable character of the Doswell brothers and explained why they should not be required to leave the state as the law would have them do. Among those who signed Doswell's petition were George W. Hardy, the future representative of the county in the Virginia House of Delegates, and of even greater significance, Jonathan A. Stokes, then–Deputy Sheriff who would soon become Sheriff of Lunenburg County.[43]

Petition of William Doswell to Virginia Legislative Assembly, 1851. Forty-seven white neighbors, including a future representative in the Virginia House of Delegates and a county sheriff, signed this 1851 petition on behalf of Willis and Andrew Doswell, so that they might be able to continue living in "their home" in Lunenburg County. (Courtesy Library of Virginia, Richmond)

Indeed, several dozen white Virginians had submitted petitions during the first half of the nineteenth century, often successfully, to the General Assembly on behalf of individual free blacks desiring to remain in the state. Doswell's petition, submitted for Willis and Andrew, was fairly typical of those requests, but at the moment faced a particularly large obstacle—a prolonged political maelstrom in the capital. Delegates from across the state had convened in Richmond to address what historian William A. Link describes as "a constitutional crisis connected to the role of slavery in the political system."[44] For eight months, representatives of the state's diverse white population would reframe the political structure of Virginia society by expanding suffrage to all white males, reapportioning representation more equally among sections, and making local judicial posts elective. The "Virginia Reform Convention," as it came to be called, "had the effect of revolutionizing the structure of state and county government."[45]

In the midst of the convention, several of the more extreme lawmakers had begun agitating for reform of the voluntary removal law passed less than a year before. For some, liberalizing the state's political process for whites necessitated increasing control over its free black population. Stephen B. Wheeler, a delegate from the nearly all-white trans-Allegheny county of Preston, called for a tenfold increase to the capitation tax imposed upon free black males by the earlier legislation (to expand efforts to colonize them in Liberia) and a measure that would encourage greater enforcement of the expulsion law of 1806 by creating a monetary incentive for "the informer or prosecutors" who would report on and prosecute free people who lived in the state illegally. Other lawmakers soon joined Wheeler in calling for a more effective voluntary removal law that would coincide with the state's new constitution.[46] Editors of *the Richmond Enquirer* similarly argued in a series of articles that constitutional reform required increased vigilance toward the state's free black population, especially now that delegates were broadening the meaning of freedom for whites previously excluded from formal politics. They wrote, "We are now about to enlarge the right of suffrage and give a more popular tone to all our institutions, and it becomes more important that the State should not be divided upon *castes*, nor, indeed, should there be a population among us, upon which such dispute could, by possibility, be raised."[47]

In an age of universal male suffrage, when the concept of citizenship had been expanded dramatically, the presence of free people who were legally and permanently excluded from such liberties apparently proved to be too great a contradiction for the *Enquirer* editors to handle. Moreover, if the new constitution would allow nonpropertyholding whites to vote and even to hold office, how much longer would it be before the free black "caste" gained a voice in state politics, agitating for greater liberties and possibly an end to slavery itself? "Our object is to separate the free negroes from direct contact with our slaves, by sending them to some other country. It matters not where that country is," *Enquirer* editors insisted. Even outside the formal political structure, they admitted, free blacks held considerable power to "remain where they are, to intermix, marry among the slaves, and foment rebellion, as they have done in every county where their strength has been permitted to assume a magnitude."[48] The *Enquirer* summed up the position of removal extremists by asking, "Is it not time that some national movement should be made for their separation and colonization?"[49]

In Willis and Andrew's petition to the General Assembly, William Doswell had carefully chosen language that might win over even those legislators who believed that free blacks, as a group, threatened social stability or were "morally and economically . . . unfit for freedom among whites" and needed to be expelled from the state, as some white Virginians would have it.[50] Doswell assured lawmakers that Willis and Andrew would live under his care if they were allowed to remain in Virginia, and he assured them that the pair would not "move about drinking and geting drunk, as is usual with free negroes, but to attend chiefly to their trade the carpenter's business." The petition appealed also to lawmakers' humane impulses and to their pride as Virginians. Willis and Andrew Doswell wanted to remain in the Old Dominion "rather than go to the northern or northwestern free states, believing from what they can learn, this condition would be worse than in this state, and fearing that their situation in Liberia would be still worse, fearing the consequence of ill health or loss of life in going or acclimating."[51] Though William Doswell was unlikely to persuade extremists that Andrew and Willis should be allowed to stay in Virginia, his petition sought to exploit the conflicted views of Virginia's moderate elite, who professed no doubt that blacks, as a class, were "morally and economically" unsuited to live as free people in the state, but many of whom also acknowledged that individual free African Americans might be peaceful, honest, and industrious enough to belong in their native state.[52]

In fact, William Doswell's phrasing of the petition articulated his own complex attitudes toward African Americans and their place in a slave society like Lunenburg's. The fifty-one-year-old preacher and his wife, Ann D. Doswell, owned six individuals as property—two men and two women in their twenties, as well as two young boys.[53] William Doswell had no problem promoting and defending the cause of two free black men he knew well and allowing them to live on his property with a free black woman and her children, as long as they expressed and exercised their freedom in ways that did not threaten his personal human property and the institution of slavery that governed his plantation and the county. Doswell's complex attitudes toward his free and enslaved neighbors were expressed in a later court document describing an incident in which Henry, a man belonging to Doswell, had beaten Milly Ragsdale, the woman who had lived with Willis and Andrew on the white Doswell's land—"the first time she had been whiped on account of a negro," the court clerk had noted. For Doswell, the chief problem lay not in the thrashing that Milly Ragsdale had suffered, but in the threat that she now posed to his valuable human property, Henry. Doswell demanded that the court secure a bond from Ragsdale guaranteeing that she would not seek vengeance and "do his negro man Henry some grievous bodily injury." Doswell succeeded in having another white citizen, Abram P. Webb, offer $25 in security for Ragsdale's future good behavior, but was careful to explain to the court that "he dose not make this complaint against the said Milly Ragsdale a free negro . . . from any hatred malice or ill will but merely for the preservation of his property from injury."[54] The security of slave property, at least in this case, trumped any intimations of justice that a free woman of color might experience after a violent assault.

William Doswell's appeal to legislators in Richmond apparently had no effect on the Lunenburg Circuit Court, which issued new summonses, again demanding that Willis and Andrew (as well as Mary) come to court on the first day of the following term, in January 1851. William Arvin Sr. was called as well, as a witness for the state.[55] Again, the black Doswells failed to appear before the court as they had been ordered to do. In the meantime, William Doswell's petition became House Bill 461 and remained on the House of Delegates docket until March, when it was tabled and buried when the legislative session ended later that month.[56]

Without an act of the General Assembly to prevent it, the Lunenburg Circuit Court issued yet another round of summonses to the black Doswells in May 1851.[57] Even though Andrew and Willis were "not found in Lunenburg" by the sheriff's deputy who apparently tried to deliver these new papers, the same procedure was followed twice more—writs calling the Doswells before the court were issued in July and again in early January 1852.[58] Apparently, Willis and Andrew had abandoned their home on William Doswell's property sometime in 1851, possibly joining their sister Mary or other relatives or friends in Prince Edward County.[59] Though Stokes and Lunenburg's other sheriffs seem not to have been trying too hard to apprehend the Doswells, even intermittent efforts to summon them to court had driven Willis and Andrew to preserve their freedom by at least temporarily leaving the county. The court had now been handling their case for nearly two years.

The January 1852 legislative session in Richmond, the first operating under the new state constitution, opened with an address by Governor Joseph Johnson, who offered a brief but forceful diatribe on "the increased numbers of our free colored population, as exhibited by the late census" and warned lawmakers that unless they could devise a solution to this problem, "it is feared that this population, which has already grown to be an evil, will increase."[60] Inspired by the governor's speech, lawmakers formed a select nine-member joint committee of House and Senate members to determine "what, if any, additional legislation be required for the better security of the slave property of the state, and for the removal of the free negroes beyond the limits of the commonwealth."[61] The Great Removal Debate of 1851–53 had begun, and lawmakers explicitly linked the issue of free black deportation with the need to protect slave property.[62] A subsequent resurgence of popular support for government action on removal accompanied, perhaps encouraged, discussion among lawmakers in Richmond. B. E. Harrison of Chesterfield County petitioned the General Assembly for a measure that would require slaveholders first to arrange for the deportation of blacks before emancipating them and would authorize any white Virginia citizen to haul before the court a free black suspected of living in the state illegally.[63] The *Daily Dispatch* of Richmond reprinted an item from a Savannah, Georgia, newspaper encouraging the wholesale removal of free blacks to the West Indies.[64] It is no surprise that in this political climate members of the House of Delegates proved reluctant to grant Willis and Andrew Doswell, two symbols of the "evil" that Johnson had vividly depicted, a law that would grant them special permission to remain in the state. At the same legislative session, however, the House refused a petition it received from Henrico County residents "asking the removal from the state of John King, a free man of color," indicating a general reluctance among legislators to empower themselves even to enforce existing state law involving illegal free black residents in local communities.[65]

Willis and Andrew Doswell saw their petition to the General Assembly going nowhere, so they adopted a new tactic that would change the terms of the removal debate then underway: they would ask permission to remain at home as slaves—provided they could select William Doswell as their new master. That change in their legal status would allow them to continue living in the house that they had constructed on Doswell's property and practicing their trade as carpenters, all in their home community, to which they belonged. Willis and Andrew now tried to gain approval from the Virginia Senate for their re-enslavement. On 30 January 1852, Lunenburg's senator, Thomas H. Campbell, moved "that the Committee on Courts of Justice be instructed to inquire into the expediency of providing by law for the voluntary enslavement of the free negroes of the Commonwealth," the first mention of such a law in Virginia or in any southern state in the mid-nineteenth century.[66]

Whereas debate over removal had up to this point fallen within the range of voluntary colonization or mandatory deportation, Campbell's legislation proposed for the Doswells allowed for another possibility. "Removal" might now apply to a change in free blacks' legal status, without any need for their actual physical relocation, and free men and women could be removed from the state without the expensive and cumbersome logistics required by colonization by a simple change in their legal status and with the stroke of a pen. Moreover, self-enslavement could operate in tandem with other more traditional forms of removal, including expulsion or colonization, as those unwilling to leave Virginia would have a legal means to remain in the state. Regardless of whether Campbell had intended for the Doswells' legislation to become either a removal measure itself or an accessory to removal propositions then under discussion, certain lawmakers understood it in these ways. As a result, Willis and Andrew's bill forever altered the debate over removal in the Virginia legislature, as subsequent proposals for state-sponsored colonization and deportation would frequently contain provisions for self-enslavement.

Removal as or in conjunction with "voluntary enslavement" appealed especially to those legislators who found it useful to suggest that the state's free blacks, because of their supposed inherent racial limitations, might actually prefer the condition of slavery to the uncertainty of freedom.[67] In addition, these same legislators were often the most uncomfortable with conferring too much power on the state, and a "voluntary" process ensured that enslavement could be a status that free blacks could themselves choose, not one to be imposed upon them by an overzealous court. Though these lawmakers could at times insist that Virginia's free blacks were "the lowest order of our population," most had always opposed any plan that would forcibly remove them from the state, let alone enslave them in mass numbers.[68]

Most important for Willis and Andrew, the proposed bill would appeal to those moderate lawmakers, such as Lunenburg's Thomas H. Campbell and George W. Hardy, who may have felt compelled by their communities to address the "problem" posed by free blacks in the abstract, but like their constituents, sympathized with individuals in their districts who had been singled out by the county courts for violating the law of 1806. It is likely that Campbell, Hardy, and others viewed the self-enslavement law as a countermeasure to the expulsion law, a legislative last resort to protect certain individuals who would otherwise be expelled from the state under the law of 1806.

The idea of self-enslavement also resonated with those less moderate white Virginians who believed that removing the state's free blacks was necessary to secure their slave property, in order to limit the influence free people might have on enslaved friends and family. For such whites, it was the impulse to preserve slavery, not any desire to offer individual free blacks further protection, which drew their support to self-enslavement. Twenty-seven men from Accomack County soon petitioned the legislature to allow "the free negroes to remain among us" and be bound out in the manner that hired slaves were, so long as those whose free labor was necessary to sustain the local economy—sailors and mechanics—were exempted.[69] Charles W. Rixey and thirty other men from Culpeper County submitted their own proposition to the General Assembly the following week. Unlike the plan put forth by the Accomack petitioners, Rixey and his neighbors argued that self-enslavement should become part of a more comprehensive program of colonization. They asked "that a law be passed at this session for the removal of Free blacks from the commonwealth of va—and as one mode of getting shut of them at as little expense as possible we humbly pray that as many as wish to remain in the state—be suffered to sell themselves to masters of their choice."[70] How could moderates denounce a more extreme removal measure as long as it allowed free blacks the option to remain in Virginia by choosing their own masters and enslaving themselves voluntarily? How could anyone argue with a plan to reduce the number of free blacks in the state that would avoid the massive expenditures presently required by colonization schemes to Liberia or elsewhere?

Rixey was the first to sign the Culpeper petition and was likely its author. A member of a prominent family (the village he lived in was called Rixeyville), he was the neighbor and acquaintance of many of the county's most powerful men but also found himself accused of violating the law from time to time. Rixey's early support of self-enslavement likely stemmed from the cases of four black Culpeper residents, Peter Miller, Stanton, Dangerfield Alexander, and Nelson Miller, who had refused several months earlier to leave for Liberia with the thirty-two other individuals freed by the will of their deceased owner Margaret Miller.[71] The insistence of these four men on remaining in Culpeper against the wishes of Miller—and others still living—had demonstrated to Rixey and the county's other hardliners that a policy of voluntary colonization was inadequate in ridding the state of free blacks and protecting the county's enslaved population from their influence. At the root of Rixey's petition (as well as other proposals at the time that sought to constrict or eliminate the liberty of Virginia's free blacks) was a widely felt but unsubstantiated fear that the very presence of free blacks—in Virginia or elsewhere in the United States—encouraged rebellion among the state's enslaved population. One petitioner at the time complained to the General Assembly that free black "neighborhoods become the very hiding places for fugitive slaves—and the hotbeds of rampant abolitionism."[72] The chief benefit of self-enslavement was not merely in reducing or eliminating the numbers of free blacks in the state and the nation, but in strengthening the institution of slavery by removing and neutralizing one of its greatest threats—those whose legal status necessarily allied them with the northern abolitionist cause.

In the convoluted slaveholding world of 1850s Virginia, though, it was possible for removal extremists to support the deportation and even enslavement of free blacks while encouraging and personally profiting from the illegal behavior of local enslaved residents. Contrary to state law (and, seemingly, the inclinations of one concerned enough about social order to petition the General Assembly), Rixey ran a "store house" where white and enslaved customers could regularly socialize and purchase alcohol, and at least once was presented by the court for allegedly buying stolen goods from an enslaved man.[73] The seeming inconsistencies in Rixey's behavior and varying attitudes toward state law help to illustrate the complex worldview held by white Virginians at the time. One could push for the wholesale deportation of Virginia's free blacks while supporting the voluntary enslavement of those unwilling to leave. Or one could be driven to petition the General Assembly for new laws intending to crack down on free black neighbors and at the same time support and participate in activities that served to undermine the legal separation of blacks and whites and the authority of a slaveholding society. Rixey himself would later become the chosen master of a free man, Thomas Grayson.[74]

Weeks then months passed, and no mention of the Lunenburg legislator's proposed voluntary enslavement law came forth from the Committee on Courts of Justice in the Virginia Senate. It looked as if the bill would never make it to the Senate floor. In late April 1852, Willis and Andrew tried again. William Doswell crafted and presented another petition on their behalf, which Thomas H. Campbell presented to the Senate, this time "praying that certain freed negroes be permitted to select their masters." This petition, too, was referred to the Committee on Courts of Justice.[75] This latest effort seemed to be the spark that legislators needed. A week later, the committee reported a measure that aimed to allow *any* free black in the state to seek self-enslavement—Senate Bill 145, "providing for the voluntary enslavement of the free negroes of the Commonwealth"—which Campbell then shepherded through the docket.[76] But the issue of self-enslavement and lawmakers' efforts to move it through the legislature would remain secondary to the debate over removal, at least in the House.[77]

In the House William H. Browne of King George and Stafford counties soon proposed the most far-reaching removal legislation in years, which for the first time incorporated a mechanism for self-enslavement to help cleanse the state of blacks bearing free legal status. Browne's bill would empower counties and towns to create "overseers of free negroes and mulattoes," who would manage the hiring of free blacks in their district as slaves "to the highest bidder at public auction"; the funds raised from these hires would be used "for the purpose of transportation of free negroes and mulattoes from the commonwealth." Methodical and comprehensive as he was, Browne took pains to show that his plan was neither ruthless nor unjust. Overseers would deport a free black individual "to the place or country of his or her own selection" with the utmost "regard to the non-separation of families and of those connected by the ties of affinity and consanguinity." Furthermore, elderly or disabled blacks would be allowed "the privilege of remaining as long as they choose in this commonwealth." Any others remaining in Virginia after 1 January 1858 would be "sold into slavery to the highest bidder at public auction." Until then, free blacks "shall at all times have the liberty of becoming the slaves of any free white citizen who will pay to the proper overseer . . . a fair compensation." To help enforce the law, Browne proposed offering the state overseers full use of Virginia's prisons and jails for incarcerating noncompliant black residents, as well as a 5 percent commission on all monies extracted from free black labor.[78]

In the Senate, legislators continued to debate how to frame a law that would allow free blacks to enslave themselves but prevent the state from enslaving those who were unwilling or unfit to choose. Of concern were issues of protection—preserving the republican concept of liberty from arbitrary state power and defending the interests of a black underclass that had rightfully received its legal status of freedom. The sanctity of liberty—its legal protection—meant a great deal to whites who governed a state whose economy was fueled by the labor, and increasingly the sale, of enslaved individuals.

Hugh W. Sheffey, a thirty-five-year-old nonslaveholding lawyer from Augusta County, offered two amendments, which raised concerns reminiscent to those articulated by critics of forced free black deportation in the late 1840s.[79] First, Sheffey demanded a clause stipulating "that no executor, administrator, trustee or other person authorised to exercise control over any person of colour, manumitted by will or otherwise, shall become the master of any such free person of colour." Sheffey's amendment would prevent newly freed petitioners from being coerced into bondage by those managing their deceased masters' estates. In other words, a modern, republican-minded society reluctant to confer freedom upon its enslaved labor force should be just as careful in how it decides to legally enslave its free residents—no matter what their color. Sheffey made clear that more was at stake here than allowing two brothers to stay in Lunenburg County or creating a law that could be used in conjunction with stricter removal regulations. At stake was the meaning of freedom to white Virginians and the degree of authority they could safely entrust to state government. Second, Sheffey sought protection for the children of free women who might decide to enslave themselves. Thus, he proposed to add another clause stating that "the children of any such female free person of colour, born prior to such time [as she enslaved herself], shall not be deemed to be reduced to slavery by such proceeding."[80]

Sheffey's provision would offer free blacks further protection by helping to guarantee that state-sanctioned enslavement would be reserved only for those men and women who deliberately sought it for themselves.

The majority of Sheffey's colleagues supported his amendments and conceived of the law in a similar way, as a measure that would almost reluctantly provide an option to free black individuals, not as license for the state to indiscriminately enslave the state's free population. Two days later, in Willis and Andrew's first legal victory, the senate passed Bill 145, which by then incorporated Sheffey's two amendments, and if passed by the House would allow any free black individual to petition the local court for permission to enslave himself or herself.[81] Once again, however, the proposal stalled in the House, where representatives were in no hurry to offer Willis, Andrew, or any of Virginia's free blacks the option of self-enslavement, and failed to debate it during the one week remaining before the legislative session ended in spring 1852.[82] The General Assembly would not meet again until November.

Back in Lunenburg, the commonwealth's proceedings against Willis, Andrew, and Mary Doswell plodded along. The court issued a new set of summonses and warnings in September and again in December 1852, which were sent to sheriffs in surrounding Prince Edward and Charlotte counties as well. All were returned unserved. Even though Willis and Andrew were apparently in communication with Lunenburg's representatives in Richmond from their temporary residence (perhaps in Prince Edward County), they were supposedly absent from the county. Indeed, rather than delegating the December summonses to a deputy, the newly minted sheriff, Jonathan A. Stokes, took it upon himself to oversee their delivery and personally declared the Doswell brothers "not found."[83] It is probable that at least Stokes, if not his three deputy sheriffs, sympathized with the Doswells and tried his best not to find them when delivering mandatory writs and summonses. At a minimum, their paper trail conveys far less interest in pursuing the cases against the three than in other pressing business. Perhaps they simply assumed that the charges against Willis and Andrew would disappear once the General Assembly passed a law allowing them to remain. In any case, the failure of the authorities to locate Mary and the brothers bought Willis and Andrew important time, enough to pursue the lengthy process of obtaining favorable legislation in Richmond.[84]

Finally, in January 1853 the House of Delegates again took up the matter of Willis and Andrew's legislation (Senate Bill 145), which had passed in the Senate the previous spring. Lawmakers proposed various amendments to the law, but interestingly enough most of the debate centered on how much the state should require a chosen master to pay for acquiring a self-enslaved person. Thomas J. Pretlow of Southampton proposed making self-enslavement as expensive as possible by charging new masters the full assessed value of the person who became their slave; there would be no discount offered prospective owners of self-enslaved petitioners. By contrast William H. Browne, whose proposed removal policy, if passed, would partially rely upon self-enslavement, suggested charging new masters only one-half the value of a new slave, thereby discounting by one-half the price of self-enslaved individuals to their new masters. Norfolk County's delegate Tapley Portlock went further; he suggested lowering the fee to only one-quarter of a self-enslaved person's assessed value. The details of this debate went unrecorded, but senators eventually agreed upon a kind of self-enslavement tax of one-third the assessed value of a person who chose self-enslavement—a tax high enough to provide the state with some revenue from the process, but not so high as to prevent determined individual free blacks from finding whites willing to become their owners at a two-thirds discount.[85]

On other aspects of the bill, however, legislators in the House were less inclined to compromise. Some opponents of self-enslavement feared that it would merely become enslavement in name only, as it appeared in the cases of Willis and Andrew, who were clearly friendly with their proposed master William Doswell. Such nominal enslavement, these legislators believed, would merely serve to undermine the institution. Others, by contrast, would not have found Sheffey's amendments adequate and would have considered *any* legislation allowing the state to legally enslave free people too unsettling to support. Still others believed the opposite—that to offer protections to free black residents was implying their citizenship and a right to accompanying protections. A minority of delegates sought first to push through a more stringent removal bill before considering one allowing self-enslavement, and they may have thought that crafting a general law concerning Virginia free blacks in response to Willis and Andrew's particular situation in Lunenburg was premature and unnecessary.

Indeed, as soon as the House had met again in December 1852, Browne had reintroduced his removal bill, which had been made "the special order of the day" later that month.[86] Still others opposed calls for additional removal legislation and sought a self-enslavement bill independent of the issue of removal. On 12 January 1853, by a decision of 48–45, the House voted not to take up the self-enslavement bill for further consideration.[87] Although Willis and Andrew had suffered another legislative setback, they might just as well have appreciated the outcome, for the time being. The brothers may have considered their as yet unsuccessful effort to win passage of a self-enslavement law in Richmond as a sort of victory in itself, as it had delayed considerably their prosecution by Lunenburg County officials without requiring them to renounce their legal freedom. As long as their request for a law allowing self-enslavement remained active in the legislature, but unrealized, they remained in convenient, indefinite legal limbo, in which their freedom was (at least temporarily) preserved and the threat of conviction—and expulsion—was lessened.

Only two days later, Thomas E. Bottom, representing Amelia and Nottoway counties, added to the removal debate by introducing a more moderate alternative to Browne's extreme proposal of mandatory removal. Bottom's plan provided that "those only are to be removed who are willing to go," a departure from Browne's measure that would allow free blacks five years to either exit the state or enslave themselves before being forced to leave.[88] The public, newspaper editors, and fellow legislators joined in the renewed, rancorous debate. A group of Goochland County residents met to urge the General Assembly to pass extensive removal legislation.[89]

The editors of the *Richmond Whig*, ever moderate on the subject of free black removal, were quick to condemn both Browne's and Bottom's proposals, calling them attempts to revive Governor William Smith's prior radical efforts to single out free blacks for the "unfeeling and tyrannical experiments of demagogues" that threatened republican government. The editors argued that Browne had "lost sight of the first dictates of justice and humanity" in his plan to drive free blacks from the state without provision for their care or to enslave them "as felons." Bottom's proposal, though "a milder measure" was no more acceptable, they added, as it sought to bring about the same result—"the expulsion of the race." They went well beyond condemning the idea of forced removal by contending that of the many complaints lodged against free blacks in recent years, "the same may be said of many whites." Indeed, they wrote, there are worthy free blacks who "perform useful functions" and "who are industrious, sober . . . useful members of the community."[90]

Editors of the *Richmond Daily Dispatch*, less inclined to sympathize with the plight of Virginia's free blacks, also condemned both proposed plans by focusing on problems of labor. Wouldn't the tens of thousands of free black farm workers, once expelled, be replaced "by a new race of white laborers, coming, probably, from the very hot beds of abolitionism?" they asked. "Will the country gain any thing by such an exchange?" The editors concluded that "one northern abolitionist (and this bill is preparing the way for 50,000,) can do more harm than all the free negroes in the State." While supporters of harsher removal laws justified their plans with calls to preserve the institution of slavery, *Dispatch* editors argued the opposite—the greatest threat to slavery would be the removal of free blacks and the onslaught of foreign or northern wage laborers in Virginia. They viewed removal policy in terms of class as well as race. They conceded that free blacks were on the lower end of the social scale, but "there are, among them, many men of industry, intelligence, and general good character. The loafing free negro is not half so bad as the loafing white man, because he is much more afraid of the law." In short, they concluded, "Of all creatures on earth, the most degraded, is a low, mean white man."[91] (One wonders if the *Dispatch* would have supported measures to deport poor whites before those in support of free black removal.)

Some critics couched their arguments in concerns over unbridled government power and sectionalism, with overtones of paternalism. The *Dispatch* followed up with an article that declared, "There is too much humanity still existing in the State of Virginia to permit such an atrocious abuse of power towards a class of persons whose helplessness, if nothing else, appeals so strongly to our better feelings." In more practical terms, they insisted that removing fifty thousand free blacks "strips Virginia of a member of Congress, and surely she can hardly afford to sacrifice one just at this time." They ended by demanding, "If this is not the free negro's country, where is it?"[92] The editors of the *Lynchburg Daily Virginian* answered, "The expulsion of free negroes in a body from the State . . . is a proposition that we have never contemplated but with abhorrence," but evidently not out of genuine compassion for the population. Free blacks were emancipated, they insisted, "By death bed cowardice and mistaken philanthropy by those who manumitted them, oftentimes in fraud of the well founded expectation of relatives. We free them to quiet our consciences, and banish them to free ourselves of the consequences of our philanthropy."[93] Irresponsible whites were to blame for the increasing presence of free blacks in Virginia, they argued, not blacks themselves.

John C. Rutherfoord, a first-term representative from Goochland County, became the spokesman for other removal extremists when he delivered a lengthy speech to the House in February 1853 urging the passage of Browne's bill. Rutherfoord presented a complicated portrait of free blacks, describing them, on the whole, as "idle, ignorant, degraded and immoral, filling our courts with culprits and our penitentiary with convicts, consuming more than they produce and diminishing rather than adding to the wealth of the state." Taken as individuals, however, they could "have the qualities to make good citizens, if our laws or prejudices would allow it." Rutherfoord echoed Rixey and others by identifying what he saw as the fundamental issue, that free blacks were "a disturbing element" in the relations between master and slave because "the slave is in daily communion with the free negro, and often connected with him by ties of blood and affinity."

In his twenty-page argument in support of Browne's proposed measure, Rutherfoord addressed the major concerns of the bill's critics. First, forced removal would not ruin the economy of Virginia, as some had asserted, because free blacks were such unproductive laborers to begin with—their labor would not be missed in the state's fields and factories. Second, their absence would not result in the loss of congressional representation for Virginia, as their deportation would instead eliminate one of the chief impulses behind whites' relocation from Virginia for western territories—the increasing presence of free blacks in their neighborhoods. Removal would "check emigration and encourage immigration," preserving state political power by augmenting Virginia's white population. Third, the bill would not bring about "hard and cruel consequences" upon free blacks themselves, as critics suggested, but would instead "confer a great blessing upon this unhappy class" by providing them with "both social and political equality" in Liberia.[94]

If in much of his speech Rutherfoord simply rehashed earlier arguments for removal, such as those of former Governor William Smith in the late 1840s, he did so in the distinctive language of a legislator still exploring his role under a new constitution drafted just one year earlier. The basic reasoning behind extremists' calls for free black removal had not evolved much since Smith had championed the cause, but Rutherfoord now had to address the broader concerns of an expanded white electorate in ways that Smith need not have. In addition, though the General Assembly had not passed any removal legislation since 1850, three sections of Article IV of the state constitution of 1852 had represented small but powerful victories for removal and proslavery hardliners, further shaping the political terrain. Section 19 reiterated the expulsion law of 1806 by stating that "slaves hereafter emancipated shall forfeit their freedom by remaining in the commonwealth more than twelve months after they become actually free, and shall be reduced to slavery under such regulations as may be prescribed by law." Section 20 empowered lawmakers to restrict slave owners from emancipating their slaves and guaranteed that they "may pass laws for the relief of the commonwealth from the free negro population, by removal or otherwise." Section 21 assured the preservation of the institution of slavery in the state.[95]

The new constitution, as well as the introduction of Willis and Andrew Doswell's self-enslavement legislation, had altered the tenor and substance of the removal debate. Rutherfoord could now legitimately argue that the Virginia constitution expressly provided for removal and that "cumpulsory removal was intended" by its framers. The constitution not only empowered lawmakers to eliminate the free black population by deportation but "by removal or otherwise," where "otherwise" now included self-enslavement. Rutherfoord condemned the idea of enslaving the whole population of Virginia's free blacks "because of its unnecessary harshness," and asserted that any law allowing for the mandatory re-enslavement of free blacks "would be an outrage upon the spirit of the age in which we live, and unworthy of our high civilization and our ancient honor." For Rutherfoord forced enslavement would express a "wantonness of power" that would violate the sacred principles of republican government reaffirmed by the new constitution, including critical limits placed upon state power. Yet Rutherfoord supported "the provision for their voluntary enslavement" in Browne's bill, which had been amended to stipulate concerning those free blacks who remained in Virginia by 1869 that "if they will not choose their own masters, they shall be sold into slavery." Rutherfoord insisted that free blacks had "no *constitutional* rights" and that a mandatory removal law, now with constitutional backing, was necessary, as it was "by high considerations of public policy, not by abstract theories of human rights, that legislative action must be determined."[96]

Rutherfoord also revealed that the deep-seated intrastate sectional tensions that precipitated the constitutional convention of 1851–52 had not vanished upon ratification of the new constitution. He pitched free black removal as a way for eastern and western men, with "becoming manliness," to come together and tackle a common, identifiable enemy. Rutherfoord addressed his "Western friends" whose "constituencies have little practical interest in the subject under discussion" to consider the long-term threat of a free black population explosion—that "sixty years hence, if we do not arrest the mischief while we can, you may suffer from it more in the West than we now do in the East."[97]

Finally, Rutherfoord explained what the purpose and function of a mandatory removal law would be in localities outside Richmond. Addressing those who agreed with the bill's object but not its content, he explained, "Though you repeal it hereafter, we will, at least, have had the benefits, for the first time, of a full, formal, legal notice from the public authorities of the state to our free negro population, that they must depart from the commonwealth. Is not this experiment worth trying, if you will go no further? Let us at least have the benefit of the notice." With little chance of passing and an even smaller likelihood of being enforced if passed, a strict removal law would at least serve as a "full, formal, legal notice," both to free blacks, who might be driven to leave the state out of fear that the law could be enforced, and perhaps more importantly to his most vocal white constituents, who sought tangible signs of removing the "evil" from their society. For Rutherfoord's radical base in Goochland, free blacks "were the link between the internal threat of slave insubordination and the external threat of abolitionism."[98] For most white Virginians, however, Browne's bill proved far too radical to support.

Though Willis and Andrew's own efforts in the legislature appeared to be stalled, self-enslavement had now entered and invigorated an already passionate debate over removal. Rutherfoord's voice and those of other extremists are often the only ones heard in historical accounts of this period, but moderates constituted the majority of the General Assembly and would easily defeat the measures advocated by Rutherfoord and Browne.[99] Thomas J. Pretlow, who represented Southampton County, countered Rutherfoord by exclaiming that he would not "remain silent in my seat and see what might seem harsh injustice inflicted on the most worthless human being that exists in my county." Browne's bill, which Rutherfoord had endorsed, "proposes to drive the free negroes forth hastily from the Commonwealth, or to sell them into slavery; which, sir, does not comport with my views of justice or humanity," he said. Pretlow proceeded to challenge Rutherfoord point by point, concluding that any mandatory removal law would strike a "deadly blow" against slavery by creating a labor vacuum to be filled by abolitionist-minded northerners and immigrants. He admonished his fellow lawmakers that those who voted in favor of the bill would quickly be voted out of office.

Pretlow also rejected self-enslavement as an effective means of "removing" free blacks from the state, likely revealing the concerns of those responsible for stalling Willis and Andrew's bill in the House. He explained, "to sell the free blacks will not be getting rid of them, nor am I inclined to think that they will be mo[r]e beneficial to the morals of our slaves—for they know that they were liberated in accordance with the laws of the land by their masters—and consequently will in my opinion not only make very bad slaves, but will prove very pernicious among our slave population." Simply changing the legal status of Virginia's blacks from "free" to "slave" would not erase their memory of or desire for liberty. Furthermore, however dangerous a burgeoning free black population might be, Virginians lived under "laws of the land" that could not be discarded in a whimsical fashion.

If the preservation of the institution of slavery was the primary object (which to Pretlow and most legislators it was), the re-enslavement of free people of any kind would have the opposite effect and sow seeds of rebellion, flight, and general discord among enslaved communities. Moreover, Pretlow speculated, a legal process of re-enslavement would aggravate class tensions among whites, because those who could afford to become the masters of free blacks sold into slavery would be exclusively wealthy slaveholders. He warned others in the House that by increasing slaveholders' property while shutting poor whites out of the process, "You would array against us a set of men who are now our friends." Drawing a clear line between the position of radicals like Rutherfoord and that of moderates like himself, Pretlow concluded, "I would willingly co-operate in any just and humane plan to gradually get rid of our free black population; but, as one of Virginia's representatives, I am not prepared to sell them and pocket the money."[100] Pretlow threw his support behind yet another removal measure that had been proposed in the House, one that was far more moderate than Browne's or Bottom's, and whose policy would depart very little from the measure that the General Assembly had passed in 1850.

Edwin T. Mapp from Accomack County also felt compelled to chastise Rutherfoord, Browne, and others for introducing and supporting "stringent legislation" that had created an air in the legislature of "levity that would better characterise a buffoon, or the cruelty of a Moloch, than the enlightened views of a Virginia statesman representing a free and christian people." Reassuring his colleagues and constituents that his opposition to the forced removal of free blacks was not "actuated by any sympathy arising from a sickly sentimentality, or suggested by feelings of any morbid sensibility," Mapp concisely voiced his central concern: "Radical and sudden changes should ever be avoided."

Mapp then elaborated upon the argument of others at the time by explaining why a stricter removal bill would never pass the House, even if most lawmakers (and white Virginians) agreed, in principle, that free blacks were a threat to Virginia's social stability. Mandatory free black removal legislation would set a precedent far more dangerous to Virginia's slave society than the presence of fifty thousand free blacks. Of removal, Mapp warned, "It is not a safe calculation to suppose that Virginia may never yield to an excitement upon this question, or that the emancipation of slavery may not be brought about by the means which I now propose to guard against." By expanding government power to enable it to deport and enslave its free black residents, the same empowered government would be well placed to bring about other sudden and far-reaching policies, including, perhaps, one to end slavery one day in Virginia.

Once again, a lawmaker's stance on policy regarding free blacks had at its root the two impulses that would guide white Virginians' positions on free blacks throughout the 1850s: the desire to preserve forever the institution of slavery and a deep skepticism of state power.[101] "Virginia without slavery is not Virginia, I mean ever to oppose all things that may tend either directly or remotely affect the institution. Believing that the very arguments and power which calls for the removal of free negroes will hereafter come with additional strength for the removal of slaves," Mapp explained. Rather than wasting one another's time in Richmond by proposing new legislation, Mapp suggested, it would be far better "to enforce the present laws, which empower the court of each county to remove all free blacks emancipated since 1806 or descendents—and in this way each county may accommodate itself to its own wishes."

The debate on the floor of the Virginia House now mirrored the larger ongoing sectional debate in the halls of Congress in Washington, but instead of calls for state's rights and regional sovereignty on issues relating to slavery, Mapp and others stressed the importance of preserving the authority of local self-government and a degree of county autonomy from the state. If the goal of Virginia's representatives in Congress was to join other southerners in pushing for limits to federal power in regard to slavery and sovereignty, the mission of Mapp and other delegates in the Virginia House was to impose limits on the power of Virginia's central government in Richmond.[102]

Though legislative issues regarding Virginia's free blacks differed greatly from those that dealt with the state's enslaved population, plans for colonization, petitions made on behalf of free black individuals, and wide-ranging proposals for deportation transcended debate centered solely on the plight, capacity, or threat of free blacks. In short, the Great Removal Debate was about slavery and its preservation. Willis and Andrew Doswell's attempt to remain in Lunenburg as slaves had shifted the terms of the removal debate, which in turn intensified Virginia lawmakers' efforts to defend their state from a perceived free black assault from within, as well as one from abolitionists from without. In his speech before the House, Mapp revealed the degree to which lawmakers believed the application of laws regarding free blacks could affect the institution of slavery. Mapp pointed to the fact that unlike neighboring Northampton County, his own Eastern Shore county of Accomack had for years liberally allowed free blacks emancipated after 1806 to petition for and receive permission to remain in the state. "What was the result?" he asked. "Why, sir, scores of slaves have attempted to runaway—some affecting their escape, and some failing, from Northampton: while a case has rarely ever occurred in Accomac. The cause was evident. Those free negroes, many of them connected by the nearest ties, were driven to the Northern cities, leaving fathers, mothers, brothers, and sisters behind, to follow the instincts of nature in seeking a re-union at the earliest opportunity;—the larger portion of which never would have attempted to leave their native homes had they not been induced by the severance of kindred ties." In Mapp's mind the willingness and propriety of the Accomack County court to allow exceptions to the law of 1806—to issue permission to free blacks to stay in the county—had little to do with white sympathy or compassion, or even free blacks themselves, and everything to do with maintaining the institution of slavery by reducing the impulse to run away among the enslaved. Perhaps further research will indeed show whether the Accomack court allowed those free blacks with family ties to enslaved individuals to stay in the county more frequently than others, and whether those Virginia counties that denied free blacks permission to stay in the state experienced greater rates of rebellion.[103] In any case, Mapp showed that he and other moderates on the removal issue could be extremists when it came to the issue of slavery, so much so that they opposed laws that allowed manumission, as well as those providing for colonization, because those who had promoted them—Jefferson, Madison, and Clay—had done so "based upon their opposition to slavery," and "looked to this quarter for its amelioration and ultimate extermination."[104]

The editors of the *Richmond Daily Dispatch* also swung at Rutherfoord, declaring his proposal, in modern terms, as downright un-American. They wrote, "we have never seen a more unsatisfactory argument." Most worrisome to the editors was that which concerned so many other white Virginians—Rutherfoord's support for a measure that would empower the government to enslave free people. Of the law of 1806 and free blacks, the editors wrote, "It is true that 'precedent' says they may be enslaved for offences against the law—but it says nothing more, and more cannot be inferred." They added that free blacks are not citizens, and "it is also true that they do not come within the provisions of the Bill of Rights. But they *are* embraced in the more comprehensive code of Human Rights and 'imperfect obligations.' We believe that the Almighty sent negroes here to be civilized, and that we cannot, at will, doff the responsibilities He has imposed." They conceded that "free negroes, as a class, are idle and vicious," but contended that their color merely marked their "poverty and debasement," rather than some inherent shortcoming in capacity and citizenship. "What right have we . . . to tear them from homes which, squalid as they are, they love to dwell in, and to condemn them, without trial, to barbarism or free soil?"[105] Once again, removal, re-enslavement, and broader sectional tensions collided on the pages of a Richmond newspaper, offering a peek into the minds of white Virginians who saw themselves as liberal, freedom-loving, law-abiding Americans who championed limited government.[106]

Thus, the actions of Virginia whites in relation to free black individuals in their communities or to legislation in the General Assembly reflected complex views toward free people and their relationship to enslaved kin and the institution of slavery itself—views that were only occasionally explained at the time and that are today difficult to discern. What is clear is the extent to which removal extremists were a minority in a legislature consisting overwhelmingly of stalwart pro-slavery defenders. In April 1853, with little hope of swaying his colleagues to support a mandatory deportation measure, the politically savvy Rutherfoord cast his vote against Browne (whose bill he had so eloquently endorsed weeks earlier) and for a moderate bill that essentially extended for five years the law passed in 1850 to encourage free blacks to leave the state voluntarily. The "Act Establishing a Colonization Board and Making an Appropriation for the Removal of Free Negroes from the Commonwealth" again committed $30,000 per year from the state treasury for colonization of free blacks, created a Colonization Board to oversee the operation, and extended the one-dollar levy on every free black male aged 21 to 54 by local commissioners of the revenue—all of which would expire after five years, unless renewed by the legislature before its expiration in 1858.[107]

Back in Lunenburg the circuit court ploddingly continued its proceedings against the Doswells, repeatedly summoning the three to court to answer the charges made against them nearly three years earlier.[108] In August 1853, however, Mary Doswell "departed this life," leaving behind three more reasons for Willis and Andrew to fight to remain in the state—three orphaned children.[109] Perhaps driven by their sister's death, Willis and Andrew soon made another attempt to jump-start their proposed legislation, which was stuck in the Virginia House. In mid-December, George W. Hardy moved that the "special committee on free negroes" place Senate Bill 145 back on the House docket. Hardy's efforts on behalf of the Doswells went unanswered.[110]

A few weeks later, Willis and Andrew attempted to begin all over again in the Senate, in an effort that might not end in self-enslavement but at least might further delay Lunenburg officials from convicting them. In late January 1854, Thomas H. Campbell presented on their behalf a petition of seventy-five Lunenburg County residents asking that Willis and Andrew "be allowed to select masters and remain in the State of Virginia as slaves." As was the routine, the petition was referred to the Committee on Courts of Justice, who apparently buried it.[111]

If Willis and Andrew's efforts to petition the state had stalled their prosecution on the local level up to this point, by the next month, Lunenburg officials finally felt compelled to act. On February 4, Willis was found—in Lunenburg County—nearly four years after his initial presentment in circuit court. Sheriff Stokes "committed him to jail," where Willis spent the next nine nights contemplating his and Andrew's next move.[112] Whereas *proposals* to the state legislature on their behalf had helped maintain the brothers' freedom since 1850, Willis and Andrew would now need the *passage* of legislation to further delay their conviction, or at the very least to allow them to choose their own master before being sentenced to public sale as slaves by the sheriff—a still unlikely, but increasingly plausible, outcome of their cases.

On February 13, Stokes released Willis on a $1,500 bond, ordering Willis to appear at the next term of the circuit court to answer the charge against him.[113] Willis moved swiftly to prepare his case. The following day, seven witnesses on his behalf were summoned to the next court meeting: William Doswell, William J. Fowlkes, Jason Woodson, Charles Smith (a former commonwealth's attorney), E. R. Chambers, Langston Arvin, and William Arvin Jr. If Willis expected William Arvin Jr. to give friendly testimony, then apparently Arvin saw Willis, and perhaps the free black population in Lunenburg more generally, in a very different way than his father, who had provided the evidence for the presentment against Willis and his siblings four years earlier.[114]

The Doswell brothers also turned their attention back to the place where they had won their only victory—the Virginia Senate. Perhaps they deemed it unlikely that either of them would escape conviction if their cases were to go to trial in the Lunenburg court. For them, self-enslavement might have been the only acceptable alternative to leaving the state, which they manifestly did not want to do. It is also possible, though, that the self-enslavement bill was not, in their thinking, the only possible course of action, but rather a form of *insurance*. If Willis and Andrew were acquitted in court and the law were passed, then no harm done, as the law would allow but not require the Doswells to enslave themselves, and if somehow the brothers were acquitted by the Lunenburg court, they could elect to remain free. On the other hand, if the law were passed and the pair were convicted in court, they could then petition to enslave themselves—yet another legal process that might delay their prosecution for many additional months. The very next day on the floor of the Senate in Richmond, Thomas H. Campbell presented one more petition, this time signed by seventy-six Lunenburg neighbors, "praying that certain slaves emancipated by the will of David M. Doswell, be permitted to select William Doswell as their master." The matter, like the petition from two weeks before, was referred to the Committee on Courts of Justice.[115]

It may have been this second petition that prodded the committee to action. On 17 February 1854, Senate Bill 287 was placed on the Senate docket, echoing the same general language of the previous (and now defunct) Senate Bill 145 in its title: "A Bill Providing for the Voluntary Enslavement of Free Negroes of the Commonwealth."[116] As he had done with the similar Senate Bill 145 two years earlier, Campbell steered this measure through the legislature. On February 24, the Senate passed the bill, but had changed its contents, and on a motion by Campbell, its title, in the process. The title of the approved bill now sent to the House read: "A Senate Bill Providing for the Voluntary Enslavement of Willis and Andrew, Free Persons of Color of the County of Lunenburg."[117] The legislative issue had become the plight of Willis and Andrew Doswell specifically, rather than whether to create an option for general self-enslavement that would apply to Virginia's entire free black population.

On 1 March 1854, awaiting a vote from the House on the Senate's bill allowing his and Andrew's self-enslavement, Willis Doswell entered the Lunenburg County courthouse and pleaded not guilty to the charge for which he had been presented back in 1850. Instead of trying him then, or even on a subsequent day during that term of court, the judge deferred the trial until the following session in September, allowing Willis another critical six months.[118] Andrew, still never having appeared before the court, was summoned again, with copies of the writ this time going also to the sheriffs in Lunenburg, Charlotte, Prince Edward, and Mecklenburg counties.[119]

On March 2, the House of Delegates took up and passed Willis and Andrew's bill.[120] The result was twofold. First, in the short term, the law would allow Willis and Andrew Doswell to petition to enslave themselves, which, if successful, would effectively end the Lunenburg Circuit Court's outstanding cases against them. Second, in the longer term, the law that Willis and Andrew fought so hard to create for themselves would become the model on which the later general law allowing *any* free people of color to petition for enslavement was based—in Virginia and elsewhere in the South.

Virginia lawmakers of different persuasions all got something that they had wanted in Willis and Andrew Doswell's law; the act's language reflected the complex and even contradictory impulses that guided legislators who reported to white male constituents who embraced a broad spectrum of opinions. Divided into six sections, the law was a labyrinth. First, Willis and Andrew were only allowed to enslave themselves to "a master or masters among the next of kin of the said David Doswell deceased," their former owner—a victory for those who saw little harm to the institution of slavery in allowing individuals to select new owners from those whites whom they knew well. In addition, the Doswells could apply for self-enslavement directly to the county court of Lunenburg, expressing in a written petition, signed by each man and two witnesses, their desire to become enslaved, and who they chose as their owner—a nod to those who believed that local authorities knew far better than Richmond lawmakers which free blacks deserved exceptional treatment by the law. The petitions would then be posted "at the front door of the court-house for one month," after which each man would be summoned back into court with his chosen master, at which time the court would "proceed to examine each party separately, as well as such other persons as said court may see fit." Those who feared an all-powerful state, empowered to indiscriminately make slaves of free people, could rest easy: "At such examination," the law stipulated clearly, "the attorney for the commonwealth shall be present and see that such examination is properly conducted, and that no injustice is done to the petitioner." Then, only if "the court shall be satisfied that there is no fraud nor collusion between the parties," and that Willis and Andrew "will be the bona fide slave of the person designated," would the court agree to legal enslavement. At that point, each man would become "the fee simple property" of his chosen master and be treated "as if such petitioner had been born a slave."[121]

The law designed for Willis and Andrew represented a political tapestry woven from compromises on many of the central concerns expressed by citizens, newspapers, and lawmakers during the Great Removal Debate over the previous several years. As a result, Virginia's first self-enslavement law, "An ACT Providing for the Voluntary Enslavement of Willis and Andrew, Free Persons of Color of the County of Lunenburg," explicitly rejected any notions of mandatory enslavement; it was Willis and Andrew, not the state, who would voluntarily strip the men of their liberty.[122] In fact, Lunenburg County authorities could deny the men's requests, if they so desired, insisting that they remain free. The law straddled the fine line between protecting free people's right to liberty and conferring legal citizenship on them, by simply making the process of enslavement difficult, time-consuming, and cumbersome.

Finally, it would strengthen, not weaken, Virginia's institution of slavery by making Willis and Andrew the "bona fide" slaves of William Doswell, as if each "had been born a slave"; in principle, the brothers' new term of absolute servitude to the white Doswell would only harden the lines between free and enslaved through ostensible (though unenforceable) assurances that once enslaved, Willis and Andrew would be true slaves, both in law and in fact. Gone were any clauses requiring chosen masters to pay a self-enslavement tax based on the black petitioner's assessed value, a sticking point in the earlier House debate over a more general self-enslavement law. What survived the amending and political wrangling in the Senate and House was thus a system of clear protections for the petitioners, which combined some lawmakers' efforts to assure their white constituents of the sanctity of liberty with others' attempts to specifically safeguard the customary rights of free black individuals.

Within two weeks, Willis and Andrew presented a joint petition, which was likely written and delivered by their lawyer, to the Lunenburg County court, asking to become the slaves of William Doswell. The document's dry legal language echoed the phrasing of the General Assembly's law and reflected a lawyer's craft more than Willis and Andrew's sincere explanation why two men who had lived as slaves and had become free would choose to renounce that hard-won freedom for permanent, absolute slavery, even if it was to William Doswell.[123] But Willis and Andrew knew that not all freedoms were equal. If legal freedom required their removal from the state, then for them, legal enslavement was preferable.

On 10 April 1854, more than eleven years after he had become free, Willis Doswell became the legal slave of William Doswell.[124] One month later, Andrew followed suit, almost exactly four years after he had been presented by the circuit court.[125] As a result, the charges against the brothers for having violated the expulsion law of 1806 were dropped by the circuit court.[126] The Doswell brothers' re-enslavement had resulted from enduring interracial neighborhood bonds that challenged certain restrictive state laws. And yet for William Arvin Sr. and other whites especially hostile to free blacks in their midst, the brothers' self-enslavement must have demonstrated just how powerful state law could be in circumscribing freedom for people of color.

William Arvin Sr.'s presence on a local grand jury four years before had initiated a chain of events that had dramatically altered the course of Willis and Andrew Doswell's lives. They had since fought for the right to remain in their community, first as free people, and ultimately as slaves. During that time, white Virginians in Lunenburg County, Richmond, and beyond had debated how to reframe the state's constitution and whether to expel free blacks from the state or simply to encourage them to leave through increased taxes, greater accountability, and expanded colonization programs. Most significantly, Willis and Andrew's sister, Mary, had

To the county court of Lunenburg humbly petitioning,—that,—Whereas An act providing for the voluntary enslavement of us, (Willis and Andrew) free men of colour of the county Lunenburg; and whereas said bill provides that we, said free men of color, shall file a petition in the county court of Lunenburg setting forth our desire to select a master or owner of the next kin to David Doswell by whom we were manumitted in his last will and testament.—

We, therefore; wishing the provisions of said law to be carried into effect, do hereby file our petition in which we desire that the privilege may be granted us to choose a master, and that we desire to select Wm Doswell a nephew of said David Doswell; & we do hereby pray your honours will cause the provisions of said act to be complied with, given under our hands this ___ day of March 1854.

Witness

                                        Willis + Doswell
                                              his mark

                                        Andrew Doswell
                                              his mark

Petition of Andrew and Willis Doswell for enslavement, 1854. Following a special law passed by the Virginia legislature allowing them to re-enslave themselves, Willis and Andrew Doswell successfully submitted this petition to the Lunenburg County court and thereby prompted a flurry of similar requests from elsewhere in the state, which led to the creation of the nation's first so-called voluntary enslavement law in 1856. (Courtesy Library of Virginia, Richmond) died, leaving behind three children in need of care. Together, Andrew and Willis would become the unlikely fathers of Virginia's first self-enslavement law. This law encapsulated—and balanced—many of the central concerns of white Virginians at the time in its carefully crafted phrases. It would become the basis of general self-enslavement legislation two years later and the model for other such laws in the mid-nineteenth-century South on the eve of the Civil War. Above all, the law had created another option—an option of last resort—for two free black brothers who had found themselves prosecuted under the expulsion law of 1806 and, for reasons that made sense to them at the time, renounced their legal liberty—forever.

CHAPTER FOUR

FAMILY AND FREEDOM IN

THE NEIGHBORHOOD

Word of Willis and Andrew's re-enslavement in spring 1854 did not spread quickly through Lunenburg County's white community, or if it did, it was met with quiet indifference. "Nothing of interest transpired at Court; fewer people than usual," noted one white man who had witnessed the application of Virginia's first self-enslavement law at the Lunenburg courthouse. More remarkable were the "great coats" worn by many, "a thing very unusual for the 8th of May," and the "great complaints about the scarcity of tobacco plants" heard among bystanders, due to extraordinarily late frosts and bitter cold.[1] Amid "the fatigue and bustle of the court house yard" that characterized such court days in mid-nineteenth-century rural Virginia, the enslavement of two free black men apparently went without public comment, even among those in the press and legislature who might have seized upon the men's decision to renounce their freedom as a vindication of pro-slavery rhetoric.[2]

Lunenburg's black community, however, had been well aware of Willis and Andrew Doswell's predicament and learned quickly how the brothers had at least averted the worst effects of Virginia's legal system—by creating and then using state law to nullify the actions of the local courts and to remain in the state, albeit as slaves. It had been rare for free black residents of Lunenburg to face prosecution for remaining illegally in Virginia, so news of the Doswells' plight would have traveled widely through the "grapevine telegraph" that linked the county's black community.[3] In this way, other free blacks living in Lunenburg in violation of the law learned two critical pieces of information: first, a presentment from the county court, however unlikely, was possible; and second, once prosecuted, one way of avoiding forced removal or sale as a slave was to secure a personal law from the General Assembly authorizing an individual's self-enslavement.

Less than one year after the court had dropped its cases against the Doswells on account of their self-enslavement, another free black resident of Lunenburg faced prosecution for living in the state illegally. In February 1855 a grand jury of the circuit court presented Araminta Frances, a twenty-four-year-old mother of two, "for remaining in this state upwards of twelve months" since her emancipation.[4] Frances's presentment had not been an accident. Years earlier, in 1848, Mary Maddux Richardson, the wife of Frances's owner, James G. Richardson, had sued for divorce, asserting that her husband was "addicted to daily habits of intoxication, and when in that state has on many occasions, inflicted upon [her] the most cruel and inhuman whippings, & at the same time threatening to kill" her.[5] Frances might have been spared her later grand jury presentment if Mary Richardson had not also stated what her neighbors may already have known: "That . . . Richardson has been guilty of the grossest Adultery with a negro slave, by the name of Araminta since [Mary] intermarried with said Richardson That the said Richardson has on more occasions than one told [her] that He never loved her and only married her for Her property, and that He would be glad to see her damned eyes closed for the last time—That the said Richardson very often drives [her] from Her own bed, and in Her presence takes to bed with Him, the sd. negro woman, and would encourage the negro woman, to insult [her] and upon one occasion made the woman slap [her] jaws."[6] Even if most Lunenburg residents were unaware of the horrors that allegedly took place on the Richardson plantation, at least Mary Richardson's brother, Washington Maddox, had heard the lurid details. Maddox had been a long-standing county court justice and justice of the peace in Lunenburg, and perhaps it was he who used his standing in the white community to facilitate an expulsion prosecution directed at Araminta Frances.[7]

Mary Richardson's efforts to combat a problem she shared with other wives of unfaithful slaveholding men in the South had won her a divorce (and the recovery of her personal property), but had done little to absolve Frances from her involvement with James G. Richardson, which had produced two children.[8] In the doublespeak of a Virginia planter, Richardson had instructed in his will shortly before his death in 1850 "that my negro child Virginia and Minty's child yet unborne" should be emancipated and each given the large sum of $1,000, leaving one to wonder whether Richardson's mention of "my negro child Virginia" was a posthumous

*Affidavit of Mary Richardson in divorce case, 1848. In addition to
alcoholism and domestic abuse, Mary Richardson described her husband's
lurid sexual exploits with an enslaved woman, Araminta, which not only won
Richardson a divorce in 1848 but helped to seal the fate of Araminta, who
would become free, then indicted for remaining in the state illegally,
then re-enslaved. (Courtesy Library of Virginia, Richmond)*

admission of rape or simply a mundane statement of fact regarding his
personal property. Frances would be manumitted as well, but only if
Richardson's daughter Sarah, to whom he had willed her, should happen
to "die without having been married."[9]

By 1852 Frances had found herself free and felt it important enough to
petition the county court for permission to remain in the county.[10] Instead
of granting Frances permission to stay in the county, however, the court
took the opportunity to appoint Jonathan L. Coleman as the guardian of
Frances's children, Virginia and William. Coleman, a "friend" of James G.
Richardson and an executor of his estate, managed the $2,000 inheritance
Virginia and William had received from Richardson, which had already
accumulated $87 in interest.[11] It may have been Richardson's bequest to

his children (or perhaps its unusual size) that prompted the court to place the children under the control of Coleman. Undeterred, Frances again sought court action when she asked to be registered at the Lunenburg courthouse in 1853. Frances, "five feet three and three fourth inches high, a scar on her forehead, dark brown complexion," became the 102nd free black resident to register in the county in nearly three years. If Frances had hoped that the clerk might not remember that she had been denied court permission to remain a resident of Lunenburg one year earlier, she must have been disappointed when he stopped short of handing her a copy of her registration, crossing out his entire eight-line entry into the county's Register of Free Negroes to begin again. He had forgotten to insert "No permission has been granted her to remain in this State" before the sentence listing her age.[12] While it mattered to the court clerk that Frances remained in the county without permission, it neither kept him from providing her with an official register nor prompted him to report her illegal residency in the county or her presence in the courthouse to the sheriff that day. This is how law worked in Virginia, through the hands of individual county clerks who decided what a register meant, exactly, and how much personal history to include on the document. Frances was not a citizen, but she sought official recognition that she belonged in the county. Though the register she obtained officially recognized her residency, it made her continuing presence in the community no less illegal.

Eighteen months would pass before George W. Hardy—Lunenburg's representative to the General Assembly—joined sixteen other grand jurors in bringing forth a presentment against Frances "for remaining in this state upwards of twelve months since [her] manumission without lawful authority upon the evidence of Jno L. Coleman, who was sent for by the grand jury and sworn in Court to give testimony."[13] Coleman, the ward of Frances's two children, was perhaps a reluctant witness, but nonetheless provided the evidence requested by the court. Frances had indeed been living in Lunenburg illegally for longer than one year. Hardy, who had been so helpful to the Doswell brothers, left no record of his position on Frances's grand jury presentment. It is not known whether he pushed for Frances to be prosecuted or dissented with (but had been overruled by) fellow jurors determined to single her out.

The court went on to pursue Frances's case in the way it had the Doswells'—in a slow, drawn-out procession of summonses.[14] By December 1855, Frances decided to combat her presentment not in the Lunenburg Circuit Court, but rather as Willis and Andrew had done, in the General Assembly in Richmond.[15] Like many free blacks, Frances took advantage of the law's many levels to make her case to multiple audiences. On the first day of the next legislative session, Hardy used the Doswells' legal precedent to help make a similar case for Frances's re-enslavement in the House; he introduced a bill to allow for the "voluntary enslavement of Araminta Frances, a woman of color," the first such measure to be proposed in the legislature since the Doswells'.[16]

News of Willis and Andrew's ironic "victory" and now of Frances's attempt to achieve the same seems to have spread beyond Lunenburg County's borders, or at least throughout the corridors of the Virginia legislature. In the following days, more free black men and women from across Virginia sought assistance from their county's representatives in Richmond in creating personal laws enabling them to enslave themselves. These included thirty-one-year-old Dangerfield Alexander of Culpeper County, who had refused to leave Virginia for Liberia upon emancipation and who had been presented by his circuit court for remaining in the state;[17] sixteen-year-old Critty Woodson from Powhatan County, whose parents had been presented by the county court and who had also refused to emigrate to Liberia;[18] Frank Harman and Charlotte Pate of Pulaski County, who had both been indicted by their county court several months earlier;[19] twenty-nine-year-old Thomas Grayson and Thomas Jones from Culpeper County;[20] Jesse Spencer of Henrico County;[21] and sixty-two-year-old Lewis Williamson[22] and a family of four—Simon, Martha, Judy, and Margaret—all of Southampton County.[23]

By mid-December 1855 the *Richmond Dispatch* reported, "So numerous are applications of this character, that it has been found necessary to introduce a general law into the Legislature for the voluntary enslavement of free negroes of the Commonwealth." The *Dispatch's* item was run, with minor variations, by several newspapers nationally under the headline "A Case for the Abolitionists" and "Voluntary Enslavement." The brief article made no mention of the underlying reason behind so many free people's petitions for enslavement—to obviate, avoid, or overcome prosecution under the expulsion law of 1806—but instead commented on the recent application to the legislature of Lewis Williamson: "He is an old man, sixty years of age, and has been lately emancipated, but is anxious to remain in a condition of servitude, which he knows by his own experience and observation, is the best and happiest condition for his race."[24] Similarly, the *Daily Richmond Enquirer* would later report that "Both the [general] law, and its cause, are curious." The paper explained, "The Virginia legislature had repeatedly been troubled with petitions from free people of color, praying for special acts (laws) authorizing them to make themselves the slaves of white persons whom they had chosen, or might choose, as owners." Echoing the earlier *Dispatch* item, the *Enquirer* smugly concluded "that such a law as one here abridged should be called for, proclaims more eloquently than all the replies to *Uncle Tom's Cabin* can proclaim, the ease, comfort, and desirableness of slavery, as it exists in Virginia, compared with Freenegroism."[25] The phenomenon of self-enslavement provided some such fodder for pro-slavery extremists and their mouthpieces, but Virginia newspapers, on the whole, stayed relatively silent on the matter, as few joined the *Dispatch* and *Enquirer* in arguing that it demonstrated blacks' genuine desire for servitude.

The individual petitions for self-enslavement in the legislature, as well as the call for a general law standardizing the process, reignited the debate among lawmakers over free black removal in early 1856, much as Willis and Andrew's first petition to the General Assembly in 1852 had done. George E. Deneale of northwestern Rockingham County represented a small group of hardliners that had never accepted the terms of the acts passed in 1850 and 1853 supporting voluntary free black migration from the state. Deneale now introduced a ten-page bill that would have repealed the act of 1853, replacing it with one that would authorize a "Virginia Colonization Board" with "full power and authority to provide for the removal, from Virginia, of such free negroes and mulattoes as are now free and residents therein, and their children, to the Western Coast of Africa, the West India Islands, or to any other suitable place." The deportation process would be funded through a system of annual taxes imposed on free blacks themselves and would involve only those who became delinquent for more than one year. A free black male who failed to pay his annual $5 tax two years in a row would "*ipso facto* forfeit all right which he might have had to remain in the Commonwealth, and shall be proceeded against as other free negroes remaining in this Commonwealth without authority of law." Significantly, Deneale's deportation plan also contained a variation on the self-enslavement process currently under discussion in the legislature. Once a free black individual had been convicted but not yet sold under the terms of his removal bill (or under the expulsion law of 1806), local authorities could, "with the consent of such free negro," sell him or her to "any responsible white person" willing to offer the court $500 in security, on condition that the new master would guarantee the black's good behavior and removal from Virginia within ninety days.[26] Deneale's bill was eventually tabled, but in the meantime it had helped to further link the idea of self-enslavement to stricter notions of free black removal, especially for those disinclined to support a general self-enslavement bill that might appear in any way to be sympathetic to free black individuals. Moreover, Deneale's support of a limited form of self-enslavement in his own removal bill likely helped with efforts to sell the general voluntary enslavement bill under consideration to more radical legislators as a kind of removal measure.[27]

The general voluntary enslavement bill moved rapidly through the legislature in the first weeks of 1856, in large part because much of its contents already had been painstakingly crafted and debated two years earlier.[28] Lawmakers had devised a draft bill for the Doswells in 1854 that would have allowed for general self-enslavement, but had scrapped it for one that pertained only to the two brothers. Tabled, but not forgotten, the earlier proposed bill now surfaced as the template for the general measure in 1856.

Bills resulting from the spate of individual petitions for self-enslavement in late 1855 also proceeded through the General Assembly with haste. Araminta Frances's measure, having been combined with that of Dangerfield Alexander, passed both houses in January 1856 and would be one of the first laws that the General Assembly would pass allowing for certain individuals to enslave themselves. Two months later, Frances became the legal slave of John L. Coleman, the guardian of her children, prompting the court to drop its charges against her.[29] Like Andrew and Willis Doswell before her, Frances had used repressive legal and political systems—at every level—to her advantage as best she could. She had petitioned and registered with the local county court, successfully stalled then annulled her prosecution by the circuit court, and with the assistance of George W. Hardy had won a state law that, as a last resort, would allow her to remain, enslaved, in her community with her free children.

In February 1856 Virginia passed the first general self-enslavement law in the nation, which mandated a process that was similar overall to that outlined in Willis and Andrew Doswell's earlier measure, but that contained several significant changes.[30] Under the general law, "any free person of color" could apply for enslavement in his or her local circuit court, as long as that person was at least eighteen years of age if female or at least twenty-one if male. The general law thus shifted the attention of free blacks who sought enslavement from the General Assembly in Richmond to their local circuit courts, thereby relieving legislators of the need to consider multiple petitions and placing the decision to accept—or deny—such requests in the hands of local authorities. In addition, by requiring the semiannual circuit courts to hear petitions, lawmakers made the process less accessible and more time-consuming for would-be petitioners and their masters than it might have been if permitted in the monthly county courts—a provision that surely would have been changed if a majority of lawmakers had viewed the law as a means to enslave large numbers of the state's free blacks.

Whereas Willis and Andrew Doswell had been restricted in their choice of a new owner to a person "among the next of kin" of their former master, a free person of color was now free to choose any willing white person to become his or her owner.[31] The new law also retained Hugh W. Sheffey's amendment to an earlier draft of Willis and Andrew Doswell's law stating that despite the self-enslavement of a mother, "the children of any such female free person of color, born prior to such term, shall not be deemed to be reduced to slavery by such proceeding."[32] Again, if most legislators at the time had been primarily driven by the impulse to enslave Virginia's free black population *en masse*, they would have removed this important protective clause from the bill.

The general law also differed from the Doswells' by imposing a kind of tax upon the process—something that had been proposed, debated, but not included in the final law passed for the Doswells. Under the law of 1856, if interviews with both a black petitioner and his or her proposed owner cleared the path for the former's enslavement, the law directed that local authorities assess the petitioner's value, as "if he or she was a slave," and that the proposed owner pay one-half that amount to the court.[33] During the remainder of 1856, at least eight free blacks petitioned their local courts for self-enslavement, followed by another nine in 1857, at least seven in 1858, and seventeen in 1859. Fifteen or more free blacks petitioned their respective local courts to forgo their freedom in 1860. Application of the general self-enslavement law extended well beyond the bounds of free black communities in Southside tobacco-belt counties like Lunenburg. Indeed, the few individuals who petitioned their circuit courts under the new law came from all corners of Virginia. The use of the general self-enslavement law by free individuals in a variety of Virginia communities largely corresponded to the degree of enforcement—or threatened enforcement—of the expulsion law by various localities. After all, it had been Lunenburg County authorities' enforcement of the law of 1806 that had prompted the self-enslavement petitions of Willis and Andrew Doswell and Araminta Frances in the first place, giving birth to the Doswells' law and now the general law, and forever linking self-enslavement to enforcement of the expulsion law of 1806.

A clearer picture, then, of how the expulsion law operated among Virginia localities in the late 1850s helps explain why and how the self-enslavement law was invoked by certain free black individuals in particular towns and counties. In their sporadic application of the law of 1806 to free blacks in their midst in the late 1850s, county officials across Virginia differed in how—and when—they applied the law to individuals. There were generally two variables in a given county's approach to the expulsion law. First, officials in a particular locality could choose whether to apply the law at all, and if so, how frequently. Then, if a grand jury presentment against a free black person did issue either from the county court or the circuit court, the prosecution could take a variety of routes. Here again, local officials had a great deal of freedom. They could choose to drop the charges quickly; prosecute haphazardly with little expectation of obtaining a conviction; regularly summon the defendant to court and thus keep alive the prospect of convicting him or her, possibly inducing the defendant to move away in the meantime; or diligently enforce the letter of the law, securing a conviction and the free person's sale into slavery. A particular locality might enforce the law only rarely, but, when it did, it could pursue the prosecution to conviction. In another locality, officials might initiate actions under the removal law fairly regularly by the 1850s, but never convict anyone they presented or indicted.

On at least seventeen occasions from 1856 to 1865, Virginia county or circuit courts convicted free blacks of remaining in the state in violation of the law and ordered them sold into absolute slavery, as permitted by the Virginia constitution.[34] In at least five instances during the same period, courts in what is now West Virginia did the same.[35] Though it is unlikely that all these individuals were actually sold into slavery, at least one, Mary Dunmore of Norfolk City, was—for $100 to H. F. Martin on 28 March 1859.[36] Others left Virginia after they were charged but before being prosecuted or enslaved.[37]

A comparison of several rare episodes of local enforcement of the expulsion law during a twelve-month period (from fall 1857 to fall 1858) illustrates the range of local efforts by whites to apply the law, as well as an equally broad spectrum of responses by those free blacks who either found themselves the objects of grand jury presentments or perhaps felt threatened by possible indictment, prompting some to petition for self-enslavement as a result. Local courts left little explanation for why certain individuals were indicted for violating the expulsion law and why others living illegally in the county were not.[38] In Frederick County, among the seventeen charged along with Thomas and Henry Champ in 1857–58 for remaining in Virginia were people with no personal property as well as others with sizable assets, such as the seventy-year-old Monday

Account of sale of Mary Dunmore, 1859. The 1852 Virginia constitution
allowed for the prosecution and sale into absolute slavery of free African Americans,
such as Mary Dunmore of Norfolk City in 1859, who illegally resided in the state.
(Courtesy Norfolk City Circuit Court, Norfolk, Va.)

Robinson, who owned among other property sixteen farm animals, a clock, and household/kitchen furniture valued at fifty dollars.[39] Some of the people targeted were apparently without employment, while others had occupations, including a gardener, housekeeper, domestic, and a "stone fence maker."[40] Though local commissioners of the revenue were frequently the ones who reported the names of free blacks living illegally to county courts (as was required by law), one cannot conclude that it was an individual's financial situation—poverty or wealth—that alone attracted the attention of the commissioner, a white neighbor, or a grand jury. In some cases, it may have been jealousy that led some who found themselves on grand juries to report such individuals. A degree of respect demonstrated toward such individual free blacks by the larger white community, however, would explain why so few of those who were indicted by grand juries were actually convicted of the offense and why such cases typically dragged on for years. In other words, it is possible that one in a few white residents used his position on a grand jury to satisfy a personal grudge or prejudice—for whatever reason—against particular free black individuals, though a majority of fellow jurors, and perhaps judges, remained indifferent.

In October and November 1857, Albemarle County court officials registered more than 110 free blacks who, it was carefully noted, had produced "satisfactory evidence of their having been born free of parents who were free previous to 1st May, 1806," an extraordinarily high number for a two-month period in any Virginia locality at the time.[41] Free blacks in Charlottesville and the surrounding area must have been responding to pressure exerted—in some form—by local whites to distinguish between legal and illegal free people in their community; pressure that drove many to seek official court recognition and protection of their liberty. Though Mary Jane House and a handful of other free blacks who lived in violation of the law also sought to register and, in the process, win court permission to become legal residents in Albemarle, few even bothered. In this instance, the court refused House her application "for leave to remain in this county," though it had granted others, including William Sindler, permission just a few months before. Though many free blacks living legally in the county felt it important enough to register at the courthouse, only a handful of those to whom the expulsion law applied attempted to register, indicating a quiet confidence among them that enforcement of the law was unlikely or impracticable and that their freedom did not rest upon obtaining a piece of paper from the courthouse. Moreover, by seeking permission from the court they might invite prosecution. Such free black residents were in effect registered in the *minds* of neighboring whites as known, useful, and upright individuals. For them, a court document stating what their neighbors knew already must have seemed redundant, even insulting, if how they carried themselves in their community far transcended the limits of law on paper. Nonetheless, at least two men at the time, John Martin and Satchell Grayson, considered themselves to be in imminent threat of indictment and, as a result of their illegal status, sought self-enslavement in order to continue living in the county.[42]

John Martin had been emancipated by the will of his former mistress, Nancy Martin, in 1852, and had lived with his enslaved wife and children for two years when the Albemarle County court indicted him for "remaining in the State Contrary to Law."[43] His case languished in court for more than three years, until county authorities began registering large numbers of free blacks in October 1857. Apparently, Martin felt a sense of urgency and began to fear that the long-standing charges against him might now lead to conviction. In addition, since his initial indictment by the court the legislature had passed the general voluntary enslavement law, thus creating a new option for those prosecuted by their courts after February 1856. In his petition to the Albemarle Circuit Court, his lawyer explained "that a presentment has been found against him in the said Court for remaining in the Commonwealth contrary to Law; and that he is advised, he has no defence against said presentment; and that a verdict against him on said proceeding will eventuate in his sale into slavery unless in the meantime, he removes from the Commonwealth . . . that he is advised furthermore that however good, his character, he would be refused by the proper authority on grounds of public policy liberty to remain in the Commonwealth;—for these reasons, your petitioner is reduced to the necessity of availing himself of the provisions of the Act of Assembly."[44] The court dropped its charges against Martin soon after he became the slave of James E. Huckstep on 11 May 1858.[45]

Satchell Grayson, a carpenter and former member of Mountain Plain Baptist Church, had been thirty-six years old when his master James Oldham died in Albemarle County in 1843.[46] He and eighteen other enslaved individuals had then become the property of their mistress, Mary Oldham. Thirteen years later, Mary Oldham died, leaving behind a will that allowed Grayson the option to become free, as long as he expressed his desire for liberty within a year of her death. In 1857 Grayson became a free man, and like Martin, assumed a legal status that had the potential to separate him from his still-enslaved wife and children. Though never indicted by Albemarle County courts for remaining in the state illegally, he nonetheless felt the effect of the expulsion law (and a spasm of increased enforcement of registration laws against free blacks in Albemarle County) and petitioned the Albemarle Circuit Court for enslavement. The court granted Grayson permission to enslave himself to John Wood Jr., who likely knew Grayson from Mountain Plain Baptist Church and knew that he was more interested in winning some form of insurance against court prosecution than in becoming his slave.[47] Grayson never followed through on the petition and clearly remained associated with Wood long after their ruse—Wood was one of two white men who posted bond for Grayson who, along with his two sons Thomas and William, had been charged with stealing two hogs from W. D. Jarman in 1867. Father and sons would be convicted of petit larceny and would apparently serve twenty days in prison.[48]

At roughly the same time as Albemarle County whites increased their vigilance against free blacks living there illegally, the Accomack County Circuit Court indicted thirteen free blacks for violating the expulsion law—including five in November 1857 for remaining in Virginia "without lawful permission" (George Evans, Adah Evans, Susan Becket, Mary Beavans, and Lavinia Phillips), and six members of the Ewell family in November 1858 (Bill, George, Bridget, Lucy, Mary, and Sarah Ewell) for remaining in the state "contrary to law." Of those indicted in fall 1857, four were acquitted or not prosecuted by the court. Susan Becket, the only one to be found guilty by a jury, was never prosecuted; her case was dismissed in 1865. Nonetheless, as a result of this crackdown in Accomack, Levin Crippin, a forty-seven-year-old "day laborer" who had not yet been indicted by the court, felt himself in need of legal protection and petitioned the county's circuit court to become the slave of neighbor Levi J. Wortham. Like Satchell Grayson in Albemarle County, however, the protection that Crippin sought was not in the form of absolute servitude to a kindly master, but in preemptive court action to delay or prevent future indictment; once his petition had been accepted by the court, Crippin never appeared in the courthouse to complete the process. In 1860, after the crackdown had subsided, Crippin still lived in Accomack County as a free man and felt confident enough to ask the court to dismiss the petition, which it did. Crippin apparently continued to live in Accomack County, unmolested by the courts.[49]

In the late 1850s, instances of removal prosecution often resulted from grand jury indictments of family groups, rather than of a broad cross-section of a county's free black community. This was the situation in Campbell County, where the circuit court presented several members of the Wood family (Nancy Ann, Wyatt, Richard, Samuel, Albert, and Walker) in March 1859, as well as in Chesterfield County in the early 1860s when John, Beverly, and Elizabeth Hix were presented together by the circuit court in April 1860, followed by the presentments of the Howlett family (Wilson, Peter, William, Robert, Fanny, Rebecca, and Sarah) in August 1861.[50] Five members of the Deeling family (Candis, Solomon, William, Dick, and Benjamin) and two of the Only family (Henry and Watt) were indicted in November 1861 by the Charles City County Circuit Court.[51] In Alleghany County, on the western border of present-day Virginia, twelve

Petition of Satchell Grayson for enslavement, 1858. Satchell Grayson likely had little intention of following through on his 1858 petition for re-enslavement, which instead acted as a kind of insurance policy should he be targeted by the Albemarle County court for continuing to live in the state illegally. (Courtesy Library of Virginia, Richmond)

free people were presented by the circuit court during a twelve-month period beginning in April 1857, among them three small (likely) family groups (Samuel and Allise Rogers, Elisha and Eliza Fox, and James William and a woman simply listed as Charlotte). Half of those charged, however, were individual men who were seemingly unrelated (James Merchant, Samuel Calender, James Matthews, William Liggins, John Blair, and John Cotrell).[52] In some cases it is unclear whether or not those indicted together by local courts were family. Among those individuals indicted for violating the law of 1806 were often groups who, even if not related biologically, had been emancipated together by the same owner, as it was with Scott, Alfred, Polly and her children in Sussex

County in April 1861, all of whom, the clerk noted, were "emancipated by the Will of Polly Winfield decd since the 1st day of May 1806."[53]

Even those local officials periodically concerned with enforcing the law of 1806, however, did so while following other laws that protected the rights of free people just as diligently. For example, in August 1856 the Alleghany County court, which later threatened twelve free blacks with re-enslavement, indicted a white man, John Reynolds, "for kidnapping William Callendar a free person, with intent to sell or use as a slave."[54] In Washington County, located in southwestern Virginia, the same court that would indict (but fail to convict) seven men for remaining in the state contrary to law on the eve of the Civil War had, several years earlier, heard and granted a petition of freedom from Eliza Powell and ten others who had been hired out illegally after their owner's death.[55] Similarly, it was not rare for officials in other localities to periodically consider and approve petitions from free black residents complaining against whites who held their loved ones "illegally detained in slavery."[56] Thus, the court records of Virginia localities tell a complicated tale, in which authorities alternately protected and threatened the liberty of free blacks through their actions (or deliberate inaction).

Many of those individuals who petitioned for self-enslavement under the 1856 law were men and women like Albemarle County's John Martin, who chose bondage to escape conviction under state laws that required free blacks and their descendants to leave the state within a year of their emancipation. From 1854 to 1864, direct enforcement of the removal law resulted in at least seventeen petitions for self-enslavement (or about 15 percent of the total number identified), as men and women who had been charged by grand juries under their county court or circuit court for violating the expulsion law sought to escape conviction and a compulsory exit from the state.[57]

In most cases, however, it appears that free individuals who applied for legal enslavement sought to avoid the chance of such court action in the future, and their petitions for self-enslavement underscore the fact that the possibility of facing charges for remaining in the state may have been real enough to worry many more free blacks than ever suffered actual enforcement. A study of self-enslavement in mid-nineteenth-century Virginia is therefore largely an examination of the dilemmas faced by individuals who were either indicted by their local court for violating state law or felt that they *might* be charged for violating the law. For example, in 1848, eight years after her liberation by her former owner in Pulaski County, Charlotte Pate had submitted a petition to the Virginia General Assembly that stated, "She is unwilling to leave the state and is advised that the law in relation to free negroes if enforced, will compel her to do so, that she prefers to return to a state of slavery rather than be compelled to leave the Commonwealth." Pate had neither been indicted nor prosecuted by the court for violating Virginia law (which she soon would be), yet in her case the *threat* of its enforcement influenced her choices and behavior in profound ways.[58] It may have been the memory of past court action in Pulaski County aimed at free blacks, news of a crackdown in another locale, or perhaps an informal warning she had received from white neighbors that impelled Pate to fear the consequences of legal freedom enough to seek enslavement. Pate was exceptional—not all free blacks who were prosecuted under (or felt threatened by) the expulsion law of 1806 petitioned for self-enslavement.

Perhaps as many as one-third of those who petitioned for self-enslavement from 1856 to 1860, however, followed the examples of Satchell Grayson in Albemarle and Levin Crippin in Accomack and likely pursued self-enslavement in their local courts only as a matter of *insurance*, without knowing what would happen. If they were indicted for living in the state illegally sometime after submitting their petition, then they could follow through with self-enslavement or leave the state, escaping further prosecution; if the court never charged them with living in the state illegally, the petition could be dismissed or simply ignored. In this way, many petitioners apparently never had any intention of renouncing their freedom at all, a fact reflected by the proportion of petitioners who actually used the general self-enslavement law to successfully enslave themselves through their local courts during these years: only one-half. Virginia's self-enslavement law of 1856 offered some free blacks a legal tool that they could manipulate to their own advantage, allowing them to avoid indictment for remaining in Virginia more than one year after manumission, to slow prosecution, to prevent conviction, or even to delay sentencing, so that they could stay in the state as free people for as long as possible or, in the worst case, choose their own master, should they find themselves convicted by their court and threatened with sale. For such individuals, the surest way to avoid being re-enslaved by sheriff's auction through conviction was to petition for enslavement.[59] The fact that self-enslavement was actively used by some free black individuals as a form of insurance against future court action is further proof that while the 1806 law was inconsistently and rarely applied, neither was it a dead letter. The threat of its enforcement—a factor difficult for the historian to observe or measure—drove several dozen individuals to take the serious and potentially life-altering step of petitioning their court for self-enslavement.[60]

As described in the Introduction, thirty-three-year-old Henry Champ of Frederick County was one who used the 1856 voluntary enslavement law to avoid further action by the court. Ironically, Champ's petitioning for self-enslavement had proved to be the most effective way of *preventing* his enslavement and ensuring his freedom. His petition bought him critical time by halting the court's prosecution of its expulsion case against him and by enabling his release from court custody, even once convicted.[61] Most significantly, Champ's request for self-enslavement allowed him to keep his family intact and to relocate to a community in which his and his children's freedom could not be declared illegal. Champ's self-enslavement petition provided him with a modicum of control within a legal system that empowered local judges, if they wished, to make slaves of free black men and women. Though Champ clearly had no intention of being re-enslaved in Frederick County, he could not have been sure that county authorities would not arrest and imprison him before he had a chance to flee the state with his family. Had he not escaped first to Ohio, Champ's petition for self-enslavement would have given him the option to choose a master—an undesirable option, but one that was better than being auctioned by the sheriff as a slave to an unknown buyer.

Thomas Champ, Henry's younger brother, used the same tactic with the court when he was convicted for violating the expulsion law in November 1859. Immediately, he petitioned to become the slave of planter James H. Carson, the next-door neighbor of William Strother Jones, whom Henry Champ had selected as his owner. If the authorities had not realized then that the Champ brothers' petitions were disingenuous, they clearly had by the time the court met again the following year; Thomas Champ had failed to show up to follow through with his enslavement but had not disappeared with his brother. Though the court seemed unable to locate Thomas Champ and continued to dutifully issue summonses for his arrest for more than one year, the census taker had no trouble that year noting Champ's location for all to see: he lived as a free man with Carson and worked as a "Gardiner."[62] The Champs would not be the last petitioners to use Virginia's self-enslavement law for a purpose other than enslavement, likely with the tacit approval of their local courts. Just as many enslaved individuals had re-made Virginia's first manumission law in the late eighteenth century by negotiating and purchasing their freedom from their owners, a significant portion of petitioners would use the self-enslavement law differently than its framers had envisioned. For Grayson, Crippin, Henry and Thomas Champ, and others, the promise of the general self-enslavement law was not in its power to make slaves of free people, but in protecting the liberty of petitioners with a lengthy judicial process that countered other legal measures of the same courts during those times in which they found their freedom most vulnerable.

In most instances, however, free blacks apparently sought enslavement (and not simply a delay in court proceedings) by applying the law in local communities in precisely the way lawmakers in Richmond had intended—namely, as a way for select individuals who might otherwise leave the state to remain in their neighborhoods, often among family, as the property of whites whom they knew well. In both its construction and its application, Virginia's self-enslavement law embodies the contradictory nature of relations between whites and blacks in nineteenth-century Virginia society. The harshness of Virginia's self-enslavement law needs little elaboration. Rather than supersede the expulsion law that applied to newly freed African Americans or the constitutional clause threatening free blacks with enslavement, the voluntary enslavement law complemented them, offering those who were singled out with a choice between freedom somewhere else and at least nominal bondage at home. In this light, there is little that was *voluntary* about the actions of those who were threatened with expulsion and chose to become slaves so that they might stay near their loved ones—those people were choosing what they saw as the lesser of two evils. No wonder, then, that most historians who have considered the self-enslavement law have concluded that it is a vivid expression of white Virginia society's callousness toward free blacks.

But the self-enslavement law also reflects a kind of intimacy between certain whites and blacks—a point so subtle that it has been frequently overlooked by historians. A reading of available county court documents, as well as other archival materials, allows the patient researcher to uncover the complicated life histories of those who did the unthinkable—who petitioned to become the slaves of other people. They did so, however, for reasons that made sense in the context of their lives and times. These life stories frequently reveal unexpected, intimate bonds between blacks and whites who worked, lived, worshipped, or socialized together in a period of history not well known for fostering such interracial relationships. How authorities conducted self-enslavement proceedings in their courts reflected a harshness and intimacy among blacks and whites at the local level that articulated the ambivalent and conflicted beliefs held by those who had fought for various protections and assurances in the voluntary enslavement law itself during its conception in the General Assembly. Commonwealth's attorneys and circuit court judges, who often were familiar with both petitioners for self-enslavement and their prospective owners, could take the letter of the law seriously and might be far less enthusiastic about a free person's desire for enslavement than indeed the petitioner was. As the law directed, free people seeking enslavement, as well as their chosen masters, were interrogated separately by the court, which was reluctant to condone either a flagrant instance of conditional servitude, whereby the petitioner might become a slave in name only, or at the other end of the scale, an arrangement in which the petitioner had been duped into self-enslavement.

During a typical self-enslavement proceeding in circuit court, Mary Elizabeth Roland of Rockbridge County "was examined carefully and cautiously" by Judge Lucas Powell Thompson and Commonwealth's Attorney David E. Moore about her petition to become the slave of Joseph Saville. Thompson and Moore inquired "whether it was of her own free will and choice that she wished to enslave herself, or had there been inducements held out to her by Mr. Saville or any other person? Had she been promised any money, or any better treatment than others of the slaves of Mr Saville?" Joseph Saville, too, "was called up and subjected to a searching examination, on oath, in order to satisfy the Court that there had been no collusion by him with the negro woman, and that he had taken no advantage of her."[63] Judge Thompson, a former state delegate and founder of a law school in Staunton, was an early proponent of professionalism in the law and asserted that "an enlightened and upright bar not only exercises a most salutary conservative influence in a free country, but that it is necessary to its very existence."[64] Even if Thompson and Moore were only paying lip service to justice during Roland's proceedings, the fact that they considered it important to give the *impression* that free blacks were being treated fairly by the court suggests that opinion among whites of public standing demanded it. The court's questioning of petitioners and proposed owners during self-enslavement proceedings illustrates the inherent contradiction in the law and one of the contradictions in Virginia society at the time. On the one hand, authorities seem to have been concerned about whether free people were being tricked or coerced by whites into absolute servitude. On the other hand, they seem to have been equally concerned about the possibility of free people colluding with whites in order to become nominal slaves, who might accept the legal condition of slavery, but live and behave as if they were still free.[65]

Many Southern lawmakers and judges in the mid-1850s were against creating a class of "favored slaves" who, in their idleness, would inspire discontent among the average slave. Quasi-emancipation schemes and individual arrangements for conditional servitude, as one North Carolina judge explained in 1860, would make so-called favored slaves "unfit for the social state which is essential to the well being, the happiness, and even the very existence of both master and slave." For those concerned primarily with preserving the integrity of the slave system, this was one danger of the self-enslavement laws—that they would tend to turn slavery into a system of social welfare, rather than the exploitative labor system that it needed to be.[66]

Circuit court judges thus dismissed cases in which petitioners seemed to contradict their professed desire to become slaves, as in the case of three black women from Fauquier County who, during their examinations before the judge and commonwealth's attorney, "declared an unwillingness to become the slaves, unconditionally," of their proposed owner.[67] In 11 percent of known self-enslavement cases, the judge denied a petitioner's request for enslavement after examining the petitioner and his or her proposed master in the courtroom—yet another indication that Virginia's self-enslavement law was neither designed by lawmakers nor applied by local white authorities as a measure to categorically enslave the state's free black population.[68] Perhaps the legislative majority did not intend to make slaves of (or to remove) the entire population of the state's free blacks, but in order to protect the institution of slavery—or to satisfy its most vocal defenders—they directed that all those who were to be self-enslaved would become slaves in name and in fact.

The contradictory nature of the self-enslavement law is further demonstrated by press coverage of individual cases, which were rarely publicized in Virginia's newspapers in the way one might expect. Occasionally, there were headlines like that in the *Richmond Enquirer* in 1858, which rejoiced in the fact that John Martin in Albemarle County had petitioned for self-enslavement. He "Prefers Slavery to Freedom," the *Enquirer* gloated. But even this story, which one would *think* would be a coup for pro-slavery propagandists, was a small paragraph buried on page two—perhaps because the story went on to explain that John Martin had re-enslaved himself "preferring the condition of a slave to that of removal to a free State."[69] Indeed, Martin's self-enslavement on 11 May 1858 to James E. Huckstep was no victory for pro-slavery extremists.[70] Publicizing the story only undermined the propaganda that free blacks were unfit for freedom and preferred bondage to emancipation. John Martin did not, as the *Enquirer* headline had stated, prefer slavery to freedom. He preferred to remain in his home community, near his wife and two children, over deportation, even if it meant that he had to sacrifice his individual, legal freedom to remain an involved husband and father. Mirroring the text of the voluntary enslavement law itself, the *Enquirer's* article tells an incomplete story. The headline, like the law's title, stressed the voluntary nature of the act and the petitioner's preference for slavery over freedom. But the article, like the body of the law, told a far different tale; one of irreconcilable dilemmas and a conflicted society that—for some—made acceptance of legal bondage the precondition for family and community life.

An article published in the *Daily National Era* communicated a very different understanding of self-enslavement than the *Enquirer*. Of voluntary enslavement, it reported, "If the instance so vauntingly proclaimed proves the affection and servility of these poor creatures, how much more forcibly does it prove the cruel oppressiveness of the laws enacted with respect to them?"[71] In fact, for every news item that flaunted a free person's "choice" of slavery over freedom, another in the North ridiculed the claim.[72] A correspondent for *the New York Times* reported in 1858, "The statutes of Virginia contain a law, the existence of which is known to but few, if any, without the limits of the State, and to a very small number within."[73] Though word of an option of last resort for those prosecuted under the expulsion law had traveled among Virginia's free blacks, few whites were aware of the law one year after its passage. Indeed, the *Richmond Enquirer* asked its readers in 1857, "Do many, even of the Virginia people, know that their statute book contains a law, providing expressly, for any negro's becoming a slave if he chooses?"[74]

Not only have many scholars incorrectly identified the voluntary enslavement law as an example of efforts by Virginia whites to re-enslave the state's free black population, but it is possible that historians in recent years invoke the law far more frequently than did contemporary antebellum Southern lawmakers and newspaper editors, who generally knew better than to flaunt the law as anything other than what it was—a concession to exceptional free black individuals who were willing to trade their legal freedom for permanent residency in the state. If pro-slavery fire-eaters and those desiring the wholesale enslavement of the South's free black population sought a measure promoting their cause, Virginia's self-enslavement law was not it.

By re-imagining the law from the perspective of contemporary free blacks and their white neighbors, we are forced to view Virginia society and the individuals who shaped and constituted it in a new light, in which contingency plays a central role. In a society in which some human beings were the fee simple property of others, self-enslavement was a peculiar legal innovation that nonetheless operated according to the logic of the petitioner. It had become in a sense a tool that free blacks could employ to their advantage—to delay, void, or overcome enforcement of the expulsion law by local courts. Though hardly a development to be celebrated by free blacks, self-enslavement allowed free people of color to maintain a number of personal freedoms—a meaningful family life and a continued connection to homeland and community—that would be lost forever if they were forced to leave the state. Of course, they took this route to a paradoxical sort of "freedom in slavery," and they did so under a threat that was every bit as grave to the few people it immediately affected as it was irrelevant to most free African Americans—that of being sold into bondage by the sheriff.

Though free people of color in the antebellum South were designated "free negro" or "free person of color" in official records that described them, individuals who possessed such labels might not have shared a single definition of freedom, as the contours and limits of one's liberty were shaped largely by individual circumstance. Those who were free shared above all the fact that they were not enslaved, that they were not the legal property of another—a significant and meaningful distinction in Virginia society. But beyond a common legal status and accompanying rights of property ownership and limited judicial participation, free blacks would have described and experienced their freedom in various ways, so that even two individuals in the same Virginia county at the same historical moment— Willis Doswell and Araminta Frances, for example—would likely have defined their freedom in very different terms, limited by different factors and protected in different ways. For men and women who found themselves free without the company of their enslaved spouse and children, the long-sought liberty of their dreams might have held a radically different meaning than for those who became free alongside their loved ones. Even individuals who were emancipated with their families on the condition of their removal from the state faced alienation from place, memory, and familiarity—from home—an alienation especially acute for those who were deported to Liberia.

Self-enslavement in Virginia and its many meanings to individual petitioners help us to understand better what freedom meant to those who had for so long been deprived of it. We are also reminded of how diverse a population the free black community was in any given Virginia county in the mid-nineteenth century, consisting of emancipated and free-born men and women performing a wide range of occupations, in varying stages of life and conditions of health. Uncovering their actions and their perspectives also offers us a glimpse of what it was they sought to achieve—in their lives and in the lives of those they cared about most. The past mattered to free black individuals; how one became free had an impact upon one's role in a community and the opportunities and relationships one forged as a free person. In the end, an examination of self-enslavement becomes an exploration of the very principles, desires, and obligations that have defined and limited individual liberty in American society.

There is no better way of understanding the phenomenon of self-enslavement in Virginia—as well as the meaning of freedom to free black individuals—than to approach the people who undertook the process and the communities to which they belonged at ground level. In November 1857, two brothers from Prince Edward County would be deported to West Africa upon the death of their owner, an event that threatened to divide their families and alienate them forever from the land of their birth. Self-enslavement became an unlikely way for James Booker and William Watson to express their values and identity as Americans, and to define their most prized possessions—love, community, and home—while rejecting the constraints of the long-awaited freedom they had won.

CHAPTER FIVE

TO LIBERIA
AND BACK

Lucy Booker of Prince Edward County, Virginia, had lived long enough to know that her master's death was nothing to celebrate—no matter what she might think of his character or temperament—having lived more than a half century as the legal property of others. In 1824 she had experienced the death of a previous owner, whose belongings had been sold and his slaves divided among various family members near and far.[1] Lucy, along with her son William and her mother Amy, had been relatively fortunate. It was unusual for a slaveowner to bequeath anything to a slave, yet Lucy and her family had received fowls, two spinning wheels, and a loom from their deceased master's estate. And more important, they had not been separated; they had become the property of their former owner's brother, John Watson, with whom they continued to live not far from their previous home, among an enslaved population of perhaps two dozen.[2]

By 1855, Lucy Booker, now sixty years old, was still surrounded by her family, which had grown considerably to include seven children and eight grandchildren in addition to her mother, "Old Amey," seventy-five years of age.[3] Two years earlier, their owner John Watson had died, leaving them not a spinning wheel or loom as his brother had done years before, but rather a simple sentence in his will that had changed their lives forever: "I do hereby give to all my slaves their freedom, to take place as soon after my death as suitable arrangements can be made by my Executors for their removal to the Colony of Liberia."[4] This was an event that most of Lucy Booker's enslaved friends and extended family in the neighborhood would experience only in their dreams.

In the lives of the enslaved, especially in Virginia in the 1850s, the death of a master or mistress promised uncertainty and life-changing circumstances that arose from wills with complicated clauses, lawsuits filed by long-lost relatives seeking to grab part of the estate of the departed, and the sale and division of the deceased's land and personal property. Upon the death of slaveholders, as with all property owners in Virginia, county officials ordered an inventory that catalogued the belongings of the deceased, including slaves. An executor or a court-appointed administrator then managed the disposition of the estate, following the directions set out in the will; often that person arranged for the sale of all or part of the estate (including its slaves) to settle any remaining debts.

During the generation or two before the Civil War, executors or administrators frequently sold enslaved Virginians for cash to slave traders, who then sold those people to buyers in the cotton states of the deep South, especially in Natchez, Mississippi and New Orleans.[5] Even when a master or mistress left behind little or no debt (as was true of John Watson), that person's will or the workings of the law in the absence of a last testament often divided the enslaved among white family members. Often enough, those distributions meant separation from one's parents, children, spouse, or friends.

John Watson, however, was one of a small group of whites in Prince Edward County who was committed to keeping his enslaved families together after his death by freeing and relocating them to Liberia, which had been established for that purpose and had recently become the first independent republic in West Africa. By carefully directing how their slaves were to be emancipated, transported to Liberia, and then supported there at least for a limited time, Watson, his neighbor Anne Rice, and a handful of others in Prince Edward County carried on the tradition of "experimentalist" manumissions begun after the Revolution and continued into the early years of the nineteenth century.[6] Though the American Colonization Society (ACS) had lost much of its luster (and political and financial backing) by the mid-nineteenth century, such experimentalists never renounced their persistent, albeit improbable, optimism that colonization was the one true path to meaningful liberty for formerly enslaved individuals and their families.[7] Experimentalists in Prince Edward clung to the belief that the colonization movement was, as Rice explained to an acquaintance, "regarded with much more favor here than before" by the early 1850s—this despite overwhelming evidence to the contrary in the continually small numbers of emigrants to Liberia from that county.[8]

Not only did experimentalists stand out from their peers in their decisions to manumit and colonize their enslaved individuals, but their ultimate goal—the gradual abolition of slavery—was fundamentally at odds with that of most white Virginians at midcentury, including those who also supported the idea of colonization but for different reasons. Female ACS manumitters were especially vocal in advocating gradual abolition and the long-term livelihoods of freedpeople. Such women broke ranks with Virginia legislators and newspaper editors, as well as with the directors of the local Virginia Colonization Society—all males—who were unquestionably pro-slavery.[9] By the 1850s, women represented only about 10 percent of slaveholders in the South, yet 21 percent of ACS manumitters were female.[10]

During the first two decades of the nineteenth century, colonization had appealed to a broad spectrum of white Virginians, who largely viewed it as an emancipationist initiative and "not just a program for ridding the state of free blacks." But beginning in the early 1830s colonization began to shift to a movement dedicated more single-mindedly toward the transportation of free blacks to Africa. By the 1850s in Virginia, proponents of colonization sought to defend the institution of slavery through their efforts.[11] Though several leading Virginia colonizationists at this time still made strong claims for black abilities and went to great lengths to see that freedpeople were equipped with the tools necessary for meaningful freedom in Liberia, the institution of slavery had never been more secure than at midcentury.[12] Indeed, many Virginia lawmakers had come to view colonization as complementary to a pro-slavery program, which had led to the passage in the General Assembly in 1850 and 1853 of measures that offered some state support toward the voluntary removal of the state's free blacks to Liberia. Individual acts of manumission and benevolent colonization, like John Watson's, become all the more remarkable in light of the beleaguered state of the ACS in the 1850s.

John Watson and other manumitters had not been alone, however, in viewing colonization and accompanying financial support for freedpeople as a just cause and perhaps the only means to dramatically improve the lives and maximize the "comfort" of the formerly enslaved. Each manumitter depended upon his or her executor(s), whom he or she could trust to carry out his or her plans for colonization after death. In the case of Watson, the burden of executing the complicated stipulations of his will, including the freedpeople's transportation to Liberia and transition to freedom, would fall upon two of his "friends"—Joseph Dupuy and Robert J. Smith—whom Watson was confident would realize his dying wishes.[13]

Joseph Dupuy, a former colonel in the Virginia militia, would assume most of the responsibilities of carrying out Watson's will, despite a "disease of the Bladder" and generally ill health.[14] In Dupuy, Watson could not have found an executor more competent, meticulous, and sympathetic to the cause of relocating his freedpeople with care to Liberia. Dupuy was part of an energetic, influential family in Prince Edward that had a history of interacting with the county's African American population in uncommon ways. Asa Dupuy, Joseph's older brother, had long served as a county justice and representative in the Virginia House of Delegates. He had proved to be a sympathetic neighbor to several free blacks and was one of the few whites in the county who commonly referred to enslaved individuals by using both their first and last names. Asa Dupuy married a woman who held even more progressive views toward the enslaved, Massachusetts-born Emily Howe Dupuy, who had come to Virginia in the 1830s as a single woman to become a schoolteacher. She continued to actively discuss slavery, sectional politics, and race relations in letters with friends and family, and would later play a major role in helping one of Lucy Booker's sons to remain in Prince Edward County. While it is unknown whether Joseph Dupuy actually endorsed Watson's mass manumission, he would show by his actions that he at least had accepted Watson's decision, and took seriously the onerous responsibilities that manumission and colonization placed on him.[15]

Many would-be colonizationists could not bring themselves to deprive their loved ones of slave property during their lifetimes and directed in their wills that their slaves be emancipated not only after their own death, but after that of their sibling or spouse.[16] Betsy Tebbs of Fauquier County articulated the worries of other emancipators when she wrote about freeing a slave named Jesse. She hoped that "none of my children will object to it even if they should consider that they have some reversionary interest in the said Jesse."[17] The deaths of people who defied community norms and the pressures of slaveholding society by embracing colonization could generate unseemly battles among the potential inheritors of their slaves.[18] After John Watson's death, Watson's brother, sisters, and several nieces and nephews contested the will, by which with the stroke of a pen Watson had erased $35,375 (more than $900,000 in 2010 dollars) of human property from their collective inheritance of $56,531—more than 60 percent of his estate's total value.[19] Such suits, filed in county courts of chancery, were not uncommon, especially when sizable manumissions dramatically reduced—or eliminated entirely—family members' inheritances. John Sale and William Witt, the executors for Timothy Rogers's estate in Bedford County, attempted to prove "the insanity of the said testator" in hopes of voiding Rogers's will, which freed his slaves, valued at more than $10,000, and provided for their removal to Liberia.[20] In another case, a man who was denied an inheritance of James Kelley's slaves in Lancaster County argued that, if Kelley's slaves were sent to Liberia, he would be denied "the means of cultivation," leaving the land he did inherit "almost useless." Legacies of land in Lancaster County in the mid-1850s, as in so many other regions of the state, seemed "of little value" unless they were accompanied by "young negro women, men and boys." Indeed, the independence—and political and economic freedom—of many white Virginia landowners was understood to depend upon an unfree "force to cultivate the farms."[21] Even in a Tidewater county such as Lancaster, where soil exhaustion and migration westward had taken their toll, many whites still believed "the best investment that can be made is to purchase negroes[,] say women[,] men[,] and boys who are young," and "that the increase of the women will be thus valuable."[22] Such black persons, after all, could either work the land in Lancaster or be sold at profit to slave traders who would take them off to the Cotton Kingdom. From 1841 to 1860, nearly half of ACS manumitters were aging slaveholders like John Watson who lived alone or with just one other white person. These people decided that liberating their human property was more important than bequeathing a substantial legacy to older, already self-sufficient children or other relatives (which did little to assuage the anger of some potential heirs who lost long-anticipated legacies in mass manumissions).[23]

Nearly all enslaved individuals, at some point in their lives, experienced the peculiar time between the death of their master or mistress and the final settlement of the estate—a time when some plantation norms might be suspended or redefined and others more strictly enforced. Lucy Booker and John Watson's other slaves were promised "their freedom, to take place as soon after my death as suitable arrangements can be made by my Executors for their removal to the Colony of Liberia" in Watson's will.[24] For those promised freedom, this interim period took on special meaning, for they learned that they would soon be free, but the gap between that moment and their actual, legal emancipation could range from a few days to many years. In the meantime, the enslaved could view themselves as people who were no longer permanent slaves but not yet free.

A small minority of slaveholders in the state remained dedicated to ideas of colonization or removal to free territory, as well, and their wills reflected a wide range of philosophies on how best to "prepare" their bondpeople for freedom, and perhaps more important to the benefactors themselves, how to buffer their own families against the loss of an inheritance of valuable slave property.[25] For Mary Frances, Tom, and the other enslaved individuals belonging to the estate of Sarah Branch in Chesterfield County in 1850, the interlude between their owner's death and legal freedom was prolonged, but their Baptist faith and regular worship at Branch's Church (formerly Hephzibah Church) sustained them.[26] Branch had directed her executor to emancipate her slaves five years after her death, at which time they were to be "removed to some free state or other place or Country, where in his estimation they may most likely enjoy the benefits of liberty." Like a number of emancipators, Branch worshipped with her slaves and extended a choice between freedom and slavery upon her death to them: "Should any of my said Negroes or slaves wish to remain in this state from any cause or notion, then those so desiring to remain shall be sold by My Executor privately at such price as he may consider reasonable permitting such slave or slaves to select his or her master or mistress."[27] During the five-year period of servitude between permanent slavery and the granting of freedom, the expectation of emancipation contributed to a decline in the authority exerted by Branch's executor and those who hired Branch's slaves for one-year increments. At different times, Mary Frances and Tom both ran away, and by 1856 the executor confessed that the slaves under his charge "have been virtually free since the 1st day of last January, this respondent not having hired them out since that time nor exercised any control over them."[28]

Hannah H. Coalter of Stafford County similarly directed in her will of 1857 that her slaves be freed, but stipulated that "if any of my said servants shall prefer to remain in Virginia . . . it is my desire that they shall be permitted by my executors to select among my relations their respective owners." Coalter's will became the subject of a lawsuit that eventually led to a ruling by the Virginia Court of Appeals in 1858, which stated that slaves, by definition, had no power under Virginia law to "have the right to elect to be free or to remain in slavery."[29] During the hearing, lawyers for Coalter's estate argued that because Coalter's will had been written after the passage of the general voluntary enslavement law in February 1856, her wish to allow her slaves to choose between slavery and freedom should be seen as falling under the act. Though Coalter's lawyers (as well as the presiding judges) were aware of the contents of the self-enslavement law devised more than one year before, it became clear, in fact, that Coalter had not known about the state's self-enslavement law when crafting her will.[30] Still other white Virginians were less committed to ideas of colonization and freed no blacks, but directed that their slaves be allowed to choose, or at least approve, those to whom they would be sold.

Margaret Miller of Culpeper County wrote in 1850 "that immediately upon my death all my slaves shall be free, subject to the restrictions hereafter mentioned and as according to the laws of the state of Virginia, they cannot remain here more than twelve months without interruption, it is my wish to make some provision for their support whilst here, and for the means of their transportation when they are ready to go away, as well as for their comfortable establishment in the country, where they may be permitted to settle."[31] Hugh Adams of Rockbridge County directed that his slaves "be emancipated and sent to the colony of Liberia" and "in no event is their emancipation to be delayed beyond 18 months from the time of my decease." Adams acknowledged that removal to Liberia would require some preparation and sought to assure his neighbors that his freed slaves would remain enslaved and supervised until their removal from the state. He wrote that his slaves should "be continued on the farm under the direction of some suitable manager, until the earliest period that my [wish] with regard to them can be carried into effect."[32]

For those promised freedom and removal to Liberia by Adams's will in 1857, the period after Adams's death that they spent "under the direction of some suitable manager" proved particularly life-changing. What was supposed to be an interval of eighteen months, as often happened in such instances, stretched out for two-and-a-half years because of legal and logistical hurdles. Though they had not been legally freed, Joshua, Sylla Jane, and others—Andy, Henry, Rosa, Mary, Isabella, and Susan—began to claim their liberty, first through small but tangible gestures, then in larger, more flagrant ways. Adams, like John Watson and other emancipators of the day, had promised most of his slaves "pecuniary legacies" in his will—in this instance, shares of the surplus or profit that would arise from the sale of his property after his death. Refusing to wait until their arrival in Liberia to begin behaving like free people, Joshua, Sylla Jane, and the others began cashing in their legacies at local stores, despite the facts that Adams's estate was far from being settled and that they were still enslaved. Joshua opened accounts at the stores of Gilkerson & McNutt and A. M. Carson, on which he charged increasingly significant purchases. In the winter of 1857, he bought an occasional small item at Gilkerson & McNutt's, including sugar, tobacco, and a thimble. The following spring, he charged three bracelets at Carson's. By 1858 Joshua was conducting regular shopping trips to both stores, spending more than $25 within one month at Carson's on a hat, a cravat, a watch, a hooped skirt, and two gold rings, and similar amounts at Gilkerson & McNutt's on red muslin, velvet ribbon, and cotton. In 1860 Joshua participated in one of the nation's newest, most commercialized holidays, purchasing "Valentines" and envelopes on February 11.[33] A few weeks before he received his free papers in April 1860, Joshua made his final purchase while enslaved, one pair of shiny "Gaiter shoes" for $3.38.[34] Though Joshua and other slaves had previously earned pocket money and made purchases at the same local stores where their owners and other prominent whites shopped (Joshua had opened an account at Patterson & Gilkerson's as early as February 1855), Adams's death and the prospect of a legacy had provided the means for more active participation in the Rockbridge County consumer economy.[35] Joshua, though still a slave of Adams's estate, had become a near-free person of means—both in his own eyes and in those of whites who willingly extended credit to him. He spent a total of $130.86, or two-thirds of his legacy, between Adams's death and his emancipation, further proof of the degree to which local merchants saw Joshua as an upstanding customer who would settle his account in good faith once Adams's will was executed.[36]

Other enslaved individuals belonging to the Adams estate began exercising their newly expanded credit too, while saving for their new lives in freedom. Sylla Jane created accounts with two local doctors for medical services while enslaved but was careful to dedicate more than enough of her and her five children's legacies to make the most important purchase imaginable in April 1860—$1,585.50 for the freedom of her husband, Bill, from his owner, Andrew Patterson. She then obtained "free papers" for herself and her children, John, Jenny Lind, Howard, Alsy, and Fanny. While still enslaved, Sylla Jane had joined the others—Andy, Henry, Rosa, Mary, Isabella, and Susan—in accumulating $252.29, $167.65, $111.76, $95.18, $50.31, $39.50, and $26.91 in purchases, respectively, at the two local stores. They bought molasses, butter, sugar, rope, and candles, as well as boots, shawls, gloves, brooms, handkerchiefs, bassinets, cups and saucers, and even spelling books, among other things. In the summer of 1858, less than a year after Adams's death, Rosa, Sylla, Andy, Henry, and Joshua together spent $40 to purchase their own buggy, which they promptly repaired, painted, trimmed, and outfitted with four new tires and fifteen spokes.[37] In all of their purchases, they spent more than $743 on credit, or nearly 14 percent of their combined legacies on consumer goods.[38]

While the degree to which enslaved individuals belonging to the Adams estate exercised their anticipated credit at local shops is extraordinary (as is the issuance of such credit by white storekeepers), generally, enslaved people's spending in local stores was anything but. In communities throughout Virginia in the late eighteenth and nineteenth centuries, people who were never earmarked for emancipation "actively participated in local economic networks" as consumers and producers. For example, archaeologist Barbara J. Heath has shown that men and women belonging to Thomas Jefferson's Poplar Forest plantation in Bedford County regularly purchased

Same Executor.
In Account with Sylla Jane and her
five Children, John, Jenny Lind, Howard,
Alex and Fanny.   Dr.

1860					
Apl 12.	To Sylla Jane's Legacy				1500.00
"	"	" John's Distributive Share			305.79¾
"	"	" Jenny Lind's Legacy		500.00	
"	"	" Jenny Lind's Distributive Share		305.79¾	805.79¾
"	"	" Howard " "			305.79¾
"	"	" Alex " "			305.79¾
"	"	" Fanny " "			305.79¾
					$3528.96

1860.		Cr.			
Apl.		By amt. of Account for sup= plies furnished & for pay= ments made	No 23	264.23	
" 2.	By Cash Pd. H. J. Foutz.	No 24	41.75	
" 5.	" " " Andr. Patterson for Sylla's husband Bill	" 29	1583.50	
" 6.	By Cash Pd. F Senebaugh.	" 28	4.20	
	" H. Sinebaugh's rent A/c.	" 29	17.50	
"	" Cash Pd. Clerks fee for re= cording deed emancipating Sylla's Husband	" 30	2.25	
"	By Cash Pd. for free papers of Sylla & her children and her husband	" 31	4.00	
"	By Morrison & Walkers Medical account	" 32	20.50	
"	By Dr J. B. Morrison A/c.	" 33	11.00	1950.93
" 12.	To Balance due them			$1577.03

Executor's account of Sylla Jane and five children, 1860. Upon becoming free, Sylla Jane immediately purchased and emancipated her husband, Bill, and secured "free papers" for herself and her five children.
(Courtesy Library of Virginia, Richmond)

items "relating to clothing, sewing and adornment"—objects bought "to supplement inadequate provisions and to express themselves in ways that plantation-issued supplies precluded."[39] Other enslaved consumers in Bedford and neighboring Campbell counties also purchased "handkerchiefs, hats, shoes, stockings, blankets, knives, pots, dishes, padlocks, combs," and other items at local stores "with cash, crops, baskets and brooms, and their own labor."[40]

In his study of Buffalo Forge, an iron foundry that relied upon skilled enslaved laborers near Lexington in Rockbridge County, Charles B. Dew uncovered an elaborate network of enslaved artisans who produced, sold, and purchased their own goods in the 1850s. The managers of Buffalo Forge relied upon an incentive system known as "overwork" to increase productivity and morale among the enslaved labor force. Overwork allowed enslaved individuals to earn their own wages for producing goods or performing services beyond the required tasks of a normal work day. A system similar to that employed by many white Virginians who hired out enslaved laborers in the mid-nineteenth century, overwork allowed a number of enslaved artisans at Buffalo Forge to earn, save, and spend their own money. One enslaved artisan in Rockbridge County, Sam Williams, even opened a savings account in a local bank, from which he occasionally drew funds for fabric, clothing, flour, sugar, coffee, and molasses—gifts for his wife and children.[41] In Virginia and elsewhere in the mid-nineteenth-century South, the institution of slavery was, in fact, an adaptable, even amorphous, creature as plantation owners, industrialists, and entrepreneurs constantly refashioned the system to adapt their enterprises to ever-evolving markets and technology, expanding their profits and protecting its survival in the process.[42] Overwork allowed business owners "to maximize labor and productivity without undue reliance on force, or the threat of force," upon which slavery necessarily rested.[43] For those enslaved individuals who did not challenge the system outright, overwork offered an opportunity to marginally improve one's life (and perhaps those of loved ones) within the bounds of chattel slavery, and it occasionally allowed individuals to purchase their own freedom and that of spouses or children.[44]

For Lucy Booker and her family, the promise of freedom and significant legacies outlined in John Watson's will brought about neither a breakdown in plantation discipline nor a flurry of purchases in local stores in fall 1855. Those belonging to the Watson estate continued to work and live as slaves, but even so, something had changed among the "Watson people." The promise of freedom altered the lives of those who were still enslaved.[45] Watson, perhaps cutting a more dramatic figure in death than he ever had in life, had directed that Lucy, her sons William Watson and James Booker, and the more than sixty others he owned "be subject to the management and contro_al of my executors until placed on board of a Vessel for Liberia."[46] As if Watson's ghost were looking over their shoulder, his executors Joseph Dupuy and Robert J. Smith not only duly abided by the will, but meticulously documented their transactions, travel, and business associated with the estate, whose property Watson's slaves remained for two years. In that time, despite Watson's benevolent designs, the usual scattering of enslaved friends and family took place—two here lent to neighboring farmers, another there to labor in the fields, nine more hired away to the Richmond and Danville Railroad, and another to the "Plank Road Comp[a]ny."[47] Those who remained on Watson's Prince Edward plantation continued to sow and harvest tobacco, wheat, and corn, which Dupuy and Smith sold to neighbors and to commercial purchasers in Richmond. It is not clear whether Watson had permitted his enslaved labor force to engage in overwork during his life, but less than a year after his death, the soon-to-be freedpeople under Dupuy and Smith's charge were cultivating corn on their own time to earn money they would spend when free. In January 1857 Smith withdrew $73.43 from estate funds "for corn made by the Est[ate] negroes." In March one or more women belonging to the estate collected $6.00 from Dupuy as a "midwife's fee" when twenty-three-year old Agnes gave birth to her third child, George Jr. Later that month, others earned $10.75 "for fodder" they had produced and sold to Dupuy.[48] Though under the "management and contro_al" of Smith and Dupuy, Lucy Booker and her extended family made the most of their situation, by performing overwork and saving for their new lives in freedom. By April 1857 eighteen months had passed since Watson's death, and Dupuy, like those still enslaved by the estate, was eager to conclude this period of his life, which had dragged on longer than he had anticipated. Rotten health, legal complications, and challenging logistical arrangements had all conspired to postpone the short trip from Prince Edward County to Norfolk, where Watson's slaves would be freed and sent along on their journey to Liberia.[49]

Soon after John Watson had died, more than two years earlier, Dupuy and coexecutor Smith had gone about realizing their good friend's dying wishes. First, Dupuy paid the estate's bills and collected its debts. He then divided the land, furniture, and household goods and distributed it all to Watson's relatives. As thoroughly and competently as he had handled the estate's other business, Dupuy saw to it that Watson's will was followed in nearly all aspects, especially those dealing with his slaves. It might have surprised Lucy Booker and the others belonging to the Watson estate that

Dupuy took this aspect of his job as seriously as he did.[50] In fact, at times, he had seemed to be almost obsessed with it. Like most executors who found themselves in his position, Dupuy knew very little about West Africa or the workings of the ACS.[51] Therefore, shortly after Watson's death, he had written William McLain, the secretary of the ACS, confessing his ignorance of the Society's procedure and of "not being well enough acquainted with the Geography of that Country" of Liberia.[52] Through an exhausting and extraordinary volley of more than twenty letters with McLain in Washington, D.C., Dupuy set a departure date for Watson's slaves, ordered the supplies necessary for their journey and resettlement, and established a procedure whereby they would receive financial support both at their departure in Norfolk and upon arrival in Liberia, as promised by provisions in Watson's will. Throughout his correspondence with McLain, Dupuy conveyed a concern and sincerity for Watson's slaves rarely seen in such letters to the ACS by Virginia executors. Also remarkable is Dupuy's desire to protect the interests of the children under his care, especially in relation to the legacies promised them by Watson's will. Dupuy insisted to McLain that in setting up a system for distributing funds from the estate to freedpeople soon to be living in Liberia, those under the age of fifteen should receive their legacies directly and not, as the will directed, have them given to their parents: "If this part of the will is strictly Complyed with, it is probible that very few of the young negroes will ever get their portion," he warned.[53]

In fact, despite McLain's assurances, Dupuy had worried constantly about the Watson freedpeople's future home in Liberia from the start, but especially as the Watsons neared their departure date. He had read obscure items in the Farmville and Richmond papers that he would have overlooked before becoming directly involved in relocating Virginians to Liberia. One month before the Watsons were due in Norfolk, Dupuy had written anxiously to McLain, "I see there is a great scarcity of provisions in Liberia, and dislike very much to see the people, sent off, at this time, but poor Creatures, they have to go."[54] Local and national newspapers recently had published scathing portraits of the ACS in Liberia which described widespread famine, destitution, and suffering among its immigrant population.[55] One wonders how reassuring Dupuy found McLain's almost mechanical responses to his concerns, one of which stated with casual disdain: "That report about 'faméne' was a great exageration." McLain also cited "the influence of the African fever" as the cause of one reporter's delusion.[56] In another letter, McLain nonchalantly admonished, "I think I omitted to mention to you that the men ought to have some *guns*—they will find plenty of use for them, if they know how to use them, it is desirable they should take them—I think six or eight guns—shot guns—would be very desirable."[57] Though McLain likely meant that firearms would be useful for hunting small game, his remark portended the tensions between the native Vai people and American emigrants that flared not long afterward along the coast of Liberia.

But the last few days had gone quickly and without event. Dupuy had boarded the Watson freedpeople on a train at Meherrin Depot near home that took them to Richmond, where he withdrew $4,000 in gold from an account of Watson's estate and sent it by "Express agent" ahead to Norfolk.[58] He then led Lucy, her sons William and James, and the others directly onto the steamship *Jamestown*, which followed an ever-widening James River past the ruins of the ship's namesake to Norfolk. They had arrived eight days early, leaving plenty of time to resolve any unforeseen problems and to ensure a smooth departure—a further testament to Dupuy's penchant for planning.[59]

On 12 November 1857, Lucy Booker looked on as her eldest son, William Watson, stood face to face with Joseph Dupuy, who had led them to the docks of Norfolk. William was thirty-nine years old and "bright mulatto" in color and one of the six Watson ex-slaves who could "Read the Bible."[60] William had lived somewhere between slavery and freedom the previous two years—knowing of his late master's emancipatory will but remaining a bondsman on Watson's plantation under the supervision of Dupuy. Now he was about to take his last steps in the land of his birth, steps that would take him "on board of a Vessel for Liberia"—his first steps as a truly free man. Joseph Dupuy stood beside William and counted out sixty dollars in gold, the first installment of the legacy that had been promised to all of John Watson's slaves when they left for Liberia. Nearby, the *Mary Caroline Stevens*, with its square sails furled upon three tall masts, gently rolled in the low waves. "Hampton Roads was full of vessels, wind bound, like ourselves, of every size and variety," a passenger aboard the previous voyage of the *M.C. Stevens* had written. "The appearance, if not the note, of preparation was manifest in all, and from many we heard the joyful chorus of the seamen bowsing up the anchors, and the sharp clink of the windlass palls. Others were loosing, hoisting and sheeting home their sails, many of the smaller fry, pilot boats and the like, were already careening to the stiff breeze and shooting towards the narrows."[61] Dupuy handed William the sixty dollars in gold he had carefully counted, followed by a thin blue sheet of paper. This money was the first share of John Watson's legacy that he would receive, he explained. A second, larger portion would find him in Liberia. To acknowledge his receipt of the gold, Dupuy asked him to mark an "X" in the margin, four lines from the bottom, next to his name, which he carefully did. Then Dupuy called for James.[62]

James Booker was Lucy Booker's second oldest son and was considerably younger than William (at twenty-four years), but one inch taller. He was described as "black" and showed a scar on his face, "on the left cheek, near the eye."[63] Freedom had been spoken, sung, and preached about for as long as either man could remember, and it was finally here—or, more accurately, in Liberia—for them to use, live, and enjoy. Like other freedpeople who had been emancipated by their owner's will and had been directed to leave the state, William and James likely weighed their options carefully. They could have remained behind with "old Cesar," who had chosen to stay home rather than go to Liberia and receive his share of gold from the Watson legacy. Cesar had shaken his head and told Dupuy that he simply "preferred staying in Virginia."[64] Three others, aged seventy-five, eighty, and ninety, had been too old for the passage. Dupuy had taken care to note for McLain the family units of those emancipated by Watson's estate, so that preparations could be made accordingly in Liberia for their housing. But again, Dupuy showed a keen sensitivity to the complexity of his task of relocating a large extended family overseas—a family, he acknowledged, which understood its own dynamics far better than he: "In classing the negroes," he explained to McLain, "we have consulted their wishes, as fair as we had an opportunity, but many of them, we have no doubt, will class themselves differently after geting to Liberia."[65] Dupuy may also have sensed a fear and disappointment in the eyes of William and James that day, a long-awaited day of freedom that less sensitive whites would have assumed was purely joyous. Dupuy, however, knew that African American family lines in Prince Edward did not correspond neatly with estate inventories and a white master's property boundaries. The Watson freedpeople, as large a group as they were, represented only a portion of a far larger family that remained enslaved in Prince Edward County.[66] For William, James, and the others, "nearly all of them, who are grown, will leave Husbands, and Wives behind," Dupuy had lamented. Many would also be forced to sever deep ties forged in faith, as they departed from their Presbyterian and Baptist church families.[67] When William and James boarded the *M.C. Stevens*, they would turn their backs on family left behind, at home, in Prince Edward County. Family—this key element of their freedom—was missing from the passenger list that day.

It had been a poignant departure from Prince Edward County, as William, James, and the others had loaded their belongings into the train at

Meherrin Depot.[68] They were free, or almost, but others there were not. William and James were going to Liberia to start new lives, accompanied by their mother, grandmother, brothers, and sisters; but not by others they had come to love growing up in Prince Edward. This would likely be the last time they would see one another. Did the mood change once the train had picked up speed? Did someone remark that those among them who had been hired by the Richmond and Danville Railroad had built the very tracks that were delivering them their freedom? Or had they discussed Liberia and their impending voyage across the mighty Atlantic, an expanse of water that none had likely ever seen? Or maybe it was the sight of Richmond that prompted talk of a different kind.

The capital was hectic. Commercial buildings and factories that processed and stored flour and tobacco lined the railroad tracks, and "coal dust made the streets & alleys look darker & more dismal than ever."[69] Dupuy had gone off to arrange financial matters, and Robert J. Smith, the other executor, directed William, James, and the others to unload their supplies from the railroad car only to stack it all into carts and carriages that would transport it to the *Jamestown*, docked a short distance away. Here were the cooking utensils, tools, hoes, axes, pot kettles, and tubs that McLain had told Dupuy to purchase for each, all "boxed up & marked with their name."[70] This was a fairly common sight these days, and Richmonders—white and black, enslaved and free—likely paused to contemplate the scene. One such bystander had mused in his diary several years before: "Saw some free negroes to-day en route for Liberia, they were in a furniture waggon with all their goods & chattels & seemed to be very well contented. They were going to the steamboat for Norfolk, there to embark."[71] Freedom in Liberia required a massive amount of provisions and enough support to make independence possible after a few months. William, James, and the others had been met with additional supplies upon arrival in Norfolk, which Dupuy had ordered in Baltimore and shipped in advance, including mattresses, bedsteads, and chairs.[72] The sixty dollars in gold that Dupuy had handed William, and now James, was yet another *thing* that proved their freedom. The tools, household goods, the locks given them for their trunks, and now the sixty dollars in gold were tangible signs of a radical change in their way of life and status. William and James could have joined Cesar in staying home and facing the consequences of defying their deceased master's will and state law. But how could Cesar have turned his back on all this? James signed an "X" beside his name on the blue sheet and returned it to Dupuy. He and William were about to be free men.

The *M. C. Stevens* left Norfolk with little of the fanfare that had accompanied its departure ten days earlier in Baltimore.[73] There, ACS officials had crowded the dock and had hailed the fifty-four emigrants who boarded with a rousing hymn, a prayer by McLain, as well as a solemn speech by the Rev. T. B. Balch, which William and James might have particularly appreciated. Balch had declared, "You are leaving the country of your birth and sundering ties which all, both old and young, must feel. But you go to the land of your ancestors, the real home of your race, the country given to the colored man by the God of Providence." Balch then expounded the meaning of freedom in terms of the equality of opportunity that they would find in Liberia. He continued, "You are going where no causes exist to retard your progress or prevent your welfare; where every avenue to social, civil and religious advancement, is open to all." Balch then "bade them God-speed," and devotions, another hymn, and a benediction quickly followed.[74]

But there had been relatively little fanfare in Norfolk. After William, James, and 108 other emigrants boarded, the crew weighed anchor, and the ship slowly slipped away. The former Watson slaves were likely seen from the docks "running up and down the different gangways, excited by the novelty of the scene and the operations of the officers and crew."[75] For Dupuy and Smith, the shrinking of the *M. C. Stevens* from the harbor, and then the horizon, closed a period of their lives marked by "considerable trouble."[76] Watson's slaves had left, at least all who were able (except for Cesar, who had declined). All that remained to do was to settle the estate's account and send the remaining legacies to Liberia, but Dupuy couldn't—or at least wouldn't—rest easy as long as these two tasks remained before him. For McLain, there was nothing remarkable about this departure of the *M. C. Stevens.* Perhaps Dupuy had been a bit more anxious than most executors who had to oversee the departure of emancipated slaves under their charge, but the Watson slaves had been but one of ten or so other groups he had coordinated for this voyage. McLain was a busy man. He received three to five letters per day from donors, emancipators, prospective emigrants, and curious executors, all of whom required prompt handwritten responses. In addition, he managed the affairs of the ACS at its headquarters in Washington, D.C., and oversaw much of the content for the *African Repository*, the society's journal that went out monthly to subscribers throughout much of the eastern United States. In short, he had little time to reflect any further on William, James, or the others once they had gone.

There were people, though, who thought of William and James after they had left and thought of them often. When the occasion arose, enslaved friends and family in Prince Edward County would give Dupuy a letter to be sent via McLain to their loved ones in Liberia. Their letters were answered, with considerable delay, in correspondence sent home through the same channels. This kind of transatlantic communication was fairly typical for families who had been split by emancipation and removal to Liberia. Often such letters were dictated to and taken down by literate blacks or whites and written directly to Dupuy or an ACS manager, who would then have read them to the intended recipients. It was common for emigrants to write their masters (or executors of their deceased masters) back home to offer news, to ask about loved ones, and especially to seek additional financial support. Letters home open windows into the lives of Virginians who found themselves starting over in Liberia, but they must be read critically, with an eye toward the author's intended reader and reaction.[77]

Cesar was the only one of the Watson freedpeople who had chosen to stay in Prince Edward County. There had been three others, all "old persons," aged seventy-five, eighty, and ninety years, who had not gone either, but it had been McLain and Dupuy, not they, who had decided that. "If they have children or Grandchildren in the Company & want to go with them— we must take them," McLain had explained to Dupuy. "But they are too old, to go for their own sakes—& it is a misfortune for the Soc. to send such— merely to die. If they can comfortably remain where they are, it would be better for them & for us."[78] And so they had stayed. At fifty-seven years, Cesar wasn't young, but he certainly wasn't an old person, at least by Dupuy or McLain's definition, and he was in good health.[79] Might it have been the fact that he had "no relations in the family" on its way to Liberia, but did among those who remained enslaved in Prince Edward County?[80] Or had it been what one former slave in nearby Amherst County had felt several years before, that he "loves the country where he was born and raised, in sight of the bigg mountains, and away from the Sea—That he wishes not to go to Liberia amongst strangers, a good country for the youthful, who can learn new things, manners-and pursuits, and form new connections in life, but to him that time is passed, he is too old to learn new things, manners or habits and he desires to form no new connections in this life"?[81] For whatever reason, Cesar had decided to stay home, a decision that many, if not most, of the others would come to regret not making for themselves.

The voyage of the *M. C. Stevens* from Norfolk to Cape Mount, Liberia, had been routine and uneventful, the *African Repository* reported; in all, it had taken less than six weeks. As Dupuy and McLain had arranged, the Watson freedpeople disembarked in Robertsport, a newly formed coastal town of several hundred people in Cape Mount named for Liberia's first president, Joseph Jenkins Roberts, a freeborn emigrant from Petersburg, Virginia.[82] Here, they were given temporary shelter in ACS housing and soon purchased land, received training, and were offered an education in the ACS school. They thus began an intensive six-month program designed to ease the transition from servitude to freedom, a program supported by the ACS, its donors, and, in part, a "specific tax" levied upon free blacks in Virginia since 1850.[83] From the perspective of Richard Stryker, the ACS representative in Robertsport, and McLain in Washington, all was unfolding as planned.

But William Watson and James Booker would tell a far different story. From the start of their journey in Norfolk, nothing seemed to go according to their plans, or so they would later attest. On board the *M.C. Stevens*, they alleged, an ACS agent had swindled them into purchasing unnecessary "quantities of cheap calico, brass jewelry, &c., assuring them that they would need such articles in their new home." Instead, they found themselves "deceived and defrauded out of their money" that Dupuy had given them in Norfolk. On top of that, upon arrival in Robertsport, "they only received a half acre of land, instead of the five acres promised" and "found provisions at exorbitant prices, and a good deal of bad treatment besides from the authorities." But perhaps most offensive, they found in their new land of liberty that a slave trade existed with the collusion of Liberian officials: "The President of the colony, if not engaged in the slave trade connives at it," they had asserted.[84] After about seven weeks, William and James had seen enough of Liberia to know that it wasn't for them. On 5 February 1858, they boarded the *M.C. Stevens* on its return, and each paid $35 for passage to Baltimore.[85] They were going home.

It is not clear when Cesar realized that his continued presence in Prince Edward County was going to be a problem, but by 15 February 1858 he had. About 460 free blacks lived in the county with him, many of whom had earned tolerance and even respect from the county's whites by living on their land, working in their businesses, or operating successfully on their own. Despite rising sectional friction that pitted growing numbers of antislavery Northerners against pro-slavery Southerners in Congress, on lecture circuits, and in major newspapers, racial tension at the national level was trumped by the nature of individual relationships that blacks and whites forged locally. Many free blacks in Prince Edward County worked hard, saved their money, and generally got along well with the white population.[86] It is true that politicians in Richmond had passed a number of laws in the 1850s aimed at circumscribing the lives of free blacks, but most knew that these laws (like many laws that applied to the county's whites) were rarely enforced and often overlooked.[87] Even the law that required free blacks to register with the county court every five years was ignored by most free blacks. Occasionally, whites in Prince Edward (as in neighboring Lunenburg County and elsewhere in Virginia), however, used the law to intimidate free blacks in their communities. Every few years since its inception, a free person had been charged under the expulsion law of 1806 with illegally remaining in the state without permission. Though apparently none in the county had been removed or sold into absolute slavery as a result of his or her conviction, the periodic enforcement of the law—or, perhaps more accurately, the threat of its enforcement—helped shape the lives of a considerable number of free blacks who had decided to remain in the county as illegals.[88] Cesar was an illegal, or at least he would be by that August.

The law stated that no person emancipated from slavery in Virginia "shall, after being twenty-one years of age, remain in this state more than one year without lawful permission."[89] Cesar had not yet been charged by the court for violating the law; strictly speaking, he had only been free for several months. Yet by February, he had surmised, or had been warned, that he was a special case.[90] The rarely enforced expulsion law might be applied to him for not having emigrated to Liberia with the others, as it had in other counties to African Americans who had refused to go to Liberia despite masters' bequests directing that they do so. In Culpeper County several years earlier, four men emancipated by the will of Margaret Miller—Stanton, Nelson Miller, Dangerfield Alexander, and Peter Miller—had chosen not to accompany the others whom Miller had freed to Liberia, as directed in her will. As a result, three (Nelson, Dangerfield Alexander, and Peter Miller) faced an uncommon presentment by the circuit court for remaining illegally in the state in 1853. Free blacks' refusal to obey the wishes of their deceased masters to emigrate to Liberia would continue to single them out for prosecution under the expulsion law. For example, Daniel, London, Phil, and Bob Rogers of Bedford County, who refused to emigrate to Liberia with the others emancipated by Timothy Rogers in 1859, were indicted by the county court for remaining in the state without lawful permission. Three were sentenced to be sold by the sheriff into absolute slavery.[91]

On 15 February 1858, Cesar met Robert J. Smith, one of John Watson's executors, and the two traveled to the county court together, where at the behest of Smith, Cesar attempted to obtain permission to be registered and to remain in the county. Though he was ordered to be registered, which was rarely denied, Cesar failed in his far more valuable request. The clerk noted flatly, "The court doth certify that no permission has been granted him to reside in this state."[92] This must have come as a great disappointment for Cesar. Singled out for not having emigrated to Liberia, he now suffered a double defeat. Not only had he failed to gain permission to live at home legally, he had increased his chances of being prosecuted by the court in the future by being formally denied permission to remain in the state and by drawing increased attention to himself. A presentment by the court did not mean that he necessarily would be convicted and sold as a permanent legal slave, which rarely happened in Virginia in the 1850s or any other decade. But the threat of prosecution was enough to encourage some African Americans to make irrevocable, life-altering decisions.

Only a little more than one month after visiting the county court, Cesar and Smith again went to court together, this time to the circuit superior court, which met only twice per year, and according to the law of 1856 had jurisdiction over all petitions for self-enslavement in the county. Here Cesar presented his petition to become a slave. He was not the first Virginian who had refused to leave the state for Liberia or elsewhere and had chosen self-enslavement as a last resort.[93] In at least four instances before Cesar's case, freedpeople who had chosen not to go to Liberia petitioned for self-enslavement to whites with whom they were well acquainted.[94] In fact, at least nine others would follow Cesar in refusing to go to Liberia and petitioning for voluntary enslavement in subsequent years.[95] Daniel Rogers of Bedford County told the executor of his deceased owner Timothy Rogers that "unless he can carry his wife with him he will remain a slave" in Bedford.[96] Instead, Daniel Rogers petitioned the county court for permission to remain in the state, so that he could stay near his wife and five children, who were all enslaved.[97] As a result, eighteen other newly emancipated slaves of Timothy Rogers refused to go to Liberia as well, as "they were induced to believe thereby that they had the same right to remain as the said Daniel."[98] After finally failing to win permission to live in the state and receiving an indictment for remaining in the state illegally, Daniel enslaved himself to the owner of his wife and children.[99]

A number of former slaves belonging to the estate of Benedict Burgess of Northumberland County also refused to emigrate when directed to in 1856. In this instance, the Circuit Court of Chancery ordered several commissioners from the county to interview all of Burgess's emancipated slaves "and report to this Court, the election or Choice of each of the said slaves," as to whether or not they wanted to remove to Liberia.[100] At least seven "refused to accept their freedom on the terms proposed," and six—Joseph Fry, Humphrey Kent, George Kent, James Hughlett, James Cockanille, and Betty Flynt—chose to stay in Virginia as slaves to chosen masters.[101]

A list of the Slaves belonging to the Estate of
B. Burgess dec'd. —

Man   James Hayes   about 40 — Chose to Stay here
       James Haughlett   about 30   Chose to Stay here
       Joe   about 34   Chose to Stay here
       Isaac   about 28   Chose to Stay here
       Jacob   about 25   chose to go to Liberia —
       Charles   about 36   Chose to go to Liberia
Woman Polley   about 55   Chose to go to Liberia
       Betsey   about 34   chose to go to Liberia
       Hiram   about 15   Chose to Stay here
       Seloma   about 12   Chose by the mother to go to Liberia
       Henderson   about 10   Chose by the mother to go to Liberia
       Jerry   about 3   Chose by the mother to go to Liberia
       Mahala   about 25   Chose to go to Liberia
       Sorenno   about 6   by the mother to go to Liberia
       Laura   about 4   by the mother to go to Liberia
       Macrinia   about 1   by the mother to go to Liberia
Man   Willowby   about 21   Chose to go to Liberia —
Woman Hannah   about 30   Chose to go to Liberia —
       Jane   about 14   Chose to go to Liberia
       Ben   about 12   by mother to go to Liberia
       Thomas   about 5   by mother to go to Liberia
       Hannah   about 3   by mother to go to Liberia
       Polley   about 1   by mother to go to Liberia
       Walter   about 18   Chose to go to Liberia
       Sidney   about 16   Chose to go to Liberia
Old   Betsey   about 60   Chose to go to Liberia
Man   George   42   Chose to Stay here
       Humphrey   40   Chose to Stay here
       { Lucey   unsound mind and not
       { capable of making choice   }

List of enslaved individuals belonging to estate of B. Burgess, 1858. Upon the death of their owners, enslaved families faced possible sale and separation. Some chose to flee, others remained. In this case, Northumberland County commissioners interviewed twenty-eight individuals belonging to the estate of Benedict Burgess as to whether they preferred to relocate to Liberia as free people or to remain in Virginia, re-enslaved. (Courtesy Library of Virginia, Richmond)

Two men belonging to the estate of James Kelley and living in Northumberland County—Armistead Currie and Jerry Glascock—also refused to emigrate and used their Baptist church connections to secure persons whom they must have presumed would be kindly masters.[102] Glascock may have spoken for all of them when he explained through a lawyer "that having been born and raised here he is unwilling to accept the provision made for him in the testators wills." He, Armistead Currie, Peter Miller, and Dangerfield Alexander all sought enslavement in Virginia over freedom in Liberia.[103]

With an unsteady hand, Cesar marked an "X" by his name, below a statement prepared and copied by his lawyer that offered no explanation for his actions. It read, "Your petitioner is over the age of twenty-one years, and desires to choose an owner."[104] In accordance with the voluntary enslavement law of 1856, Cesar's petition was ordered to be posted on the courthouse door for one month, and both he and Smith were summoned to the court's next meeting in August. Cesar had waited fifty-seven years to gain his freedom. Before the end of summer, he would once again be legally enslaved, this time to Smith.

On 22 March 1858, the *M. C. Stevens* landed in Baltimore.[105] Within days, William Watson and James Booker's return to the United States hit the news. The *Richmond Enquirer* ran an article that declared the two men's homecoming humiliating to "the 'Freedom Shriekers' of the North" and nothing less than a vindication of the institution of slavery itself. The author, under the alias "South Side" and likely writing from Prince Edward County, pronounced that all of the other Watsons taken to Liberia "are anxious to return, and are only prevented from doing so by the want of funds; all knowing that they could not stay in Virginia without having the bond of slavery thrown around them again." The return of William and James, the author continued, gave "the lie to the thousands of calumnies which have been heaped upon the Southern Slaveholders, by the Abolitionists of the North."[106] Soon another article appeared, this time in the *Farmville Journal*, which recounted the trials and tribulations that William and James allegedly faced on the outbound journey and in Liberia. The headline proclaimed "Liberia a Swindle."[107] The portrait of Liberia portrayed by James Booker and William Watson was a dismal one and the version reprinted in various newspapers was likely even more so, as the story of two free men returning to the land of slavery provided excellent propaganda for pro-slavery extremists. It is also possible that Booker and Watson purposely exaggerated their claims of fraud and corruption in Liberia, figuring that the only way they might be allowed to return to Prince Edward to be reunited with their families was by placating those whites who had been most vocal about the dangers of free blacks in their midst and the need to defend the institution of slavery—those who had been most insistent they leave in the first place. In addition, to return to Virginia after one's emancipation and departure was illegal, and to attempt a reunion with family that defied their deceased master's wishes and state law required an explanation far more compelling than simple longing or homesickness.

Within a month of their return, William and James were standing in the Prince Edward County court alongside Smith, as Cesar had two months earlier. Like Cesar, William and James hoped to register and gain permission to stay in the county. As Cesar had, they won a court order to be registered, but lost the request for permission to remain there lawfully.[108] In regard to granting permission to free blacks who had left the state and returned, Virginia law was clear: "Such permission shall not be granted to any person who, having removed from this state, shall have returned into it."[109] In seeking permission, Cesar might have made the case that he had never left the state, but for William and James, their round trip to Liberia was a nonnegotiable disqualification, even if they were now celebrities in the eyes of pro-slavery propagandists. Though both men were likely aware of the 1856 Virginia law that allowed for self-enslavement, it would not have been their first choice upon returning to Prince Edward as free people. William and James had returned home to live as free men and because the expulsion law was so rarely applied to free blacks in the county, they may have been surprised that they had been denied permission to settle again in the county. Nonetheless, it soon became clear that county authorities would not embrace their homecoming unless it contributed to a larger narrative that slighted the efforts of ACS emancipators and defended slavery as the natural state for Virginia's blacks. Edmund Ruffin and other pro-slavery apologists used the men's return to make the case that blacks were unfit for freedom whether at home or abroad and that many other freedpeople "would rejoice to leave [Liberia], if they were able to pay their passage, or were not too lazy to earn as much, even if to return to their former slavery." James Booker and William Watson, Ruffin contended, were even willing to travel "under great difficulties, and danger of being arrested as runaway slaves, to their former home in Prince Edward County, Virginia," where, "as they expected and desired, they were again enslaved, being sold for that purpose at public auction, and were bought by the persons whom they preferred as their masters."[110] Joseph

Dupuy, who presumably did not doubt that African Americans were capable of leading meaningful, productive lives as free people, fretted about the "great deal said in the publick Newspapers" and the use of James Booker and William Watson's return by pro-slavery ideologues.[111]

At about the time that Smith stood next to William and James in county court, Dupuy was busy scribbling a letter to William McLain in Washington, explaining the maddening news that two of John Watson's manumitted blacks had returned aboard the very ship on which Dupuy had sent them away. He wrote, "Two of the people, who went out at the same time, Came to my House, and informed me they had returned in the same Vessel to Baltimore,—which I regret very much, as it was their Masters wish for them to go to Liberia & remain there, and We Were at considerable trouble, and expense, in sending them away, and I have no doubt they would have become satisfyed, had they remained long enough to become acquainted with the Country and people."[112]

But Dupuy's frustration at seeing William Watson and James Booker was quickly overtaken by his concern for the others he had sent to Liberia. What if William and James were correct and colonization to Liberia truly was a swindle? Had he and his old friend John Watson been duped? At least William and James were safe. The others had written him letters and seemed "very well pleased with their new homes," but newspaper reports regarding Liberia, combined with the published reports of William and James's assessment of the country, haunted him. He wrote to McLain, "I however noticed in a paper a few days ago, that the Native Chiefs in the neighbourhood of Cape Mount, where Mr Watson's negroes have settled have commenced their old practice of kidnapping, for the purpose of procuring emigrants to send abroad—and if you should think Mr Watson's servants are in any danger by remaining at Cape Mount, I wish you to give directions for their removal to some more secure place."[113] McLain kept his composure, replying simply, "I fully appreciate what you say about the return of those two Watsons. They did not remain there long enough to form any opinion of the place or people." As for the report of kidnapping in Cape Mount, McLain insisted, "There is no foundation for that report in the papers," and he assured Dupuy that he would relocate any Watson freedpeople who might find themselves in danger in Liberia, should there be a need.[114]

Beginning two days later, on a Sunday, those who had remained in Liberia did find themselves under siege, not from Vai slave raiders as Dupuy had feared, but from disease. Little George Washington Watson, a one-year-old, was the first to die. The next week, William and James's elderly grandmother Amey died, followed by other members of the extended family—Billy, Isaac, Mary, Jane, and Ellick Watson.[115] Lucy Booker, the mother of William and James, also became ill and prepared to follow the others in death. Had she seen freedom as a prelude to death, even if that death might bring a victorious deliverance to a better world? Did she take a moment to reflect on her life in Prince Edward County, her emancipation, and her move to Liberia? Her sons, William and James, the two who had left Liberia for home: were they still healthy? Would death continue to visit her family, taking more of her loved ones from the life of freedom they had finally attained? The sad news from Robertsport traveled slowly back by sea in the form of a letter from ACS officials in Liberia to McLain, who then printed it in the *African Repository*, which made its way to Moore's Ordinary in Prince Edward County, where Joseph Dupuy received his mail. Dupuy then told William and James of their mother's death, which by then had occurred months before.[116]

In Washington, the only news from Liberia that mattered at the moment was that conveyed by William Watson and James Booker on their return, now appearing in newspapers across the nation. The brothers' reports of fraud, mistreatment, and Liberian involvement in the slave trade were still being repeated more than a month later in May. If McLain had appeared unflappable in his letter to Dupuy, he showed himself irate and at wit's end in urgent communications to those employed by the ACS in Liberia. At pains to refute the words of these two men from Prince Edward County, McLain sought testimony to quell the firestorm once and for all. On 31 May 1858, he sent two letters to Liberia. In the first, to Richard Stryker, the ACS agent in Cape Mount, he included a clipping of the *Farmville Journal* article. "Liberia a Swindle" would be the first thing that Stryker would read when he opened the envelope. In the accompanying note, McLain wrote: "I inclose you a paragraph from a newspaper, which is going the round of all the papers opposed to us and of many that are friendly with the inquiry, 'are these things so!' It is doing us immense injury. The charges it makes you will see affect you. What have you to say in answer to them? I beg of you to make out the best statement you can—get the testimony of some members of the Watson family, pl[ease] send it to me by the first opportunity. Unless we can clear up this business your settlement will be permanently injured by it."[117]

McLain's second letter, to H. N. Dennis, the ACS agent in Monrovia, Liberia, was similar in tone, but confessed, "I am in doubt what to say *about the half acre of land* affair. I want more light. Can you help me to it? We are greatly embarrassed & discouraged at the present time, not only by this, but also by many other untoward things!" McLain included with his note an article from a Richmond newspaper that detailed the "other untoward things" being said: "a report of what the two *Watson* people saw & heard & suffered &c."[118] McLain's supporters soon mounted a wave of propaganda aimed at discrediting the public testimony of William Watson and James Booker and destroying the credibility of the two men. Reverend Alex M. Cowan, an agent for the Kentucky Colonization Society who had traveled on board the *M. C. Stevens* with the former Watson slaves on their way to Liberia, published a lengthy rebuttal in the Frankfort, Kentucky, *Commonwealth* titled, "The Statement of Two Emigrants Returning to Slavery Refuted." Cowan offered a detailed history of the Watson group's journey and settlement, assuring readers that he had personally met with the Watson family in Robertsport and had asked them, "Are you all well? Have any of you been sick? Do you get enough to eat?" He reported, "The answers were, all of us are well."[119] Cowan's article, as well as McLain's responses, had an effect. Dupuy, for one, concluded, "Many of the statements made by these negroes, I was disposed to doubt."[120]

But rumors continued to circulate in the press. One report confused Cesar's petition for self-enslavement posted on the courthouse door with the plight of William Watson and James Booker. It said that Watson and Booker had "resigned themselves to their former bondage—one of the Executors purchasing them as his slaves."[121] However, the rumor, reprinted in the *African Repository*, helped to change the debate introduced by William and James from one strictly about the ACS and its operations in Liberia into one centered on the meaning of freedom for former slaves—in Virginia and Liberia. Dupuy tried to set the record straight. He wrote to McLain in July: "The two Watson Servants, who returned, have not been purchased by one of the Executors, as stated in the last African Repository, they will probibly petition our next Superior Court to remain in the state, and go back into slavery, as the only chance of remaining with their family, and only one speakes of choosing either of the Executors as their owner as the Law allows him to do."[122]

Several days later, McLain began receiving responses to the angry letters he had sent to Richard Stryker and H. N. Dennis in Liberia. Stryker's note was attached to "some evidence of exoneration," with promises of "other evidences being forwarded, sufficient to satisfy any inquiry respecting the money of the Watson people."[123] The most important evidence was a letter signed by nine Watson men, including Cornelius, a brother of William Watson and James Booker. The Watsons' letter condemned William and James's statements as "libelous" and vigorously defended the validity and significance of their freedom in Liberia. Though they were living in "town lots" and had not yet received enough land to farm, they argued, "Considering what has been our condition in the past, and our prospects for the future, we are qualified to say, that our present condition is not made worse by our coming to this country and do cheerfully remain."[124]

There were other letters from defenders of the ACS. Reverend Edward Weir, a black missionary from the Presbyterian Church who had traveled to Liberia with his wife on the same voyage as the former Watson slaves, declared of the reports from Prince Edward County: "There has been much said about this settlement at Cape Mount, and but little or no truth in all that I have heard about it." Weir proceeded to dismiss the criticism of James Booker and William Watson point by point: "It has been said we are engaged in the slave trade, but it is not so; that the emigrants are ill treated on their arrival, this is not so; also, that the agent of the American Colonization Society sells the provisions of the people, but I do not think that is so."[125] Another pastor living in Liberia, James W. Wilson, wondered, "As for my Part I do not know What William & James Watson return for unlest it Was for the Whipe." Wilson, a former slave and emigrant himself from Georgia, described Liberia as a land of plenty and a promised land for free people of color. "I can not see What a man of Coller Want to go Back to the united States to Live for un Lest he has no Sol in him, for Whare thire is a sine of a sole With in a man, it Panc [pants] for fredom in this Life & the Life to come."[126]

Others who wrote to McLain were equally emphatic, arguing that the journey from slavery to freedom was a difficult one, and some (like Booker and Watson) had not been up to it. Ralph Moore, a former slave from Mississippi who now served as district attorney and chief military officer in Robertsport, wrote that the account of William and James "is a downright falsehood" and went on to explain the larger problem facing recent emigrants—freedom. He explained, "You will know what kind of people Emancipated slaves are, never had their own way and now are free and dont know how to use their freedom just [having emerged] from the [slave] quarters." He asked, "What can you expect from them they are free but dont know freedom?"[127] H. N. Dennis, the white ACS representative in Monrovia, dismissed William and James's words as "unfounded and unreasonable," but, like Moore, he used the affair to condemn the newly emancipated for the damage and emasculation he believed slavery had wrought on them. Of William Watson and James Booker's complaints about Liberia, Dennis wrote, "Such statements of the ignorant & indolent, & who are so far sunken, from the effects Slavery, as to prefer the Shackles to

Liberty, are false. Those parties not having been accustomed to provide for themselves & being too lazy to work, return with an ill report of us, which, to my mind, is principally to serve as an excuse for their unmanliness in returning to bondage."[128]

Richard Ford, who had emigrated to Liberia in 1853, echoed Moore's sentiments, but wrote from the perspective of one who had been a slave but who believed he had successfully distanced himself from his former life "by being honest and Industrious." Of William and James, he wrote, "These 2 men never went 1 mile from the town the whole time they were here (45 days) what time they were here they employed themselves how? Why sir in Eating and Drinking like gluttons. And I will also state a fact not generally known, that is that Emancipated slaves [who are] sent out here have an Appetite that its impossible to satisfy for the first 6 or 8 months after their arrival here in this Country. Hence the complaint that they did not get enough to eat." Ford went on to acknowledge both the challenge of providing for oneself in freedom (which he said had yielded him "a Large Frame house and a good farm") and the sacredness of that freedom, a sacredness that outweighed any hardship encountered in Liberia. He and other established emigrants invariably "prefer this land of Freedom with its little privations to all the Grog Shops and Plantation Kitchens in the world."[129]

Neither grog shops nor plantation kitchens were on the minds of James Booker or William Watson as they stood in the Prince Edward County Circuit Superior Court in mid-August 1858. They were asking—or praying, in the legal language of the day—that the court make them legal slaves again. The price of being at home, and of having the meaningful family life they had returned for, was enslavement.[130] Less than a week earlier, Cesar had stood in the same courtroom and had become the legal slave of Robert J. Smith. The Commonwealth's attorney and the judge had separately interrogated first Cesar, then Smith. Though it must have been clear to all that Cesar's legal enslavement to Smith would bring little change to Cesar's everyday life, the court was willing to state unequivocally that "there is no fraud nor collusion between the parties"—a required step in the self-enslavement process. Three men attending court that day, W. B. Brightwell, N. Cunningham, and A. R. Venable, then valued Cesar at $375, half of which Smith was required by law to pay the court. Without fanfare and little press, Cesar had become the property of Smith.[131]

By 1858, it was James and William's turn. Though they had not joined Cesar in his refusal to go to Liberia in the first place, they had come back, even though that turned out to mean joining him in petitioning for a return to slavery. The two submitted their terse petitions, each marked with an "X," to the circuit superior court, stating, "Your petitioner is over the age of Twenty one years and desires to choose an owner."[132] James selected as his prospective owner Emily Howe Dupuy, Joseph Dupuy's abolitionist-leaning sister-in-law, someone whom the court could be sure would never treat James as a common slave, no matter what assurances she might offer to the contrary.[133] As Cesar had, William asked to enslave himself to Smith. The Prince Edward Circuit Court would have understood perfectly well that James and William were following Cesar's example in asking to become slaves in name only; that the kind of bondage they sought through the voluntary enslavement law of 1856 was legal and conditional—precisely the kind of quasi slavery that a portion of Richmond lawmakers had sought to prevent by opposing self-enslavement measures. Nonetheless, here was the nexus between the harsh expulsion law of 1806 and the requirements of everyday life in a complex rural society shaped by slavery. In the eyes of the court, James and William could not be given permission to resettle in the county as free people, but neither would public opinion allow officials to forcibly remove or enslave the two, as the law permitted. Self-enslavement offered free people an option of last resort that could satisfy the concerns of whites on both extremes of the political spectrum at the same time—from hawkish removal extremists to those genuinely concerned about the rights of free black individuals whom they knew well.

More than three years into his role as John Watson's executor, Dupuy sounded more eager than ever to conclude the estate's business, but he was anything but expedient in his efforts to tie the remaining loose ends of the estate. Here, again, Dupuy went beyond what many other executors might have done and actively sought to see that the remaining legacies due the Watson freedpeople in Liberia were properly distributed. In February 1858 he wrote to McLain, explaining that the Watson freedpeople needed to sue John Watson's estate if they were ever to receive their money, a process he would facilitate with McLain's assistance. He wrote, "I wish to get you to send a paper to Liberia for the Watson people to [affix] there names too, requesting some Lawyer to bring suit against the Executors for the balance of the money in their hands, we wish this done, that the money may be paid to them under an order of Court."[134] Despite the efforts of Dupuy, the chancery case he initiated in order to settle the estate's finances outlived him, and would not be settled until 1873, six years after his death.[135]

In February 1859, during the one month or so that William's and James's petitions hung on the Prince Edward courthouse door, the men received messages via Joseph Dupuy from the family they had left behind in Liberia. Limus, Rial, Simon, George, and Doctor Watson, likely aware of Cesar, William, and James's efforts to re-enslave themselves, wrote a letter that extolled the virtues of Liberia as a land of liberty even as it evinced a burgeoning homesickness and a desire to return to Prince Edward County themselves. They wrote, "Tell Ceaser all of us says come over the enjoyment here is great we would not be back in Virginia on no Condition whatever." They continued, "Tell James Booker & William that if they were here and had seen as much of the Country as we have they would never return again," adding proudly, "We all have Improved ourselves and send you our own Signatures." In addition to receiving an education, the men were enjoying the material fruits of freedom in Liberia: "We have 2 stores doing tolerable good busines. The stores belong to George, Lymus Ryal, Simon, & Adam. We have sent to England for a supply of goods."[136] But by this second year in their new homes, a degree of nostalgia had set in, and some of their words belied the rosy image they were otherwise attempting to project. They explained, "George says the only thing would ever bring him back but his wife and Children And so says all the Rest of us. Lymus says he will not return only to pay you a visit and please write us whether their would be any difficulty in our Coming back on a visit." The men then sent an implicit message to their wives: that they had remained true to their loved ones at home. They averred, "Simon and all the rest say the same none of us have got married yet except Sally."[137] In fact, each of the men longed for his wife and family at home in Prince Edward County; each was eager to return home, if only for a visit, and George and others may even have thought at times, however fleetingly, of coming back for good. True freedom, it seemed, encompassed more than emancipation, the right to keep the fruits of one's remunerative work, and greater educational opportunities. It also required the liberation of one's loved ones and the reunification of families. In letters back home, the sentiments of those who did not return to Prince Edward County illuminate those of the few who did. Though James Booker and William Watson apparently left no lasting record of their thoughts or feelings about returning home and their re-enslavement, reunion with still-enslaved family was most likely their primary objective in leaving Liberia.

Joseph Dupuy again wrote to William McLain in Washington. True, he had complained about William and James's return; he had also been inclined to doubt their hyperbolic stories of Liberia. But the welfare of those who remained in Robertsport nagged at him. Might William and James have been right about the ACS after all? Had he sent Watson's former slaves into a death trap? Dupuy wrote to McLain that he was eager to "hear from the Watson people" and "would be glad to receive any news you may get." He then wrote, "I fear they may be in some danger of being Captured, if they remain at Cape Mount."[138]

In mid-March 1859, William Watson returned to Prince Edward's Circuit Superior Court, accompanied by Robert J. Smith, his chosen owner. After an examination of both petitioner and prospective owner, the court declared William the legal slave of Smith and ordered Smith to pay $475 to the court, or one-half the assessed value of Watson.[139] Later that summer, in similar proceedings, James Booker became enslaved to Emily Howe Dupuy.[140]

Yet another letter arrived from Liberia, this one written by George, Rial, Limus, Doctor, Simon, Adam, and other unnamed former Watson slaves. There is no record of McLain's having responded to Dupuy's latest anxieties, but it is possible that instead of ignoring Dupuy's letter, McLain had asked ACS officials in Liberia to solicit a direct response from the Watson freedpeople that would help to calm Dupuy's nerves. The letter's contents, however, would not satisfy Dupuy's conscience and sense of duty. Though the group of Watson freedpeople assured Dupuy in their message that "we are all well and doing tolerable well," they explained that "we have spent our money very fast but it is in building our houses and hope we may have a better chance hereafter to save it, we are all nearly done building at this time." The tone of this letter signaled a significant change in the welfare of the former Watson bondpeople since the previous spring, or simply, with time, a more realistic assessment of how hard it would be to begin new lives abroad, even as free people. "Persons just come here cannot succeed as well at first as they need experience every thing here is so different from America and every thing is very high indeed and farming is hard as all has to be done with a hoe there is no horses nor oxen here," they wrote. "Rice, Potatoes and Cassavia are our principal bread stuffs here we have to labour very hard indeed on this account and as we have engaged in trading to help us along." Most importantly, the portrait of challenging lives in Liberia served to support the ultimate aim of the letter—to pressure Dupuy to send the remainder of their legacies, "our money," which had been promised to them in the will of John Watson long ago.[141]

Most distressing to Dupuy, the men ended their letter by confessing their homesickness and desire to see those in Prince Edward County once again. "There are a few of us would like to come back on a visit to you and our friends please write us how it would be with us as we would be happy to see them but we wish to hear first from you if their would be any difficulty we all believe that if there is any difficulty you will let us know we all of us will look anxiously for a answer from you," they wrote. "Remember us to Jim Booker and Ceaser," they added, "tell them we are all well and that if they had staid here until this time they would not have went back without any experience but its too late now it cant be helped." They concluded by sending "our best respects to all of our wives and acquaintances and all others." If earlier letters had brimmed with pride and satisfaction in their lives as free people in Liberia, this one was pervaded by a longing for home that had only deepened. Whereas they had earlier been convinced that if William and James "had seen as much of the Country as we have they would never return again," now those writing from Liberia argued that "if they had staid here until this time they would not have went back without any experience." The value of Liberia was no longer necessarily or solely as a place to build a future; it might merely provide "experience" with which one could then return home.

This was exactly the kind of letter that Dupuy did not want to read from those whom he hoped he had sent away to lives of freedom and prosperity. As a result, in September 1860 he was still second-guessing his decision to send the Watsons to Cape Mount, as opposed to another settlement in Liberia. More important, he doubted whether the ACS had the best interests of the Watsons in mind at all. Dupuy was particularly upset that the Watsons had not received enough land in Cape Mount to farm upon. In an angry rough draft of a letter to Stryker, he complained that "as Executor of John Watson, and acting as agent for his Negroes, I feel unwilling for them to hold Town Lots, in lue of farming Lands, when they were not raised as trading or Commercial people." He proposed that "they should now have the privilege of giving up their lands given them either at Cape Mount or some other place where they would be protected and let their Town Lots, with the improvements they have made, be sold, or taken back by the government, and for them to receive pay for their improvements." Dupuy, having done his research, even went so far as to suggest an alternative site to which they should be moved—"Careysburg, or some healthy place, where they will be sufficiently protected to engage in farming, and [such]."[142] Three days later, Dupuy reviewed his letter and drafted a new one to McLain whose language flowed more smoothly, more politely, yet even more directly. "I never would have sent them to Cape Mount, nor, any other place, to be settled on town Lots," he wrote resolutely.[143]

McLain responded to Dupuy's missive with predictable coolness. He assured Dupuy that adjustments in living arrangements could be easily made; that recent violence in the Cape Mount area and the interior had been quelled: "There is no difficulty in the people making the exchange" of their town lots for farmland, he wrote. "It is often done." And as for Robertsport being a dangerous place for the Watsons, "It is perfectly safe now for them to go any where interior of C[ape] Mount—as [President Stephen Allen] Benson was up there last winter & spring and settled all their troubles."[144] In McLain's letters to Dupuy, conflict in Cape Mount was always described in the past tense, yet as something that had *just then* been resolved. Indeed, there is no evidence that the ACS formally removed any of the Watsons to another settlement in Liberia. Instead, many of the Watsons simply removed themselves to other locations in West Africa, never to return again to Robertsport.

Letters from Liberia kept arriving in Prince Edward County. Just before the outbreak of the American Civil War, Agnes Watson's note arrived at Moore's Ordinary, where Dupuy read the latest from Cape Mount. Generally, the news was not good. Three more former Watson slaves had died and, Agnes explained, "Lymus is gone down to the leaward George Simon Andrew Rial Albert is gone to Seirraleon Corneus is gone to war 500 miles of[f]." Apparently, at least seven of the Watson men, including Cornelius, the brother of William and James, sought livelihoods elsewhere—on the Leeward Coast, in Sierra Leone, and "to war" somewhere five hundred miles away, presumably in coastal West Africa, perhaps along the Gold Coast. Agnes asked Dupuy to send her a care package of cotton, thimbles, and needles "in a little Box," as well as "som[e] money if you can." She also asked Dupuy to "remember my love to James an[d] William[.] I sen[d] my love to all Mr R Smith an[d] his family." Nearly three years after William Watson and James Booker had left the others in Liberia for their old home, the connection to family and home in Prince Edward remained painfully strong for Agnes—a connection that William and James had been unwilling to sever after their arrival in Liberia.[145]

Cesar, William, and James remained enslaved in Prince Edward County through the Civil War. When their second freedom came in April 1865, the men could count themselves as three of several dozen Virginians who had been emancipated twice, though the meanings of liberty in the first and second instances differed considerably. Their first emancipation had freed them—but not their loved ones who had belonged to someone other than John Watson—from a legal, social, and economic condition they had inherited, and that had placed them from the first day of life at the mercy of a slave system that fostered precariousness and coercion. Their second emancipation, which now brought liberty to all of their friends and family,

Robestport G C M,
Febuary 12th 1861

Dear Sir

I take the responsability on my self to drop you a few lines hoping that it my find and your family in good state of health ads for my part an family they or we all are well and also them that are living, there are three deceased Elving Watson & Denis Watson & abraham, but I thank god that all the rest are Still alive Lymus is gone down to the leaward George Simon Andrew Pial Albert is gone to seiraleon Cornens is gone to war 500 miles of we would write now the mail did not cam by I want to how is your family Abraham is dead an Denis is dad Elvia is dead Denis was member of the P Church Elvia a member of the Baptist church I am perfess of religion Please to sen me a bale of spun cotton sen me two dosyen of thimble sen me three dosyen paper of nedle an sen them to Agnes watson sen me three spool of thread mary going to school every day you is our friends an hope you will rem ain so remember my love to James an William

Letter of Agnes Watson to Joseph Dupuy, 1861. Letters from Liberia conveyed news and messages to loved ones at home. Agnes Watson asked the executor of her former owner in Prince Edward County to "remember my love to James an[d] William," two men who returned to Virginia in 1858 only to become re-enslaved after a brief stint in Liberia as free men. (Courtesy Library of Virginia, Richmond) had come after a term of six or so years of conditional servitude to masters who had owned them, in a legal sense, but who had every intention of buffering them from the worst effects of the slave system—sale, relocation, and physical punishment. Joseph Dupuy also survived the war and lived just long enough to see the three men establish themselves—once again—as free people in Prince Edward County.[146]

CHAPTER SIX

FAMILY BONDS AND
CIVIL WAR

One day in 1875, long after the Civil War had ended, Betsy Payne of Rectortown, in Fauquier County, Virginia, took a moment to reflect upon the contents of a letter that had just been read to her. It was signed by "your granddaughter Nellie B. Francis"—a name she did not recognize—and was mysteriously postmarked Providence, Rhode Island. Betsy Payne had lost track of her large extended family, especially those who ended up in the North.[1] She turned to the woman who had just read the letter to her and asked which of her grandchildren now called themselves "Francis," and how this granddaughter came to be in Rhode Island.[2] In the confusion and turmoil of the Civil War, many of the links that had held Betsy Payne's family history together were broken and now, more than a decade later, collective memory was required for their repair.

The war had come early to Fauquier County; soldiers and supplies circulated in and around Rectortown long before fighting broke out in nearby Manassas in July 1861.[3] Fauquier authorities reordered residents' everyday lives according to the needs of war; soon after fighting broke out, public buildings were converted to hospitals "for sick & wounded Mississippians or others" who fought in defense of the South and of slavery.[4] The burdens of war fell heavily on African Americans—enslaved and free—who lived and worked in the county's plantations and small towns. State law, implemented by county authorities, required black men to assist in the construction of defensive forts for the Confederacy.[5] Sometime during that next year, amid the confusion and freedom that the presence of Union troops nearby had delivered, critical pieces of Betsy Payne's world came undone.[6] Her daughter, Jane Payne, died, probably of disease, along with many others in Rectortown.[7] Shortly afterward, Betsy's granddaughter, Mary Elizabeth ("Betty") left with other enslaved individuals to claim their liberty behind Union lines.[8] Months later, Betsy Payne was contacted by a man working with the Union Army, who had arranged for Betty's adoption by a white couple somewhere in the North. Grandmother Betsy consented, and that was the last she heard of her granddaughter.

Betsy Payne's family history had been complicated before the war, too. Much of that story had gone unspoken; and the silence had obscured certain difficult facts and allowed for the emergence of competing narratives and rumors among family members and within the larger Rectortown community, white and black. For example, it had been clear to all that planter Charles R. Ayres had maintained sexual relationships with at least three of his enslaved women (including Betsy Payne's daughter Jane Payne) until his violent death "in a street fight" with a neighbor in 1859.[9] But it had been less certain which of Ayres's young slaves could claim him as their father.[10] As so often happened in antebellum Virginia, color lines had bled into the unspoken fabric of family. In his will, Ayres articulated his version of plantation genealogy when he chose to free several of his twenty-odd slaves, including, apparently, only women with whom he had had sexual relations—Jane Payne, Mary Fletcher, and Annah Gleaves Poters—and the offspring of those unions.[11] Ayres charged his executors with relocating Payne, Fletcher, and Poters and their children to a free state and providing them with at least five hundred dollars for their settlement there. Several of the manumitted children were also to be given support when they reached the age of ten—"one hundred dollars annually apiece to be applied in raising & educating them."[12] But one of the executors of Ayres's estate, William H. Payne, found it difficult to follow the terms of Ayres's will, which directed him to remove the women and children to the North: "They refused to go," he complained.[13] Payne, Fletcher, and Poters were unwilling to trade their homeland and their familial connections in Fauquier for freedom in an unknown place.

Shortly after Ayres's death and the subsequent manumission of Payne, Fletcher, and Poters, war "was upon the very year of breaking out between this & the free states, indeed was declared but a few days thereafter," William H. Payne remembered. Even if the women had consented to leaving the state, as Ayres had directed, "It was impossible," Payne later explained, "to execute this special clause of the will."[14] For free people of color, not only were the circumstances of their emancipation important factors in shaping the contours of their lives as free people, but the timing of their emancipation proved critical as well. William Payne suggested that amid the crisis of disunion that gathered at the time of Payne, Fletcher, and Poters's emancipation, he had proved unable to persuade and unwilling to force the women to leave their community for the North. If Ayres had died a few years earlier, and his estate had been settled before the onset of civil war, perhaps William Payne would have succeeded in removing the women from the state, as other executors had done previously with emancipated slaves in their charge.[15]

Payne, Fletcher, and Poters, having lived together under Ayres's watch and given birth to children who shared Ayres as their father, found themselves in a terrible predicament by 1860. By accepting their freedom but refusing to leave Rectortown and Virginia, they faced the possibility of indictment and conviction for unlawfully remaining in the commonwealth, under the terms of the expulsion law of 1806. If they chose to leave Virginia, however, they could not legally return, forsaking long-standing bonds with family and community.[16] In addition, for their children who had been promised future financial support in Ayres's will, leaving the state would add to the uncertainty of the children's legacy and make claiming their inheritance sometime in the future all the more complicated and unlikely.

Thus, in terms of family and social connections, as well as the best financial interests of their children, it made sense for Payne, Fletcher, and Poters to insist on staying in Rectortown, where they were known and had grown up. In Fauquier County, as well as in Prince Edward, Lunenburg, and other Virginia counties at the time, a large proportion of the free people who remained in their communities lived in defiance of the expulsion law of 1806 and made no effort to register with the county court clerk or to petition the court for formal permission to remain in the county.[17] By September 1860, after living less than a year as free people, Payne, Fletcher, and Poters nonetheless had reached a crucial and no doubt painful decision and had chosen not to risk life in Rectortown as free women—they had too much to lose. Unlike those of their neighbors who had been emancipated by will or had purchased their own freedom several years before, Payne, Fletcher, and Poters found themselves free in Fauquier County at a particularly inauspicious moment. For several years, anti–free black sentiment had once again flared in the Virginia legislature and the press, as a vocal minority of lawmakers and civic leaders pushed for mandatory removal as a panacea for local and national political problems that seemed now, more than ever, to threaten their way of life and the institution of slavery that underpinned it. In addition, a recession in 1857 reinvigorated the lingering discussion among white Virginians over the effect of an ever-growing free black population on the availability of jobs for white laborers.[18] Also, in March of that year, the Supreme Court answered one of the key questions raised in past debates in Virginia over free black removal: were free people of color entitled to any benefits of citizenship under the U.S. Constitution? In the so-called Dred Scott decision, the Court famously ruled that African Americans, whether free or enslaved, had no claim to protections guaranteed to white citizens in the Constitution—a decision that would further justify extremists' views on mandatory removal from the state.[19] Finally, radicals in other Southern states began to lobby their respective legislatures for measures requiring the deportation or re-enslavement of free blacks, assuring like-minded Virginians that they belonged to a regional political movement, even if they were still only a fringe group in Virginia and elsewhere.[20]

Of immediate concern to some white Virginians in 1857 was the future of the state-sponsored voluntary removal program, through which Virginia had offered up to $30,000 per year to aid the colonization of free blacks to Liberia since 1850. In 1853, the legislature had renewed and revised the program, but with a five-year expiration date, which was now rapidly approaching. In anticipation of the next legislative session—and the debate over removal and colonization that was bound to ensue—readers aired their views on the subject in Virginia newspapers. The *Daily Richmond Enquirer* generously offered one reader space on its pages for five lengthy articles in August and September of that year, all bearing the title: "On the Necessity of Removing or Reducing to Slavery the Free Negroes of the Commonwealth." The author, identified only as "Ollin," aimed to lobby two influential audiences—lawmakers preparing their agendas for the upcoming legislative session in Richmond and readers who might be inspired to prod their representatives into action. Ollin directed his remarks primarily toward those in the first group who had previously refused to support measures in favor of mandatory removal or re-enslavement; those responsible for the "legislative timidity upon the free negro question." The acts of 1850 and 1853 promoting voluntary colonization were "ineffectual," he argued, and he called upon lawmakers to pass enforceable legislation encompassing four gradual measures to finally "relieve old Virginia of the free negro curse": "voluntary removal," "compulsory removal," "voluntary enslavement," and "compulsory enslavement." As a few others had tried but failed to do in 1853, Ollin attempted to define self-enslavement as a removal measure and an instrument that could help facilitate the wholesale enslavement of those free blacks unwilling to leave the state. He argued, "By 'removal' we do not simply mean transportation out of the State, but include every means by which they shall cease to be free negroes in the State, whether by enslavement or transportation."²¹ Ollin chided rural whites for permitting existing laws regarding the state's free black population to go unenforced. He observed, "The laws on the subject of free negroes are so loosely executed in many of our counties, that they amount to a mere nullity."²² But Ollin saved his harshest criticism for those lawmakers who continued to insist that free blacks, as residents of the state once home to Thomas Jefferson, were entitled to certain inalienable and natural rights. "The great decision in the Dred Scott case," he wrote, had settled the matter. A free black individual had "no Constitutional rights—that he is denied, very properly, the rights of citizenship," and "in removing the free negro, then, or in selling him, we violate no Constitutional provision. Ours is a government of white men—the black man has no part or portion in it." Why hadn't Virginia's elected representatives had the courage to take stronger action in the past? Because "most of the barbers of the State and waiters of hotels are free negroes, and the members of the Legislature feared they would suffer great personal inconvenience if they were banished," he insisted. Ollin ended his final article with a call for grassroots political mobilization: "Let the *people* take this matter in hand. Let them hold meetings in every county—pass resolutions on the subject; urging and demanding legislative action. This is the only way to make a Legislature act, that constantly needs the whip of popular opinion to make them do their duty."²³

Readers in at least two counties accepted Ollin's call to crack "the whip of popular opinion" on the issues of free black removal and enslavement. Meeting at their courthouse in September, a group of Dinwiddie County residents adopted several resolutions based on the premise that "the negro is not a citizen and his natural condition is slavery." They concluded that free blacks were universally despised as a class and thereby unable to enjoy their liberty in Virginia. To live as truly free people, they were obliged to leave the state. In addition, they alleged that the free black laborer, who "works for half pay per day, and steals double per night" took jobs from hard-working white citizens. Thus, these residents from Dinwiddie urged the General Assembly, as a "dernier resort," to take the action "of forcibly expelling them from our midst." In so doing, they insisted, lawmakers should allow free black individuals "a few years . . . to prepare and go from among us, or if they prefer to remain, to do so under the regulations and laws of slavery."²⁴ Citizens in King William county also called "a meeting, to be held at their next court" the same month "for the purpose of considering the expediency of disposing, in some manner, of the free negroes of the State, and of urging legislative action in the premises."²⁵

The efforts of some determined white citizens to make free black removal a political issue in the fall of 1857 had an effect. In his opening address to the General Assembly in December, Governor Henry A. Wise privileged the issue in a way that had not been done by a Virginia head of state for a decade. Unlike his predecessor William "Extra Billy" Smith in the late 1840s, however, Wise positioned himself closer to the political center, which by the late 1850s had shifted only slightly toward a more radical stance on the issue. "But what is to be done with them?" he asked of free blacks. One idea, he asserted, would be to send freedpeople to the North, but such a cruel plan would lead to their demise: "They are not fit for freedom or frost, unless they are among friends who will provide for them." Another "more humane" and "more just" proposition would be "to take from them their liberty at once, and sell them wholesale into slavery, without their consent. But the moral sense of our people would revolt at a violation of individual and personal rights like this, and no such usurpation would be tolerated by public sentiment." In short, Wise concluded, "We ought to colonize as many as we can in Liberia; [and] to take back under masters as many as are willing to return to the patriarchal protection of slavery." Wise also recommended that the tax levied on free black males to raise funds for colonization be repealed and "that a free negro be allowed in the future, after a given day, to hold no land or real estate beyond a small number of acres for a homestead; and no house or lot in a city or town; and that they be prohibited from lending money on interest to a white person at all; and from holding slaves."[26] Though Wise had suggested a new course for the legislature, his removal program relied upon two core initiatives that had been linked since Willis and Andrew Doswell sought a special law for their self-enslavement in 1852—colonization and voluntary enslavement. As described in Chapter 3, John C. Rutherfoord, Thomas E. Bottom, and other legislators had tried to fashion a mandatory removal law complemented by large-scale voluntary enslavement in the early 1850s, but they had failed on both counts. Not only had they been unable to win a stricter removal measure than that passed by the legislature in 1853 (which merely encouraged voluntary colonization to Liberia), but the Doswells' law passed in 1854, followed by the general voluntary enslavement law in 1856, had provided an option of last resort for those free blacks who feared prosecution under the expulsion law of 1806. Since 1856 the use of the general law by only a few dozen free black individuals proved that, as written, it was not, and would never be, the instrument of large-scale re-enslavement that a few pro-slavery propagandists desired it to be. It contained far too many protections for petitioners, it charged chosen masters too much for taking in a self-enslaved individual (one-half the petitioner's value), and the procedure took far too long to conduct in local circuit courts, which typically met only a few times per year. If Ollin, Wise, and their colleagues were to refashion self-enslavement as a tool of removal (in the broadest sense), the 1856 general law would need to be rewritten.

Two days after Wise's address to the legislature, a select committee was formed in the House to consider the governor's ideas concerning the state's free black population.[27] In January 1858 voluntary enslavement, now a key item on the governor's agenda, entered formal legislative discourse when Lunenburg County's George W. Hardy motioned to amend the general voluntary enslavement law of 1856 so as to give county courts concurrent jurisdiction with the circuit courts on that subject.[28] Did Hardy, who had once made special efforts to shepherd legislation through the House on behalf of Andrew and Willis Doswell as well as Araminta Frances, believe that more free blacks would employ self-enslavement to protect themselves against prosecution if the process were made easier and more accessible in monthly county courts? Or had Hardy become more radical with age and the times, joining Wise and Ollin in viewing self-enslavement more as a desirable kind of removal? Hardy's motion died in committee, but the idea of revising the voluntary enslavement measure resurfaced later that month in the Virginia Senate, when extremist George E. Deneale of Rockingham County proposed to amend the law by requiring individuals chosen as masters to pay only for the court proceedings rather than an additional tax of one-half the value of the petitioner.[29] Deneale's proposal stuck and by March 1858 a Senate select committee, with Deneale as chairman, had proposed a bill "to amend the act passed February 8th, 1856, providing for the voluntary enslavement of the free negroes of the Commonwealth."[30]

As senators in Richmond considered changes to the state's voluntary enslavement law, a handful of delegates in the House worked diligently toward a more effective removal policy, which would rely heavily upon a revised self-enslavement measure to reduce the number of Virginia's free blacks in the future, as the governor had urged. William M. Howerton of Halifax County proposed a bill that would give Virginia's free blacks three years to exit the state or voluntarily enslave themselves, before facing sale as absolute slaves by the state. The bill—designed and promoted by radicals—was for this reason destined to fail, unless it could be amended enough to satisfy the concerns of moderate Virginia lawmakers, who were ever wary of unnecessarily expanding state power and of violating the individual and property rights of free black residents, even if such rights were customary and not legally protected by either the state or federal constitutions. More important, the objects of such proposed legislation were real people—women like Fauquier County's Payne, Fletcher, and Poters, and their children—whom whites in their community knew well. A measure proposing expulsion or re-enslavement of anonymous individuals was one thing; it was another to subject neighbors with familiar names and faces to the full force of such a law. A Richmond correspondent for the *New York Herald* predicted of the bill, "I doubt whether it will pass in any form, the prevailing considerations of its inhumanity being such as to overrule the moral and social necessities which are advanced as pleas to justify its passage."[31] In order to keep the measure alive in the House, radicals were forced to amend its contents. John C. Rutherfoord of Goochland County successfully moved to extend the grace period for free blacks from three to twelve years, before they would face forced sale into slavery. Howerton offered his own alterations, which would allow for further delay in one's sale as a slave, as long as an individual was in the process of leaving the state, about to depart the state, "or have bona fide commenced legal proceedings for voluntary enslavement."[32] In this way, a harsher removal policy would be tempered by a revised, more accessible self-enslavement process, allowing large numbers of free blacks to choose re-enslavement over physical removal.

Only the most radical proponents of removal and re-enslavement supported Howerton's bill. *The South-Side Democrat* championed the measure, arguing that there should be no in-between people in Virginia, that either one should be black and enslaved or white and free: "There should be no other caste, estate or condition separate and distinct from both of these." In fact, the paper argued, self-enslavement was preferable to removal to Liberia, as absolute servitude was "certainly the most consistent with the theory of Southern society."[33] But the paper acknowledged its minority position, complaining that "there are not a few to be found among us, who, professing the most devoted attachment to the Southern cause, and inveighing lustily against abolitionism in every shape and form, throw up their hands in holy horror at the bare suggestion of a plan to remove the incubus of free-negrodom."[34] Indeed, such critics of Howerton's bill would win the day. No matter how much extremists amended the bill to delay or mollify its provisions, it would rely upon the forced enslavement of free individuals by the state, an action unacceptable to most Virginia lawmakers and their constituents. Shortly after Howerton's removal bill fizzled in the House, the Senate tabled the bill to amend the state's voluntary enslavement law, which, up to that point, had moved quickly through the docket. Apparently, a revised self-enslavement law would be of little value without a complementary removal measure in place, as the laws would operate in tandem.

Though it is true that some white Virginians in the late 1850s rallied for extreme measures against the state's free blacks, moderates never lost control of the issue. Wise, who would later become famous for signing the execution papers for John Brown after his ill-fated raid on Harpers Ferry in 1859, had proposed to continue a state-supported program of voluntary colonization that relied more heavily upon self-enslavement, but even this measure failed to make it out of the Senate in spring 1858. The voluntary colonization measure of 1853 expired without renewal.[35] During this latest debate over how or whether the Virginia legislature should remove the free black population, local officials in a number of Virginia counties began enforcing the expulsion law of 1806 in their rural communities more strictly, if still sporadically.[36] Fauquier County officials were among those who targeted certain individuals for living in the state illegally, with chilling results. In April 1858 the Fauquier County Circuit Court charged Archie and Mima, a free couple, with living in the state contrary to law. By September, they had left the county, and the case against them was dismissed.[37] A short time later, the Fauquier County court indicted Sarah Ann Shepherd, a free woman with eight children, for living in the state illegally. Shepherd petitioned for permission to remain in Fauquier, but an unsympathetic county court denied the request. The acting justices declared that "the said Sarah Ann Shepherd is required to leave said Commonwealth."[38] Perhaps the case that had the largest impact on Fauquier's free black community, however, was that against Eliza Payne, who was indicted by the county court in November 1858 and then pleaded guilty to remaining in the state for more than one year after her emancipation. If Payne had hoped that her guilty plea would elicit compassion from the court, she had miscalculated. Instead, the court clerk noted, "It is considered by the court that she forfeit her freedom and be sold as a slave—and that the costs of the proceedings in this case be retained by the sheriff." Though there is no available evidence that Eliza Payne was in fact sold, her case no doubt made an impression upon the county's free black population and communicated a frightening willingness on the part of county officials to enslave at least some free people in the community.[39]

Just in case the message from the county's courts—conveyed through indictments, summonses, and convictions—had not been clear enough to Fauquier's free black residents, the county court had appointed a committee of five men in April 1859 "to take into consideration and prepare a memorial to the next legislature of Virginia in regard to free Negroes of this county as being . . . a decided nuisance thereto—setting forth the evils under which we live thereby—and suggesting a proper remedy therefor."[40] Soon after, Charles Ayres was killed, leaving behind his will that would free Jane Payne, Mary Fletcher, Annah Gleaves Poters and their children. Manumission was not the kind of "proper remedy" that the Fauquier County court had envisioned, and from the perspective of the women, their emancipation could not have come at a worse time. No doubt racial tensions, insecurity over national sectional politics, and the local courts' newfound eagerness to prosecute free blacks under the law of 1806 crystallized in the minds of Payne, Fletcher, and Poters. In order to remain at home in Fauquier County, they chose to enlist the services of a lawyer, who began proceedings by which they would renounce their legal freedom and become the slaves of William H. Payne, one of the executors of Ayres's estate.

Though drafted by a skilled attorney in legal language most likely to sway the minds of local authorities, each woman's petition contained some personal information and reflected distinct reasons why she preferred to remain in Fauquier County rather than accept legal freedom elsewhere. The petition of Annah Gleaves Poters was the most formulaic in wording and construction of the three, but nonetheless expressed her individual dilemma as a free woman of color. Her petition stated, "She prefers to remain a slave in Virginia amongst her friends and relations, than to go amongst strangers, helpless and encumbered with her child, who is several years too young to enjoy the benefits of her master's will."[41] Poters's petition displayed the complex set of factors that she balanced in deciding whether to accept exile in the North as a condition of her enduring freedom. The pull of "friends and relations" far outweighed that of the prospect of freedom in a place where she would be surrounded by "strangers." Not the least of her concerns was the substantial monetary support provided to her child by Ayres's will—yet another reason to stay put. But Poters and her attorney must have thought that they would win sympathy with the court by highlighting the social aspects of her dilemma and the alienating effects of state law on well-intentioned mothers like Poters. How could officials, in good conscience, deny a poor mother the family and community connections needed to raise her child, not to mention forcing her to relocate to the hostile North?

Jane Payne's petition also emphasized that removal to the North would have meant a complete break with her existing social and family networks, her "kindred" and "friends," and that her child was still too young to receive the support Ayres had promised in his will. Payne's petition communicated an additional motivation for wanting to remain in Rectortown, however: she was in poor health. Her petition explained, "That your petitioner is of delicate health & that to go alone, encumbered with a helpless child, amongst strangers would subject her to great hardship, to avoid which, she declares, that she desired to become a slave."[42]

Despite certain basic similarities to the others' petitions, Mary Fletcher's revealed a great deal about her family life—that she was married to an enslaved man with whom she had likely had children (who were not mentioned in Ayres's will). Her petition asserted, "your petitioner respectfully represents that she has been born and raised in the county of Fauquier, that all her kindred and friends are now living in that county—that she is married and her husband is a slave who could not accompany her. That she has several children, besides those provided for by the will of her late master, all of whom are young and helpless—and that if she goes away, she parts from all whom she has ever known, & goes a friendless stranger to a new state encumbered by helpless children. In view of all these facts, your Petitioner declares that she deliberately prefers slavery in Virginia to freedom outside of it."[43]

In eight available petitions submitted to Virginia county courts, Virginia circuit courts, and the Virginia General Assembly from 1856 to 1864, free men and women revealed motives of this sort for seeking self-enslavement. As in Payne's, Fletcher's, and Poters's petitions, deeply felt family ties between free women and enslaved family members were the main motivations for many free individuals who sought self-enslavement in Virginia during this period. Sinah Ambers in neighboring Loudoun County sought enslavement to "the owner of her husband."[44] Margaret Price, a resident of the city of Richmond, selected a new owner who was "the master of her father."[45] Lavinia Napper, who had successfully enslaved herself in Fauquier County shortly before Payne, Fletcher, and Poters submitted their petitions, sought to stay in the county because that was where "all of her relations and friends" lived.[46] For men, too, self-enslavement served as a way to remain with enslaved family members, the benefits of which clearly trumped any inducements to individual freedom outside Virginia. The petition of John Martin in Albemarle County explained "that he has a wife & two children, slaves, to whom he is naturally attached, and is unable to purchase and unwilling to abandon."[47] Satchell Grayson of the same county also pursued enslavement so that he could remain with "his wife and children."[48] Both Dennis Holt of Campbell County and Thomas Hill of Greensville County sought to enslave themselves to men who owned their wives.[49] The petition of Lewis Wilkerson (or Wilkenson) of Amelia

County stated that "he has a wife now living in the State of Virginia," and that of Daniel Rogers of Bedford County explained that "he has a wife and five children who are slaves the property of Robert C. Mitchell of this county, and he hereby selects the said Robert C. Mitchell as his master."[50] For a number of free men and women in Virginia, it was the existence of enslaved family members—a spouse or child—that made exiting the state without them unthinkable and self-enslavement, as a last resort, palatable. Petitions for self-enslavement stand as poignant reminders that free black individuals felt they belonged in their communities and believed that if they were able to explain their circumstances to authorities, their voices just might be heard.[51]

Though family considerations guided the decisions of many free Virginians to self-enslave, the prospect of choosing one's own master or mistress offered petitioners some control over their new circumstances and served to lessen some of their concerns about permanently renouncing their legal freedom. In most cases, petitioners knew those whom they selected to be their new owners well. In fact, family relations also played an important role in determining who free men and women chose to be their new owners, inasmuch as many petitioners considered only close relatives of their deceased owners as candidates. Free men and women took advantage of close, often multigenerational connections with white families to defend their own kin groups against a legal structure that might otherwise break them apart. For example, Thomas Gardner and Mary Anderson of Hanover County selected Elizabeth C. Clarke, the wife of their former master, as their new owner.[52] Mary Roland of Rockbridge County and half a dozen enslaved residents of Northumberland County all chose to enslave themselves to sons of their deceased masters.[53] Others petitioned to enslave themselves to nephews, grandsons, or brothers-in-law of their former owners, to whom some petitioners may have been biologically related.[54]

In Lavinia Napper's petition for self-enslavement to the Fauquier County Circuit Court, her lawyer took great pains to explain why Napper "deliberately prefers slavery in Virginia to freedom out of it," but apparently had to revise the statement in court, since a married woman's property belonged to her husband under the law (with certain exceptions). The petition explained, "She desires to become the slave of Edwin Smith of the said County—your petitioner represents, that her proposed Master has is married a member of the family to which she formerly belonged. That she has known her from childhood, and has frequently been in heris service, and feels assured that he will be a kind Master to her."[55] Napper, however, had sought not merely the general condition of self-enslavement, but enslavement to a particular person, Mary H. Smith, whom she had known since childhood and about whose personality and character she was sure. In a courtroom charged with upholding the customs and laws of a society written by and for white males, though, Napper and Mary H. Smith were required to concede the arrangement to Mary's husband, Edwin, who was ordered to "hold the said Lavinia Napper as his Slave for life."[56] Unhappy with the outcome, Napper spent the next month pressuring Mary H. Smith to gain legal control of her, so that Napper could live in peace, free from the possibility of being sold by Edwin Smith to settle one of his debts. In an extraordinary turn of events, Napper succeeded in securing a document from Edwin Smith that declared, "Whereas it was the wish of said negro to be secured to the said Mary H. Smith and the children of the said Mary H and Edwin Smith free from all liability for the debts and obligations &c. of the said Edwin Smith, now this indenture witnesseth that in considerations of the promises and of the natural love and affection which he the said Edwin Smith hath for the said Mary H Smith his wife, he the said Edwin Smith gives grants & conveys unto the said Mary H Smith during her life, all his right title and interest in and to the said slave Lavinia Napper and her increase: to have & to hold the same during her natural life to her sole and exclusive use and benefit free from all liabilities whatsoever of the said Edwin Smith."[57] Napper, already enslaved, had revised the terms of her bondage to reflect her original desire, to be under the charge of Mary H. Smith. However, Napper's negotiated conditional status, at least in this respect, would come to an abrupt end should Mary H. Smith die before her husband, as Edwin Smith would then have the right to sell Napper (and any children of hers born during her second enslavement), should he so desire. In addition, Napper's condition (and that of any of her children) would remain unchanged should Smith decide to leave Virginia for another slave state.[58] Thus, Napper's bondage was absolute, and she could be bought and sold as any other legal property could in Virginia at the time. The indenture further reiterated the fact that her chosen status would be inherited by any and all of her children, who upon the death of Mary H. and Edwin Smith, would "be equally distributed amongst the children of the said Edwin & Mary H Smith."[59] Though the law protected the freedom of children born prior to their mother's self-enslavement, children born during one's period of second slavery inherited the legal status of their mother—a fact that might have discouraged more than a few free black women from seeking self-enslavement.

Napper was not alone among Virginia women who were willing to enslave themselves but feared their subsequent sale by male owners needing to settle their debts. For example, Mary Phelps (or Phillips) of Frederick County sought enslavement to Hiram O'Bannon, but only on the condition that she be immediately held in trust by another man, John Avis, whose wife would protect her from future sale. Phelps's petition explained: "She desires to reduce herself to slavery and to choose Hiram O'Bannon as her master he having agreed with her that upon this court granting your petitioners prayer that he will at once convey her to John Avis to be by him held as Trustee for the sole and exclusive use of the wife of the said John Avis . . . and her children now living and hereafter to be born of the said John Avis. free from the debts, control and marital rights, of the said John Avis."[60] It is unclear why John Avis hadn't simply volunteered to become Phelps's new owner in the first place.

Male petitioners for self-enslavement also sought protections from future sale by brokering sometimes complex arrangements with potential owners that manipulated Virginia's legal system to win greater personal protections than the state's self-enslavement law specifically provided. For example, Nicholas Poindexter of Orange County selected Bettie C. Towles as his new owner in 1861, but only "on the following terms and conditions": that he become Towles's slave "and be held by a trustee for her sole and separate use for and during the term of her natural life . . . and that he should not become liable in consequence thereof in any manner for the payment of the present or any future debts of her said husband, nor for the payment of any debts of the said Bettie C. Towles heretofore contracted." Thomas R. Towles, Bettie's husband, would "be & act as the trustee for his said wife in this behalf, and [would] hold legal title to him for the sole and separate use of the said Bettie C. Towles upon the terms and conditions aforesaid." The circuit court judge, apparently unconcerned by this explicit legal guarantee of Nicholas Poindexter's conditional status as a bondsman, approved of the unusual arrangement, and Poindexter agreed to renounce his legal freedom.[61]

If not relatives of deceased owners, those chosen as masters and mistresses were more often than not acquaintances, neighbors, housemates, or fellow congregants of those seeking self-enslavement. Lewis Wilkerson, Armistead Currie, Araminta Frances, and a woman known only as Mary were among those who chose to enslave themselves to executors of their former owners' estates, as had Payne, Fletcher, and Poters.[62] Thomas Hill, William Williamson, Levin Crippin, Mike Ailstock, Thomas Goings, and Jane Horton were among those who selected neighbors they knew well as owners.[63] Both Celia Hale of Bedford County and Tom Squire of Halifax County selected those with whom they already lived to be their owners, suggesting that, despite their assurances in court to the contrary, voluntary enslavement would, in practice, change little in the lives of the petitioners.[64]

In some cases, self-enslavement arrangements between petitioners and their chosen owners were the products of decades-long relationships, which endured years after the close of the Civil War. For example, in the 1830s William Williamson of Campbell County had made a deal with his owner, Deboux Williamson: if he were able to pay his master his value (perhaps as much as $800) through overwork and other activities done on his own time, the black Williamson would earn his freedom.[65] Indeed, by the time of his master's death in 1838, William Williamson had done just that. Instead of granting him immediate freedom, however, Deboux Williamson stipulated in his will that William "should be free after the death of my wife," Martha. Perhaps as a concession to him in the meantime, Deboux bequeathed William "a horse. The one that is now a colt two years old."[66]

For four years William Williamson lived as the property of Martha Williamson, during which time he visited his enslaved wife, Maria, and their children (living less than three miles away on the plantation of Joel Franklin) as often as he could.[67] When Martha Williamson died in December 1842, William was finally emancipated. He remained in the neighborhood, used the horse he had inherited to make a living, and lived next to or near Thomas H. Rosser, whose family had lived nearby and had associated with the white Williamsons for years.[68] By 1850, forty-five-year-old William Williamson had established himself as a "prosperous" farmer, plowing and sowing a one-hundred-acre parcel of land he had recently acquired from the Rossers.[69] Confident, astute, and increasingly wealthy, Williamson knew the value of freedom and sought to protect the fruits of his labor. He registered himself as a free person at the Campbell County courthouse in that year.[70] Williamson was also aware that perhaps, having remained in the state now for eight years since his emancipation, someone would challenge his right to remain in residence.

Just before Christmas in 1850, Williamson petitioned the General Assembly for formal permission to remain in Campbell County as a free man, offering a snapshot of one man's life in freedom, circumscribed by the bonds imposed upon him and his enslaved family by the structure of a slave society. His petition explained, "that about 1830 he was married to a slave woman the property of Joel Franklin (then & now) and they have ever since lived together as man & wife in the greatest harmony—and have 8 living children—7 of which are in this County & 4 of these with his wife's master—all the children being slaves. That he is owner of 100 acres of land in this County & a farmer thereon by occupation; that he is not in debt but [in] prosperous circumstances and lives within 3 miles of his wife's master."[71]

Forty-seven white neighbors signed the petition, beneath a testimonial of their own. Of Williamson, they attested that they "have known him for *many years*. They believe him to be a man of honesty—not addicted to drunkenness, gaming, or any other vice. We are his neighbors and *all* of his neighbors," they assured the General Assembly, "and are willing and indeed desirous that the legislature pass a law permitting him to remain in this state as he is not only an honest, prosperous man but in truth a most useful and accommodating man to his neighbors & all with whom he has any thing to do." Finally, Williamson's white supporters avowed, "We further certify that we know of no one in this community who is unwilling that he should remain." Williamson (as well as his white supporters) almost certainly knew that this last statement had been an exaggeration, if not altogether untrue—plenty of neighboring whites had not signed the petition, including one of great importance—Robert O. Doss, the county commissioner of the revenue who lived a short distance from Williamson. The petitioners had made their point, however; those in the neighborhood should be able to decide how to administer state law in their community, in ways they deemed appropriate. In this and many other residency petitions sent to Richmond at the time, whites not only supported the claims of one or several free black individuals to belonging in their neighborhood but, less explicitly, challenged the idea that Richmond-made law could be applied monolithically across the state, trumping local knowledge and practice. In this way, such petitions can be read as intense expressions of white localism and neighborhood solidarity, as well as evidence for the existence of strong interracial bonds between free people.

Williamson's petition for legal residency was rejected in Richmond, but he seems to have been undiscouraged. He continued to expand his farming business and accumulate personal wealth by cultivating tobacco and corn. By 1853, when Doss visited Williamson to collect his annual property taxes, Doss reported that Williamson owned one horse, twelve cattle, sheep, or hogs, and household or kitchen furniture worth $25. Of twenty-six free black property owners in the county that year, Williamson was the second wealthiest.[72] Three months later, despite Williamson's prominent standing in the community—or perhaps because of it—a grand jury of the Campbell County Circuit Court presented him for remaining in the state illegally, after he had been living as a free man there for eleven years. The reason for his charges rested upon the discontent of one of his neighbors—"the Information of Robert O. Doss Commissioner of the Revenue." Anticipating conviction by the circuit court, Williamson wasted no time in ceding 100 acres, along with "two horses, all of his stock of cattle, hogs, crop of Tobacco now on hand, all of his corn now on hand, and all of his plantation tools, and household furniture of every description, and all of the present crop, now growing" to another long-standing neighbor, Thomas H. Rosser.[73]

Though Williamson was far more proactive than the circuit court was efficient (the case against him languished in the court for more than three years), he nonetheless decided to make use of the voluntary enslavement law and chose none other than Thomas H. Rosser, now the owner of his former farmland and personal property, as his master in May 1859.[74] Almost certainly Williamson's transfer of his property to Rosser, followed by his self-enslavement to the same, allowed Williamson to continue living in his house, tilling what had been his soil, and making use of the very tools, animals, and household goods he had for years. Most important, he remained within a short walk of his wife and children at Franklin's plantation. Neighborly bonds between William Williamson and Thomas H. Rosser formed first while Williamson had been enslaved, strengthened through Williamson's fifteen-year term of freedom, and continued after the Civil War emancipated Williamson once again and made his wife and children free for the first time. In 1871, after Williamson's death, Rosser legally transferred to Williamson's widow, Maria, the one-hundred-acre tract of land that he had received from her husband on the eve of his re-enslavement seventeen years earlier.[75] Williamson's case was indeed extraordinary, but it represents only a more extreme example of common connections that many enslaved people sought to maintain with former owners long after achieving their liberty. Such bonds were important for free blacks in staking and maintaining claims of belonging in the community and determining the terms of those claims.

For Payne, Fletcher, and Poters, the idea of becoming the nominal slave of a chosen master, as Williamson had to Rosser, was appealing. William Payne was the executor of their former owner's estate and one they knew well. As slaves in name only, they could remain in close contact with their family and friends, while continuing to live as they had for several months now, as free women. Self-enslavement might change their legal status, but not their status in everyday relations with whites they already knew well.[76] Becoming the ostensible slaves of Payne would also increase the women's chances of seeing that their children would receive their legacies from Ayres's estate, which Payne managed.

To give up one's legal freedom, however, no matter how clear the oral agreement might have been with a chosen owner that such bondage would be conditional, was a profound, irreversible act. Though they had not lived long enough as free people to experience many tangible legal benefits of their liberty, Payne, Fletcher, and Poters knew that the law viewed the free differently than it did the enslaved, even if to be free and black in Virginia in 1860 meant living as second-class citizens.[77] Despite all of the inadequacies and frustrations of their freedom, their joint decision to re-enslave themselves and their children could not have been an easy one, even if the process seemed to offer the best alternative in a world in which their options seemed severely limited.[78]

The arrangement also may have appealed to the humane impulses of William H. Payne, the women's proposed master, who had committed himself to executing as best he could the will of his deceased friend, Charles R. Ayres. Or perhaps Payne did not have any strong humanitarian motivation for agreeing to become the women's new owner, and only reluctantly agreed to participate in the proceedings once he had been asked.[79] In either case, according to law, he would be required to pay half the assessed value of Payne, Fletcher, and Poters to become their owner—money he figured he could raise from sympathetic acquaintances of Ayres, including fellow executor James S. Green.[80] William Payne had overestimated his colleagues' generosity, however. In an angry reply to Payne's request for a contribution toward the purchase of the freedwomen as slaves, Green scribbled: "With regard to the emancipated Negroes I will say emphatically that I will not give one Dollar, to any one to purchase, after selection under your law. If the advantage of having such as slaves, is not inducement enough to pay the price, I can't help it." He concluded wryly, "The negroes can get good homes, where the money will be cheerfully paid, and all will be peace and harmony."[81] Without contributions from others, and with William Payne being unwilling to front the entire sum required to purchase the women himself, Payne, Fletcher, and Poters hit their first roadblock to self-enslavement.

Soon another obstacle appeared. Under the self-enslavement law of 1856, Payne, Fletcher, and Poters were not permitted to enslave their children along with themselves, which they had decided to do. The law read: "The children of any such female free person of color, born prior to such term, shall not be deemed to be reduced to slavery by such proceeding."[82] Several other Virginia women had encountered the law's child protection clause when petitioning for self-enslavement and had used it in their favor, in hopes that they could preserve the integrity of their family—and the freedom of their children—when they became enslaved themselves; they had bound out their free children (an otherwise common practice at the time) as apprentices to their chosen master for a finite period. In Lunenburg County in 1856, Araminta Frances had bound her two children to her chosen owner.[83] The next year in Fauquier County, Betsy Taylor had petitioned for self-enslavement to Charles B. Tebbs, the grandson of her former owner. Though Taylor died before her petition could be approved by the court, her two children, William Taylor and Laura Taylor, were ordered to be bound out "as apprentices to Charles B. Tebbs Jr., the boy, until he arrives at the age of twenty-one years, to learn the art of farming, and the girl, until she arrives at the age of eighteen years, to learn the art of a house servant." At the end of his term of service, William was to receive $100 and Laura $50 from Tebbs.[84] The situation was different for Celia Hale of Bedford County the same year, who selected Jesse Minter as her new owner precisely because already "four of her children have been bound as apprentices to Jesse Minter of this county to be kept by him until they arrive at lawful age."[85] In this way, free women of color who had made the difficult decision to enslave themselves negotiated with their chosen owners and obtained legal assurances that in the best scenario, their families would remain intact, and in the worst their children would preserve their freedom and acquire remunerative occupations.[86]

Unlike most women in their position before or after, Payne, Fletcher, and Poters sought in 1860 to enslave themselves *and* their children. To do so required special legislation from the Virginia General Assembly which would allow their children to become legal slaves to the same person whom they would choose as their new owner. Though atypical, they were not the first Virginia women to seek the enslavement of their children. The self-enslavement law had been designed to stem the flow of free black petitions to the General Assembly, but ironically free blacks from around the state had continued to petition the Virginia House and Senate since 1856 to grant exceptions to the self-enslavement law itself. These petitions largely fell into one of two categories: those of free women of color who sought to enslave their children along with themselves,[87] and those of men or women who asked to be enslaved without requiring their chosen owner to pay the court one-half their assessed value, as the law stipulated.[88] In fact, in neighboring Culpeper County, a woman named Mary had recently asked the General Assembly for a law allowing for both exceptions in her case—the enslavement of her and her six children and an exemption from the required fee for her proposed master. She had succeeded, but representatives to the Virginia Senate, in their deliberations over the bill granting her request, made clear how controversial the issue of enslaving free children could be. Adults choosing for themselves whether to renounce freedom or not was one thing, but allowing parents to enslave their underage children was another. The bill was initially rejected by the Senate, 29 to 12, and only passed after significant alterations had been made.[89] Mary had nonetheless obtained the law she needed, and her case likely served as a model for Payne, Fletcher, and Poters. By seeking a similar measure from the General Assembly, the women would be able to enslave themselves and their children at little cost to William Payne.

In February 1861, the Fauquier women's petition went to the General Assembly, where several weeks earlier representatives in the House and Senate had launched a coordinated effort to overhaul the general voluntary enslavement law of 1856.[90] Nearly three years had passed since Howerton, Deneale, and other lawmakers had attempted to craft compulsory removal legislation and a more permissive self-enslavement law to complement it. In the aftermath of Abraham Lincoln's victory in the presidential election of November 1860 and the subsequent secession from the union by South Carolina, Mississippi, Florida, Alabama, Georgia, Louisiana, and then-most-recently Texas, legislators in Virginia took a break from rancorous debates over whether their state should also secede in order to consider perceived dangers posed by free blacks.[91] Those who sought to redefine self-enslavement as a means of re-enslaving masses of free people still numbered in the minority, but their influence had grown since 1858. Individual petitions to the General Assembly over the previous year from free blacks requesting a waiver of fees for masters in self-enslavement cases also bolstered the position of those lawmakers who insisted that the natural condition of African Americans was that of servants and that most, if not all, free blacks would voluntarily enslave themselves if the process were made easier and less expensive.[92] If ever there had been a moment for removal and re-enslavement extremists to claim the necessity for forceful, wide-reaching measures, this was it; Lincoln had been inaugurated, southern whites perceived slavery to be under attack, and one might argue with renewed fervor that African Americans would undermine Virginia's peace and security in the future if they were permitted to remain in the state as free people.

Most Virginia lawmakers, however, remained unwilling, even in the spring of 1861, to pass a measure that would empower the state government to re-enslave large numbers of Virginia's free blacks, inasmuch as such an act would have violated the very principles they sought to protect from a perceived assault from the federal government, now under the control of so-called Black Republicans—limited central authority, local self-determination, and the sanctity of liberty itself, even when enjoyed by blacks. In this respect, the debate over the bill in 1861 echoed that in the legislature of the late and early 1850s, as moderates criticized the "audacity and rascality for a majority to pass a vote to enslave a minority, in a republican State of the Union," and decried a dangerous expansion of government power that could just as well lead to "the enslavement of the poor white population" down the road.[93] As more extreme lawmakers pushed to eliminate entirely the fee imposed upon masters for the enslavement of petitioners (thereby "facilitating enslavement," according to one legislator), more moderate legislators motioned for greater protections for free blacks against being coerced into slavery and, if enslaved, from being sold to settle the new master's debts.[94] Those in favor of making self-enslavement nearly free of cost for prospective owners argued that "this would enable white men in humble circumstances to become slave-owners, and thus extend the institution, and enlarge and more widely diffuse the interest in its preservation." But others fought to maintain the tax imposed upon new owners in such cases, as they believed that eliminating the cost of self-enslavement for participating whites "would put the free negroes into the hands of persons, some of whom may be worthless."[95] In this way, the issue of how difficult it would be to reduce free blacks to slavery intersected with some Virginians' concerns about class differences among a diverse white population in the state. And the debate itself showed yet again that white Virginia never behaved with the uniformity that pro-slavery propagandists claimed.

Some of the same lawmakers who supported changes in the law to make self-enslavement easier endorsed counterbalancing measures designed to protect free individuals from being coerced into bondage and, once enslaved, treated as common slaves. For example, after voting in favor of eliminating the fee for self-enslavement, Delegate Nathaniel Riddick of Nansemond County proposed "that such slave or slaves shall not at any time be sold or mortgaged, or in any way be made liable for the debts of the master or mistress existing at the time of such enslavement, except for taxes and county levies."[96] But even moderates had trouble agreeing on the proper extent to which free blacks should be protected under the law. Edward C. Burks of Bedford County captured the complicated views of fellow moderates on the issue in a letter written after a day of vigorous debate in the legislature. He wrote that the self-enslavement bill under consideration "will pass our House, I think, but it is said will probably be defeated in the Senate. The negro enslaved is *protected* against the debts of the master selected and his heirs and legatees. I tried to amend in part in this respect by striking out 'heirs and legatees,' but was ruled out of order . . . There are some other objections to the bill, but I think I shall vote for it on its passage."[97] Burks was only partly correct in his prediction: the bill passed the House with Riddick's protection clause intact, but faced substantial revision in the Senate that included the removal of Riddick's provision but the insertion of still others. Thus, the debate among the majority was not whether to incorporate protections of blacks into the new bill, but rather which protections to adopt.

On 13 March 1861, the General Assembly passed a special law enabling Payne (and her daughter Betty Payne), Fletcher (and her daughters Vianna, Fanny, and Sally Fletcher), and Poters (and her daughter Selina) to petition their local court for enslavement to a master of their choice.[98] Several weeks later the legislature approved "An ACT for the Voluntary Enslavement of Free Negroes, without Compensation to the Commonwealth," which replaced the general law of 1856 and streamlined self-enslavement. In addition to removing the fee that owners who gained slave property through the process had been required to pay, the revised legislation contained another concession to those lawmakers interested in popularizing the process and increasing the number of re-enslavements in Virginia. It eliminated the need for petitioners to submit a formal written petition to their circuit courts that would be posted on the courthouse door for one month. The new law allowed a person seeking self-enslavement with a chosen owner to simply apply to his or her local circuit court, which would immediately "proceed to examine each party separately, as well as such other persons as said court may see fit." By doing away with the one-month waiting period (which typically became three or more months because circuit courts convened semiannually in a given county), legislators had devised a way to discourage applicants from using their petitions to self-enslave as a tactic to delay their prosecution for violating the expulsion law. Under the new measure, once an individual applied to the court for self-enslavement, the court was to conduct its proceedings the same day, or at least during the same term of court.

Extremists had indeed made their mark on the law of 1861, but the measure was by no means a radical departure from the earlier law of 1856. In fact, for every concession made to re-enslavement radicals in the law's language, moderates had inserted new protections. For example, the new law contained a provision whereby the "debts and liabilities" of applicants for self-enslavement would be paid by their new owner—an added incentive to self-enslave for those individuals who had come under hard times after their emancipation, but more importantly a powerful disincentive to those who might consider becoming their masters. It is possible that this provision served as the moderates' weaker substitute for the requirement that the new master pay half the value of the self-enslaved person. Whereas the law of 1856, under which Payne, Fletcher, and Poters first sought self-enslavement, had merely prevented the children of petitioners from being enslaved along with their parents, the law of 1861 required the owners of self-enslaved mothers (or fathers, if the mother were no longer living), "to have and to take the custody, control and services of such of the children of said father or mother as are free, until the females arrive at the age of eighteen, and the males at the age of twenty-one." Most important was the law's provision that the new master or mistress "shall pay for [their new slaves' children's] services at the expiration thereof, so much and for such years as the court may order."[99] Not only would children of the self-enslaved remain free, as they always had; they would now be required to remain alongside their enslaved parent(s), and, upon coming of age, they were to receive compensation for their labors.[100] The law of 1861 also contained a new passage that directed local authorities to interrogate applicants for self-enslavement more closely. Before anyone could be enslaved under the measure, commonwealth's attorneys and judges were to "be satisfied, by personal examination of the said negro, that he fully understands the nature and object of the proceedings, and that the act on his part is free and voluntary."[101]

As a result of the changes made to the legal self-enslavement process by Virginia lawmakers—including the several additional protections offered for petitioners—the law of 1861 did not "fling back into the seething hell of American Slavery between SIXTY and SEVENTY THOUSAND FREEMEN," as editors of the *Weekly Anglo-African* feared it would.[102] In fact, the new law apparently did not even result in increased numbers of self-enslavements, which surely contributed to the lack of press the law received from contemporary pro-slavery newspaper editors and politicians.[103] Individuals who might have considered petitioning for enslavement under the 1856 measure with no intention of actually going through with it—using the process instead merely as insurance against prosecution for violating the expulsion law—were now less inclined to participate in an expedited process that might produce self-enslavement in as little as one day. Indeed, the new law ensured that the few petitioners who employed it were much likelier to end up enslaved than had been true under the original general self-enslavement law of 1856. Of at least thirty-one free men and women who applied to their circuit courts for self-enslavement after the outbreak of the Civil War, twenty-eight, more than 90 percent, were successfully enslaved, typically in a court process that lasted no more than one day. By comparison, only thirty-four of the sixty-three free individuals known to have petitioned local Virginia courts for self-enslavement from 1854 to 1861 were enslaved, in processes that commonly took months or years to complete. In 1861, at least ten free people applied to their local courts for enslavement. The number apparently dropped in 1862 (perhaps as few as four individuals sought enslavement in Virginia that year), but rebounded somewhat in 1863 and 1864, when at least ten, then twelve, applied for self-enslavement throughout the state. At least one free person was still seeking self-enslavement as late as November 1864, nearly two years after the Emancipation Proclamation and, as it turned out, only five months before Lee's surrender.[104]

Priscilla Rich of Richmond County took full advantage of the law's changes, including its added provisions regarding the care of petitioners' children. As part of a one-day proceeding in circuit court in 1861, Rich's prospective master, Albert F. Yerby, agreed to "have and take custody, control and services" of Rich's three children—aged six, two, and one—until the two girls reached the age of eighteen and the boy twenty-one, at which time Yerby would pay the children $80, $50, and $175, respectively.[105] In the midst of civil war in 1864, Betsy Stevens and Morgan Hancock petitioned the Circuit Court in Halifax County for the right to enslave themselves to Stephen D. Tucker, to whom Betsy Stevens bound seven of her children. Before enslaving herself to Tucker, Stevens negotiated an arrangement with him whereby five of her sons would receive "the Sum of one hundred Dollars on the day that they respectively arrive at the age of 21 years." As for Nora, her daughter, she would earn "the Sum of Seventy five dollars on the day that She arrives at the age of 18 years" in return for her service. Betsy Stevens's arrangement with her prospective owner was crucial to her willingness to enslave herself. Stevens was willing to join her then-husband Morgan Hancock in slavery, as long as she could first be assured that her children would forever be free and that they would receive compensation from her new owner, so that they could care for themselves when they became of age.[106]

Though the majority of petitioners for self-enslavement in Virginia were individuals who had experienced slavery first-hand and then had been emancipated, perhaps as many as 15 percent of those who sought enslavement from 1854 to 1864 were *free-born* individuals, most of whom applied under the revised law of 1861. Free-born men and women who petitioned for self-enslavement, especially during the Civil War, largely did so because of the general deprivation affecting most layers of free society, white and black—poverty and a lack of available options to improve their lives. In Virginia's urban centers, especially Richmond, "even in the first year of the war, many residents of the city were driven to desperation," as supplies ran short and prices on medicine, clothing, food, and other necessities rose dramatically. Though the lives of city dwellers at every level were shaped by wartime scarcity and inflation, the poor suffered the most.[107] One even wonders whether some whites might have availed themselves of the option of self-enslavement, had it existed for them during the Civil War.

Anderson Hatter had been born free in Albemarle County, and his mother Maria Hatter had always taken pains to protect his freedom. She had led her son into the county court clerk's office not long after he learned to walk, so that the two-year-old Anderson could be registered; the clerk noted "satisfactory evidence of his freedom" and described him as "two feet high, light complexion."[108] Years later, at the age of twenty-six, Anderson Hatter registered again, this time gaining a critical phrase in his free papers; the clerk now recorded "satisfactory evidence of his having been born free of parents emancipated prior to the 1st day of May 1806," which would protect him from the kind of court harassment that had plagued other free-born individuals whose mothers had not been born free themselves.[109] Though safe from prosecution under the expulsion law, Hatter could not escape the attention of the court in another matter—his nonpayment of taxes in 1863. "A. Hatter" was one of nine free black men (or about 3.3 percent of free black males in the county) who were reported as delinquent that year; as was typical, the court identified 162 white men (roughly 2.6 percent of the total white male population) as remiss in their taxpaying duties that year as well.[110] Likely destitute and short on options to improve his situation, Hatter petitioned for self-enslavement in May 1863 to Benjamin F. Abell, one of the larger slaveholders in Charlottesville. As provided by the law of 1861, Abell agreed to "pay the debts and liabilities of said Anderson alias Andrew Hatter existing prior to this date."[111]

Mike Ailstock, also born free in Albemarle County, similarly fell on hard times during the Civil War after he had been drafted into service of the Confederate military in September 1861.[112] In May 1864, Ailstock sought enslavement to next-door neighbor Shepherd S. Moore in order to escape his debts.[113] During the final year of the Civil War, free-born Ailstock remained Moore's legal slave.

Nicholas Poindexter was born free in Louisa County in 1830 and worked as a "Laborer" there, where he lived with white brickmason John W. Walker and his family by 1850. That year he registered as a free person on Christmas Day with the Louisa County court clerk.[114] Poindexter's fortunes seemed to fluctuate annually. In 1851, he possessed no personal property, but by the next year he had saved enough to acquire one piece of silver valued at $8. By the following summer, however, despite having been working as a mason, Poindexter did not pay his state tax of $1.[115] Without property and now delinquent to the Louisa County commissioner of the revenue, Poindexter decided to try his luck by relocating north to neighboring Orange County.[116] During the next four years, he traveled back and forth between the two locales, likely securing work where he could, periodically visiting friends and family in Louisa, and, in 1856, finding time to renew his free papers at the Louisa County courthouse.[117] By 1859 Poindexter had settled in Orange, though the move seems not to have improved his financial situation. Shortly after the outbreak of the Civil War, Poindexter petitioned the Orange County Circuit Court to become the slave of Bettie C. Towles.[118]

Five free-born women and men in southeastern Sussex County also petitioned for self-enslavement during the Civil War to avoid "the poor house under the Overseers of the Poor." Though Sussex County authorities had charged several free blacks with violating the expulsion law in recent years, Coriceda Reid, Martha Reid, Louisa Myrick, Billy Barlow, and Arthur Barlow were born to mothers who had been free before the law of 1806 took effect. It was a desperate "need of assistance," not the threat of expulsion or court prosecution, that hastened the individuals' petitions in 1863 and 1864.[119] Billy Barlow was the first of the five to petition for self-enslavement. In October 1863, twenty-eight-year-old Barlow became the legal slave of Dr. William E. Prince, with whom he had been living for at least three years.[120] The following April, at the beginning of what would be the final twelve months of legal slavery in the United States, Arthur Barlow, aged twenty-six, followed suit by applying successfully to become the slave of Prince as well.[121] Next was nineteen-year-old Louisa Myrick, who enslaved herself to neighbor William G. T. Clements.[122] Coriceda Reid and Martha Reid followed. Coriceda, twenty-three years old, bound out her three children to James R. Graves and became his legal slave.[123] Thirty-year-old Martha selected James D. Howle, the next-door neighbor of Graves, as her chosen owner, to whom she apprenticed her eight children.[124]

Celia Hale had been born free in Campbell County before moving with her mother to Bedford County at the age of four. By the time she was twenty years old, Hale had settled in the neighborhood of Jesse Minter, a white farmer who owned several slaves in the southern part of the county. Soon thereafter, Celia moved into the household of Minter, to whom she apprenticed four of her children.[125] Two years later, Hale had approached Minter, suggesting that she become his slave. A disinterested—and perhaps nonplussed—Minter sent Hale to local attorney James F. Johnson in possession of the following note: "I send you this by Celia Hale a free woman of color, who, for the sake of future protection and support wishes to become my slave.—Please give her your views of the subject as a man and a Lawyer. If she persist, institute the necessary Proceedings forthwith. Let her sign the petition in the presence of several *good* citizens, and send me a note by her stating the willingness or reluctance with which she did so. I am wholy indiferent about it, and will not consent to it unless it is her own deliberate act cheerfully consented to in my absence and out of my influence. She has served in the family long enough to know us, and is old enough to judge for herself."[126] Though unenthusiastic, Minter was willing to go along with Hale's plan for enslavement, but only as long as her intentions were validated by people whom he saw as "*good* citizens." One month later, Johnson crafted a petition expressing Hale's desire to become the slave of Minter, explaining "that she is prompted to do this from no undue influence, but from a conviction that her condition will be bettered, and from a desire to do so after being made fully aware of all the consequences of such a step."[127] In October 1858, Hale and Minter went together to the courthouse where they expected to formalize the arrangement. Indeed, the court clerk had already painstakingly drafted a bond that stated: "Celia Hale, a free woman of colour, hath petitioned the Circuit Court of Bedford County, to allow her to choose as her Master and owner Jesse Minter of said County, the prayer of which petition the said Court hath granted."[128] The form would never be signed, however. After examining Hale and Minter separately, "for reasons appearing to the Court," Hale's petition was rejected by the judge.[129] Neither in theory nor in practice did Virginia's self-enslavement law serve as a vehicle to re-enslave the state's free black population. As Celia Hale's case demonstrates, even those few individuals who petitioned their local courts for self-enslavement could not take the outcome for granted.

Free-born and formerly enslaved blacks who sought enslavement under the state's laws represented a wide range of backgrounds, including young single mothers (or perhaps more commonly, mothers whose spouses were enslaved), young men with enslaved wives and children, other single people without children, and older men and women, some frail or in ill health.

In at least one unusual case, an entire family attempted to remain together and further their interests in their community, first by seeking freedom and then by seeking re-enslavement to a chosen owner. Simon, his wife Martha, and their two daughters Judy and Margaret of Southampton County had patiently anticipated their promised freedom for more than twenty years. John Williamson, their owner, died in 1844, leaving behind a complicated will that divided all of his slaves equally among Williamson's two sisters and friend, John C. Summerall, for as long as the three should live.[130] Summerall outlived the others, and when he died in January 1850, Simon, Martha, Judy, and Margaret should have been emancipated along with at least twenty-nine others who were the property of Williamson's estate, but they were not.[131] Instead, they remained in bondage under the control of Edwards Butts, the administrator of Williamson's will. Butts hired many of them out annually to local planters, who paid Williamson's estate a pittance for their labor.[132]

One year later, Simon was named as the lead plaintiff in a drawn-out suit that aimed to secure the freedom of Williamson's former slaves, as well as partial payment for their labor since Summerall's death. The court action, having been initiated by enslaved individuals and taken on by a white lawyer sympathetic to their cause, caused quite a "rumpus" in the local white community and prompted Butts, the estate administrator who was being sued, to complain about "the extraordinary and unusual trouble that has fallen on his hands in consequence of the institution of a suit for the freedom of the negroes belonging to John Williamson."[133] Even if a few in the white community objected to Simon and the others' case against Butts, they failed to influence the outcome. The court ruled in favor of Simon and his fellow plaintiffs in late November 1855 and ordered Butts not only to free Simon and all those under his charge, but also to pay each $45.12 (with interest calculated from November 1 of that year) and to cover the court fees associated with the suit and "all the expenses of obtaining Registers of Freedom for the emancipated slaves."[134] Eleven years after the death of their owner John Williamson, and five years after they should have been legally manumitted, Simon, Martha, Judy, and Margaret formally registered their hard-won freedom with the Southampton County court clerk. Freedom had come late in life for Simon, who was sixty-nine years old when he won his lawsuit. Having persisted so long in his quest, and he and his family having won combined damages of $180.48 for having been wrongly kept in bondage, they might have been expected to defend their newfound freedom relentlessly.[135] Yet less than three months after winning their victory in court, Simon, Martha, Judy, and Margaret petitioned the Virginia

General Assembly for self-enslavement.[136] Did Simon and Martha's advanced ages compromise their ability to care for their family? Or had raising a disabled child—one daughter was "subject to fits"—imposed demands that the family could not meet in freedom? Might re-enslavement have been the idea of younger daughter Margaret, who may have concluded that she alone would be unable to provide for a household of four? Perhaps some combination of the above factors led the family to ask the state's lawmakers for a special law that would allow them to seek self-enslavement. Less than one month after submitting their petition to the state legislature, Simon, Martha, Judy, and Margaret won a measure allowing them to select a forty-year-old farmer, Willis Bradshaw, as their new owner.[137] A "suit for freedom," like that of Simon and others in the Southampton Court of Chancery, was employed rather frequently by free blacks in Virginia's courts. Such petitions typically took the form of a petition delivered to a circuit court complaining of a person's having been "illegally detained." For example, one petition submitted to the Southampton Circuit Court on behalf of the children of Mason Freeman—Adolphus Freeman (aged eleven) and Sam Freeman (aged eight)—alleged "that sometime in the year of 1853, in the fall of that year, James Worrell took bodily possession of your petitioners, and has ever since retained them against their will and without any legal authority whatever . . . compelling them to labor without any compensation of any kind." In this instance, the court ruled that the young men were indeed "illegally detained" and ordered them discharged from the control of Worrell.[138]

Simon, Martha, Judy, and Margaret were among twenty-four men and women who had petitioned the Virginia General Assembly directly for special self-enslavement laws by the time Jane Payne, Mary Fletcher, and Annah Gleaves Poters secured their own measure from the legislature in 1861.[139] Having obtained what they needed from the legislature, Payne, Fletcher, and Poters decided to abandon their previous individual petitions to the Fauquier County Circuit Court for self-enslavement, in which they had selected William Payne as their prospective owner, and instead entered a new joint petition to the circuit court asking to be collectively enslaved to Ann M. Rector, "the sister of our late master," and the aunt of their five children.[140] Perhaps the women had changed their course upon learning of William Payne's unwillingness to pay for their enslavement proceedings—which itself may have arisen from a change of heart on Payne's part about becoming the legal owner of the three women and their children. In any event, living with Ann M. Rector would allow Jane Payne, Mary Fletcher, and Annah Gleaves Poters to remain in Rectortown as the

Petition of Jane Payne, Mary Fletcher, and Annah Gleaves Poters for enslavement, 1861. When Jane Payne, Mary Fletcher, and Annah Gleaves Poters were questioned about their unusual joint petition for re-enslavement, they confessed that none intended to renounce their freedom, regardless of the outcome of the legal proceedings. (Courtesy Library of Virginia, Richmond) ostensible slaves of a presumably kindly mistress who was a blood relation of their children.

But the plan quickly unraveled. Self-enslavement proceedings under the law of 1861 (as under the previous law of 1856) could be rubberstamped by Virginia's legal authorities, but frequently they were not. Circuit court judges—men who had been chosen in part for their commitment to supporting the pillars of Virginia's slaveholding society—might look upon the voluntary enslavement law in two different ways. On the one hand, it offered a practical solution to the plight of those free blacks deemed worthy of remaining in the state. But the law also might threaten the integrity of the institution of slavery if applied irresponsibly, by producing a class of quasi slaves exercising freedoms that contradicted their servile legal status.[141] As the law directed, the act of reducing oneself to a slave was not to be taken lightly—by petitioner, proposed owner, or judge. While the law contained a series of protections for free blacks who might otherwise be coerced or fooled into enslaving themselves, it also incorporated safeguards against those free blacks and proposed masters who might make a mockery of the self-enslavement process and of the institution of slavery itself by fashioning their own arrangements involving nominal or conditional enslavement.[142] Whatever the intent of the law, many judges proved perfectly willing to allow free blacks to broker the terms of their own re-enslavement. From county to county, there was great variation in how seriously judges took the letter of the law.

One day after the surrender of Fort Sumter and two days before Virginia would vote to secede from the Union, Jane Payne, Mary Fletcher, and Annah Gleaves Poters filed into the Fauquier County courthouse. As dictated by the legislation passed a month earlier by the state's General Assembly, each was interrogated by the circuit court judge and commonwealth's attorney, separately and apart from Ann M. Rector, their proposed mistress. Each of the black women, when asked by the court whether she would be willing to become Rector's slave *unconditionally*, unequivocally refused—for that was not the arrangement they had agreed upon. Discovering either that Rector and the three women had colluded to deceive the court, or that Payne, Fletcher, and Poters had simply misconceived their proposed new legal status, the judge promptly dismissed their petition.[143] And indeed, it is likely that the three women had chosen to pursue self-enslavement not to become legal slaves, but rather to preserve key elements of their newfound freedom, rooted in relationships with familiar people and in vibrant lives they had forged in Fauquier.

The Fauquier women were not the only Virginians to find a court unsympathetic to their petitions for self-enslavement. Mary Elizabeth Roland of Rockbridge County faced an equally rigorous examination by the circuit court when she attempted to enslave herself to William Miller, the son of a man who had owned her a few years before. After examining Roland and Miller separately, the clerk noted, "Whereupon the Court being satisfied that there is good reason why the prayer of the said petition should not be granted, doth reject the same." The clerk offered no further explanation of the judge's decision to void Roland's petition, but one year later, once Roland had selected a different prospective owner, a new petition of hers was granted.[144]

In at least one instance, a circuit court judge apparently denied applications for self-enslavement that hinted at impropriety on the part of the proposed master. In Madison County, in 1859, three brothers, Jeptha, Thadeus, and Timothy Chapman, each submitted two petitions for enslavement—one asking to become the slave of Nathaniel Tatum (the executor of the estate of their former owner Isham Tatum), and another proposing self-enslavement to long-time acquaintance and neighbor Nathaniel S. Wayland.[145] The court rejected without explanation the brothers' petition selecting Nathaniel Tatum as their owner; a letter Tatum had sent to the Virginia General Assembly several months earlier suggests why. In it, Tatum referred to his father's will, which manumitted Jeptha, Thadeus, and Timothy Chapman, and noted that the three did not have "the means of leaving the commonwealth and will be left a burthen upon the public, without masters or protectors, contrary to public policy and in violation of the laws of this State." "Under these circumstances," Nathaniel Tatum had therefore asked "that said slaves may be sold for the benefit of the said testator's estate and that an act of the General Assembly may be passed to meet the necessities of the case which cannot be adequately provided for by the Courts of the Commonwealth."[146] The General Assembly had denied this attempt by Tatum's son to cash in on slaves his father had wanted to liberate, despite the supposed risk that taxpaying whites in Madison County would have to support the supposedly destitute freedpeople with public funds.[147] Apparently unwilling to allow the Chapman brothers to become the legal property of one who had already sought to sell them as slaves, the Madison County Circuit Court judge had also denied their petition selecting Nathaniel Tatum as their owner. Though the court subsequently permitted Jeptha Chapman and Thadeus Chapman to enslave themselves to Nathaniel S. Wayland in August 1859, the petition of Timothy

Chapman was again "rejected at the costs of said Timothy" without further explanation.[148] Though one might assume that those petitioners whose applications for self-enslavement were denied would promptly leave the state, at least a few such individuals did no such thing. Rather than flee, Timothy Chapman decided instead to visit the Madison County court later that month to register with the clerk, which he was allowed to do.[149] The fact that Timothy now lived in Madison County in violation of the expulsion law of 1806 seemed not to matter to the clerk, who efficiently registered him and provided him with legal documentation of his freedom.[150]

Similarly, Payne, Fletcher, and Poters remained in Fauquier County after their joint petition for enslavement was dismissed in April 1861, while Virginia seceded and joined the Confederacy and war broke out on the county's fringes. Weeks later, Fauquier County's circuit court system stalled, and with it, the legal machinery that had the sole authority to make slaves of free people. The county's social order crumbled as well. Whereas general emancipation had seemed highly unlikely just a few months before, slaveholders and the enslaved now sensed a sea change, and many who had lived their lives in bondage saw a chance to seize their freedom—or so white people feared.[151] A number of blacks who had remained the human property of Payne, Fletcher, and Poters's deceased owner's estate after his death were sold by William Payne in 1862 "to prevent their loss" to liberty behind Union lines during the war.[152] Those who could, fled.[153]

In 1862 both Jane Payne and Mary Fletcher died, leaving Poters and various relatives to care for their orphaned children.[154] Whereas Poters, along with Payne and Fletcher, had refused to leave Fauquier County just one year earlier and had fought for a way to remain in the county legally even as slaves, by the fall of 1862 Poters had decided to leave home and family behind as she joined others who sought liberty behind Union lines.[155] With her went her daughter Selina, three of Mary Fletcher's daughters, and Jane Payne's only daughter.[156]

Much has been written about the effect of the Civil War upon enslaved Americans, but far less has been said about how the war and the social upheaval it wrought dramatically reshaped the lives of free black individuals and families.[157] While the escape of tens of thousands of enslaved individuals to Union lines is well documented, free blacks joined Union soldiers in camps by the thousands as well, claiming a new kind of freedom in the process—a freedom which, however, like that of many escaped slaves, entailed a break with community, extended family, and the past.[158] Fanny Fletcher vividly remembered her family's flight from Fauquier County in

1862 to the Fairfax Seminary near Alexandria, Virginia. She later recalled, "My sisters Viana and Sally in company with two colored men named Uncle Ben & Uncle Bill and other slaves walked; my sisters & Uncle Ben & Uncle Bill carrying me until we met Mrs. Catherine Lawrence with whom I have lived ever since."[159]

Fanny Fletcher's arrival in Alexandria with Viana, Sally, "Uncle Ben & Uncle Bill and other slaves" marked the close of a childhood in Rectortown and in the South. In the company of more than four thousand free and enslaved African Americans who had fled difficult circumstances at home in the Upper South, Fanny and the others, even as they remembered the people, sounds, and spaces of their childhood in Rectortown, now began building new lives as young women in the North. Fanny's memory of life on a plantation focused by the 1870s on striking details, recalled from the perspective of a small child: "I remember Ann Rector, and I remember Mr. Rector the husband of Grandma Kidda. I remember the cook and her little girl Nanny; also that Mr. Rector had false teeth; also a slave known as old blind Nat who used to pound hominy, & take care of horses. I remember that they sent sister Sally away a week before we left, to work; and she came back the night we started for Fairfax Seminary."[160]

It was in the so-called contraband camp in Alexandria that Fanny, Viana, and Betty—and those who brought them there—began to define for themselves the boundaries of freedom off the plantation and the possibilities for forging new beginnings under federal supervision.[161] Fairfax Seminary, like other gathering places of African Americans who had left their communities for new lives behind Union lines, became a place of reunion amid wartime disorder. Catherine Lawrence, a "hospital nurse for the Union Army" in 1862, recalled meeting Fanny Fletcher and her sisters at Fairfax Seminary and witnessing there the discovery of old friends who had been separated by the slave society from which they had fled.[162] She remembered,

> They said they were the slaves of Charles Rufus Ayres who had then recently died, and that their mother's name was Mary Fletcher and they spoke of her death, they said their Grandmother Kidda told them to come into the Union lines as soon as she was dead—that this grandma Kidda was the mother of Charles R. Ayres.
> ... They said they had walked from Rectortown to Fairfax Seminary Viana, Sally and the men mentioned alternately carrying the child Fanny. And while at Fairfax Seminary several fugitive slaves from

Rectortown & vicinity saw these girls in my care and recognized them calling them by their names Viana Sally and Fanny and generally calling Viana "Rufus Ayres" on account of her likeness to her father.[163]

Betsy Payne and others who had remained behind in Rectortown were unaware of the chapters of their family's history that unfolded after the girls' departure from Fauquier County. This history began with the trek to and stay at Fairfax Seminary and then unfolded in various Northern cities, as one by one the surviving children of Jane Payne, Mary Fletcher, and Annah Gleaves Poters were adopted by white families with connections to those serving at the Union camp in Alexandria. In the process, the girls' journey from Fauquier County north was imprinted in their ever-changing names, which reflected their new homes and the families to which they became attached.

At her home in Rectortown, Virginia, in 1875, Betsy Payne had posed a profound question to the reader of a letter from someone claiming to be her granddaughter. Which of her descendants might Nellie B. Francis of Providence, Rhode Island, be? James Jefferson, an African American veteran of the war, could have answered Betsy Payne's questions regarding the identity of her granddaughter Betty, who now went by the name of Nellie B. Slocum. Jefferson recalled:

I first became acquainted with her [Nellie B. Slocum] in 1863 in Virginia. I was barber for the 12th R.I. Volunteers and she came with some Slaves from Rectortown to where the regiment was. She was then a small child and was in charge of her grandmother. I asked her name and they told me it was Betty Payne. When I came home with the regiment I told an acquaintance of Mine, Mr. John C Francis about this little girl Betty and about another little girl I saw there, Mr. Francis said he would like to have such a little girl to bring up in his family and I told him if I went South again I would try to get one of them for him. In 1864 I went South again and found little Betty, and her grandmother consented to me bringing her North which I did. Betty's full name was Mary Elizabeth Payne. Mr. and Mrs John C. Francis adopted her and had her name changed to Nelly B. Francis. I was on intimate terms with the Francis family and kept run of the little girl while she lived with them. Both her adopted parents are now dead and Nellie married Charles Slocum of Pawtucket R.I. some 8 or ten years ago . . . She was a delicate little thing when I took her and she never has been rugged or strong since . . . She is now residing with her husband in Pawtucket R.I.[164]

Nellie B. Slocum would reveal her story and the evolution of her identity in a court deposition given thirty years after the death of her father, Charles R. Ayres. Slocum, thirty-two years old and in ill health, sat in her home at 19 Elm Street in Pawtucket, Rhode Island, in November 1889 and answered definitively the question her grandmother had asked fourteen years earlier: "I was born in Rectortown, in the State of Virginia in 1857. My mother's name was Jane Payne. My mother died when I was three or four years old in Rectortown. My own name before marriage was Nellie B. Francis. My name was originally Mary Elizabeth Payne or as I was called in the South for a nickname 'Betty' Payne. I came North just before the close of the war. I came North with a man named James Jefferson. I was then about 6 or 7 years old. Mr Jefferson brought me to Providence R.I. and there I was adopted by John C. Francis and his wife, Lucretia A. Francis. At my adoption my adopted parents had my name changed from Mary Elizabeth Payne to Nellie B Francis. Mr and Mrs Francis are both dead. I have lived in Pawtucket nearly ten years."[165] Nellie Slocum had been discovered by those charged with finally settling Ayres's estate and distributing the individual legacies Ayres had promised in his will to his formerly enslaved children so long before. Slocum's inheritance, now valued at $406.85, was part of a legacy that helps explain why her mother, Jane Payne, and the other two newly emancipated women, Mary Fletcher and Annah Gleaves Poters, had been so reluctant to leave Fauquier County in 1860. Payne, Fletcher, and Poters had even attempted to legally enslave themselves first to William Payne, then to Ann M. Rector—all for the sake of their children's future—a future which Slocum had now realized through the life she had forged in Pawtucket by 1889.[166]

CHAPTER SEVEN

THE BARBER OF

BOYDTON

In April 1867 African Americans in Mecklenburg County, Virginia, commemorated the second anniversary of general emancipation by parading through the town of Boydton. According to a rhapsodic contemporary account, Watt Love, a 35-year-old barkeeper and businessman, was among those "mounted on fiery steeds, their white sashes flying, and batons in hand," leading a procession of "some twelve or fifteen hundred souls" in "files of four" that "extended from one end of Boydton to the other." While the men, women, and children in attendance ate, drank, and engaged in "general jollification," Love employed his "oratorical powers" to inspire the crowd and to urge them to vote for his friend John Watson, "a freedman cobbler," in an upcoming election for the constitutional convention that would charter a new, free Commonwealth of Virginia in which both black and white citizens would play a role.[1] Like many black leaders who rose to prominence in the state during Reconstruction, Watkins (Watt) Leigh Love was wealthy, literate, light-complexioned, professionally successful, and had been a free man before the war.[2] What distinguished Love from his colleagues in Mecklenburg politics as well as from those citizens who joined him in the Boydton gathering that day was the fact that he had been one of the few Virginians who had risen to social, financial, and political prominence first as a free man, then as a dynamic *self-enslaved* entrepreneur during the war.

Born in 1832, Love had become an accomplished barber while enslaved to Fleming J. Jeffress. Jeffress singled Love out in his will as the only one of his slaves he thought deserving of emancipation upon his death, which occurred in 1859. Love found himself a free man and established himself in Boydton, where he quickly was deemed "the barber of that village" for his superior skills in dying, shampooing, and trimming the hair of the county's male elite.[3] Barbering opened doors for Love in Boydton society, as it had for many free blacks who pursued the trade in Virginia and throughout the South before and after the Civil War.[4] Love saved his earnings, invested wisely, and used his position to forge lasting relationships with his white customers, many of whom were prominent in county legal affairs, business, and politics.[5] Love formed such strong personal connections with his white clients that one regular customer, J. J. Daly, "while Wat was taking off his beard," had even asked Love to accompany him and his family on a tour of the American and Canadian West. Daly recalled that Love "replied that it would please him exceedingly, and that he would go." Daly later recollected:

> Wat made his appearance in due time at the depot in Clarksville, [Roanoke Valley Railroad] and took his departure with us for the great West. As we approached Baltimore Wednesday morning we were informed by the clerk of the boat, that before we could proceed West it would be necessary for us to give bond and security, that Wat was free . . . . This difficulty being met and overcome, no other similar obstruction presented itself during our trip. We thought it not improbable, that in our transit across the States of Ohio, Illinois and Indiana, Wat might be, to some extent, annoyed by abolition emissaries. But nothing of the sort occurred even though on our return trip we passed through Hamilton, Canada West, which is the Northern terminus of the main trunk of the Underground Railway. Our freedom from molestation in this regard, we attribute in the main, to Wat's superior intelligence and to his strong attachment to home in Virginia for though wonderfully pleased with St. Louis, and impressed with the belief, that in that city he could make a fortune quickly and easily, he nevertheless expressed himself as preferring Boydton over all other places on the earth's surface for a permanent abode.[6]

Acquainted with the ways of the larger world and well connected in his Mecklenburg community, Love went about expanding his business upon returning from his monumental tour of the West. Though prosecutions were rare in the county for black men and women who remained as residents for more than one year after gaining their freedom, Love was certainly aware of the law of 1806 and of the Virginia constitution that authorized one's indictment by the county or circuit court for such an offense. In March 1860, less than twelve months into his newfound freedom,

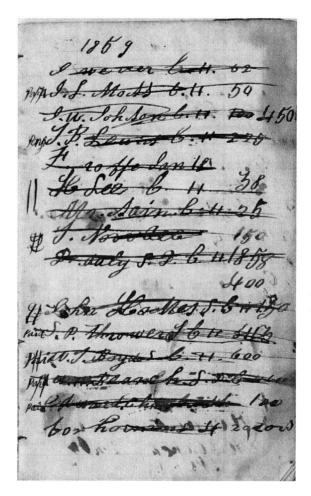

Watkins Love barber book, 1859. The barber books of Watkins Love, taken by the Mecklenburg County court as evidence in a case after the Civil War against his former business partner, are a who's who of Mecklenburg County's white elite, who regularly visited the once-free and twice-enslaved barber for haircuts, trims, and shaves. (Courtesy Library of Virginia, Richmond)

Love apparently decided to protect himself, his newly acquired property, and his burgeoning business interests in Boydton by filing a petition for self-enslavement—the first of *three* such petitions he would submit to the Mecklenburg Circuit Court.[7]

In Love's first request for re-enslavement, his petition was succinct and composed of boilerplate language proffering nothing more than what was minimally required. It stated: "Your petitioner Watkins Leigh Love respectfully represents that he is a free man of color resident of the . . . county of Mecklenburg Virginia over the age of 21 years & that he desires to enslave himself and wishes to select James W Love as his master or owner your petitioner therefore prays that he be allowed to select the said James W. Love as his master or owner upon the terms prescribed by the act of assembly."[8]

His proposed master, James W. Love, was the brother-in-law of his deceased owner, Fleming J. Jeffress, and a man he knew well (and to whom he was possibly blood related).[9] The two men acting as witnesses for his petition, S. R. Johnson and J. W. Mackasey, were regular patrons of Love's—Mackasey for haircuts, Johnson for cuts and dyes.[10] And the man who drafted his petition, Thomas F. Goode, was a leading lawyer in Mecklenburg and a loyal customer of Love's who periodically stopped by for a shave.[11]

Not all petitioners for self-enslavement in Virginia at the time were as well off or as proactive as Watt Love. For some men and women of color whose age, infirmity, or poverty highly circumscribed their freedom, self-enslavement seemed a reasonable alternative in a society that presented few options for those who could not take care of themselves.[12] By the late 1850s, a number of private benevolent societies operated in Virginia, mostly in the state's larger towns and cities. Such charitable organizations were largely organized and run by white women who were driven by what historian Suzanne Lebsock has called a "persistent personalism" in their attempts to assist mainly fellow females and their children who did not "'deserve' their poverty." For many elderly women and men of both races who were unable to provide for themselves, support came from extended networks of relations or their children. If they lacked children "willing or able to care for them, old people often found themselves completely destitute." Among the young too, "victims of debt as well as those born to poverty, or those suffering from physical or mental disabilities, sometimes found themselves on the county poor list."[13] Fanny Gillison, a sixty-year-old woman living in Fauquier County, had received her freedom by deed from her owner Richards Payne just after Christmas in 1859. Within four months, however, Gillison had decided to return to slavery, as her lawyer explained in a petition to the circuit court: "She has heard the laws of Virginia require her to leave the state within twelve months after her emancipation that in as much as she is of an advanced age her years numbering nearly sixty with no reason to believe that from her own labor she will be able to support herself in comfort for any great length of time: that having been born raised & having resided up to this time of her life in said County she could be entirely friendless outside of the state of Virginia—she after mature Consideration deliberately declares slavery in said state is to her preferable to freedom out of it."[14] Gillison's age had been the primary reason behind her decision to enslave herself, but there had been other important factors—the fear of being prosecuted for remaining in the state illegally and her unwillingness to leave friends and family in Virginia.[15]

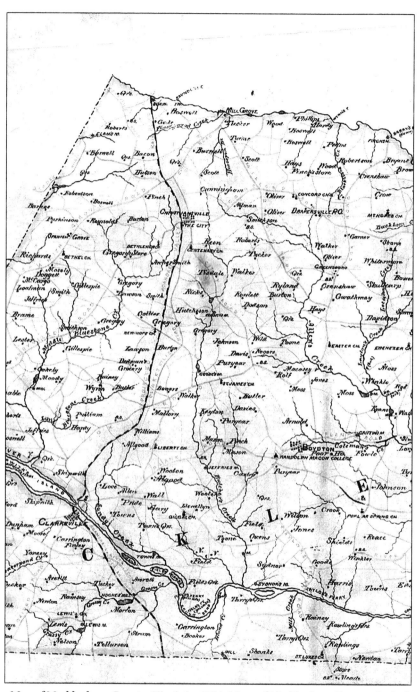

Map of Mecklenburg County, Virginia, 1864. Maps of Mecklenburg County drafted for the Confederate States of America during the Civil War depict geographical features, roads and bridges, and the property of poor and wealthy whites, including slave quarters, as well as the homesteads of free blacks (denoted by "F.N."). They serve as spatial representations of the names listed in the barber books of Watkins Love. (Courtesy Virginia Historical Society)

Of the multiple issues confronting fifty-three-year-old Dennis Holt of Campbell County, who petitioned to enslave himself in October 1860, of central concern was "that by reason of his infirmity of body, and imbecility of mind [he] distrusts his ability to take care of himself."[16] If he had been able to provide for himself as a free man, perhaps he would have set out to do what his father had, which was to work industriously, save his earnings, and purchase his loved ones in order to set them free.[17] Lewis Wilkerson of Amelia County had been born during the Revolutionary War and lived as the property of Polly Morris when she had died in 1851, at which time he had registered with the county court clerk.[18] The clerk had noted that Wilkerson was "a free man of colour of dark complexion about seventy years of age . . . the little fingers of the left hand stiff in the joint."[19] Unable to care adequately for himself six years later and perhaps suffering from worsening arthritis in his hands, Wilkerson declared "his wish and desire to return again into slavery" in a petition to the circuit court.[20] Gillison, Holt, and Wilkerson were among a small fraction of petitioners for self-enslavement in Virginia from 1854 to 1864 who stand in marked contrast to those like Watt Love—they were older, physically impaired, or impoverished.

More common among petitioners for self-enslavement were those who had at one time been presented, indicted, or convicted by their local courts for violating some Virginia law. The majority of these individuals had fallen victim to their county's uneven enforcement of the state's expulsion law of 1806. Less common were those who petitioned for self-enslavement after facing charges for other crimes. In 1860 Walker Fitch was living comfortably in the town of Staunton, Virginia, where he worked as a laborer. The next year he had been arrested for forgery, and while in custody at the Augusta County jail, decided to petition for self-enslavement to his employer, Michael G. Harman, the owner of his wife and children.[21] In Mecklenburg County, Matthew Feggins, a forty-year-old man of humble means who had been free since at least 1851, entered his application for self-enslavement to Armistead G. Boyd on the same day that Watt Love submitted his own petition. Feggins was without personal property and had been convicted by the county court a year and a half earlier for stealing $10 worth of corn from a white man's corn crib. For the offence, Feggins had received a jail sentence of thirty days and "thirty nine lashes upon his bare back well laid on."[22] The witnesses for Feggins's self-enslavement application, S. R. Johnson and J. W. Mackasey, were the same two men who later signed Love's petition for self-enslavement. The nearly simultaneous appearance of Watt Love, a respected businessman, and Matthew Feggins, a poor convicted felon, at the Mecklenburg courthouse to present almost identical petitions for self-enslavement illustrates vividly the range of complex circumstances that could have motivated formerly enslaved people in a single Virginia county to petition for self-enslavement.

A third Mecklenburg man, thirty-one-year-old Isaac Burnett, submitted his own petition for self-enslavement just one week after Love's and Feggins's appearances in the circuit court.[23] Burnett, who had sued for and won his freedom just one year earlier, likely shared with Love a fear of future prosecution for remaining in the state illegally, and asked to become the slave of Thomas F. Goode—with the seemingly ubiquitous J. W. Mackasey again serving as a witness along with William F. Small, yet another of Watt Love's business associates.[24]

The manner in which each Mecklenburg petitioner subsequently pursued (or ignored) his petition once submitted to the circuit court further demonstrates the multiple meanings that self-enslavement applications represented to freedpeople, even among those who petitioned from the same county. By September 1860, just six months after submitting his petition, Matthew Feggins changed his mind about re-enslavement and asked the court to dismiss his petition.[25] Isaac Burnett also had a change of heart. In April 1861 he asked the court to dismiss his initial petition, in which he had selected Thomas F. Goode as his new owner, only to submit another application five days later that requested Charles R. Edmonson, another business associate of Watt Love's, as his chosen master.[26] This second petition of Burnett's would sit inactive on the docket for five years as an insurance policy of sorts—if Burnett were ever indicted for remaining in the state illegally, he could hope to stymie or indefinitely stall the prosecution by proceeding with self-enslavement. If absolutely necessary, he would enslave himself to Edmonson, rather than be forced from the state or re-enslaved through public auction.[27] Watt Love, too, decided not to pursue the petition he had initiated but, like Burnett, he did not want his case dismissed outright. Rather, Love skipped his scheduled court appearance before the circuit court judge, claiming to be "sick and unable to attend," and failed to ask the court for a makeup date. His petition would remain on the court's docket for four years. Like Burnett, should Love ever happen to be indicted by a grand jury for remaining illegally in the state, he could point to his self-enslavement petition already underway (but dormant) as protection. Having his application for self-enslavement on file at the courthouse might also compensate for his increasing audacity as a free black entrepreneur in Boydton.[28] By 1860, Love had plenty of work. He created partnerships with local whites and used his solid reputation as a barber to diversify his business to include enterprises other than barbering, services that his wealthy clientele desired or needed once their faces were smooth and their hair clipped short. Within two years, he had "entered into copartnership with Wm. A. Homes as equal partners in the name & style of 'Wm. A. Homes' for the purpose of Keeping a *Hotel or Bar* in Boydton in this county and for the purpose of running hacks, wagons & horses." The enterprise lasted until 1865.[29]

Working as a team during these years, Homes and Love "purchased and jointly owned a valuable stallion 'Jack Morgan' and . . . they made two seasons with him." As owners of one of the more prominent enterprises in town, Love and Homes "did an extensive and profitable business with the bar, hacks &c. and stallion and made considerable profit in money and *corn*—(The season of mares let to the stallion being payable in corn)."[30] Customers employed and accepted the interracially operated enterprise and seemed not to care or remember which of the proprietors they had dealt with when conducting business.[31] At the same time, while Love managed numerous behind-the-scenes facets of this partnership (including bookkeeping), the business remained officially in the name of Homes, who frequently served as the enterprise's front man in everyday financial dealings. Perhaps there were limits to what Love could be *seen* doing.[32]

Even the arrival of war failed to slow the activities of Watt Love. It was in September 1862 that he purchased in furtherance of his joint enterprise with William Homes one hack, one mare, "one buggy & Harness," "one brake waggon," and one bay horse, for a total of $430.[33] By January 1863, Love and Homes had more than $400 "Cash on hand." From 1863 to mid-1865, the men brought in at least $3,488 in revenue from their various businesses together and earned more than $1,090 in profits.[34] Unlike those free people of color who joined tens of thousands of Virginia's enslaved in fleeing for safety, freedom, and new lives behind Union lines during the Civil War years, Watt Love stayed put, expanding his businesses in Boydton, purchasing property. In June 1863, when other free blacks were being drafted to construct fortifications for the Confederacy, Love received a rare exemption, facilitated by one of his customers. He later explained how it had happened:

When I was called upon—when they was getting up hands here they called upon me to go—Mr. Winfree came out here to carry hands down. I went with him to Keysville with the hack & horses and hands—when we got there he gave me a furlough back to fetch the hack & horses— told me I was to meet him in Richmond on such a day—which I did, told me before I started from Keysville to meet him in Richmond and he would get me exemption papers—which I met him there and he gave them to me. I paid him $150:—in money and the hacks carried him to Keysville which was a hundred dollars more making $250. for which he gave me these papers which I brought back home. On getting back I showed them to Mr. Homes. Mr. Homes told me he would keep them and if any one asked me about them tell them to go to him—that he had the papers. A short time after getting back home I met Mr. Sam Farrar which was getting up hands at that time or had got up hands, he asked me what I was doing back I told him I had the papers to come back on to go to Mr. Homes—he went to Mr. Homes I suppose and I suppose saw the papers—he didnt come back to me any more.[35]

The wealth, power, and privilege that Love had gained and exercised in the business world of Boydton had its perquisites, but by 1864, it had also brought him the attention (and likely sparked the envy) of some of his white neighbors. In April grand jurors serving the Mecklenburg Circuit Court charged Love with four counts of selling liquor illegally.[36] Four men, including one of the grand jurors, provided evidence against him.[37] The next day, Love offered a rare confession, admitting to the charges and accepting responsibility for a total court fine of $240, a significant sum, but still less than he had paid to exempt himself from Confederate service in the war. Likely reckoning that his conviction for selling liquor was only the first of other charges to come, Love decided the same day that he would revive the idea of self-enslavement—not to James W. Love, whom he had designated in his previous petition to the circuit court, but to James Bowers, who may have been the father of his future wife, Martha Bowers.[38] The court refused the latest petition, however, after examining both Love and Bowers.[39] Undeterred, Love immediately changed his request and filed his third self-enslavement petition with the court, this time asking to be bound to Allen S. Mason "as his Master or owner."[40] After another searching examination by the court, with longtime associate and customer Thomas F. Goode acting as a witness, Love became the legal property of Allen S. Mason. He was apparently the first—and last—person ever to be self-enslaved in Mecklenburg County.[41]

Despite the apparent diligence of Virginia's circuit court judges and their best attempts to ensure that there was "no fraud nor collusion between the parties" in self-enslavement cases—as the laws of 1856 and 1861 directed—in practice some free blacks did what authorities feared they would; they formulated the terms of their own self-enslavement and used the law to become the legal property of others while continuing to live as free people for all practical purposes. Watt Love did exactly this and in fact prospered financially and politically while doing so. Though Love sufficiently satisfied the court's questions to succeed in becoming Mason's property, 5 April 1864—the day on which he formally renounced the legal freedom he had won from the will of his former owner—did not become a major turning point in his life. In fact, the act of legal re-enslavement made such a small impression on him and was so insignificant to the way he lived his life that only a few years later, he was unable to recall to whom, exactly, he had been re-enslaved. On one occasion, Love recollected a time "before I was turned over to Mr. Bowers. I mean the time I chose Mr. Bowers for a master," referring to James Bowers, the man to whom he had chosen to enslave himself in his second petition to the court, which had been refused.[42] Curiously, Bowers similarly recalled that "before the emancipation of slavery he was the owner of Wat who was then a slave."[43] Later, Love correctly identified Allen S. Mason as the man who had become his new owner, but further confused the facts by incorrectly insisting that James Bowers at one time had become his owner too. He remembered hazily, "I then enslaved my self to Mr. Mason and then to Mr. Bowers."[44] By comparison, Love's memory proved to be razor sharp when discussing other details of his life during and before 1864, especially those concerning his business activities and the war.[45]

Watt Love never forgot, for example, that he had deposited two certificates of deposit (one valued at $300 in 1861 and another at $450 in 1862) in the Boydton Savings Bank, which had collected 5 percent interest while he had been free, during the period in which he had been enslaved to Mason, and in his two years of legal freedom after the close of the Civil War. Exercising his knowledge of the county's court system, Love successfully sued the bank for the certificates' entire value, including interest and "damages for nonpayment" in 1867.[46] Love also seemed to remember details of events that occurred during or before his period of self-enslavement to Mason quite vividly. He described General Sheridan's pickets sweeping through Boydton as well as the raids of Sheridan and General Sherman "which passed through this country." In so doing he recalled hiding his personal property in nearby North Carolina, where it would be safe from plundering Union forces, at the same time that he bargained for Yankee goods in Boydton.[47] Somehow he had even managed to acquire "two horses and one mule the property of the U.S." by the close of the war.[48]

Because Love's behavior had never changed as a result of his legal enslavement to Mason, those in the neighborhood continued to refer to him

$100 ‡ for my exemption papers and I paid
$150. out of my pocket for the same. —
Question by same. Please state the dates of
these transactions?

Answer. — I dont recollection the dates but
they were before I was turned over to Mr. Bowers.
I mean the time I chose Mr. Bowers for a
master _____ which was at the Term Cir. Ct. 186
See Exhibit here filed marked E.
It was a short time before this. —

Question by Com. In one of the books
in evidence there seems to be a balance in hand
after paying expenses on account of the hacks
of $1090.25 on the 5th day of Jany. 1865 and
in another place in the same book there appears to be a charge made against you
"Jany 5th 1865 settled up to date $526.33"
Can you explain for what that charge was
made if you know? —

Answer. — There ought not to be anything
charged here against me — The concern owed
me the $1090.25 which was there as before
stated. —

And further this deponent saith not. —
                              Watts Love

Williams A. Homes the Deft. introduced by
Defts counsel being sworn deposes & says
Question by some. Defts counsel. — State
the facts in regard to the purchase of the

*Deposition of Watkins Love, 1871. Depositions in chancery cases, like this made
by Watkins Love in 1871, serve as important repositories of voices from the past.
Though filtered, interpreted, and often communicated through a clerk's cryptic
shorthand, the responses nonetheless convey details, texture, and personality rarely
documented in other archival sources. (Courtesy Library of Virginia, Richmond)*

as "a Free man" during the period of his dubious enslavement.[49] Lucy Homes remembered that Love "faired as the white family" in everyday affairs; he "was fed from the table" when he ate with the Homes family.[50] Even the clerk of the Mecklenburg Circuit Court had difficulty describing Love's new status, as evidenced by a summons he directed to "Watt Love a free person of color, but now the Slave of Allen S Mason."[51] But the most illuminating portrait of Love's peculiar lifestyle as Mason's supposed slave came in 1871, when Love again drew upon his vast experience with the county's court system to sue his one-time business partner William A. Homes for property owed him from their wartime business collaboration, when he had ostensibly been a slave. During an examination by Homes's attorney, Love's long-time associate and former Commonwealth's Attorney Thomas F. Goode, who had served as witness for his enslavement proceedings to Mason, found himself having to explain to the court how Love, a legal slave, had been able to purchase an expensive piece of property from him in 1864. Goode was asked searchingly, "State if you remember that at the time you were about to settle with [Love] for the house and lot referred to by you, if [Love] was not at that time in a state of quasi slavery, and if he did not offer you payment for the same and did you not advise him to get some white person to pay the money and take your receipt for him?" An artful lawyer himself, Goode appeared unflappable. He replied, "I recollect that [Love] proffered to close the contract with me in regard to the sale of the house and lot,—whether he actually offered the money or not I do not recollect. I told him that he was in no situation to make such a contract and suggested to him that he should get some white person and I think named Mr. Homes as a suitable person to make the arrangement for him. I suggested Mr. Homes because of the business relations existing between them."[52] For once, Love's status as a self-enslaved person had had a discernible effect: though he had been accepted by Goode and other local white elites as a businessman, Love had had to recruit a white man—Homes—as his broker for an important transaction.

On another matter, Homes's attorney again prodded Goode about the unusual nature of Love's re-enslavement, asking incredulously, "Please state if you do not now remember that [Love] was at that time a slave and whether or not you believe you would have paid so large an amount of money to him—Knowing him to be a slave at that time?" Again, Goode remained articulate and unshaken. In his response, he revealed an important truth about how the two men and others in their circle had operated before the close of the Civil War, as well as the nature of Watt Love's self-enslavement. Goode stated, "I recollect that [Love] was at that time a slave he had however my entire confidence. I had been in the habit of borrowing money from him and paying money to him for services rendered by the hacks and teams of Homes & Love and I do not think that the fact that he was a slave would have kept me from paying him that amount of Confederate Currency."[53] While technically enslaved to Mason, Love not only continued to rent wagons, horses, and oxen with William A. Homes, but also operated "the only bar room Kept in Boydton at that time" out of Homes's house, where he lived "all the time." Love expanded his unlicensed, and therefore illicit, business of providing alcoholic beverages to serve a wide range of Boydton residents—from the enslaved to the slaveholding, "black & white."[54] Love not only knew how to run a profitable illegal enterprise, but knew how to take advantage of his enslaved status to protect himself from potential customers whom he thought might not pay for the spirits they consumed. One frustrated customer, Mary Beard, recalled, "I used to go down there very often to get liquor when the Homeses was not at home. Wat Love would ask me if I had the money & I would tell him no.— he would then say what belongs to the boss does not belong to me. . . . if it was mine I Could do as I choose with it, but if the liquor is gone & the money is not here I will be held responsible."[55] That Love was the principal owner of the bar did not impede him from using his supposedly subordinate status to avoid extending credit to certain black customers by claiming "that the bar belonged to the Homses & not to him."[56]

Even more remarkable is the fact that Love continued to earn the trust and "confidence" of the county's white leaders, all the while lending money to Thomas F. Goode and even to his supposed master, Allen S. Mason, who owed Love at least three hundred dollars by September 1864.[57] By the close of the war, Love had expanded his business network to include a number of prominent blacks and whites involved in county politics, connections that would prove important once peace returned and Reconstruction radically reshaped Mecklenburg society.[58] Love's standing in the community, as well as his wealth, made him an important ally for aspiring Mecklenburg politicians. In addition to bankrolling black Republican candidates for local offices, Love helped to solidify connections between emerging African American political leaders and white power brokers—many of whom were long-time customers and acquaintances. For example, Love's relationship with Goode, which began while Love was enslaved and deepened during Love's brief stints as a free, then self-enslaved man, was an important factor in the rise of freedman Ross Hamilton to political prominence in Mecklenburg County during Reconstruction. Goode, a Democrat in a black- and Republican-majority county, regularly "spent many hours closeted" with Hamilton talking politics, a ritual that maintained Goode's connection to the most powerful politicians in the county at the time and likewise strengthened Hamilton's influence in white society.[59]

By April 1867 Watt Love had carved out a place for himself in the Boydton business world that would make him one of the most powerful men in Reconstruction-era Mecklenburg County. After leading the massive procession commemorating emancipation, during which he delivered one of the lively "harangues," Love went on to coordinate local social and political gatherings in support of "the colored True Republicans," a new political organization that held biracial barbecues and frequently backed blacks in contests for seats in the state legislature.[60] Love's ability to navigate the black and white worlds of Mecklenburg positioned him for a major role in the True Republican organization, whose leaders called for the "beginning of peace and harmony" in a state where Reconstruction politics up to this point had been a "war of the races."[61] Love also acquired a vast seven-hundred-acre "plantation," farmed by black tenants, which included a stone house, three log cabins, two tobacco sheds, a shedded barn, and three log barns.[62] As with many of Virginia's black leaders, Love's political influence was an outgrowth of his financial stature and his prominent social position in the county, which he had forged while free and enslaved before, during, and after the Civil War.[63]

Throughout the Reconstruction period and into the 1880s, Watt Love worked tirelessly to help create a black political machine known as "the Court House clique," a powerful grassroots organization that bridged racial lines in electing Ross Hamilton to the Virginia House of Delegates and keeping him there. Love, who never ran for political office himself, helped to fund and rally support for "Hamilton's party," or "Hamilton's faction," which successfully routed its Democratic opponents in state elections for two decades. Hamilton was the longest-serving African American representative in the Virginia legislature in the nineteenth century, thanks in no small part to Watt Love, the influential man who had gotten his start as the barber of Boydton and then amassed a small fortune as a self-enslaved entrepreneur.[64]

CONCLUSION

A brief front-page article in Richmond's *Daily Dispatch* in 1856 reported that Caroline Banks and Mary Frances, sisters who recently had been emancipated in Virginia and then sent to New York, had returned with their children and now were willing to give up their hard-won liberty for the right to live at home. The two women desired legal re-enslavement, the newspaper pronounced, "a condition far preferable to the 'pleasures' of freedom they had experienced among the flinty-hearted abolitionists at the North." Banks and Frances's arrival in Richmond offered "something for Abolitionists to Reflect Upon" and afforded *Dispatch* readers "a fair illustration of the actual benefits of bondage to the negro race."[1] Occasionally during the 1850s, as the *Dispatch* article demonstrates, the Southern press relished the decision of a few free black individuals to renounce their liberty and used such instances—as rare as they were—to promote the idea that the natural condition of African Americans was that of slaves. Scholars of the Civil War era frequently mention self-enslavement laws passed in seven Southern states during the period as among the most repressive measures on the books—devised, and even flaunted, by white Southerners to effect the re-enslavement of free blacks. But the *Dispatch* editors knew better, as did their readers. In their internal tensions and contradictions, Virginia's self-enslavement laws passed in 1856 and 1861 mirrored the complicated society that produced them. For years, historians have seen in these laws a widespread, bitter, incorrigible white southern antipathy to black freedom—an interpretation that ignores the complex origins and functions of the legislation. The *Dispatch* story above can be read in different ways—for its shameless use of two freedwomen to vindicate racist, pro-slavery ideology, or as a record of a difficult moment in the lives of two young free women who returned to Virginia with their children, contrary to state law, and decided to put *place*—community, family, home—above their legal freedom. This study of self-enslavement in Virginia is but one of a number of recent attempts to present underexamined legal, political, and social dimensions of a conflicted and contradictory Southern society from the perspective of African Americans.

Any study of free African Americans before or during the Civil War is to some degree a study of an exceptional group, and this is even more true of an examination of those individuals who petitioned for self-enslavement. Few men and women sought to enslave themselves in Virginia from 1854 to 1864, though their numbers (at least 110) are greater than previously thought. Exceptional lives can reveal ordinary practices, however, and the actions of a small group of free blacks in this case illustrate quotidian ways that individuals who were marginalized by law nonetheless saw themselves as belonging to neighborhoods that comprised the very society that excluded them from political, economic, and social life on many levels. These anomalous, well-documented individuals, when viewed together, serve as a core set of diagnostic tracers, charting a trail through the legal, political, and social layers of Virginia society at the time, and illustrating aspects of daily life otherwise obscured. For example, the experiences of those who petitioned for self-enslavement illuminate the stresses that might attend the period between one's owner's death and one's promised emancipation, the nature and perils of the journey that some newly freed people made to Liberia, and the role of one's past—identity, reputation, and neighborhood—in defining new-found freedom and the edges of belonging, in new ways.

This study is as much an investigation into individuals' relationship to Virginia's expulsion law of 1806 as it is to the state's self-enslavement laws of 1856 and 1861. Most free people of color living illegally in Virginia before the Civil War were not prosecuted for remaining in the state longer than one year after their emancipation, as the law threatened. Though local courts were permitted to offer exemptions to an individual who had been singled out by a grand jury for expulsion, a free man or woman could be convicted under the law, and in at least one case between 1854 and 1864, be sold at public auction as an absolute slave. In the relatively few instances when the expulsion law was applied, personal relationships and the interests of individuals went far toward determining how the process would unfold and what it would mean to the individual free black men and women.

Sometimes, a free black was indicted for remaining in the state illegally because a hostile white neighbor happened to sit on the local grand jury that day. At other times, free blacks were implicated for breaking the law when local whites, who themselves had been indicted for infractions of the law, presented evidence to the court. In this way, African Americans could become caught up in the justice system almost by happenstance. In still other instances, suspicion fell on a free black person because he or she had spent time in the North, or had done something else that white neighbors objected to. In nearly every case, it is abundantly clear that free blacks knew state law and how best to avoid, navigate, or overcome it. They regularly engaged the services of white lawyers who, even in spite of personal racial ideologies or dependence upon the institution of slavery, represented their black clients as they did others.

Freedom mattered to Virginians in the 1850s. African Americans did everything they could to secure and preserve their legal liberty. Individuals who sought legal self-enslavement usually did so only after exhausting all available alternatives. In fact, many of those who petitioned for enslavement likely did so hoping that they would not have to go through with it. Applying to the state legislature or to one's local court for self-enslavement allowed some to delay their prosecution or conviction for violating the expulsion law—and sometimes a long delay could amount to a dropping of the case. In short, rather than an attempt by the state legislature to re-enslave Virginia's free black population, the so-called voluntary enslavement law was intended to be, and was used as, a buffer against the expulsion law, available to exceptional free black individuals. For some free blacks, the freedom to live in one's home community and to have a meaningful family life could be more significant than legal freedom, if the latter would have required their removal from the state. Liberty was something that was defined personally, according to one's particular circumstances.

Freedom mattered to white Virginians as well, and their representatives in Richmond did all they could to defend their right to own slaves and protect themselves and their property from excessive state intrusion. At the same time, even many extreme pro-slavery advocates proved unready to empower the state government to forcibly remove free blacks from their midst. Most Virginia legislators in the decades before the Civil War saw themselves as liberal, modern, freedom-loving champions of limited government. They bore a deep skepticism of state authority and consistently resisted any measures to raise taxes or expand government power, even for the purpose of expelling the state's free black population, which many agreed was desirable in principle. But there was something beyond this general desire to limit government that prevented white Virginians from expelling or re-enslaving the free black population. White Virginians who sat as judges, served as commonwealth's attorneys, or provided basic legal services to free black petitioners or defendants saw themselves as law-abiding, moral citizens, and perhaps more important, wanted others to see them the same way. Free blacks employed white attorneys who believed themselves to be impartial Christian followers of law to submit petitions, take depositions, and even draft legislation on their behalf, no matter that the whites themselves were by no means racial egalitarians.

Free and enslaved African Americans knew the law and used it to their advantage whenever possible. Enslaved people who had been promised their freedom in a deceased master's will contested their detainment before county and circuit courts. Free people who found themselves held in bondage also found ways to use the law, which held legal liberty sacred, to restore their rights as free noncitizens. When state laws made deportation a condition attending the manumission of black individuals, new laws were adopted to offer an option of last resort, allowing the few blacks threatened with expatriation to remain connected to life and family even if that meant renouncing one's legal liberty. Some used the process of self-enslavement to shield themselves from the law, so that they might continue living and working as if they were free.

That Virginia's first self-enslavement law was passed at the initiative of two free black brothers so they could remain at home in Lunenburg County highlights both the resilience and creativity of African Americans who beat the odds by using a convoluted and coercive legal system against itself to secure meaningful lives. The self-enslavement laws did not express a popular desire to expel free blacks *en masse*, as some historians contend; still less were they designed as vehicles that anyone believed might actually effect such a goal. Even so, that the same two free black brothers, and others like Caroline Banks and Mary Frances, had to resort to *enslavement* to remain in the state among family and community illustrates vividly one of the central tragedies of southern and American history.

Notes

The following abbreviations are used throughout the notes and bibliography:

CAB	Herbert A. Claiborne Account Book, Virginia Historical Society, Richmond, Virginia
CirCt	Circuit Court
CirSupCt	Circuit Superior Court
CLOB	Common Law Order Book
CoCt	County Court
DB	Deed Book
FNSR	Free Negro and Slave Records, Library of Virginia mss, Richmond, Virginia
LOC	Library of Congress, Washington, DC
LVA	Library of Virginia, Richmond, Virginia
MB	Minute Book
OB	Order Book
PPTB	Personal Property Tax Book, Library of Virginia microfilm
SRC	State Records Center, Richmond, Virginia
SupCt	Superior Court
VBHS	Virginia Baptist Historical Society, Richmond, Virginia
VGALP	Virginia General Assembly Legislative Petitions, 1776–1862, Library of Virginia
VHS	Virginia Historical Society, Richmond, Virginia
WB	Will Book

PROLOGUE

1. Mark Bowes, "33 Workers Arrested in Immigration Raid," *Richmond Times-Dispatch*, 7 May 2008.

2. VGALP, Accomack County, 13 January 1838, reel 1, box 1, folder 85, LVA microfilm; VGALP, Accomack County, 2 January 1838, reel 1, box 1, folder 82, LVA microfilm; VGALP Fauquier County, 6 December 1827, reel 51, box 73, folder 46, LVA microfilm; VGALP Campbell County, 18 December 1815, reel 33, box 46, folder 78, LVA microfilm.

3. While many free African Americans successfully avoided court action against them, others faced tremendous legal hurdles to residency, as a result of certain white neighbors. For example, on 12 August 1855, Thomas B. Brooks wrote to the Louisa County court to complain about Jim Chicken, who had been manumitted by the

estate of Jack Hope. Chicken, Brooks explained, "has for sometime been an incomberence on my hands." Apparently, the eighty-year-old Chicken lived on Brooks's land with an aging freedwoman, Viney, whom Brooks asked the court to "appoint a *master*, or direct her to be sold for her support." See "Thos B. Brooks' letter" in Louisa County FNSR, 1851–64, box 1, LVA mss.

4. VGALP, Essex County, 15 December 1825, reel 48, box 67, folder 78, LVA microfilm.

5. Declaration, Mothershead V. McCarty, April 1861, Richmond County Loose Papers, 1849, 1853–68, box 19, SRC. Suits initiated between male neighbors over perceived slights to honor supplanted challenges to duels as a more socially acceptable way to save face by the mid-nineteenth century. Alleged instances of dueling continued into the 1860s, however. See, for example, Norfolk County OB 14, 1858–74/172, LVA microfilm; Northumberland County CirCt OB 2, 1854–77/64, LVA microfilm; Fluvanna County CirCt OB 6, 1860–68/10, LVA microfilm; Amherst County CirCt OB 6, 1855–60/417, LVA microfilm; Smyth County CirCt OB 4, 1857–73/49, LVA microfilm.

6. Isaac Forman to William Still, 7 May 1854, in Still, *Still's Underground Rail Road Records*, 65.

INTRODUCTION

1. In an unforgettable scene in *Uncle Tom's Cabin*, Harriet Beecher Stowe depicted the escape of an enslaved woman, Eliza, across a partially frozen Ohio River: "Eliza made her desperate retreat across the river just in the dusk of twilight. The gray mist of evening, rising slowly from the river, enveloped her as she disappeared up the bank, and the swollen current and floundering masses of ice presented a hopeless barrier between her and her pursuer." Stowe, *Uncle Tom's Cabin* 121 (quotation). See Morrison, *Beloved*.

2. 1860 federal census.

3. See Frederick County PPTBs 1851, 1852, 1853, 1854, 1855, 1856, 1857, LVA microfilm.

4. In the 1850 federal census, Henry Champ was listed as a "Blacksmith." See also 1860 federal census, Stephensburg, Frederick County, Virginia. Anna Champ worked as a "washer." See Frederick County PPTB 1851, LVA microfilm. For birthdates and names of Henry and Anna Champ's children, see 1860 federal census, Barnesville, Ohio (Belmont County); Frederick County, Virginia, Register of Births, 1853–1912 (A–Ha)/61, LVA microfilm.

5. "A List of Free Negroes Who Have Failed to Pay Their State Tax for the Year 1853," Frederick County, Virginia, FNSR, 1795–1871, box 12, LVA mss.

6. "Henry Champs Certificate," Frederick County FNSR, 1795–1868, box 5, LVA mss.

7. See Scott, "Paper Thin." Those looking for lost free papers created a subgenre of classified advertisements in Virginia newspapers through the Civil War. See, for example, the 1851 advertisement of John Stewart, in search of papers that had been lost "by my coat going overboard into James River." See Petersburg FNSR, 1809–59, box 1,

LVA mss. Another man, Robert Morse, advertised in the *Richmond Daily Dispatch* in July 1859 for "my *Free Papers*, in a Cigar Case," lost between Byrd and Twelfth Streets in Richmond. See Henrico County FNSR, folder: Misc. Free Negro Papers, 1816–64 (quotation), LVA mss. For the significance of being free "but having no free papers," see Comm. v. Jno Parramore, Jan 1848, Princess Anne FNSR, 1771–1862, box 1 (quotation), LVA mss.

8. "Henry Champs Certificate," Frederick County FNSR, 1795–68, box 5, LVA mss. A 1662 Virginia statute stated that "all children borne in this country shalbe held bond or free only according to the condition of the mother." See Hening, *Statutes at Large* 2:170.

9. Sally Hadden points to the creation of early Virginia laws defining the legal status of mixed-race children, or mulattos, as evidence that whites, Africans, and Native Americans "engaged in interracial intercourse" and regularly transgressed "the cultural boundary dividing slavery from freedom." See Hadden, "Fragmented Laws of Slavery," 264.

10. Smith, *Civic Ideals*, 58.

11. Ariela Gross convincingly argues that "trials of racial identity in the United States turned less on legal definitions of race as percentages of 'blood' or ancestry than on the way people presented themselves to society and demonstrated their moral and civic character." See Gross, "Race, Law, and Comparative History," 557. For the intersection of race and law at work in the courthouses and neighborhoods of early Virginia, see Breen and Innes, *"Myne Owne Ground,"* 68–109.

12. See, for example, Hebron Church, Frederick County, Virginia, Private Register of W. S. Ryland, VBHS; Frederick County CirCt OB 10, 1853–68, LVA microfilm; 1860 federal census, Frederick County, Virginia.

13. On the number of free blacks living in Virginia contrary to the 1806 expulsion law, see the estimate provided by John H. Russell in *Free Negro in Virginia*, 156.

14. *Code of Virginia* 1849, 466.

15. For relative populations of free people of color in Virginia's counties, see 1860 federal census. The spirited roundup of free people living illegally in Frederick County from 1857 to 1858 was one of the few that occurred in Virginia counties in the 1850s.

16. Restrictive laws targeting free blacks mattered, but customary practices in Virginia communities did not end with their passage. For a similar argument regarding pigkeeping laws and everyday life in nineteenth-century New York City, see Hartog, "Pigs and Positivism," 924–25.

17. Frederick County CirCt OB 10, 1853–1868/205, 237, LVA microfilm.

18. Melissa Milewski argues, however, that "even after African Americans had lost many of their other rights, the courts remained a possible avenue for justice for some black southerners." See Milewski, "From Slave to Litigant," 724.

19. As many as one-third of petitioners for self-enslavement in Virginia from 1856 to 1864 avoided, delayed, or overcame prosecution for violating the state's expulsion law, with little intention of enslaving themselves. See Maris-Wolf, "Liberty, Bondage, and the Pursuit of Happiness," 141–51.

20. Ibid., 270, 289. For William Strother Jones, see 1860 federal census and slave schedule, Frederick County, Virginia.

21. Frederick County CirCt OB 10, 1853–1868/289, LVA microfilm. Apparently, William Strother Jones never paid the court the $200 he had promised in security of Henry Champ.

22. Barnesville, Ohio, in Belmont County, is on the eastern border of the state with what would become West Virginia (St. Clairsville is the county seat). Many free blacks from Virginia and North Carolina found themselves in the southeast corner of the state, in the areas roughly bounded by the towns of Steubenville, Columbus, and Portsmouth. On free black migration into Ohio and white Ohioians' efforts to slow the migration during the first half of the nineteenth century, see Gerber, *Black Ohio and the Color Line*, 14–18.

23. I share Paul Finkelman's interest in explaining the intersections among "statutes, constitutions, local ordinances, and customs that functioned as laws" in the antebellum South. See Finkelman, "Exploring Southern Legal History," 85. My approach to the study of Virginia law and society has been greatly influenced by the work of Ariela Gross, who argues that "law is part of the way people conceive of their identities, which make sense to them only in relation to others." See Gross, "Beyond Black and White," 683. Laura F. Edwards's emphasis on "That tangled web of social networks" that bound community members to a localized legal world is also especially relevant here. See Edwards, *People and Their Peace*, 44. See also Tomlins, *Law, Labor, and Ideology*, 48–49 and Caldwell, "When the Complexity of Lived Experience," 568.

24. Ariela Gross has shown how important "reputation evidence" was to an individual's relationship with the law at many levels. For example, see Gross, *What Blood Won't Tell*, 9, 24, 54. Other scholars continue to explore the power and politics of race and reputation in the antebellum southern courtroom. See Kennington, "River of Injustice"; Kennington, "Law, Geography, and Mobility"; Turner, "Rights and the Ambiguities of Law"; Welch, "People at Law"; Smith, "Mulatto Bend"; Twitty, "Slavery and Freedom in the American Confluence."

25. Karsten, *Heart Versus Head*, 20.

26. Rebecca J. Scott has shown how one's legal status in a community could be determined by how one "looked and behaved" to longstanding neighbors. See, for example, Scott, "Paper Thin," 1082.

27. See, for example, the efforts of Asa Hawkes of Nottoway County in April 1861 in Nottoway County CoCt MB, 1860–1864/43, LVA microfilm. Historians have recognized this phenomenon in various localities in Virginia (and the South, more generally), but this study takes the entire state of Virginia as its scope.

28. See Gross, "Beyond Black and White," 688–89; Gordon-Reed, *Race on Trial*, 4.

29. Kirt von Daacke makes a similar argument in describing the "highly personal face-to-face culture" of nineteenth-century Albemarle County, Virginia, in *Freedom Has a Face*, 112. Rebecca J. Scott similarly employs court records and other documentary evidence to reveal "the web of social solidarities, reciprocities, and deceit within which" local legal systems operated. See Scott, "'She . . . Refuses to Deliver Up Herself,'" 121.

30. On the same day that Mary Dunmore had been sentenced to absolute slavery, the cases of Joe Cooper, Daniel Jackson, and William Reid—the other free blacks who had been charged along with Dunmore, one month before, with violating the expulsion law—were dismissed. See Norfolk City Hustings Court OB 39, 1857–1859/138, 313,

LVA microfilm. See also Comm. v. Mary Dunmore, 27 April 1858, Norfolk City Hustings Court Ended Law Causes, January–June 1859, Norfolk City Circuit Court, Norfolk, Va.

31. Of the twelve individuals convicted for remaining in the state illegally, nine were sentenced to be sold into absolute slavery and two were temporarily hired out to cover jail fees. It is unclear whether any of the nine sentenced to be sold actually were. See Campbell, *Slavery on Trial*, 156.

32. I have been inspired by the work of others before me who have written important and informative history while embracing the enduring obscurities and ambiguities that surface in their fragmentary documentary sources. See, for example, Scott, "Afro-American Sailors," 39, 45 and Sweet, *Domingos Álvares*, 56, 80, 144.

33. Powhatan County, Virginia, Register of Free Negroes, 1820–1865/89, #716, 6 February 1854 ("Dark brown," "on the left"), LVA microfilm; ibid., #653, 7 May 1851 ("a scar").

34. Throughout this study, I have used the terms "freedom" and "liberty" interchangeably. Though there exists legitimate scholarly debate over whether these terms signify the same meanings, I accept Isaiah Berlin's argument for using the terms as synonyms. See Isaiah Berlin, *Four Essays on Liberty* and *Liberty*.

35. Answer of Creed Taylor, 4 May 1850, Powhatan County Chancery, 1856–010 ("to provide for"), LVA mss; Deed—Henly Cullins to Creed Taylor, 26 June 1846, Powhatan County Chancery, 1856–010 ("free from," "an ample," "the remainder"), LVA mss.

36. Deed—Henly Cullins to Creed Taylor, 26 June 1846, Powhatan County Chancery, 1856–010, LVA mss. See also Powhatan County WB 9, 1831–1836/256, LVA microfilm.

37. Answer of Creed Taylor, 4 May 1850, Powhatan County Chancery, 1856–010, LVA mss.

38. Judy Cullins married William Brooks on 6 May 1848. See Powhatan County Marriage Register, 1777-1853/151, LVA microfilm.

39. Powhatan County CoCt OB 28, 1848–1851/412-13, 498, LVA microfilm. See also Powhatan County CoCt Commonwealth Causes, 4 March 1851, LVA mss.

40. Bill, 6 Feb. 1850, Nancy Cullins & others v. Cullins' admor & others, Powhatan County Chancery, 1856–010, box 62, LVA mss.

41. Judy Cullins was one of few free blacks in Virginia during the 1850s to adhere to the letter of the law, which required one to register with his or her local court once every five years. Cullins registered twice in the Powhatan County court. See Powhatan County Register of Free Negroes, 1820–1865/89, #716, 6 February 1854, LVA microfilm; ibid., #653, 7 May 1851.

42. Petition of Judy Cullins to be allowed to choose W. C. Scott as Master, Aug. 1858, Powhatan County CirCt Ended Causes, LVA mss; Powhatan County FNSR, box 4, LVA mss.

43. 1860 federal census, Powhatan County, Virginia.

44. In short, the actions of Judy Cullins and others described below help to answer at least a few of the key questions raised by Jon-Christian Suggs, who asked, "When there can be no black voice in the court and no black hand drafts the legislation, who owns the legal narrative of slavery?" See Suggs, *Whispered Consolations*, 4 (quotation).

45. This is a point underscored by Susan Eva O'Donovan in *Becoming Free in the Cotton South*, 111–61.

46. In her study of self-enslavement in the antebellum South, Emily West concludes that the primary factor behind the self-enslavement petitions of free people of color was the desire to remain with family, rather than be subject to expulsion from their home communities. See West, *Family or Freedom*, 93–122. The relevant circuit court records (Common Law Order Books or Circuit Court Order Books, as they are sometimes called) for twenty-nine Virginia localities are either incomplete, missing, or destroyed, thus making it difficult to conclude exactly how many free blacks petitioned for self-enslavement from 1854 to 1864. For the purposes of this study, only those counties situated within the current boundaries of the state of Virginia are considered. Clear evidence for the phenomenon of self-enslavement exists in those counties that form today's West Virginia, however. For example, Flora Jones of Jefferson County petitioned the Virginia General Assembly in December 1861 that she and "her child" become the slave of Annie E. Wager. See *Journal of the House of Delegates*, 1861–62, 12, 39 (quotation); "Jones, Flora, Petition (ca. Dec. 1852) to Va. General Assembly," Mss 2, J7155a1, VHS [note that the date given for the petition is incorrect].

47. See Chapter 26, "An Act for the Voluntary Enslavement of Free Negroes, without Compensation to the Commonwealth," *Acts of the Virginia General Assembly*, 1861, 52–53.

48. There were petitioners for self-enslavement who were aged, impoverished, or physically disabled. Fifty-three-year-old Dennis Holt of Campbell County complained of his "infirmity of body, and imbecility of mind" in his petition for enslavement. See Petition of Dennis Holt, 24 Oct 1860, Campbell County FNSR, 1791–1867, box 4 (quotation), LVA mss. Soon after Jerry Glascock's re-enslavement in Northumberland County, he was described as "being very old & infirm & unable to work." See Northumberland County CoCt OB, 1861–1871/50 (quotation), LVA microfilm. Fanny Gillison of Fauquier County was fifty-seven years old when she requested enslavement because she had "no reason to believe that from her own labor she will be able to support herself in comfort for any great length of time." See petition of Fanny Gillison, Fauquier County Chancery, 1860–090, LVA online; Fauquier County CirCt OB G, 1860–1872/17 (quotation), LVA microfilm. In Amelia County, seventy-six-year-old Lewis Wilkerson suffered from arthritis when he applied to re-enslave himself. See Amelia County Register of Free Negroes, 1835–1855/129, #399, LVA microfilm.

49. Of 109 identified individual petitioners in Virginia, the ages of only 77 could be calculated—24 women and 53 men.

50. Ferguson, Lapidus, and Wilentz, *Liberty and the American Revolution*, lvi (quotations).

CHAPTER ONE

1. The 1850 federal census lists Daniel Hickman as a sixty-three-year-old "Laborer." Hickman's undated register in the Accomack County Register of Free Negroes explains that he was "born about the year 1785." See Accomack County Register of Free Negroes, 1807–63/n.p., #523, LVA microfilm.

2. Ira Berlin, *Making of African America*, 89. See also Eliga H. Gould's engaging essay, "The Laws of War and Peace," 52–58.

3. Budros, "The Antislavery Movement in Early America," 945–47.

4. Wolf, *Race and Liberty*, x–xi. Virginians voiced various motives for prohibiting slave importation during the Revolutionary era. Though less adamant than Maryland's Luther Martin, who argued that the slave trade "was inconsistent with the principles of the Revolution and dishonorable to the American character," Virginia legislators like George Mason persuaded their colleagues that "this nefarious traffic" must be stopped. See Deyle, *Carry Me Back*, 23 (quotations).

5. Virginia's manumission law of 1782 nullified the state's existing law of 1723, which had prohibited manumission "except for some meritorious services, to be adjudged and allowed by the governor and council." Virginia's leaders had first attempted to discourage manumissions in 1691, with a measure that had required slave owners "to pay for the transportation of their manumitted slaves out of the colony." See Matison, "Manumission by Purchase," 148 (quotations). See also Klebaner, "American Manumission Laws," 443.

6. *Code of 1819*, 434.

7. Jefferson, *Writings*, 264.

8. Several New England states allowed property and voting rights to free blacks in the new republic, however. See Rogers M. Smith, *Civic Ideals*, 65, 254; Van Cleve, *Slaveholder's Union*, 195–96. James Madison argued that "the prejudice of the whites, prejudices which proceeding principally from the difference in colour must be considered as permanent and insuperable" and overruled those republican principles that would have made freedpeople citizens. See Bradburn, "The Great Field of Human Concerns," 91–92 (quotation).

9. Barbara Young Welke writes that from the outset, only "a few states recognized free blacks as citizens." See Welke, *Law and the Borders of Belonging*, 34. Kunal M. Parker illustrates how Early National legislators in Massachusetts attempted to prevent African Americans from becoming citizens, at least in part by making "foreigners" of emancipated slaves. See Parker, "Making Blacks Foreigners," 81, 84. See also Zolberg, *Nation by Design*, 76–77; Novak, "The Legal Transformation of Citizenship," 90–91; Bradburn, *Citizenship Revolution*, 22–42.

10. Egerton, *Gabriel's Rebellion*, 51 ("death or Liberty"). On the memory of the Revolutionary War and its legacy in African American society, see Quarles, *Negro in the American Revolution*, 182–200; Frey, *Water from the Rock*, chaps. 5–7; Gilbert, *Black Patriots and Loyalists*, 248–57; Nash, *Forgotten Fifth*, chaps. 1, 3; Pybus, *Epic Journeys of Freedom*, 3–20; Schama, *Rough Crossings*, 3–18, 401–22; Egerton, *Death or Liberty*, 3–14, 222–47; Countryman, *Enjoy the Same Liberty*, 85–124.

11. See Morgan, "Slavery and Freedom," 5–29; Hamilton, "Revolutionary Principles," 531–56. Barbara Young Welke argues that to a large degree, the privileges and freedoms of able white men in the long nineteenth century "rested on the legally forced dependence, subjection, ownership, and exclusion of others." Welke offers examples of expanded white male suffrage in Connecticut (1818) and New York (1821) that corresponded with a simultaneous disfranchisement of free blacks in both states. See Welke, *Law and the Borders of Belonging*, 15, 124.

12. Alison Freehling, *Drift toward Dissolution*, 90 ("would not yet bear"). See also Nash, *Race and Revolution*, 11–13. On white cultural diversity in Virginia, see Freehling, *Drift toward Dissolution*, 26–30; Shade, *Democratizing the Old Dominion*, 25–26; Isaac, *Transformation of Virginia*, 115–38.

13. Alison Freehling, *Drift toward Dissolution*, 89.

14. In 1787 a proposed amendment to the manumission law of 1782 in the legislature called for the forced removal of free blacks within twelve months of their emancipation or re-enslavement if they remained. Though this amendment was defeated fifty-six to thirty-two, it foreshadowed a later Virginia law (and section in the state constitution) that mandated the expulsion of free blacks from the state. See Wolf, *Race and Liberty*, esp. 112–14; McDonnell, *Politics of War*, esp. chaps. 8–10.

15. Eva Sheppard Wolf concludes that "previous estimates of the number of people emancipated in Virginia after the Revolution . . . are wrong: many fewer people were freed than has been thought." See Wolf, *Race and Liberty*, xi (quotation), 53 ("the Laws," "Morality"). Rhys Isaac has written that manumission "did not happen on a scale sufficient to transform prevailing social patterns, but the incidence was great enough . . . to show that the traditional conception of authority had been fundamentally disturbed." See Isaac, *Transformation of Virginia*, 310 (quotation). Douglas R. Egerton similarly contends that the Revolution and its aftermath "created a climate of social insubordination and violence" that "damaged patriarchalism and control" and boosted "black confidence." See Egerton, *Gabriel's Rebellion*, 7 (quotation). In Virginia and beyond, the Revolution forever altered African Americans' relationship to the law and empowered some enslaved people to seek their freedom through suits lodged at various legal levels. See, for example, Schweninger, "Freedom Suits," esp. 35–42.

16. In her examination of manumission in Virginia during the Early National period, Eva Sheppard Wolf finds that "enslaved Virginians who purchased their own freedom and free blacks who emancipated friends and family members accounted for 14 percent of the deeds of manumission filed in the eight counties from 1782 to 1806 and in the years 1794–06 they accounted for 18 percent, nearly one-fifth of all acts of manumission." She suggests that "enslaved Virginians helped shape manumission" and that "manumission might have modified slaves' and masters' behavior toward each other." See Wolf, *Race and Liberty*, 66 ("enslaved Virginians who purchased"), 64 ("enslaved Virginians helped," "the possibility"). On the importance and prevalence of self-purchase for African Americans in Virginia, see James Hugo Johnson, *Race Relations in Virginia*, 6–8. On guilt among Virginia's gentry as an impetus for manumission, see Egerton, *Gabriel's Rebellion*, 13.

17. Tyler-McGraw, *African Republic*, 11; Ford, *Deliver Us from Evil*, 29.

18. 1790 and 1800 federal census. See also Heinegg, *Free African Americans*, 7.

19. *Code of 1819*, 437–38, 440–41; Wolf, *Race and Liberty*, 117.

20. Taylor, *Internal Enemy*, 40–42.

21. For an exploration of the meaning of the neighborhood in the complex interracial setting of the American South, see Kaye, *Joining Places*, 51–82. Melvin Patrick Ely argues that "many Southern whites felt secure enough to deal fairly and even respectfully with free African Americans partly because slavery still held most blacks firmly in its grip." See Ely, *Israel on the Appomattox*, x (quotation).

22. David Brion Davis, *Inhuman Bondage*, 159. On Saint-Domingue and its influence on Virginia's slave society and African American community, see Hunt, *Haiti's Influence*; Dubois, *Avengers of the New World*.

23. For detailed accounts of Gabriel's failed rebellion and its immediate aftermath, see Nicholls, *Whispers of Rebellion* and Schwarz, *Gabriel's Conspiracy*.

24. *Code of Virginia*, 1849, 466.

25. A number of historians have viewed Gabriel's plot and the subsequent expulsion law of 1806 as a clear turning point in the state's race relations and the quality of life for Virginia's free blacks. Marie Tyler-McGraw concludes that with the passage of the expulsion law, "the modest liberalizing tendencies of the 1780s and 1790s were effectively halted in Virginia." See Tyler-McGraw, *African Republic*, 12 (quotation). Eva Sheppard Wolf writes that the law "helped to mark the end of the Revolutionary era." See Wolf, *Race and Liberty*, 126 (quotation). Similarly, Douglas R. Egerton argues that the 1806 law turned "free blacks into a closed class." He continues, "Those who yearned to become free now viewed any change in their status as a mixed blessing. Slaves who bought their freedom or heard it pronounced in an aged master's will had either to petition the legislature for an exemption or to stay and risk re-enslavement." See Egerton, *Gabriel's Rebellion*, 166–67 (quotations).

26. See Ely, *Israel on the Appomattox*, 379. For changes in manumission rates after 1806, see Wolf, *Race and Liberty*, 162–95.

27. James Hugo Johnson, *Race Relations in Virginia*, 44. Johnson writes, "On the one hand are documents, signed by more than a hundred citizens, who declare that all the free Negroes are worthless and that they should be exiled from the State; on the other hand are documents, again signed by more than a hundred citizens, who certify that a particular Negro, by the name of John, Tom, or Harry is a skillful workman and an honest man, whose exile would inflict loss upon them and upon the commonwealth."

28. In some cases, such a study might prove difficult, as county court clerks sometimes did not document in their minute books the causes of grand jury indictments.

29. For example, in her study of African American freedom in nineteenth-century Cumberland County, Virginia, Ellen D. Katz concludes that "passage of the 1806 manumission law brought to an end relatively large-scale manumissions by white slaveowners" in the county, but that "within a decade of the enactment of the 1806 law, lax enforcement coupled with liberalizing amendments undermined its efficacy." See Katz, "African-American Freedom," 948–49. In his examination of Albemarle County, Kirt von Daacke likewise concludes, "For three decades after the passage of the removal law in 1806, no one in the county appeared concerned about the numerous free blacks living in the area, in clear violation of the law." See von Daacke, *Freedom Has a Face*, 84.

30. In fact, John H. Russell, one of the few historians to appreciate this fact, may have been too conservative when he wrote that "by 1860 probably from one fourth to one third of the free colored population in Virginia were unlawful residents under the provisions of the act of 1806." See Russell, *Free Negro in Virginia*, 156. By comparison, Ellen Eslinger suggests that the number of illegal free black residents in Virginia may have been significantly less because of the power of residency laws to deter newly emancipated people from remaining in the state. See Eslinger, "Free Black Residency," 263. Indeed, one finds occasional references to free African Americans leaving the state

after experiencing harassment from their local courts over the 1806 law. See, for example, Comm. vs. Nelson Talbert Gant, 1850, in Loudoun County Loose Papers, Loudoun County courthouse, Leesburg, Va. In fact, by 1850 authorities in Loudoun County had designed special preprinted legal forms designed to facilitate the process of prosecuting local free blacks living in violation of the 1806 law.

31. Luther Porter Jackson, *Free Negro Labor*, 33 ("despite the avalanche"); "and," Jackson adds, "they prospered"—a proposition that need not be weighed in the present discussion. Jackson seems to have been at odds with John H. Russell, who concluded "As an immediate consequence of spasmodic attempts to enforce the law and of fears on the part of manumitted slaves that the law would be enforced against them, a noticeable egress of negroes took place from Virginia to the Northern States and to the States bordering on Virginia on all sides." See Russell, *Free Negro in Virginia*, 71 (quotation). As evidence of such migration caused by the law, Russell points to reports presented to surrounding state legislatures, such as one from white residents in Maryland complaining that "Virginia has passed a law [expelling certain free negroes] and many of her beggarly blacks have been vomited upon us." In an excellent study of antebellum Richmond, Gregg D. Kimball concludes that, despite the 1806 statute, "Richmond's free-black population grew almost 60 percent in the 1820s, fueled by post-Revolutionary emancipations and migration to the city." He observes less growth in the city's free black population by the 1850s, in the midst of "renewed calls for re-enslavement and further legal restrictions." See Kimball, *American City, Southern Place*, 129.

32. 1820 federal census; Ford, *Deliver Us from Evil*, 194.

33. See Staudenraus, *African Colonization Movement*; Tyler-McGraw, *African Republic*, chap. 1.

34. See the *Virginia Emigrants to Liberia* project at http://www.vcdh.virginia.edu/liberia/index.php?page=Home.

35. VGALP, King George County, 20 December 1815, reel 102, box 133, folder 44, LVA microfilm.

36. VGALP, Lunenburg County, 23 December 1835, reel 117, box 150, folder 79, LVA microfilm.

37. Powhatan County CoCt OB 28, 1848–51/494–95. See also Comm v. Rachel a free negro, 4 March 1851, Powhatan County, CoCt, Commonwealth Causes, 1851, LVA mss.

38. Schafer, *Becoming Free, Remaining Free*, 151. For details on the self-enslavement case of Peter Pearson (or Beason) in Fauquier County, see "The Tired Freeman," *The Cleveland Herald*, 28 September 1850; "Voluntarily Sold into Slavery," *The Mississippian*, 8 November 1850.

39. Accomack County Register of Free Negroes, 1807–63/n.p., #523 ("light Black"), LVA microfilm. See also Accomack County WB, 1828–46/63, LVA microfilm.

40. Richard H. Smith Jr., *Accomack County*, 64–65. By 1831 a small minority of free black men and women owned land in Accomack County. See entries for Frank Bayly, George Custis, Littleton Dennis, Leah Elliott, Solomon West, Isaac West, and Joshua Wiggin in Accomack County Land Tax Book, 1831b, LVA microfilm. Twenty-one free people of color in Accomack owned thirty horses, subjecting them to personal property tax the same year. See "List of Free Negroes and Mullatoes Subject to Tax,"

Accomack County PPTB 1831b, LVA microfilm. Some free blacks were able to use Virginia laws—and their local court—to their advantage. For example, George Scarburgh and Jim Scarburgh successfully sued the administrator of their former owner's estate for their freedom in 1856. See Accomack County CirCt OB, 1850–57/415, LVA microfilm. Other free people of color also sued for their freedom, sometimes successfully, other times unsuccessfully. See ibid., 419, 420. Though free people living in Accomack County in violation of the expulsion law of 1806 were commonly refused permission to remain in the county, throughout the nineteenth century individuals seemed undeterred from attempting to secure legal permission to reside in the county from local courts, even (and perhaps especially) when others were being indicted for violating the law. For example, see Accomack County CoCt MB, 1857–59/n.p., 30 November 1857 and 28 June 1858, LVA microfilm.

41. The Virginia General Assembly passed a number of laws pertaining to the state's African Americans during the months following Nat Turner's rebellion. See *Supplement to the Revised Code of the Laws of Virginia*, 246–48. See also Cromwell, "The Aftermath of Nat Turner's Insurrection," 220–23. For a vivid account of the effects of Turner's rebellion on discussions of slavery at the state level, see Curtis, *Jefferson's Freeholders*, 134–38. On the effects of Nat Turner's rebellion on race relations and religious worship in Virginia, see Hillman, "Drawn Together, Drawn Apart."

42. Accomack County SupCtCLOB, 1831–42/45, LVA microfilm.

43. Alison Freehling, *Drift toward Dissolution*, 124 ("The present crisis"), 124–25 ("until slavery"). Only among a small Quaker minority were there calls for an immediate restoration of the "inalienable rights of the African race." See ibid., 126 (quotation).

44. Shade, *Democratizing the Old Dominion*, 20 (quotations).

45. Historian Alison Goodyear Freehling has written, "To base voting and office holding on ownership of land, and representation on counties and districts, everywhere violated the principle of equal political rights for white men," now a central tenet of American republican politics. See Freehling, *Drift toward Dissolution*, 37. See also Ford, *Deliver Us from Evil*, 361–89.

46. VGALP, Accomack County, 21 January 1845, reel 1, box 2, folder 15, LVA microfilm. There is no available evidence to suggest that the other ten individuals convicted in 1838 were sold, as Ewell had been to Rew.

47. *Journal of the House of Delegates*, 1845–46, 7–17. The only explicit mention of African Americans in Governor James McDowell's address to the legislature in December 1845 was his call to reform state psychiatric hospitals to "provide for the insane amongst our slaves." See ibid., 16 (quotation).

48. Potter, *Impending Crisis*, 18–62; William Freehling, *Road to Disunion*, 488–507.

49. *Journal of the House of Delegates*, 1846–47, 7–20, esp. 10 (quotations).

50. *Code of Virginia*, 1849, 464–68, esp. 466, 468.

51. Interestingly, instead of passing removal legislation, the Virginia House and Senate passed laws allowing three free individuals, Lucy, Thomas Duncan, and George Scott, to remain in the state, though they had been emancipated after 1806. See *Journal of the House of Delegates*, 1846–47, 248 (Lucy); 103, 242, 244, 248 (Thomas Duncan); 128, 222, 248 (George Scott).

52. *Daily Richmond Enquirer*, "The Free Negroes of Virginia," by "An Eastern Virginian," [a letter to the editor], p. 2, col. 4, 19 December 1846.

53. *Daily Richmond Enquirer*: "*For the Enquirer*" by "H.," p. 2, col. 6, 5 January 1847.

54. *Daily Richmond Enquirer*: "*For the Enquirer*" by someone in Essex County, p. 2, col. 7, 5 February 1847.

55. *Richmond Daily Whig*, "Governor's Message" [editorial], p. 2, col. 1, 8 December 1846.

56. The position of legislators against widespread, mandatory removal measures from the 1840s to 1860s served to stymie all efforts of extremists on the issue to pass such legislation.

57. The *Richmond Whig and Public Advertiser* would later write that "some, under the influence of the clamor against free negroes raised some years ago by Ex-Gov. Smith, went off half-cocked, and gave in to the absurd notion that all the evils in the State resulted from free negroes." See "Removal of Free Negroes," p. 2, col. 1., 3 February 1853.

58. See text of Bill No. 68 printed in *Journal of the House of Delegates*, 1846–47, n.p. (quotation). Bill No. 68, "A bill concerning free negroes and mulattoes," passed the House on 26 January 1847. See ibid., 37, 67, 71, 106, 110. The bill was rejected by the Senate, however. See ibid., 168.

59. *Richmond Whig and Public Advertiser*, "Free Negroes" by "Essex," p. 2, col. 4 25 June 1847.

60. These words belong to William Smith, who in his second address to the legislature referred to the feelings of critics of his removal plan. See *Journal of the House of Delegates*, 1847–48, 10–34, esp. 21 (quotation).

61. *Journal of the House of Delegates*, 1847–48, 19–22, esp. 21 (quotations).

62. Ibid., 23 ("with the great west"); *Richmond Whig and Public Advertiser*, "The Governor's Message" [editorial], p. 1, col. 1, 10 December 1847 ("leading topics").

63. *Richmond Whig and Public Advertiser*, "The Governor's Message" [editorial], p. 1, col. 1, 10 December 1847.

64. *Journal of the House of Delegates*, 1847–48, 48, 50, 69, 84, 87. Attempts to strengthen the law of 1806 "so as to throw the burthen of proof on the free negro" for his freedom were unsuccessful. See ibid., 50, 105 (quotation). Citizens of Clarke County petitioned unsuccessfully to remove free blacks from their county. See ibid., 186, 191, 373, 392, 401. House Bill 140, "prohibiting free negroes, mullatoes and slaves from raising owning or carrying dogs about with them in the county of Mathews" was passed, however. See ibid., 155, 188, 193, 432, 436.

65. *Journal of the House of Delegates*, 1848–49, 21 ("deport"), 30 ("impairing essentially," "sapping seriously"), 22 ("By our law").

66. VGALP, miscellaneous, 12 June 1850, reel 238, box 301, folder 65, LVA microfilm, 2–3 (quotations).

67. Brown, *Plan of National Colonization*, 437–569, esp. 499–500 (quotations).

68. Tucker, *Dissertation on Slavery*, 30, 96, 90. See also Hamilton, "Revolutionary Principles," 535–36; Van Cleve, *Slaveholder's Union*, 206–11; Curtis, *Jefferson's Freeholders*, 133–34.

69. *The Richmond Enquirer*, "To the Legislature of Virginia—On the Subject of Free Negroes" by "B.," p. 2, col. 4, 19 December 1848 (quotation).

70. VGALP, Rockingham County, 30 January 1849, reel 177, box 226, folder 36, LVA microfilm (quotations).

71. VGALP, Augusta County, 5 March 1849, reel 14, box 18, folder 63, LVA microfilm. A petition submitted to the Virginia General Assembly by American Colonization Society representative R. W. Bailey the following year shares several passages with the Augusta petition. See VGALP, miscellaneous, 12 June 1850, reel 238, box 301, folder 65, LVA microfilm.

72. VGALP, Frederick County, 8 March 1849, reel 62, box 84, folder 81, LVA microfilm.

73. See *The Richmond Enquirer*, "Free Negroes," by "W.," p. 2, col. 3, 23 December 1848 (quotation).

74. VGALP, Augusta County, 5 March 1849, reel 14, box 18, folder 63, LVA microfilm.

75. See, for example, *Richmond Whig and Public Advertiser*, "Force of Habit," p. 2, col. 1, 16 February 1849; ibid., "Colonization Society of Virginia. General Meeting," p. 1, col. 5, 22 February 1849; ibid., "Colonization in Liberia" by "Laocoon," p. 1, col. 5, 27 February 1849; ibid., "The Colonization Society," p. 4, col. 1, 27 February 1849, in which the editors reaffirm their "steady and consistent support to the scheme of Colonization."

76. Blight, *Frederick Douglass' Civil War*, 125 (quotation).

77. *Journal of the House of Delegates*, 1848–49, 40, 43, 185, 199, 295, 311, 352, 419, 421, 558, 591–92.

78. Accomack County CoCt OB, 1848–51/112 ("age and infirmity"), LVA microfilm. William Riley owned eight slaves in 1850 and housed David Crippin, a free black "Laborer." See 1850 federal census and 1850 federal census slave schedules.

79. See the brief description and portrait of Judge George P. Scarburgh in Bryson, *Legal Education in Virginia*, 557–59. Though the 1850 census lists Miers W. Fischer's occupation as "lawyer," he also managed the labor of sixteen slaves (with the help of overseer Jonathan Richardson, who lived with him). See 1850 federal census and slave schedules.

80. Accomack SupCt CLOB, 1842–50/392 ("for ready," "at the"), LVA microfilm. Unlike many of those convicted in 1839, however, Daniel Hickman was not convicted by the decision of a jury. See Accomack County SupCt CLOB, 1831–1842/242–45, LVA microfilm.

81. 1850 federal census, Accomack County.

82. The 1850 federal census slave schedules show Topping as the owner of fifteen slaves.

83. In 1850, William Riley was seventy-six years old, owned eight slaves, and possessed at least $6,000 in real estate. See 1850 federal census.

84. William P. Moore Jr. owned nineteen slaves and at least $16,000 in real estate in 1850. See 1850 federal census and 1850 federal census slave schedule. The other two justices present during Hickman's visit to county court in 1849 were Edward O'Finney and Edward L. Bayly, both of whom had free blacks living in adjacent households in the 1850 census.

85. See von Daacke, *Freedom Has a Face*, 204.

86. Brian Balogh has described early nineteenth-century Americans' preference for inconspicuous government in "Enduring Legacy," 271-76.

CHAPTER TWO

1. David Walker to Thomas Lewis, 8 December 1829, Executive communications–1830, January 7, box 14, folder 61, accession #36912, LVA misc. microfilm reel 5391; Walker, *Walker's Appeal*, 1.

2. Walker, *Walker's Appeal*, 18, 23, 59 (quotations).

3. Ibid., 74, 45 (quotations). Walker references the unjust and restrictive "laws of Virginia" on 17.

4. William B. Giles to Linn Banks, 7 January 1830, 1-2 (quotations), Executive communications–1830, 7 January, box 14, folder 61, accession #36912, LVA misc. microfilm reel 5391.

5. Walker, *Walker's Appeal*, xi-li.

6. This estimate stems from my reading of every intelligible page of every extant circuit court order book in Virginia for the years 1856-65 and a broad sample of the extant county court minute books for Virginia counties from 1806 to 1865.

7. For examples of free African Americans in a range of circumstances receiving court-appointed attorneys in one Virginia county during the antebellum period, see Daniel, *Bedford County*, 118-41. County court minute books frequently list those attorneys who received compensation for their court-appointed defense of free blacks. For example, see Southampton County CoCt MB, 1861-1870/96, LVA microfilm. See also Fredericksburg City Hustings Court OB H, 1819-1827/26-27, LVA microfilm. Enslaved people also received court-appointed counsel. For example, see Richmond City Hustings Court MB 10, 1828-1831/494, LVA microfilm. Recent scholars have shown that a surprising number of free blacks won their cases in these instances, even when defendants were charged with serious crimes like arson or rape. See, for example, Sommerville, *Rape and Race* and Campbell, *Slavery on Trial*.

8. For an excellent study of northern free black intellectual life and leadership during the nineteenth century, see Kantrowitz, *More Than Freedom*. Others are more wary than I of characterizing free African Americans' actions in localized antebellum Southern legal systems in terms of individuals' expression of rights or citizenship. For example, Laura Edwards argues that "to understand a localized law system in terms of individuals or individual rights is to misconstrue its most basic dynamics, stretching the standards of a single, developing area of law at the state level not only backward, but well beyond its reach." See Edwards, *People and Their Peace*, 11 (quotation).

9. For examples of scholars who have written well-documented histories of slavery and freedom in Virginia based almost purely on the text of law, see Ballagh, *History of Slavery in Virginia* and Ira Berlin, *Slaves without Masters*. Others have acknowledged state laws but focus instead on the frequency and severity of such laws' application. See McLeRoy and McLeRoy, *Strangers in Their Midst*.

10. Maris-Wolf, "Liberty, Bondage, and the Pursuit of Happiness."

11. Ira Berlin, *Slaves without Masters*; Wolf, *Almost Free*; Grivno, *Gleanings of Freedom*, 5, 153, 190.

12. Herbert A. Claiborne Account Book (hereafter cited as CAB), 23, VHS, Mss 5:3c, 5213:2.

13. *Code of Virginia*, 1849, 466. On the number of free blacks living in Virginia contrary to the 1806 expulsion law, see Russell, *Free Negro in Virginia*, 156.

14. It is difficult to give an exact number of attorneys who practiced law in Richmond in the 1830s. In addition to those who lived and worked almost exclusively in the city, a number of lawyers from surrounding localities, including Chesterfield and Hanover Counties, often took on cases and clients in Richmond courts.

15. Claiborne's clientele included whites and blacks associated with the First Baptist Church of Richmond and the Second Baptist Church of Richmond. Though Claiborne was a member of neither establishment, he was acquainted with people in—and drew clients from—both congregations. An enslaved woman named Rachel who was owned by Claiborne joined the First Baptist Church in 1834 and may have helped draw clients from that congregation. Mike Whitt, personal communication with author, 8 June 2012, VBHS, Richmond, Va.

16. For example, in Cumberland County, it is likely that individuals like Hezekiah Ford, who appears in many legal transactions involving free blacks in the county, were particularly approachable to free blacks. Though the nature of the relationships between Ford and his free black acquaintances remains uncertain (as he might have been "a manipulative figure who provided credit and used his authority as tax collector to exploit free blacks in the county"), he clearly was woven into the free black community in ways that most whites and other attorneys were not. His case suggests that certain whites, because of their positions, status, access, or personality, became go-to people for free blacks who needed legal services. See Ellen D. Katz, "African-American Freedom," 979 (quotation).

17. Herbert A. Claiborne will, Richmond City WB 9/103, LVA microfilm.

18. Campbell, *Slavery on Trial*, 96 (quotation), 152.

19. Herbert A. Claiborne will, Richmond City WB 9/104, LVA microfilm.

20. Here I invoke Barbara Young Welke's conception of "belonging," as registration in one's city or county court often defined one of the legal "borders of belonging" for free African Americans in Virginia. See Welke, *Law and the Borders of Belonging*.

21. VGALP, Essex County, 6 December 1811, reel 48, box 67, folder 64, LVA microfilm.

22. For a sophisticated discussion of the structure and intent of such petitions, see Wolf, *Almost Free*, 56, 58, 66, 70, 101–8.

23. VGALP, Essex County, 6 December 1811, reel 48, box 67, folder 64, LVA microfilm; VGALP, Chesterfield County, 15 February 1848, reel 40, box 56, folder 65, LVA microfilm; VGALP, Accomack County, 12 December 1815, reel 1, box 1, folder 50, LVA microfilm; VGALP, Bath County, 18 December 1828, reel 16, box 21, folder 70, LVA microfilm.

24. VGALP, Accomack County, 14 December 1815, reel 1, box 1, folder 52, LVA microfilm.

25. VGALP, Buckingham County, 25 October 1814, reel 30, box 41, folder 102, LVA microfilm.

26. VGALP, Cumberland County, 7 December 1813, reel 44, box 61, folder 78, LVA microfilm.

27. VGALP, Amherst County, 27 December 1833, reel 10, box 12, folder 81, LVA microfilm.

28. VGALP, Accomack County, 13 January 1838, reel 1, box 1, folder 85, LVA microfilm; VGALP, Accomack County, 13 January 1838, reel 1, box 1, folder 86, LVA microfilm; VGALP Accomack County, 2 January 1838, reel 1, box 1, folder 82, LVA microfilm.

29. VGALP, Fauquier County, 6 December 1827, reel 51, box 73, folder 46, LVA microfilm.

30. Kantrowitz, *More Than Freedom*, 6.

31. VGALP, Accomack County, 2 January 1838, reel 1, box 1, folder 82, LVA microfilm.

32. VGALP, Amelia County, 28 January 1836, reel 8, box 10, folder 14, LVA microfilm; VGALP, Amelia County, 28 January 1836, reel 8, box 10, folder 15, LVA microfilm.

33. VGALP, Campbell County, 18 December 1815, reel 33, box 46, folder 78, LVA microfilm.

34. Ibid.

35. VGALP, Essex County, 15 December 1825, reel 48, box 67, folder 78 ("intermarried"), LVA microfilm; VGALP, Bedford County, 8 December 1830, reel 17, box 24, folder 46 ("married"), LVA microfilm; VGALP, Amherst County, 27 December 1833, reel 10, box 12, folder 81 ("wife"), LVA microfilm.

36. VGALP, Bath County, 18 December 1828, reel 16, box 21, folder 70, LVA microfilm.

37. VGALP, Bedford County, 8 December 1830, reel 17, box 24, folder 46, LVA microfilm.

38. VGALP, Campbell County, 27 December 1824, reel 33, box 47, folder 12, LVA microfilm.

39. VGALP, Chesterfield County, 12 January 1850, reel 40, folder 56, folder 81, LVA microfilm.

40. Attorneys, court-appointed or otherwise, were often mentioned by court clerks when documenting criminal cases (especially commonwealth causes) and, less often, civil suits.

41. Richmond City Hustings Court MB 12, 1835–1837/34, LVA microfilm.

42. On 25 July 1835, Claiborne noted a charge for $5 to Pheby Kemp "To motn for your Register in Hustings Court." See CAB, 226 (quotation).

43. Richmond City Hustings Court MB 12, 1835–37, LVA microfilm.

44. CAB, 37, 243.

45. Henry Family Papers, Account Book—Henry, William Wirt, 1853–57, 41, VHS Mss1 H3968a694.

46. Ibid., p. 46.

47. CAB, 66, 152, 174.

48. Dabney, Mss1D1124b2578, Section 23, Account Book, 1832–65 of Charles William Dabney, VHS Mss, n.p., entry dated 11 July 1836.

49. CAB, 36. Richmond Hustings Court minutes identify Betsy Ham's son as "Robertson Ham." See Richmond City Hustings Court MB 11, 1831-1835/271, LVA microfilm.

50. Richmond City Hustings Court MB 12, 1835–1837/290, LVA microfilm.

51. Attorneys like James Lyons were periodically hired to defend free blacks in Richmond courts. For example, in July 1831 a man named Garms hired Lyons to defend his brother for $10. See James Lyons, Memorandum and Day Book, 1830–36, Robert Alonzo Brock Collection, misc. reel 5261, LVA microfilm.

52. Edwards, *People and Their Peace*, 8, 24, 27, 58, 167, 236.

53. VGALP, Richmond City, 5 February 1833, reel 223, box 279, folder 68, LVA microfilm.

54. CAB, 80.

55. In 1847 Alfred Winfield notified the Sussex County court that he would, "by my attorney," petition for permission to remain in the state, which his attorney apparently succeeded in obtaining. See "Petition of Alfred Winfield, free Negro, for residency, #1847-72," Loose Court Papers of Sussex County, Virginia, 1754–1870, Sussex County courthouse, Sussex, Virginia. I am grateful to Gary M. Williams for supplying this information.

56. It is unclear whether any of the nine sentenced to be sold into absolute slavery actually were. See Campbell, *Slavery on Trial*, 156.

57. I make this case in detail in Maris-Wolf, "Libery, Bondage, and the Pursuit of Happiness," especially chapters 1–3.

58. Accomack County CirCt OB, 1857–1866/69, 170, 190, 275, LVA microfilm.

59. A woman noted only as "Rachel" was apparently indicted three times by the Highland County courts for illegally remaining in the state—in 1849, 1856, and again in 1857. The first two cases against Rachel were dismissed, while a grand jury found her guilty in 1857 and ordered her to be auctioned as a slave. See Highland County CoCt OB 1, 1847–1858/119, 128, 132, Highland County courthouse, Monterey, Virginia; Highland County CirCt OB 2, 1848–1860/166, 179, 194, 203, 217, 233, Highland County courthouse, Monterey, Virginia.

60. Accomack County CirCt OB, 1850–1857/377, LVA microfilm; Accomack County CirCt OB, 1857–1866/96, 97, LVA microfilm.

61. Accomack County CirCt OB, 1857–1866/199 (quotations), LVA microfilm.

62. CAB, 160. See also ibid., "Solomon Adams," 260.

63. On Pharoah Sheppard and his father of the same name in relation to Gabriel's failed rebellion in 1800, see Nicholls, *Whispers of Rebellion*, 143–45. See also CAB, 43.

64. CAB, 97.

65. Ibid., 229.

66. Ibid., 217.

67. Ibid., 76.

68. Garrit Minor Legal Account Book, 1806–31, Fredericksburg City microfilm reel 101, p. 61, 72, LVA microfilm.

69. CAB, 93.

70. Ibid., 196, 214.

71. Henry Family Papers, Account Book—Henry, William Wirt, 1853–57, p. 84, VHS Mss1 H3968a694.

72. CAB, 314.

73. Ibid., 258.

74. J. J. Chew Account Book, 1830–69, p. 103, Fredericksburg City microfilm reel 88, LVA. See also Fredericksburg City Hustings Court DB O, 1845–1848/409–11, LVA microfilm; Frederick City Hustings Court OB K, 1841–1845/490, LVA microfilm.

75. J. J. Chew Account Book, 1830–69, 72, Fredericksburg City microfilm reel 88, LVA.

76. CAB, 23.

77. Henry Family Papers, Account Book—Henry, William Wirt, 1853–57, 69, VHS Mss1 H3968a694.

78. CAB, 110.

79. Ibid., 215.

80. Ibid., 137, 145, 255.

81. Henry Family Papers, Account Book—Henry, William Wirt, 1853–57, 25, VHS Mss1 H3968a694.

82. Melissa Milewski, "From Slave to Litigant," 727, 745 (quotations).

CHAPTER THREE

1. William Arvin Sr. held at least twenty-two individuals in bondage in 1850. See 1850 federal census, slave schedule.

2. Ericson, *Slavery*, especially 164–85; Howe, *What Hath God*, 792–836; Fehrenbacher, *Slaveholding Republic*, 205–94; Davis, "Culmination of Racial Polarities"; Wills, *"Negro President,"* 1–13; Potter, *Impending Crisis*, 93.

3. Gaines, "Virginia Constitutional Convention," 95; William W. Freehling, *Road to Disunion*, vol. 2, 505–6.

4. See the address of Governor John B. Floyd in *Journal of the House of Delegates*, 1849–50, 20 (quotations).

5. Susan Dunn argues that "the reluctance of Virginians in the early nineteenth century to dismantle slavery and launch practical plans to improve their state and enrich the lives of ordinary Virginians would condemn the Old Dominion to irrelevance and poverty." See Dunn, *Dominion of Memories*, 14 (quotation). By comparison, William G. Shade concludes that "the Old Dominion was a huge and diverse state that during the period from the end of the War of 1812 through the mid-nineteenth century underwent the same dynamic economic and social development that characterized the country as a whole." Indeed, this study and its incorporation of contemporary legislative journals, newspapers, and county court records tends to support Shade's assertion that "the economic decline of the Old Dominion and the exceptionalism of Virginia have been grossly exaggerated." See Shade, *Democratizing the Old Dominion*, 6 (quotations). While Virginia experienced a decline in national political influence over these years, public works, internal improvements, and large profits from a modern-

izing slave society in the state's eastern region contributed to an increasingly prosperous and powerful state economy and vibrant civil society, in spite of its internal political tensions.

6. Men were frequently charged with betting at the game faro or exhibiting a gaming table in many Virginia counties in the 1840s and 1850s, prompting religious leaders like Richmond's George Roper to lament "the evils of the faro table." See Roper's letter to George K. Crutchfield, 18 September 1834 in Crutchfield Family papers, section 1 MSS1 C8895a8–46, VHS. For accounts of faro in various Virginia courts, see Floyd County CirCt OB 2, 1853–1859/317, LVA microfilm; Mecklenburg County CirCt OB 5, 1853–1859/210, 317, LVA microfilm; Montgomery County CirCt OB 4/126, LVA microfilm; Halifax County CirCt OB 5/246, 250, LVA microfilm; City of Norfolk CirCt OB 7, 1859–1866/175, 186, LVA microfilm; City of Petersburg CirCt OB 6, 1853–1858/352, LVA microfilm; Lynchburg City OB 7, 1855–1858/272, 280–83, 409, 413, LVA microfilm; Lynchburg City OB 8, 1859–1865/300–306, 308–38, 432–39, LVA microfilm. Faro had worldwide appeal in the eighteenth and nineteenth centuries. For one of the more vivid descriptions of the operation of high-stakes faro in Russia, see Pushkin's "Queen of Spades" in Pushkin, *Complete Prose Tales*, 273–305. John A. Bishop, who had served as constable in the lower end of the county in 1848, was presented with "knowingly permitting a gaming table commonly called a faro bank to be established in his tavern while in his occupation." See Lunenburg County CirCt OB, 1843–1851/217, LVA microfilm; Lunenburg County CirCt OB, 1852–1866/21, LVA microfilm. John J. Peace was a commissioner of Lunenburg County schools and was charged with "betting at the game commonly called Faro Bank." See Lunenburg County CoCt OB 29, 1842–1848/304, 366, LVA microfilm; Lunenburg County CoCt OB31, 1856–1865/66, LVA microfilm.

7. Lunenburg County CirCt OB, 1843–1851/214, LVA microfilm.

8. William A. Link asserts that "many Virginia masters believed that their authority was eroding" in the 1850s, as "slaves seemed more willing to challenge masters, usually by individual acts" and "by stealing, refusing to work, or confounding the 'efficiency' of the plantation." See Link, *Roots of Secession*, 7 (quotations). For national political developments centering on the issue of slavery at the time, see Potter, *Impending Crisis*, 83–98. Many whites were implicated by neighbors for allowing enslaved people "to go at large and trade" as free people. See, for example, York County CirCt OB, 1845–1860/360 (quotation), LVA microfilm; Middlesex County CirSupCt OB, 1843–1857/341, LVA microfilm; Page County CirCt OB 2, 1860–1865/10, 28, LVA microfilm; King George County CirCt OB 15, 1843–1870/296, LVA microfilm; Isle of Wight County CirCt OB, 1855–1885/29, LVA microfilm; Clarke County CirSupCt OB B, 1848–1865/323, LVA microfilm; Charlotte County CirCt OB 5, 1851–1863/224, LVA microfilm.

9. Beverly J. Winn was presented for selling liquor to King, Bob, and Jim, men belonging to George Inge, James Inge, and Robert Burnett, respectively. Winn was also charged with selling "ardent spirits" to George Inge and James Inge. See Lunenburg County CirCt OB, 1843–1851/214, LVA microfilm.

10. The law was unequivocal on the matter of selling alcohol to slaves: "If any person sell wine, ardent spirits, or any mixture thereof, or any intoxicating liquor, to a

slave without the written consent of his master, he shall forfeit to the master four times the value of the thing sold, and also pay a fine of twenty dollars." See *Code of Virginia* 1849, 459 (quotation).

11. *Richmond Whig and Public Advertiser,* "Free Negroes" by "Essex,": p. 2, col. 4, 25 June 1847 (quotation).

12. For examples of whites selling liquor to enslaved or free blacks, see Halifax County CirCt OB 6, 1858–1866/391, 392, LVA microfilm; Pittsylvania County CirCt OB 8, 1854–1859/450, LVA microfilm; Bedford County CirCt OB 12, 1857–1859/10, LVA microfilm; Middlesex County CirCt OB, 1857–1865/60, Middlesex County courthouse, Saluda, Va.; Caroline County CirCt OB 3, 1858–1870/2, Fredericksburg Heritage Center, Fredericksburg, Va.; Surry County CirCt OB, 1839–1867/272, Surry County courthouse, Surry, Va. For examples of whites playing cards and gambling with enslaved or free African Americans, see Patrick County CirCt OB, 1855–1881/55, LVA microfilm; Pittsylvania County CirCt OB 9, 1859–1869/134–35, LVA microfilm; Halifax County CirCt OB 6, 1858–1866/391, 392, LVA microfilm; Scott County CirCt OB 3, 1852–1867/152, 201, LVA microfilm; Floyd County CirCt OB 2, 1853–59, LVA microfilm; Henry County CirCt OB, 1850–1867/n.p., entries between 2 April and 3 September 1857, Henry County courthouse, Martinsville, Va. For an example of whites hunting with enslaved individuals, see Culpeper County CirCt OB 6, 1856–1866/332, LVA microfilm.

13. For examples of whites socializing with free blacks, see Culpeper County CirCt OB 6, 1856–1866/332, LVA microfilm; Russell County CirCt OB 4, 1850–1871/321, LVA microfilm; Charles City County CirCt OB, 1853–1863/133–35, LVA microfilm; Lynchburg City CirCt OB 8, 1859–1865/84, LVA microfilm. See also Bedford County CirCt OB 13, 1859–1866/78 ("free and easy conversation"), LVA microfilm. For examples of alleged romantic relations between whites and free blacks, see Accomack County CirCt OB, 1857–1866/211, LVA microfilm; Mathews County CirCt OB 3, 1853–1863/407, Mathews County courthouse, Mathews, Va.

14. *Journal of the House of Delegates,* 1849, 25 (quotations). On 18 December 1849, a number of citizens of Rockbridge County petitioned the General Assembly for an appropriation of an annual sum from the state treasury for the transportation of free blacks to Liberia. See VGALP, 18 December 1849, reel 175, box 223, folder 50, LVA microfilm.

15. *Acts of the General Assembly,* 1849–50, 7–8.

16. For an earlier example, see Alison Goodyear Freehling, *Drift toward Dissolution,* 85–87.

17. Lunenburg County CirCt OB, 1843–1851/175–76, LVA microfilm.

18. In her examination of interracial rape cases in nineteenth-century Virginia, Diane Miller Sommerville concludes that class had as much to do with race in determining a court's decision. See Sommerville, *Rape and Race,* 5, 258. For a particularly insightful study of stratified white society in nineteenth-century South Carolina, see McCurry, *Masters of Small Worlds,* especially chapters 3 and 4. See also Lunenburg County CirCt OB, 1843–1851/217, LVA microfilm. See also the registers of Andrew, Willis, and Mary Doswell (registers 119, 120, and 121, respectively) in Lunenburg County, List of Free Negroes (1818–50), LVA microfilm.

19. Arvin may have also been inspired by the county's recent but unsuccessful attempt to convict Gray Winn of remaining in the state in violation of the expulsion law. See Lunenburg County CoCt OB 29, 1842–1848/85, LVA microfilm; Comm. v. Gray, CoCt, Commonwealth Causes, 1700–1924, box 1, 11 March 1850, SRC. James Hugo Johnson found a significant quantity of testimony from white Virginians in petitions to the state legislature in which they communicated their view "that the free Negroes were undesirable members of society." See Johnson, *Race Relations in Virginia*, 42–71, especially 42 (quotation).

20. On 8 June 1846, Thomas Arvin was charged with a breach of peace for "striking" William Doswell. See Lunenburg County CoCt OB 29, 1842–1848/165, 205 (quotation), LVA microfilm. But William Arvin Sr. and William Doswell were neighbors and regularly participated in neighborly activities, such as dividing a neighbor's estate and regulating "the hands that work on the roads of which Richard Crofton and Thomas Staples are surveyors." See, for example, Lunenburg County CoCt OB 29, 1842–1848/261, 336 (quotation), LVA microfilm.

21. See VGALP, Lunenburg County, 6 January 1851, reel 117, box 151, folder 5, LVA microfilm and Comm. v. Willis, summons, 27 June 1854 (quotation), Lunenburg CoCt Judgments 1854, folder: September 1854, LVA mss. According to the 1850 federal census slave schedules, Langston Arvin owned nine enslaved individuals.

22. For examples of people who apparently received presentments from circuit courts because of the presence of particular jurors, see Amelia County CirCt OB 5, 1853–1872/244–45, LVA microfilm; Brunswick County CirCt OB 2, 1843–1867/520, LVA microfilm; Madison County CirCt OB 4, 1861–1887/1, LVA microfilm; Fluvanna County CirCt OB 5, 1856–1860/6, LVA microfilm; Rockbridge County CirCt OB, 1852–1867/432, LVA microfilm; Powhatan County CoCt OB 28, 1848–1851/412–13, 498, LVA microfilm.

23. Lunenburg County CirCt OB, 1843–1851/175–76, esp. 175 (quotations), LVA microfilm. In fact, it was likely another incidence of "domino justice" that brought on thirty-two of the presentments made on 6 May 1850, the day the Doswells were charged by the grand jury. The grand jury had learned that Spencer Inge had struck Edmund P. Winn at Booth's Grocery. Winn had reported Inge to the authorities and, while he was doing so, used the opportunity to get even with John A. Bishop, who ran an illegal gambling operation. See ibid., 212–17.

24. See VGALP, Lunenburg County, 6 January 1851, reel 117, box 151, folder 5 (quotation), LVA microfilm; Lunenburg County CoCt OB 29, 1842–1848/257, LVA microfilm. On William Doswell's activities as minister, see Lunenburg County WB 13, 1846–1851/223, 411, LVA microfilm. William Doswell would also serve as a county school commissioner from 1853–55. See Lunenburg County CoCt OB 30, 1849–1856/520, LVA microfilm.

25. Prince Edward County WB 7, 1828–1837/413 (quotations), LVA microfilm.

26. Lunenburg County List of Free Negroes, 1818–50, Register no. 120 ("bright yellow"), LVA microfilm; ibid., Register no. 119 ("dark brown," "short and wooly"), LVA microfilm. For Willis's and Andrew's ages, see 1850 federal census, Lunenburg County. Though the records are incomplete, there is no evidence that either man was delinquent in his taxes for the years 1842–50. See Delinquent Free Negroes for 1849, 14

January 1850, Lunenburg County, Commonwealth Causes, Various Series, 1700–1924, box 1, SRC; Lunenburg County PPTBs 1842–49, LVA microfilm. Willis and Andrew appear on the 1850 personal property tax list as among those "free negroes from 21 to 55 paying a specific Taxe of 1$ according to late act of assembly." See Lunenburg County PPTB 1850 (quotation). The two appear on a delinquent tax list of 1852, owing $1 each, only after they had been charged by the circuit court and had apparently "removed" from the county. See Delinquents Taxable property, 12 January 1852, Lunenburg County, Commonwealth Causes, Various Series, 1700–1924, box 1, SRC (quotation). But neither appears in a list of delinquents for the following year. See "A List of Revenue Tax Returned at Feb. Court—1854, Delinquent and non Resident—for the non payment of Taxes for the year 1853," Lunenburg County, Commonwealth Causes, Various Series, 1700–1924, Box 1, SRC.

27. The nature of the relationship between Milly Ragsdale and the Doswell brothers remains unclear. See 1850 federal census, Lunenburg County.

28. See VGALP, Lunenburg County, 6 January 1851, reel 117, box 151, folder 5 (quotation), LVA microfilm.

29. Prince Edward County WB 7, 1828–1837/413 (quotation), LVA microfilm. It seems that Mary's two sons successfully registered with the Lunenburg County court in August 1849, but their registers were revoked soon thereafter. See Lunenburg County List of Free Negroes, 1818–50, registers 143, 144, LVA microfilm. Mary and her sons are listed in the 1850 federal census as living in Prince Edward County by 25 September 1850. In the census, Mary Doswell's sons are listed as "Sam Mack" and "Alphious [Mack]," both having been born in Prince Edward, indicating that Mary had at least been living in Prince Edward when the boys were born, seven and four years earlier, respectively. See 1850 federal census, Prince Edward County, Virginia.

30. According to the 1860 federal census, 257 free people of color lived in Lunenburg County, among a population of 7,305 enslaved and 4,421 white individuals.

31. For lists of occupations of a portion of free people of color in Lunenburg, see "List of Free negroes & mulattoes above 12 years of age in the County of Lunenburg, 1851," in Lunenburg County PPTB 1851, LVA microfilm; "List of Free negroes & mulattoes above 12 years of age in the County of Lunenburg, 1852," in Lunenburg County PPTB 1852, LVA microfilm. By correlating the Lunenburg County Register of Free Negroes with lists of free blacks and mulattos in the PPTBs, it is clear that much of the county's free population lived in violation of the law of 1806. Most individuals listed in the PPTB lists never bothered to register themselves with the county court, though several people did, even more than once.

32. The 1850 federal census for Lunenburg County shows that 16 of 820 households were composed of "whites" and "blacks," eight of "whites" and "mulattoes," and six of "whites," "blacks," and "mulattoes." The census also showed thirteen all-"mulatto" households, twelve all-"black" households, and five mixed "black" and "mulatto" households.

33. See the list of free African Americans in Lunenburg in Lunenburg County PPTB, 1840 ("Hireling"), LVA microfilm. Gray Winn was presented on 8 June 1846, "by the information of Geo. L. Bayne, who was sent in by the Court to give information." See Lunenburg County CoCt OB 29, 1842–1848/204 (quotation), LVA microfilm. See also

Comm. v. Gray, 11 March 1850, Lunenburg County CoCt Commonwealth Causes, box 1, SRC.

34. Lunenburg County CoCt OB 29, 1842–1848/251, LVA microfilm.

35. Ibid. 241 (quotation).

36. For example, extremist Henry Shackleford, a state senator from Culpeper County, unsuccessfully proposed an amendment to disallow manumission to the removal bill under consideration in the Senate on 5 March 1850; Shackleford's amendment was rejected by a vote of 21 to 3. See *Journal of the Senate*, 1849–50, 136. The next day, he proposed that all free blacks convicted of felonies (except for those punishable by death) be transported "to the Coast of Africa." See *Journal of the Senate*, 1849–50, 141 (quotation). In May 1852 Shackleford would propose that slaves no longer be allowed to have their sentences commuted instead of being executed. See *Journal of the Senate*, 1852, 350.

37. Lunenburg CirCt OB 1843–1851/217, 223, LVA microfilm. The three jurors in Bishop's trial were William L. Bragg, William H. Hatchett, and Jonathan L. Cralle; Bragg and Cralle were both convicted for betting at faro in Bishop's tavern and fined $30, while Hatchett was acquitted. See Lunenburg CirCt OB, 1843–1851/232, 234–36, LVA microfilm.

38. The summons directed Willis and Andrew "to appear before the judge of our Circuit Superior Court of law & chancery for Lunenburg County, at the Courthouse, on the first day of the next term, to show cause, if any they can, why an information should not be filed against them upon a presentment of the grand jury made against them in the said Court, on the 6th day of May 1850, for remaining in the County of Lunenburg in the Commonwealth of Virginia, more than twelve months after their emancipation." The filing of an information would be the next step in a long process of prosecution. On the reverse, Stokes had noted that the summons had been "Executed on Willis," that Stokes had found him at home and had delivered it to him. See Summons, 27 June 1850, Comm. v. Willis, September 1854, Lunenburg County Court Judgments 1854, folder: September 1854 (quotations), LVA mss. Significantly, Stokes was one of the Doswell brothers' neighbors to sign a petition eight months later requesting that the Virginia state legislature allow them to remain in the state. See VGALP, Lunenburg County, 6 January 1851, reel 117, box 151, folder 5, LVA microfilm.

39. Lunenburg County CoCt OB 30, 1849–1856/115 (quotation), LVA microfilm. Note that the brothers are here referred to as "Andrew Doswell" and "John Willis Doswell."

40. Lunenburg CirCt OB 1843–1851/256, LVA microfilm.

41. Summons, 3 January 1851, Lunenburg County Court Judgments 1854, folder: September 1854, LVA mss.

42. It was noted on the reverse of a summons sent to the Prince Edward County sheriff that Mary Doswell "departed this life August 4th 1853 leaving three children at the high bridge." See Comm. v. Mary, 1 September 1853, Lunenburg County Court Records, Various Series, 1700–1924, box 4 (quotation), SRC.

43. See VGALP, Lunenburg County, 6 January 1851, reel 117, box 151, folder 5, LVA microfilm.

44. Link, *Roots of Secession*, 13.

45. Francis Gaines, "Virginia Constitutional Convention," 252 (quotation).

46. Preston County had listed only fifty-nine free blacks in the 1850 census, or 0.5 percent of its total population of 11,708 residents. *Journal of the House of Delegates,* 1850–51, 54, 136 (quotation), 514. Wheeler was appointed to a new committee charged with considering his proposals, but Bill no. 478, "A Bill Concerning Free Negroes," went nowhere in the House. See ibid., 138, 261 (quotation).

47. *Richmond Enquirer,* "Free Negroes," 1 March 1851.

48. Kettner, *Development of American Citizenship,* 287–333; Smith, *Civic Ideals,* 215; *Richmond Enquirer,* "Jamaica and the Free Negroes," p. 4, 5 March 1851.

49. *Richmond Enquirer,* "The Free Blacks," p. 4, 16 April 1851.

50. John C. Rutherfoord of Goochland County, Virginia, was a champion of expulsion and asserted in 1853 that free blacks "have proved the most troublesome where their privileges have been greatest." See Rutherfoord, *Speech of John C. Rutherfoord,* 6.

51. See VGALP, Lunenburg County, 6 January 1851, reel 117, box 151, folder 5, LVA microfilm.

52. Even John C. Rutherfoord, who argued at the time that Virginia's free blacks were "idle, ignorant, degraded and immoral," admitted that there were exceptions. "These exceptions," he said, "form the most intelligent and respectable of these people," and were "industrious laborers" and "mechanics." See Rutherfoord, *Speech of John C. Rutherfoord,* 13. It should be noted that none of the Doswells appear on the delinquent tax lists submitted by the Lunenburg Commissioner of the Revenue for the years 1849 and 1850. See "Delinquent Free Negroes for 1849," 14 January 1850, "Delinquent Property Tax 1850," 10 March 1851, and "Delinquents in County levy for 1850," 13 January 1851, all found in Lunenburg County Commonwealth Causes, Various Series, 1700–1924, box 1, SRC.

53. 1850 federal census, slave schedules.

54. Milly Ragsdale v. Comm., 4 February 1856 (quotations), Lunenburg County Commonwealth Causes, Various Series, 1700–1924, box 1, SRC.

55. Comm. v. Willis and Comm. v. Andrew, summonses dated 17 January 1851, Lunenburg CoCt Judgments 1854, folder: September 1854, LVA mss.

56. *Journal of the House of Delegates,* 1850–51, 131, 250, 423.

57. Lunenburg County CirCt OB 1843–1851/280, LVA microfilm.

58. Summonses dated 28 July 1851 ("Not found") and 3 January 1852, Lunenburg County Court Judgments 1854, folder: September 1854, LVA mss.

59. Two documents submitted to the court by the Lunenburg Commissioner of the Revenue list Andrew and Willis as having "removed" or no longer residing in the county. See Delinquents Taxable property, 12 January 1852 (quotation), and Delinquents County levy, 12 January 1852, both found in Lunenburg County Commonwealth Causes, Various Series, 1700–1924, box 1, SRC. Of the 69 persons listed on the Delinquents Taxable property list, 9 were noted as free blacks. Of the 193 individuals found on the Delinquents County levy, only 11 were listed as free blacks.

60. *Journal of the Senate,* 1852, 16.

61. Ibid., 33.

62. *Journal of the House of Delegates,* 1852, 78.

63. VGALP, Chesterfield County, 26 January 1852, reel 40, box 56, folder 87, LVA microfilm.

64. *Richmond Daily Dispatch*, "Free Blacks in the West Indies," p. 2, col. 2, 29 January 1852.

65. *Journal of the House of Delegates*, 1852, 280 (quotation), 466.

66. *Journal of the Senate*, 1852, 71 (quotation). The evidence linking Thomas H. Campbell's motion for a "voluntary enslavement" law to Willis and Andrew Doswell's plight is circumstantial but compelling. It was Sterling Neblett, Lunenburg's representative in the House, who had introduced William Doswell's initial petition supporting Willis and Andrew's residency in the county, but Campbell would soon take the lead in advocating for the brothers. Campbell would present two petitions on behalf of Willis and Andrew to the Senate the following year. See *Journal of the Senate*, 1853–54, 194. On southern legislators' uses of euphemism in race-based law, particularly after the Civil War, see Welke, *Law and the Borders of Belonging*, 132–33.

67. John McCardell writes that a number of southern extremists in the early 1850s came to pronounce arguments in support of those "who endorsed slavery not as a paternalistic system but as a necessary condition for an inferior race." See McCardell, *The Idea of a Southern Nation*, 71–72 (quotation).

68. *Richmond Whig and Public Advertiser*, "House of Delegates," p. 1, 1 March 1853 (quotation). See also Ira Berlin, *Slaves without Masters*, 343–80.

69. VGALP, Accomack County, 18 February 1852, reel 2, box 2, folder 50, LVA microfilm. See also VGALP, Accomack County, 18 February 1852, reel 2, box 2, folder 51, LVA microfilm, which is virtually identical.

70. VGALP, Culpeper County, 24 February 1852, reel 43, box 60, folder 68, LVA microfilm.

71. Three of these men, Peter, Dangerfield, and Nelson, would be presented for violating the law of 1806 in November 1853, the same day that the grand jury charged Charles W. Rixey "for attempting in the said County to bribe Robert J. Irving a witness sworn to give evidence before the grand jury at the last term of the Court." See Culpeper County CirCt OB 5, 1850–1856/272 (quotation), LVA microfilm. For information regarding those emancipated by the will of Margaret Miller, see Culpeper County WB R, 1847–1857/244–45, LVA microfilm; Culpeper County WB R, 1847–1852/449, LVA microfilm; for estate of Margaret Miller, see also Culpeper County WB N, 1833–1836/25, LVA microfilm; Culpeper County WB P, 1839–1843/359, LVA microfilm; Culpeper County WB R, 1847–1857/244, 449, LVA microfilm; Culpeper County WB S, 1852–1854/22, 96, 198, LVA microfilm; Culpeper County WB T, 1854–1857/320, LVA microfilm; Culpeper County WB U, 1857–1862/22, LVA microfilm; *African Repository* 27 [December 1851], 354.

72. The same petitioner also complained that "the female free negroes keep their husbands and families from emigrating to Liberia." He added that "they are held back by a stubborn refusal of their wives to accompany them." See VGALP, Norfolk City, 23 March 1852, reel 215, box 270, folder 46 (quotation), LVA microfilm.

73. Charles W. Rixey would be indicted for selling liquor to slaves but found not guilty on 5 November 1855. See Comm. v. Charles W. Rixey, 5 November 1855, drawer 3, CirCt Judgments, 1856–58, Culpeper County courthouse, Culpeper, Va. See the indictment against Joseph Selvey for selling ardent spirits "at the store house of Charles W Rixey in the County of Culpeper to slaves without the written consent of the

masters of said slaves" in Culpeper County CirCt OB 5, 1850–1856/271, LVA microfilm. See also Culpeper WB S, 1852–54, 96–98, 198–99, LVA microfilm.

74. Thomas Grayson would enslave himself to Charles W. Rixey in 1856 after the white family with whom he had lived for many years sold its land and moved to Missouri. See Culpeper County CoCt MB 23, 1853–1858/282–83, LVA microfilm. John J. Settle and Achsah Settle sold their landholdings to Benjamin F. Miller and M. A. Browning and settled in Platte County, Missouri, by 1870. See Culpeper County DB 13, 1856–58, LVA microfilm; 1870 federal census, Platte County, Missouri.

75. *Journal of the Senate*, 1852, 277. William Doswell's petition could not be located.

76. Ibid., 301, 312, 371.

77. Lawmakers' attention to issues surrounding removal helps to explain why so little was apparently written at the time about proposed self-enslavement legislation. Richmond newspapers remained silent on the issue, other than simply reporting the proposed Senate Bill 145.

78. All quotations come from the text of William H. Browne's proposed House Bill 470, "providing for the Removal of Free Negroes and Mulattoes from the Commonwealth." See Virginia, General Assembly, House of Delegates, "Bill No. 470. A BILL of Mr. Browne of Stafford and King George, providing for the Removal of Free Negroes and Mulattoes from the Commonwealth," VHS mss, E445.V8.A154 c.1. See also *Journal of the House of Delegates*, 1852, 458, 564.

79. For debates concerning the deportation of free blacks from Virginia in the late 1840s, see Chapter 1. Hugh W. Sheffey appears on the 1850 federal census as a single man living in the "Virginia Hotel" along with several dozen others, including single women and men born in Maryland and Germany. Sheffey does not appear on the slave schedule of the 1850 census. By 1860, however, Sheffey lived on a farm and owned at least eight slaves. See 1860 federal census, slave schedule.

80. *Journal of the Senate*, 1852, 371 (quotations).

81. Unfortunately, there is no record of the roll call for this vote. *Journal of the Senate*, 1852, 374.

82. *Journal of the House of Delegates*, 1852, 526, 571.

83. Comm. v. Willis and Comm. v. Andrew, summonses dated 29 December 1852, Lunenburg County Court Judgments 1854, folder: September 1854 (quotation), LVA mss.

84. Lunenburg County CirCt OB 1852–1866/5–6, LVA microfilm; Comm. v. Willis and Comm. v. Andrew, summonses dated 3 September 1852 and 29 December 1852, Lunenburg County Court Judgments 1854, folder: September 1854, LVA mss.

85. *Journal of the House of Delegates*, 1852, 169.

86. Ibid., 73, 104, 156, 235 (quotation).

87. Ibid., 169.

88. John C. Rutherfoord, delegate from Goochland County, criticized Thomas E. Bottom's plan for being too soft. See Rutherfoord, *Speech of John C. Rutherfoord*, 12 (quotation).

89. *Journal of the House of Delegates*, 1852, 230; *Journal of the Senate*, 1852–53, 160.

90. *Richmond Whig and Public Advertiser*, "Free Negroes," p. 2, 25 January 1853.

91. *Richmond Dispatch*, "Removal of Free Negroes," p. 2, 26 January 1853 (quotations). See also *Richmond Whig and Public Advertiser*, "Removal of Free Negroes," p.1, 3 February 1853, for similar arguments.

92. *Richmond Daily Dispatch*, "Removal of Free Negroes," p. 2, 15 February 1853.

93. *Lynchburg Daily Virginian*, "Removal of Free Negroes," p. 2, 23 February 1853, quoted in Delaney and Rhodes, *Free Blacks of Lynchburg*, 27, 29.

94. Rutherfoord, *Speech of John C. Rutherfoord*, 4 ("idle, ignorant," "disturbing element"), 5 ("slave is in"), 8 ("check emigration," "hard and cruel"), 9 ("confer a great," "both social and political"), 20 ("have the qualities").

95. *New Constitution of Virginia*, Article IV, sections 19, 20, and 21.

96. Rutherfoord, *Speech of John C. Rutherfoord*, 9 ("cumpulsory removal"), 11 ("no *constitutional* rights," "by high considerations"), 15 ("provision for," "if they will not"), 16 ("by removal," "unnecessary harshness," "outrage upon the spirit," "wantonness of power").

97. Ibid., 18 ("Western friends," "little practical interest"), 19 ("sixty years hence"), 20 ("becoming manliness").

98. Ibid., 7 ("formal legal notice"), 19 ("though you repeal"); Link, *Roots of Secession*, 143 ("were the link").

99. Historians have tended to focus on the most vocal extremists in describing the removal debate of 1851-53. See, for example, Ira Berlin, *Slaves without Masters*, 360-63; Link, *Roots of Secession*, 142-44.

100. *Richmond Whig and Public Advertiser*, "House of Delegates," pp. 1-2, 1 March 1853 (quotations).

101. William Link contends that in the 1850s, "the governing tenet, especially in eastern Virginia, remained the protection of slavery" and that throughout Virginia, even in the largely nonslaveholding west, "the protection of slavery [was] an article of faith." See Link, *Roots of Secession*, 63 (quotations). William Shade reminds us that while both main political parties in Virginia at the time were pro-slavery, "this evidence fails to support either the claim that other concerns were less important in determining political behavior or the assertion that the parties took the same position on the sundry slavery-related issues." See Shade, *Democratizing the Old Dominion*, 12 (quotation).

102. In the early 1850s, Whigs, who predominated in Virginia's towns and cities and typically represented commercial enterprises, pushed for the interests of larger planters and advocated government support of infrastructure, especially in the realm of transportation. Democrats, on the other hand, commonly represented the interests of small farmers and small entrepreneurs, usually in more rural areas. According to William Shade, "The Democrats favored limiting legislative action in all areas . . . by circumscribing the assembly's power to spend, tax, and pledge the state's credit to improvements projects." By comparison, "The Whigs were quite willing to risk legislative activism in order to encourage economic development and to elevate the moral tone of the society." Members of both parties, however, could agree on a set of basic libertarian values and republican ideals, at least when it came to forging common ground on the issue of free black removal. As it had been with issues relating to constitutional reform during the 1850-51 convention, removal proved to be a "policy that sometimes followed and sometimes cut across party lines." See Shade, *Democratizing the Old Dominion*, 15-16 (quotations). See also Link, *Roots of Secession*, especially 5.

103. *Richmond Whig and Public Advertiser*, "Remarks of Mr. Mapp," p. 4, 29 March 1853.

104. Ibid.

105. *Richmond Daily Dispatch*, "Removal of Free Negroes," p. 2, 9 March 1853 (quotations).

106. My use of the term "liberal" here is primarily informed by the excellent studies of William G. Shade and William A. Link. Shade concludes that by the mid-nineteenth century, "as religious controversy splintered society and elevated individual agency in the struggle for salvation, expansion of the economy and the multiplying forms of economic activity further fostered a pluralism of personal experience that encouraged the culture of political liberalism in the Old Dominion." Shade, *Democratizing the Old Dominion*, 30 (quotation). Link similarly contends that in the early 1850s, "believing fervently in republican institutions and the Union, Virginians embraced national notions of business enterprise and public culture. Most were enthusiastic capitalists, connected to the outside world and acutely aware of the market revolution." Link, *Roots of Secession*, 6–7 (quotation).

107. *Acts of the General Assembly*, 1852–53, 58; *Journal of the House of Delegates*, 1853, 537.

108. Lunenburg County CirCt OB 1852–1866/29, LVA microfilm; Comm. v. Willis and Comm. v. Andrew, summonses dated 2 June 1853 and 26 November 1853, Lunenburg County Court Judgments 1854, folder: September 1854, LVA mss.

109. It was noted on the reverse of a summons sent to the Prince Edward County sheriff that Mary Doswell "departed this life August 4th 1853 leaving three children at the high bridge." See Comm. v. Mary, 1 September 1853, Lunenburg County Court Records, various series, 1700–1924, box 4 (quotation), SRC. Though it is possible that Mary Doswell died from complications in the birth of her third child, she may have fallen victim to a smallpox outbreak "in the lower part of the county" within the previous year. See Lunenburg CoCt OB 30/277 (quotation), LVA microfilm.

110. *Journal of the House of Delegates*, 1853–54, 83.

111. *Journal of the Senate*, 1853, 194.

112. Comm. v. Willis summons dated 26 November 1853, Lunenburg County Court Judgments 1854, folder: September 1854, LVA mss.

113. Ibid.; Lunenburg County CoCt OB 29, 1842–1848/204, LVA microfilm; ibid., bond dated 13 February 1854.

114. Comm. v. Willis summons dated 14 February 1854, Lunenburg County Court Judgments 1854, folder: September 1854, LVA mss.

115. *Journal of the Senate*, 1853–54, 249.

116. Ibid., 255.

117. Ibid., 279, 284; *Journal of the House of Delegates*, 1853–54, 368.

118. Lunenburg County CirCt OB 1852–1866/68, LVA microfilm.

119. Ibid., 69.

120. *Journal of the House of Delegates*, 1853–54, 401, 408.

121. *Acts of the General Assembly*, 1853–54, 131 ("a master," "at the front"), 132 ("the court," "At such," "the attorney," "the court," "will be," "the fee simple").

122. Ibid., 131 (quotation).

123. Willis and Andrew Petition, 8 May 1854, Lunenburg County, CoCt, Common-wealth Causes, 1700–1924, box 1, SRC; Lunenburg County CoCt OB 30, 1849–1856/382–83, LVA microfilm.

124. Lunenburg County CoCt OB 30, 1849–1856/388–89, LVA microfilm.

125. Ibid., 399.

126. The Lunenburg County Circuit Court did drop its charges against Willis and Andrew, but not immediately. The court was at first unconvinced that the men's self-enslavement absolved them of their alleged crime. On June 27, the court directed the Lunenburg sheriff to summon William Arvin Sr. and John S. Bayne as witnesses for the court and William Doswell, William J. Fowlkes, [?] Woodson, Charles Smith, E. R. Chambers, Langston Arvin, and William Arvin Jr. "to testify on behalf of Willis" in a trial scheduled for September 1. On September 2, however, the court dismissed charges against both men. See Comm. v. Willis summons dated 27 June 1854, Lunen-burg County Court Judgments 1854, folder: September 1854, LVA mss.

CHAPTER FOUR

1. See unpaginated entries for 10 April 1854 ("Nothing of interest"), 8 May 1854 ("great coats," "a thing," "great complaints"), in William Haynie Hatchett, *Diary, 1853 Feb. 27–1855 Aug. 3*, Misc. microfilm reel 282 (quotations), accession #28643, LVA mss.

2. "A/C Lunenburg County to Wm H. Cole," 8 June 1848, Lunenburg CoCt Records, various series, 1700–1924, box 4 (quotation), SRC. During sessions of the county court, attested one northern visitor to Virginia, "all the landholders and gentlemen of a neigh-borhood become mutually acquainted, and lay the foundation for friendly and hospi-table reciprocities, which may be continued for life. The whole texture of society has a tincture from this intermingling." See Shepard, "'This Being Court Day,'" 459 (quota-tion). For descriptions of court days in other parts of the South, see Edwards, *People and Their Peace*, 75–78 and Gross, *Double Character*, 22–46.

3. A number of contemporary African Americans referred to an extensive word-of-mouth network, a "grapevine telegraph," which free and enslaved people employed in Southern communities to transmit important news and information during the first half of the nineteenth century. See, for example, Yetman, *When I Was a Slave*, 47 and Ira Berlin, *Generations of Captivity*, 189, 202.

4. Lunenburg CirCt OB, 1852–1866/125, LVA microfilm.

5. Bill, 17 June 1848, Mary Richardson by H v. James G. Richardson, Lunenburg Chancery, 1850–003, case #3, folder 14A, LVA microfilm.

6. Affidavit of Mary Richardson, 10 Nov. 1848, Mary Richardson by H v. James G. Richardson, Lunenburg Chancery, 1850–003, case #3, folder 14A, LVA microfilm. See also Lunenburg County WB 13, 1846–1851/432, LVA microfilm.

7. The most vivid details of Mary Richardson's testimony against her husband (and his sexual relations with Araminta Frances) were recorded by her brother, Washing-ton Maddox. See Affidavit of Mary Richardson, dated 10 November 1848, Mary Rich-ardson by H v. James G. Richardson, Lunenburg Chancery, 1850–003, case #3, folder 14A, LVA microfilm. Mary Richardson later named Maddox the executor of her estate. See Lunenburg County WB 14, 1851–1916/42, LVA microfilm; Lunenburg County

CoCt OB 30, 1849–1856/364, LVA microfilm. Washington Maddox served as a justice of the Lunenburg County court from 1830 to 1852. See Bell, *Old Free State*, 1: 328, 330, 339.

8. In the Richardson divorce settlement, James G. Richardson was ordered "to surrender all the slaves received by him on his marriage with Mrs. Richardson, and the increase of the female slaves, two beds and the other furniture belonging to Mrs. Richardson, & the clothes of Mrs. Richardson." See Final Decree, 8 October 1850, Mary Richardson by H v. James G. Richardson, Lunenburg County Chancery, 1850–003, case #3, folder 14A, LVA microfilm. James Hugo Johnson concluded that "in many cases the lust of the white master for the black bond woman destroyed the peace and happiness of the slaveholder's home," not only in Virginia, but "in the other southern states the records show that white wives attempted to divorce their husbands for adultery with slave women." See Johnson, *Race Relations in Virginia*, 248–49 (quotations). See also Fox-Genovese, *Within the Plantation Household*, esp. 94–99.

9. Lunenburg County WB 13, 1846–1851/432 (quotations), LVA microfilm. The appraisal of James G. Richardson's estate made upon his death listed twenty-nine enslaved individuals, including "Minta & 2 children" valued at $900. At least eight individuals were sold in January 1851 in order to settle the estate. See ibid., 451, 465, LVA microfilm.

10. Lunenburg CoCt OB 30, 1849–1856/234, LVA microfilm.

11. Lunenburg County WB 13, 1846–1851/432 ("friend"), LVA microfilm; Lunenburg County OB 30, 1849–1856/244, LVA microfilm; Lunenburg County Fiduciary Book 1, 1851–1855/219, LVA microfilm. The court would continue to dutifully oversee the disbursement of funds to Virginia and William Richardson until at least 1865, when in August of that year, their inheritance amounted to $2,339.28. See Lunenburg County Fiduciary Book 4, 1863–1868/223, LVA microfilm; Lunenburg County Fiduciary Book 3, 1859–1863/318, 500, 626, LVA microfilm; Lunenburg County Fiduciary Book 2, 1855–1858/158, 275, 419–20, 599, LVA microfilm.

12. Lunenburg County Register of Free Negroes, 1850–1865/19 (quotation), LVA microfilm. See also "Free Negroes to be registered," Lunenburg County, Commonwealth Causes, 1700–1924, 8 August 1853, SRC; Lunenburg County OB 30, 1849–1856/337, LVA microfilm.

13. Lunenburg CirCt OB 1852–1866/125 (quotation), LVA microfilm.

14. Ibid., 166.

15. Araminta Frances skipped her court date scheduled for September 1, 1855. See ibid.

16. *Journal of the House of Delegates*, 1855, 42.

17. Dangerfield Alexander: *Journal of the Senate*, 1855–56, 155; Culpeper County CirCt OB 5, 1850–1856/272, LVA microfilm; Culpeper County WB R, 1847–1852/449, LVA microfilm; *African Repository* 27 [Dec. 1851], 354.

18. Critty Woodson: *Journal of the Senate*, 1855–56, 55; Powhatan County CoCt OB28, 1848–1851/412, LVA microfilm; Powhatan County CoCt OB 29, 1851–1856/13, 65, 116, 134, 180, 224, 240, LVA microfilm; Powhatan County Register of Free Negroes, 1820–1865/85, register 690, LVA microfilm. See also court order for register in Powhatan County CoCt OB 29, 1851–1856/181, LVA microfilm; Powhatan County CoCt OB

29, 1851–1856/191, LVA microfilm; Charles Seldon to William McLain, ACS, Incoming Correspondence, Domestic Letters, 10 August–31 December 1853, LOC mss.

19. Frank Harman: *Journal of the House of Delegates*, 1855–56, 285; Charlotte Pate: *Journal of the House of Delegates*, 1855–56, 170; Pulaski County CoCt OB, 1850–1862/259, LVA microfilm.

20. Thomas Grayson: *Journal of the House of Delegates*, 1855–56, 173; Thomas Jones: *Journal of the Senate*, 1855–56, 152.

21. Jesse Spencer: *Journal of the Senate*, 1855–56, 157.

22. Lewis Williamson: ibid., 147.

23. Simon, Martha, Judy, Margaret: ibid., 222.

24. *Boston Evening Transcript*, "News and Miscellaneous Items," p. 4 (quotations), 17 December 1855. See also *Baltimore Sun*, "A Case for the Abolitionists," p. 4, 18 December 1855; *Macon Weekly Telegraph*, "Voluntary Enslavement," p. 2, 25 December 1855; *Charleston Mercury*, p. 2, 17 January 1856.

25. *Daily Richmond Enquirer*, "Voluntary Enslavement of Free Negroes," p. 2, col. 2 (quotation; italics added), 14 May 1857.

26. Virginia; General Assembly; Senate; "A bill to provide more effectually for the removal of Free Negroes," 2 ("Colonization Board," "full power"), 7 ("ipso facto"), 8 ("with the consent," "any responsible"), VHS mss, E445.V8.A15.

27. Deneale also played an active role in the debates over the enslavement bill, which revolved around a clause requiring chosen owners to pay a one-time tax on self-enslaved individuals. Deneale moved to eliminate any tax whatsoever to be charged upon those enslaving free blacks under the bill, a measure that might facilitate the process by making it more affordable and more appealing to a broader cross-section of whites. See *Journal of the Senate*, 1855–56, 70.

28. *Journal of the Senate*, 1855–56, 70, 149, 156; *Journal of the House of Delegates*, 1855–56, 172, 364.

29. *Journal of the House of Delegates*, 1855, 42, 189, 210; Lunenburg County OB 30, 1849–1856/547–48, LVA microfilm.

30. The general law differed in significant ways from all of the individual laws passed up to that point, which had allowed Lewis Williamson, Araminta Frances, and Dangerfield Alexander to enslave themselves in their respective localities.

31. The law did not specify that free blacks must select a white master, but another Virginia law, already on the books, was clear on this point: "No free negro shall be capable of acquiring (except by descent) any slave other than the husband, wife, parent or descendant of such free negro." See *Code of Virginia*, 1849, 458 (quotation).

32. *Acts of Virginia*, 1856, 37–38, esp. 38 ("The children").

33. Ibid.

34. For the known instances of courts convicting free blacks of remaining illegally in the state and ordering them sold into absolute slavery, see Accomack County CirCt OB, 1857–1866/168 (Ninna or Nina Phillips), LVA microfilm; ibid., 171–72 (Scipio Phillips); ibid., 271 (Jacob Bayly); ibid., 318 (Richard Mason); Bedford County CirCt OB 12, 1857–1859/49, 187 (Ann Durrett), LVA microfilm; Bedford County CirCt OB 13, 1859–1866/186, 366 (Henry), LVA microfilm; Bedford County CoCt OB 33, 1858–1861/480

(London Rogers, Phil Rogers, and Bob Rogers), LVA microfilm; Charles City County CirCt OB, 1853–1863/n.p. [18 November 1861] (Benjamin Deeling, Candis Deeling, and Watt Only), LVA microfilm; Frederick County CirCt OB 10, 1853–1868/320 (Ellen Apts), LVA microfilm; Fauquier County CoCt MB, 1857–1859/210, 222 (Eliza Paine), LVA microfilm; Highland County CirCt OB 2, 1848–60, 203 (Rachel), Highland County courthouse, Monterey, Virginia; Loudoun County CoCt MB, 1856–1858/7 (Sinah Ambers/Ambrose), LVA microfilm; Comm. v. Mary Dunmore, 27 April 1858, Norfolk City Hustings Court Ended Law Causes, January–June 1859, Norfolk City Circuit Court, Norfolk, Virginia (Mary Dunmore).

35. On one occasion in late 1857, four women were "sold by order of the Court for remaining in the State contrary to law," "in front of the Court House in Charlestown." See *Virginia Free Press* (Charleston), "Sale of Negroes," p. 2, col. 2 (quotation) 31 December, 1857. See also Link, *Roots of Secession*, 302, n 23.

36. On the same day that Mary Dunmore had been sentenced to absolute slavery, the cases of three of the four other free blacks who had been charged along with Dunmore a month before with violating the expulsion law (those of Joe Cooper, Daniel Jackson, and William Reid) were dismissed. See Norfolk City Hustings Court OB 39, 1857–1859/138, 313, LVA microfilm. See also Comm. v. Mary Dunmore, 27 April 1858, Norfolk City Hustings Court Ended Law Causes, January–June 1859, Norfolk City Circuit Court, Norfolk, Virginia. Such sale into absolute slavery should not be confused with the periodic "sale" of free blacks into a limited period of servitude, frequently ordered by county courts for nonpayment of taxes but unevenly executed. See, for example, Halifax County CoCt MB 19, 1859–1862/380, LVA microfilm, in which 107 free blacks were ordered "sold" for nonpayment of taxes in 1860 and 1861. See also Greenesville County CoCt OB 12, 1852–1866/233, LVA microfilm; "A List of free Negroes in the Parrish of Nottoway to be sold," Southampton County FNSR, LVA mss. See also "Memorandum of Free Negroes Hired by order of Court," Westmorland County FNSR, 1780 c.a.–1870, box 1, LVA mss, in which thirteen free African Americans were hired out in 1818 for terms of six months to three years. One entry reads: "No person will purchase the fiddler." On other occasions, county courts sold free people "into absolute slavery" for allegedly assisting slaves to escape or into virtual slavery after being arrested without their free papers. Washington Brown, a free man of color, was ordered sold by the Southampton County court in August 1862. See also W. P. Fowler to James Morgan, 19 March 1853, Petersburg City FNSR, 1809–59, box 1, LVA mss. See Southampton County CoCt MB, 1861–1870/61 ("into absolute slavery"), LVA microfilm. John Harris, who had been "confined in jail as a runaway without his register" by the Halifax County court, was ordered to be sold "for the shortest time that he can," in order to pay off the jail fees and associated expenses from his arrest. Instead, Harris was "hired" to William G. H. Ligon for one thousand dollars "for the term of twenty five years" in November 1864. See "John Harris Order to Hire Out," 29 November 1864, Halifax County Judgments, Halifax County courthouse, Halifax, Virginia. See also Dinwiddie County CoCt, MB 3, 1863–1866/64. Apprentice indentures for African American children used similar language, stating that youths were "bargained, sold, and delivered" to whites for a certain number of years. See, for example, apprentice indentures in Southampton County FNSR, LVA mss.

37. Henry Champ, one of those free blacks convicted during the Frederick County roundup of 1857–58, left the state after receiving a conviction. See Introduction.

38. One Chesterfield County court document of 14 June 1853 describes the process of (though not the rationale behind) a systematic roundup in that locality: "Ordered that the constables of this County summon to attend at the next term, all free negroes in their respective Districts who they have reason to believe are remaining in this Commonwealth contrary to law, or going at large without being duly registered and furnished with copies of such registry." See Chesterfield County FNSR, 1790–1862, box 1, LVA mss.

39. Frederick County CirCt OB 10, 1853–1868/206, LVA microfilm. See also Frederick County PPTBs 1855–58, LVA microfilm.

40. See entries in the 1860 federal census, Frederick County, for the occupations of Thomas Champ, Catharine Bell, Henry Bullet, and Henry Walker, respectively.

41. It is unclear whether all those free blacks who had registered with the Albemarle County court in fall 1857 had indeed shown "satisfactory evidence of their having been born free of parents who were free previous to 1st May, 1806," as the court clerk had claimed. It is possible that in some cases, county officials willingly overlooked individuals' illegal status by fudging their entries in their county's Register of Free Negroes. For example, in his examination of free black registrations in Prince Edward County, Virginia, Melvin Patrick Ely concluded that such collusion between court clerks and individual free blacks might have occurred. See Ely, *Israel on the Appomattox*, 251–55, 372–73, 394.

42. For lists of those free blacks ordered registered by the Albemarle County court in October–November 1857, see Albemarle County CoCt MB, 1856–1859/184–90, 200–203, 346 (quotation), LVA microfilm. For Mary Jane House's application, see ibid., 346 ("for leave"). For William Sindler's application made in April 1857, see ibid., 81–82.

43. Albemarle County WB 18, 1847–1848/407, LVA microfilm; Albemarle County WB 21, 1851–1852/492, LVA microfilm; Albemarle County WB 21, 1851–1852/493, LVA microfilm; Albemarle County CoCt MB, 1856–1859/142 (quotation), LVA microfilm.

44. Petition of John Martin, Oct 1857, in Free Negro & Slave: Petition for Voluntary Enslavement folder, Albemarle County FNSR, 1796–1870, box 2 (quotation), LVA mss. Martin's petition is referenced in Albemarle County CirCt OB, 1857–1865/71, LVA microfilm.

45. Albemarle County CirCt OB, 1857–1865/113, LVA microfilm; Commonwealth v. John Martin, June 1858, Albemarle County Commonwealth Causes, 1858, box 46, LVA mss.

46. See entries dated 15 June 1834 and 23 February 1839 in Mountain Plain Baptist Church, Albemarle County, MB, 1833–69, 1886, accession# 29393, LVA mss.

47. Albemarle CirCt OB, 1857–1865/137, LVA microfilm; Albemarle County, FNSR, 1796–1870 ca., box 2, LVA mss. See entry dated 1 June 1851 in Mountain Plain Baptist Church, Albemarle County, MB, 1833–69, 1886, accession# 29393, LVA mss.

48. "Comm. v Satchell Grayson, Thomas Grayson, William Grayson CoCt 1867 Aug.," in Albemarle County, Commonwealth Causes, box 55 (1867), LVA mss.

49. Accomack CirCt OB, 1857–1866/69, 170, 190, 275, LVA microfilm.

50. Campbell County, Unspecified Court Records, box 22 (Wood family), SRC; Chesterfield County CirCt OB 4, 1856-1873/225-26, 289, LVA microfilm (Hix and Howlett families).

51. Charles City County CirCt OB, 1853-1863/n.p., dated 18 November 1861, LVA microfilm.

52. Alleghany County CirCt, OB 3, 1854-1872/105, 147, Alleghany County courthouse, Covington, Virginia.

53. Sussex County CirCt OB, 1831-1866/388, Sussex County courthouse, Sussex, Virginia.

54. See Alleghany County CoCt OB 5, 1849-1859/434 (quotation), LVA microfilm.

55. Washington County CirCt OB E, 1859-1870/91, LVA microfilm (indictments of David Bird, Nelson Wellington, Dock Hill, Enoch Mosely, Thomas Banks, Henry Wilson, and James Goff). See also Washington County CirCt OB D, 1853-1859/243, LVA microfilm (Eliza Powell et. al).

56. Culpeper County CirCt OB 6, 1856-1866/188 (quotation), LVA microfilm. Even free blacks indicted and found guilty by local courts of felonies could be granted new trials. See, for example, Cumberland County CirCt OB, 1849-1860/555, LVA microfilm; Lynchburg City CirCt OB 8, 1859-1865/442, 444, LVA microfilm.

57. Those individuals who were charged by their local courts for remaining in the state illegally included John Martin of Albemarle County, Daniel Rogers of Bedford County, William Williamson of Campbell County, Dangerfield Alexander and Peter Miller of Culpeper County, Henry Champ and Thomas Champ of Frederick County, Araminta Frances, Willis Doswell, and Andrew Doswell of Lunenburg County, Maria Nimmo of Norfolk City, Judy Cullins of Powhatan County, Charlotte Pate of Pulaski County, Tom Hart and Littleton Hart of Surry County, James Goff of Washington County, and Henry Wilson of Washington County.

58. VGALP, Pulaski County, 7 January 1856, reel 166, box 212, folder 33, ("she is unwilling"), LVA microfilm. See also Charlotte Pate's deed of emancipation, dated 13 May 1848, and recorded 6 September 1848, in Pulaski County DB 2, 1846-1856/163, LVA microfilm. Pate never re-enslaved herself to Phillip L. Woolvine, a fifty-one-year-old saddler, as she had requested in her petition, and she was indicted "for remaining in the State Contrary to law." See Pulaski County CirCt OB 2, 1857-1876/49, 70, 82 (quotation), LVA microfilm. Instead, it is likely that Pate moved north to Botetourt County, where she lived "At Home" in the household of Moses Parmer by 1870. See 1860 federal census, Pulaski County, Virginia; 1870 federal census (quotation), Botetourt County, Virginia.

59. In his groundbreaking study of free blacks in North Carolina, John Hope Franklin indicated a different use of self-enslavement by free blacks who found themselves in trouble with the law. He writes, "Another way out of the difficulties which beset the free Negro was to seek enslavement." See Franklin, *Free Negro in North Carolina*, 218 (quotation).

60. Several scholars have dismissed Virginia's expulsion law as entirely ineffective. Luther Porter Jackson, for example, declared it "for the most part a dead letter." See Jackson, "Manumission in Certain Virginia Cities," 298 (quotation).

61. Frederick County CirCt OB 10, 1853–1868/287, 310, 319, 330, 341, 364–65, LVA microfilm; Thomas Champs Petition, 12 November 1859, Frederick County, FNSR, 1795–1871, box 12, LVA mss; 1860 federal census, Frederick County, Virginia.

62. Frederick County CirCt OB 10, 1853–1868/287, 319, 330, 341, 364–65, LVA microfilm; "Thomas Champs Petition," 12 November 1859, Frederick County, FNSR, 1795–1871, box 12, LVA mss; 1860 federal census.

63. *New York Herald*, "Prefers Slavery to Freedom," p. 4, 25 September 1860 (quotations); See also *Spectator*, "A Sensible Negro," 25 September 1860. Roland's case is referenced in Rockbridge County CirCt OB, 1852–67 (continued)/368, 384–85, 402, LVA microfilm.

64. Bryson, *Legal Education in Virginia*, 597.

65. See Morris, *Southern Slavery*, 422.

66. Ibid.

67. Fauquier County CirCt OB G, 1860–1872/48, LVA microfilm.

68. At least 110 individuals submitted at least 121 petitions for self-enslavement in what is now Virginia. At least one hundred of those petitions were deliberated upon in county or circuit courts. Eleven of these were rejected by the judge. Those whose petitions were rejected include: Celia Hale of Bedford County; Mary Fletcher, Jane Payne, and Annah Gleaves Poters of Fauquier County; Sinah Ambrose of Loudoun County; Jeptha Chapman, Thadeus Chapman, and Timothy Chapman of Madison County; Watt Love of Mecklenburg County; Ann Bannister of Pittsylvania County; and Mary Elizabeth Roland of Rockbridge County. A few individuals petitioned the court twice or three times for self-enslavement. Some whose first petition was denied were allowed to enslave themselves but only after they had changed their choice of owner.

69. *Richmond Enquirer*, "Prefers Slavery to Freedom," p. 2, 18 May 1858.

70. See Albemarle County CirCt OB, 1857–1865/113, LVA microfilm.

71. *Daily National Era*, "Voluntary Enslavement," p. 2, 10 March 1854.

72. See, for example, *Boston Atlas*, "Prefers Slavery," p. 1, 11 February 1857.

73. *New York Times*, "Affairs in Virginia," 15 October 1858.

74. *Daily Richmond Enquirer*, "Voluntary Enslavement of Free Negroes," p. 2, col. 2 (quotation), 14 May 1857.

CHAPTER FIVE

1. "Memos of James Watson's Will & estate," Accounts of Joseph Dupuy and Robert J. Smith as Executors of John Watson, Prince Edward County, 1854–66, 22 December 1824, p. 4, 8, Dupuy Family Papers, 1810–66, accession #21781c, LVA mss.

2. For family relations of Lucy Booker, see "A List of Sixty Six negroes Emancipated by John Watson decd. . . ." Prince Edward County Chancery, Dosha etc. vs. Exrs of John Watson, etc., 1873–001/cc, LVA mss. It is difficult to discern how many enslaved individuals lived on John Watson's Prince Edward County plantation in the 1820s. By the mid-1850s, Watson would own sixty-seven individuals who lived in Prince Edward and Charlotte counties. See Prince Edward County CirCt WB, 1833–1899/73–74, LVA microfilm. For a description of John Watson's Prince Edward County estate, including

twenty-nine slaves who lived there, see John Watson Inventory, 29 September 1855, Prince Edward County, CirCt Court Records, August 1854–August 1855, box 74, LVA mss. For items left by James Watson to his female slaves exclusively, see "Memos of James Watson's Will & estate," Accounts of Joseph Dupuy and Robert J. Smith as Executors of John Watson, Prince Edward County, 1854–66, 22 December 1824, p. 4, 8, Dupuy Family Papers, 1810–66, accession #21781c, LVA mss.

3. In an inventory and appraisal of John Watson's estate dated 8 October 1856, "Lucy Booker" is noted as being sixty years old, and "Amy" seventy-five. See Prince Edward County CirCt WB, 1833–1899/73–74, LVA microfilm. Though biologically possible for there to have been only a fifteen-year age difference between Amey and her daughter Lucy Booker, it is certainly possible that those noting the women's ages got it wrong. For slight variation in the women's ages, see also John Watson's Inventory, 29 September 1855, Prince Edward County CirCt Court Records, August 1854–August 1855, box 74 ("Old Amy"), LVA mss. Amey is listed as the seventy-five-year-old "Mother of Lucy Booker" in "A List of sixty six Negroes emancipated by John Watson ded.," 12 November 1857, Dosha etc vs. Exrs of John Watson, Prince Edward County Chancery, 1873–001/cc, box 23, LVA mss.

4. John Watson's Will, Dosha etc vs. Exrs of John Watson, Prince Edward County Chancery, 1873–001/cc, box 23, LVA mss.

5. From 1790 to 1860, hundreds of thousands of Virginians were sold into a thriving domestic slave trade from the upper South to the Deep South. See Walter Johnson, *Soul by Soul*; Berlin, *Generations of Captivity*, especially 159–244; Gudmestad, *Troublesome Commerce*; Deyle, *Carry Me Back*, especially 15–93. For an example of an account book detailing the sale and transfer of enslaved individuals from Southside Virginia to New Orleans, Louisiana, and Natchez, Mississippi, from 1835 to 1851, see Lunenburg County (Va.) Beasley Jones and Wood Slave Trade Account Book, 1835–51, Local Government Records Collection, Lunenburg County Court Records, misc. reel #410, LVA microfilm.

6. For a more detailed description of "experimentalists" and their cause, see Burin, *Slavery and the Peculiar Solution*, 54, 59, 103.

7. In her study of the American Colonization Society's efforts in Virginia, Marie Tyler-McGraw concluded, "The Society's membership and resources dwindled from the 1840s until the Civil War." During this time, Tyler-McGraw writes, "Society members talked mostly to themselves. The center of the struggle had moved away from them." See Tyler-McGraw, "American Colonization Society in Virginia," 2–3 (quotations), 6.

8. Ibid., 48–49, especially 49 (quotation). In his now-classic study of the American Colonization Society, P. J. Staudenraus writes, "Through the 1850s the forlorn hope for a miraculous revival of public confidence animated the faithful few who still clung to the aging Colonization Society." See Staudenraus, *African Colonization Movement*, 239 (quotation). For examination of manumission and colonization in Rockbridge County, Virginia, in the mid-nineteenth century, see Young, *Ripe for Emancipation*, 127–88.

9. Varon, *We Mean To Be Counted*, 61–62 (quotations). See also Burin, *Peculiar Solution*, 49–52, especially 51.

10. Ibid., 49.

11. Tyler-McGraw, "American Colonization Society in Virginia," 17, 219. See also Hickin, "Antislavery in Virginia," 1: 274–320.

12. Hickin, "Antislavery in Virginia," 1: 334.

13. John Watson's Will, Dosha etc vs. Exrs of John Watson, Prince Edward County Chancery, 1873–001/cc, box 23, LVA mss.

14. Dupuy to McLain, 11 July 1857, ACS, Domestic Letters, Incoming Correspondence, LOC mss. For statements on Dupuy's health, see also letters from Dupuy to McLain dated 16 October 1856 and 24 July 1857, Ibid.

15. Dupuy, Emily Howe, Papers, 1834–83. Mss1D9295b, especially sections 5–10, VHS. See also Ely, *Israel on the Appomattox*, 209, 300. See also Adams, "New England Teacher in Southside Virginia."

16. Benedict Burgess of Northumberland County stipulated in his will that his slaves be freed and removed to Liberia only after the death of his wife. See Will of Benedict Burgess, Benedict & Samuel Burgess, Exrs vs. Gamaliel T. Burgess, et als., Northumberland County Chancery, 1867–015, LVA mss. See also the will of John Terrell, who freed his slaves after his wife's death, in Albemarle County WB 24/390–91, LVA microfilm. William Kelly of Lancaster County agreed to emancipate his slaves after the death of his brother, James. See Wm Kelly's Will, Northumberland County Chancery, 1856–003, Kelly v. Kelly, LVA mss.

17. Fauquier County WB 24, 1852–1853/125–27, 125 ("none of my"), LVA microfilm.

18. Hickin, "Antislavery in Virginia," 331.

19. Watson, *Notes on Southside Virginia*, 131. Williamson, "Seven Ways to Compute."

20. Timothy Rogers v. Daniel et als, Bedford County Chancery, 1859–036, 7 ("the insanity"), Bedford County courthouse, Bedford, Virginia.

21. Bill, 11 April 1856, James W. Kelley v. James Kelley, Northumberland Chancery, 1856–003, LVA mss.

22. Deposition of J. A. Harding, 11 August 1856, James W. Kelley v. James Kelley, Northumberland Chancery, 1856–003, ("the best investment"), LVA mss; 11 April 1856, James W. Kelley v. James Kelley, Northumberland Chancery, 1856–003, ("that the increase"), LVA mss.

23. Burin, *Peculiar Solution*, 48, 181 n. 38.

24. John Watson's Will, Dosha etc vs. Exrs of John Watson, Prince Edward County Chancery, 1873–001/cc, box 23, LVA mss.

25. Eric Burin concludes that emancipators did not "intend to leave their children penniless." He finds that almost half of all ACS emancipators "lived either by themselves or with just one other person (enslaved African-Americans notwithstanding)." See Burin, *Peculiar Solution*, 49 ("prepare").

26. See lists of "Coloured members" and "Female members" in Branch's Church, Chesterfield, MB, 1825–58, VBHS.

27. Chesterfield County WB 19, 1850–1852/158–59 (quotations), LVA microfilm. For an example of another emancipator who offered his slaves a choice between freedom in Liberia and slavery in Virginia in the 1850s, see Extract from the Last Will and Testament of Edwd Poindexter, ACS Reel 313, Wills, A–P, LOC mss. For emancipators who offered their slaves a choice between freedom or slavery, see the will of Mary

Oldham in Albemarle County WB 24, 1856–1857/9, LVA microfilm. See also the will of David M. Doswell in Prince Edward County WB 7, 1828–1837/413, LVA microfilm.

28. Answer of W. L. Watkins, 14 April 1856, Watkins, Adr. of Sarah Branch (Decd) Petition, November 1873, Chesterfield County Chancery, 1873–033, box 75, ("have been virtually free"), LVA mss. For Mary Frances's escape to Richmond and capture, see Chesterfield County WB 20, 1852–1855/254, LVA microfilm. See also The Estate of Sarah Branch deceased, Doc. 8, Watkins, Adr. of Sarah Branch (Decd) Petition, November 1873, Chesterfield County Chancery, 1873–033, box 75, LVA mss. For Tom's escape and capture, see Chesterfield County WB 20, 1852–1855/254, LVA microfilm. See also The Estate of Sarah Branch deceased, Doc. 8, Watkins, Adr. of Sarah Branch (Decd) Petition, Nov 1873, Chesterfield County Chancery, 1873–033, box 75, LVA mss. Flight of slaves after the death of masters seems to have been fairly widespread. See, for example, Account of the Estate of Timothy Rogers, 24 June 1851, Bedford County WB, 1851–1853/131, LVA microfilm.

29. Grattan, *Reports of Cases*, 14: 394–408, especially 395 ("if any of"), 396 ("have the right"). The Virginia Court of Appeals decided that "allowing a slave to elect whether he would accept freedom was not a method of manumission recognized by the laws of Virginia." See Hickin, "Antislavery in Virginia," 342 (quotation). See also "Legal Decisions in Virginia," *African Repository* 34 (1858), 359–60.

30. Grattan, *Reports of Cases*, 14: 406.

31. Will of Margaret Miller, Culpeper County WB R, 1847–1857/244–45, LVA microfilm.

32. Rockbridge County CirCt WB 1, 1809–1874/136–38, LVA microfilm.

33. On Valentine's Day and its emergence as a frenzied national holiday, see Schmidt, "Fashioning of a Modern Holiday," 214–18. For the participation of Virginians in Valentine's Day activities, see "St. Valentine's Day," *Richmond Daily Dispatch*, p. 2, col. 1, 14 February 1852.

34. For Joshua's accounts at local stores, see Exr of Hugh Adams vs. Legt(s) of Hugh Adams, Rockbridge County Chancery, 1860–065, 189–99; 485–90, LVA online.

35. Exr of Hugh Adams vs. Legt(s) of Hugh Adams, Rockbridge County Chancery, 1860–065, 486, LVA online.

36. Ibid.

37. For the expenses and legacies of Sylla Jane and family, see ibid., 134. David A. Gileson reported on 7 February 1859, that he had received $40, "the price of a Buggy bot of me by the negroes belonging to the estate of said Adams." See ibid., 313. For an account of the buggy's remodeling, see ibid., 297.

38. Ibid., 140–43, LVA online.

39. Heath, "Slavery and Consumerism," 1 ("actively participated"), 4 ("relating to," "to supplement").

40. Heath, *Hidden Lives*, 50–58, especially 51–53 (quotations). See also Schlotterbeck, "Internal Economy of Slavery," 170–81.

41. Dew, *Bond of Iron*, 171–86, especially 172, 180, 183. See also Dew, "Sam Williams, Forgeman," 199–239.

42. James Oakes has made this argument forcefully in Oakes, *Slavery and Freedom*, especially 80–136.

43. Dew, *Bond of Iron*, 367.

44. For a powerful description of the promise and pitfalls of overwork in the lives of Virginia's enslaved population, see Grandy, "Narrative of the Life of Moses Grandy."

45. McLain to Dupuy, 20 July 1858 ("Watson people"), ACS, Domestic Letters, Incoming Correspondence, LOC mss. On how the mere expectation of freedom changed the behavior of the enslaved, see Answer of W. L. Watkins, 14 April 1856, Watkins, Adr. of Sarah Branch (Decd) Petition, November 1873, Chesterfield County Chancery, 1873–033, box 75, LVA mss. See also Exr of Hugh Adams vs. Legt(s) of Hugh Adams, Rockbridge County Chancery, 1860–065, LVA mss.

46. John Watson's Will, Dosha etc vs. Exrs of John Watson, Prince Edward County Chancery, 1873–001/cc, box 23, LVA mss.

47. Joseph Dupuy Account Book, Mss 5:3, D9295:1–2, Mss1D9295c8, VHS.

48. Accounts of Joseph Dupuy and Robert J. Smith as Executors of John Watson, Prince Edward County, 1854–66, Dupuy Family Papers, 1810–66, p. 7, accession #21781c, LVA mss. "George, Jr." is listed as "8 months" old in November 1857, placing his birth in March 1857. See "A List of Sixty Six negroes Emancipated by John Watson decd. . . ." Prince Edward County Chancery, Dosha etc. vs. Exrs of John Watson, etc., 1873–001/cc, LVA mss. Other Virginia emancipators at the time explicitly prohibited their freedpeople from engaging in certain activities. For example, Sarah Branch of Chesterfield County directed her executor to "hire out all my negroes for five years but they are not to be hired to work at any Coal Mine or to go on the River or canal." See Chesterfield County WB 19, 1850–1852/158–59, LVA microfilm.

49. Dupuy to McLain, 31 March 1857, ACS, Domestic Letters, Incoming Correspondence, LOC mss.

50. Other executors in Virginia in the 1850s undertook the unusual task of emancipating and removing a deceased friend's slaves to Liberia, but apparently none approached the task with as much care and meticulousness. Like other executors throughout Virginia at the time, however, Dupuy acted honestly, diligently, and, seemingly, sincerely. See, for example, Burin, *Slavery and the Peculiar Solution*, especially chapter 2.

51. See Staudenraus, *African Colonization Movement*; Tyler-McGraw, *African Republic*, chapter 1.

52. Dupuy to McLain, 24 July 1857 ("not being well enough acquainted"), ACS, Domestic Letters, Incoming Correspondence, LOC mss; see also ibid., letters of Dupuy to McLain dated 30 September 1856, 18 October 1856, 31 March 1857, 11 July 1857, as well as ibid., McLain's replies to Dupuy dated 14 October 1856, 20 October 1856, 9 February 1857, 1 April 1857, 2 April 1857, 15 July 1857, and 25 July 1857.

53. Dupuy to McLain, 30 September 1856, ACS, Domestic Letters, Incoming Correspondence, LOC mss.

54. Dupuy to McLain, 3 October 1857, ACS, Domestic Letters, Incoming Correspondence, LOC mss.

55. Reports of famine in Liberia were widespread in the media in mid-1857, as seen in such articles as "Destitution and Suffering among the Liberia Colonies," *New York Daily Times*, p. 1, 10 September 1857. The ACS responded forcefully to such allegations. See, for example, *Liberator* (Boston), "Bad News from Liberia," p. 147, no. 137,

col. C, 11 September 1857, and *Daily National Intelligencer* (Washington, D.C.), "The Famine in Liberia," no. 14, col. D, 11 September 1857; see also McLain's response to such reports in "Condition and Prospects of Liberia," *African Repository* 33, no. 10 (October 1857), 289–96.

56. McLain to Dupuy, 5 October 1857, ACS, Domestic Letters, Outgoing Correspondence, LOC mss.

57. McLain to Dupuy, 13 October 1857, ACS, Domestic Letters, Outgoing Correspondence, LOC mss.

58. Accounts of Joseph Dupuy and Robert J. Smith as Executors of John Watson, Prince Edward County, 1854–66, Dupuy Family Papers, 1810–66, 7, accession #21781c, LVA mss.

59. Ibid., 9.

60. See copy of William Watson's register in William ex parte Petition, 15 March 1859, Prince Edward County, CirCt, Law Papers, March 1856–August 1858 [mislabeled; should be 1868], box 117, SRC. The six who "Can Read the Bible" were: Jim Price, Billey, Doctor, George, William, and Mariah. See Dupuy Family Papers, 1810–66, Personal Papers, Dupuy Account Book, 1856–65, accession #21780, p. 170, LVA mss.

61. "Voyage to Liberia. 'Getting under Way,' " *Maryland Colonization Journal* 9, no. 2 (July 1857): 17.

62. "Money paid to 66 of the Slaves, Emancipated by John Watson, in Norfolk . . ." 12 November 1857, Dupuy Family Papers, 1810–66, Accounts of Joseph Dupuy and Robert J. Smith as Executors of John Watson, Prince Edward County, 1854–66, accession #21781c, p. 9, LVA mss.

63. Prince Edward County, CoCt OB 27, 1853–1862/263, Prince Edward County courthouse, Farmville, Virginia.

64. Dupuy Account Book, 1856–65, p. 170–171, especially 171 ("preferred staying in Virginia"), Dupuy Family Papers, 1810–66, Personal Papers, accession#21780, LVA mss.

65. Dupuy to McLain, 3 September 1857, ACS, Domestic Letters, Incoming Correspondence, LOC mss.

66. Dupuy to McLain, 15 July 1858, ACS, Domestic Letters, Incoming Correspondence, LOC mss.

67. Dupuy to McLain, 3 September 1857, ACS, Domestic Letters, Incoming Correspondence, LOC mss. In a letter written from Liberia after the death of Dennis and Elvira, Agnes Watson would remind Dupuy that "Denis was member of the P Church Elvia a member of the Baptist church." See Agnes Watson to Joseph Dupuy, 12 February 1861, Dupuy Family Papers, 1810–66, Accounts of Joseph Dupuy and Robert J. Smith as Executors of John Watson, Prince Edward County, 1854–66, accession #21781c, LVA mss.

68. On Tuesday, 3 November 1857, Dupuy paid $70.20 for "Expenses of Negroes from Meherrin depot to Richd." See Accounts of Joseph Dupuy and Robert J. Smith as Executors of John Watson, Prince Edward County, 1854–66, p. 7, Dupuy Family Papers, 1810–66, accession #21781c, LVA mss.

69. Kimball, *American City, Southern Place*, 3–36, 3 ("coal dust"). For a vivid description of Richmond during this time, see Takagi, *"Rearing Wolves,"* 16–17.

70. McLain to Dupuy, 15 July 1857, ACS, Domestic Letters, Outgoing Correspondence, LOC mss.

71. William Ludwell Sheppard, Diary, 1853–54, entry for 1 May 1854, Personal Papers Collection, accession #24772, LVA mss.

72. Dupuy to McLain, 24 July 1857, ACS, Domestic Letters, Incoming Correspondence, LOC mss. For a detailed list of recommended provisions, see McLain to Dupuy, 17 September 1857, ACS, Domestic Letters, Outgoing Correspondence, LOC mss, in which McLain suggests that "*Each one* should have a knife & fork, a table & tea spoon, a cup & saucer or mug, two or three plates, a hoe/either hilling or weeding,—each man should have an axe—each family should have a tub, two buckets, or two pots, a frying pan, an oven, a tea kettle, a tea pot, a hammar or hatchit, a saw, a keg of nails, (i.e. each family that will keep house for themselves—or in which there are men to use a saw &c.) some tin cups—tin pans, wash basin;—there should be say half a doz. spades."

73. Marie Tyler-McGraw writes that "the ACS and its Virginia agents frequently attempted to orchestrate the scene of departure for maximum sentiment, with speeches, specially composed hymns, and prayers." Apparently, none of this occurred before the departure of the *M.C. Stevens* in fall 1857. See Tyler-McGraw, *African Republic*, 77 (quotation).

74. "Third Departure of the Mary Caroline Stevens . . ." in *African Repository* 33, no. 12 (December 1857): 354.

75. Quotation describes the scene on the previous voyage of the *M. C. Stevens* from Norfolk. See "Voyage to Liberia. 'Getting under Way,'" *Maryland Colonization Journal* 9, no. 2 (July 1857): 19.

76. Dupuy to McLain, 19 April 1858, ACS, Domestic Letters, Incoming Correspondence, LOC mss.

77. See Joseph Dupuy to William McLain, 9 October 1860, ACS, Domestic Letters, Incoming Correspondence, LOC mss, in which Dupuy refers to "a letter to one of the Watson people at Cape Mount, sent by a servant here." For letters apparently written in the hand of freedpeople in Liberia, see Agnes Watson to Joseph Dupuy, 12 February 1861, and Allen Watson to Joseph Dupuy, 13 February 1861, in Dupuy Family Papers, 1810–66, Accounts of Joseph Dupuy and Robert J. Smith as Executors of John Watson, Prince Edward County, 1854–66, accession #21781c, p. 13, LVA mss. See Miller, *"Dear Master"*; Wiley, *Slaves No More*; Starobin, *Blacks in Bondage*, especially part 3; Blassingame, *Slave Testimony*, 61–111. Blassingame's collection includes a letter written by Lewis Johnson, an emancipated slave from Augusta County, Virginia, who accompanied the Watson freedpeople on their journey aboard the *M. C. Stevens* and settled with his wife Emma Johnson in Careysburg, Liberia; see ibid., 111–12.

78. McLain to Dupuy, 20 October 1856, ACS, Domestic Letters, Outgoing Correspondence, LOC mss.

79. See county court register of Cesar, dated 15 February 1858, Prince Edward County CoCt OB 27, 1853–1862/255, Prince Edward County courthouse, Farmville, Virginia. In the inventory of John Watson's Prince Edward estate, "Ceasar" was valued at $350, a price that exceeded that of others who were younger and, apparently, healthy. See "Inventory & appraisement of the personal & Perishable Estate of John

Watson . . ." 17 September 1855, Prince Edward County, CirCt Court Records, August 1854–August 1855, box 74, LVA mss.

80. "Register of the Emancipated Slaves of John Watson . . . ," Dupuy Family Papers, 1810–66, Personal Papers, Dupuy Account Book, 1856–65, accession #21780, pp. 163–72, especially 168, LVA mss.

81. McLeRoy and McLeRoy, *Strangers in Their Midst*, 24.

82. On Roberts and other Virginians who were active in the formation and expansion of Liberia, see Tyler-McGraw, *African Republic*, 151–70, especially 152–53.

83. Hickin, "Antislavery in Virginia," 1: 319. See also Ely, *Israel on the Appomattox*, 327, 330 ("specific tax"). It is interesting to note that in the years preceding the outbreak of the Civil War, the federal government too supported such training programs in Liberia with public dollars. Such training for freedpeople, especially at public expense, was unthinkable in the United States. See, for example, Fehrenbacher, *Slaveholding Republic*, 173–204.

84. "The Statement of two Emigrants returning to Slavery refuted," *African Repository* 34, no. 7 (July 1858): 199.

85. Ibid., 202.

86. Ely, *Israel on the Appomattox*, 558 n. 9, 345–401.

87. Many scholars contend that from 1806 to 1861, Virginia laws directed toward free blacks became increasingly harsh and restrictive, an assertion that is well supported by a chronological comparison of the text of the laws themselves. See, for example, Guild, *Black Laws of Virginia*, especially 96–122. A number of historians have looked at such laws and have concluded that Virginians—white and black—largely lived according to them; that whites passed and generally attempted to enforce laws aimed to restrict free blacks, and blacks generally abided by the same. For examples of scholars who have written well-documented histories of slavery and freedom in Virginia heavily based upon the text of law, see Ballagh, *History of Slavery in Virginia* and Ira Berlin, *Slaves without Masters*. Others have acknowledged state laws but focus instead on the frequency and severity of such laws' application. Melvin Patrick Ely concludes, "Life's realities emerge much more accurately from the authorities' day-to-day behavior than from laws recorded in statute books." See Ely, *Israel on the Appomattox*, 251 (quotation). See also McLeRoy and McLeRoy, *Strangers in Their Midst*. McLeRoy and McLeRoy write that though "the reins on free coloreds grew ever tighter" during the course of the nineteenth century, "state laws were often ignored or adapted to suit local conditions," and that "the extent to which this was true varied from an urban to a rural setting," 12 ("the reins"), 13 ("state laws").

88. Section 19 of the Virginia constitution of 1852 stated unambiguously that "slaves hereafter emancipated shall forfeit their freedom by remaining in the commonwealth more than twelve months after they become actually free, and shall be reduced to slavery under such regulations as may be prescribed by law." See *New Constitution of Virginia*. On the expulsion law, see *Code of Virginia*, 1849, 466.

89. *Code of Virginia*, 1849, 466.

90. According to Cesar's register, he was emancipated by the will of John Watson, dated 22 September 1854, and was recorded in the circuit court on 13 August 1856. It is clear, however, that Cesar did not gain his freedom until at least November 1857,

around the time when the others left for Liberia. I am using the latter date as the date of his emancipation; thus, by November 1857, Caesar would have been considered an illegal in the eyes of county officials. Typically, African Americans in Virginia were not prosecuted under the expulsion law until several years after they had become illegal. See Prince Edward County CoCt OB27, 1853–1862/255, Prince Edward County courthouse, Farmville, Virginia.

91. See Culpeper County WB R, 1847–1852/449, LVA microfilm; *African Repository* 27 [Dec. 1851]; Culpeper County CirCt OB 5, 1850–1856/272, LVA microfilm. Alison Goodyear Freehling concluded that Virginia's "free blacks remained unwilling to remove," because of "dismal accounts of famine, destitution, disease." Alison Goodyear Freehling, *Drift toward Dissolution*, 228 (quotations). See Bedford County Chancery, September 1859, 1859–036, Timothy Rogers ETC v. Daniel ETC., Bedford County courthouse, Bedford, Virginia; Bedford County CoCt OB 33, 1858–1861/400, LVA microfilm; Comm. v London Rogers, 27 November 1860, Bedford County Criminal, 1860–69, folder 1, Bedford County courthouse, Bedford, Virginia; Comm. v Phil Rogers, ibid.; Comm. v Bob Rogers, 27 November 1860, ibid.; Bedford County CoCt OB 33, 1858–1861/400, LVA microfilm.

92. Prince Edward County CoCt OB 27, 1853–1862/255, Prince Edward County courthouse, Farmville, Virginia.

93. See, for example, *Richmond Daily Dispatch*, "Something for Abolitionists to Reflect upon," 17 November 1856. The identical story ran in the *Daily Richmond Examiner*, p. 2, 18 November 1856.

94. See Culpeper County CirCt OB 6, 1856–1866/376, LVA microfilm (Peter); Culpeper County CoCt MB 23, 1853–1858/313, LVA microfilm (Dangerfield); Northumberland County CirCt OB 2, 1854–1877/103, LVA microfilm (Jerry Glascock); Lancaster County CirCt OB, 1854–1869/52–53, LVA microfilm (Armistead Currie).

95. See Bedford County CirCt OB 13, 1859–1866/191, LVA microfilm; Rogers, Daniel Pet. to become slave to Robert C. Mitchell, 25 April 1862, Bedford County FNSR, 1862, Bedford County courthouse, Bedford, Virginia (Daniel Rogers); Northumberland County CirCt OB 2, 1854–1877/230, LVA microfilm (Joseph Fry); Northumberland County CirCt OB 2, 1854–1877/230, LVA microfilm (Humphrey Kent, James Hughlett, James Cockanille [Cockanill/Cockarill], and Betty/Bettie Flynt); Northumberland County, Judgments, 1860 Apr–Petition of George Kent, LVA mss (George Kent); Rockbridge County CirCt OB, 1852–1867/432–33, LVA microfilm (Joshua Johnston); *Journal of the Senate*, 1855–56, 55 (Critty Woodson/Collier).

96. Applicants for a Passage to Liberia, 1 October 1853, ACS, Emigration, List of applicants for passage to Liberia, 1850–93, LOC mss.

97. In Daniel Rogers's 1862 petition for self-enslavement, his attorney, James F. Johnson, wrote that Daniel "has a wife and five children who are slaves the property of Robert C. Mitchell," his proposed owner. See Rogers, Daniel Pet. to become slave to Robert C. Mitchell, 25 April 1862, Bedford County FNSR, 1862, Bedford County courthouse, Bedford, Virginia. On Daniel's initial petition to the CoCt to remain in the state, see Bedford County CoCt OB 33, 1858–1861/220, LVA microfilm.

98. Bill, Bedford County Chancery, 1859–036, Timothy Rogers ETC v. Daniel ETC., Bedford County courthouse, Bedford, Virginia. It was alleged in this bill "that Daniel's

refusing to go was the cause of the other eighteen of the said Negroes remaining behind."

99. Bedford County CirCt OB 13, 1859–1866/191, LVA microfilm; Rogers, Daniel Pet. to become slave to Robert C. Mitchell, 25 April 1862, Bedford County FNSR, 1862, Bedford County courthouse, Bedford, Virginia; Bedford County CirCt OB 13, 1859–1866/202, LVA microfilm.

100. Account & Report of S. B. Burgess & B. C. Burgess Executor of the Will and Administration on the Estate of Benedict Burgess, decd., 1 Mar 1858, Benedict & Samuel Burgess, Exrs vs. Gamaliel T. Burgess, et als., Northumberland County Chancery, 1867-015, LVA mss. There was a precedent for such a decision. An untitled loose paper signed by "Critcher" in Benedict & Samuel Burgess, Exrs vs. Gamaliel T. Burgess, et als., Northumberland County Chancery, 1867-015, LVA mss, reads: "If your honor should be of opinion that the slaves of the decd. are emancipated unconditionally, comrs. might be appointed as in [Wlder vs Elder], 4 Leigh, to examine the slaves privily after explaining to each the provision of the will and the place of their destination, to ascertain whether they are willing to accept of their freedom, taking the election of the mother for her infant children." It cites "Code of '49. p. 465. s8."

101. Report of William Harding, W. C. Rice & Thomas Flynt Commissioners appointed to examine slaves belonging to the estate of B. Burgess, 6 April 1858, Benedict & Samuel Burgess, Exrs vs. Gamaliel T. Burgess, et als., Northumberland County Chancery, 1867–015, LVA mss. For Joseph Fry, see Northumberland County CirCt OB 2, 1854–1877/230, 257, LVA microfilm. For Humphrey Kent, James Hughlett, James Cockanille, and Betty Flynt, see Northumberland County CirCt OB 2, 1854–1877/230, 256, LVA microfilm. For George Kent, see Northumberland County, Judgments, 1860 Apr–Petition of George Kent, LVA mss.; Northumberland County CirCt OB 2, 1854–1877/275, LVA microfilm.

102. "Register of Coloured Members," dated 15 May 1844, Moratico Church, Lancaster County MB, 1844–79, VBHS. The author would like to thank Thomas A. Wolf of the Northumberland County Historical Society for clarifying the whereabouts of Armistead Currie and Jerry Glascock after the death of James Kelley. For Peter Miller, Stanton, Nelson Miller, and Dangerfield Alexander's use of Baptist church connections in their self-enslavement cases, see Gourdvine Church, Culpeper County, MB, 1812–32, n.p., entries of 15 April 1832, 15 September 1849, 16 September 1849, VBHS.

103. Petition of Jerry a free man of color, Northumberland County, Judgments, 1857 April, LVA mss; Northumberland County CirCt OB 2, 1854–1877/84, LVA microfilm.

104. See the awkwardly drawn "X" marked by Cesar on his petition for self-enslavement in Caesar Exparte Petition, 12 Aug 1858, Prince Edward County, CirCt Law Papers, March 1856–August 1858 [mislabeled; should be 1868], box 117, SRC. See also Prince Edward County, CirSupCt OB, 1853–1870/191, Prince Edward County courthouse, Farmville, Virginia; Prince Edward County CirSupCt MB, 1846–1870/n.p., entry dated 18 March 1858, SRC.

105. For a list of vessels that made landfall in Baltimore on 22 March 1858, including the M. C. Stevens, see Baltimore American & Commercial Advertiser, "Marine Intelligence," p. 1, 23 March 1858.

106. *Richmond Enquirer*, "Another Nut for the Abolitionists to Crack," p. 2, 2 April 1858.

107. The *Farmville Journal* article is described in "Liberty not worth having," *African Repository* 34, no. 6 (June 1858): 191.

108. For James Booker, see Prince Edward County, CoCt OB 27, 1853–1862/263, Prince Edward County courthouse, Farmville, Virginia. For William, see ibid., 262–63; William ex parte Petition, 15 March 1859, Prince Edward County, CirCt, Law Papers, March 1856–August 1858 [mislabeled; should be 1868], box 117, SRC.

109. *Code of Virginia*, 1849, 466.

110. Ruffin, *African Colonization Unveiled*, 14 (quotations); reprinted in *Debow's Review* 27 (1859):68.

111. Dupuy to McLain, 15 July 1858, ACS, Incoming Correspondence, Domestic Letters, LOC mss. For an analysis of ACS detractors in the 1850s, see Burin, *Peculiar Solution*, 117–120.

112. Dupuy to McLain, 19 April 1858, ACS, Incoming Correspondence, Domestic Letters, LOC mss.

113. Ibid.

114. McLain to Dupuy, 2[3?] April 1858, ACS, Incoming Correspondence, Domestic Letters, LOC mss. For an ACS rebuttal to allegations of slave trading in Liberia, see "(From the Richmond Whig)," *African Repository* 34, no. 8 (August 1858): 235–36.

115. See "Latest from Liberia," *African Repository* 34, no. 8 (August 1858): 243–45. For family relations of Lucy Booker, see "A List of Sixty Six negroes Emancipated by John Watson decd...." Prince Edward County Chancery, Dosha etc. vs. Exrs of John Watson, etc., 1873-001/cc, LVA mss. See also "Deaths," Dupuy Family Papers, 1810–66, Accounts of Joseph Dupuy and Robert J. Smith as Executors of John Watson, Prince Edward County, 1854–66, accession #21781c, p. 2, LVA mss.

116. Dupuy to McLain, 22 September 1858, ACS, Incoming Correspondence, Domestic Letters, LOC mss.

117. McLain to R. Stryker, 31 May 1858, ACS, Outgoing Correspondence, Letters to Liberia, 31 July 1856–7 March 1862, LOC mss.

118. McLain to H. N. Dennis, 31 May 1858, ACS, Outgoing Correspondence, Letters to Liberia, 31 July 1856–7 March 1862, LOC mss.

119. Alex M. Cowan, "The Statement of two Emigrants Returning to Slavery Refuted," *African Repository* 34, no. 7 (July 1858): 199–203 (quotations, 202).

120. Dupuy to McLain, 15 July 1858, ACS, Incoming Correspondence, Domestic Letters, LOC mss.

121. "Liberty not worth having," *African Repository* 34, no. 6 (June 1858): 191.

122. Dupuy to McLain, 15 July 1858, ACS, Incoming Correspondence, Domestic Letters, LOC mss.

123. R. Stryker to McLain, 30 July 1858, ACS, Incoming Correspondence, Letters from Liberia, 11 January 1858–29 February 1859, LOC mss. See also "A friend to A.C.S." to Member of the ACS, 2 August 1858, ACS, Incoming Correspondence, Letters from Liberia, 11 January 1858–29 February 1859, LOC mss.

124. Adam Watson, Limus Watson, Doctor Watson, Allen Watson, Henry Watson, Ryal Watson, Georg Watson, John W. White, Cornelius Watson to Executive Committee

of the ACS, 4 August 1858, ACS, Incoming Correspondence, Letters from Liberia, 11 January 1858–29 February 1859, LOC mss. The letter likely was dictated to Stryker or another ACS official in Robertsport, and its contents were perhaps heavily influenced by them, which casts some doubt on their credibility.

125. "The Rev. Edward Weir . . ." in *African Repository* 34 (1858): 328. McLain corrected the spelling and grammar of Weir's letter prior to publication in the *African Repository*. For the contents of Weir's original letter, see Rev E Weir to Executive Committee of ACS, 4 August 1858, ACS, Incoming Correspondence, Letters from Liberia, 11 January 1858–29 February 1859, LOC mss.

126. Wilson's letter is transcribed in Wiley, *Slaves No More*, 244–45 (quotations, 245). A heavily edited version appeared in the *African Repository*. See "From the Rev. J. A. Wilson, (who emigrated from Georgia.)," *African Repository* 34, no. 11 (November 1858): 332–33. For the original letter, see James W. Wilson to William McLain, 5 August 1858, ACS, Incoming Correspondence, Letters from Liberia, 11 January 1858–29 February 1859, LOC mss. Eric Burin concludes that the voices of naysayers like William Watson and James Booker were overpowered by Liberia's promoters. See Burin, *Slavery and the Peculiar Solution*, 73 n. 184, 154–55.

127. Ralph Moore to McLain, 5 August 1858, ACS, Incoming Correspondence, Letters from Liberia, 11 January 1858–29 February 1859, LOC mss. It appears from the letter's contents that McLain believed that Moore had a persistent drinking problem, which had been addressed by McLain at least on one occasion previously. For a description of the power struggles between Moore and Thomas Morris Chester in the management of the emigrant communities in Robertsport (as well as the allegations of drunkenness made against Moore), see Chester, *Thomas Morris Chester*, especially 20–24. Ralph Moore appeared in a census of Monrovia, Liberia, made by the U.S. government in 1845; he was twenty-six years old, it noted, "Reads and writes," and emigrated to Liberia with his brother and sister, Gabriel and Margaret Moore in April 1835. See *Tables Showing the Number of Emigrants*, 321 [also numbered as p. 150].

128. H. N. Dennis to McLain, 16 September 1858, ACS, Incoming Correspondence, Letters from Liberia, 11 January 1858–29 February 1859, LOC mss.

129. Richard Ford to McLain, 7 Aug 1858, ACS, Incoming Correspondence, Letters from Liberia, 11 January 1858–29 February 1859, LOC mss.

130. Eric Burin concludes that "many freedpersons were not content to waste away in such a dismal place" as Liberia; as a result, "hundreds quit" the colony and returned home. Three-eighths of those who left Liberia departed within the first twelve months of their settlement there. See Burin, *Peculiar Solution*, 144 (quotations). Cases of self-enslavement involving those who were supposed to have gone to Liberia (such as Cesar) indicate that even those who did not leave the state—but who had been directed to do so by their deceased masters—were tainted, as well.

131. Caesar ex parte Petition, 12 August 1858, Prince Edward County, CirCt, Law Papers, March 1856–August 1858 [mislabeled; should be 1868] ("there is no fraud"), box 117, SRC. See also Prince Edward County, CirSupCt OB, 1853–1870/200, Prince Edward County courthouse, Farmville, Virginia; Prince Edward County CirSupCt MB, 1846–1870/n.p., entry dated 12 Aug 1858, SRC; Dupuy Family Papers, 1810–66, Personal Papers, Dupuy Account Book, 1856–65, accession #21780, p. 171, LVA mss; Au-

ditor of Public Accounts, Voluntary Enslavement Reports, 1857–60, 12 August 1858, LVA microfilm. Cesar's self-enslavement was reported in a small item in the *New York Times*, "Personal," p. 8, 22 April 1858.

132. For James's petition, see James ex parte Petition, 18 August 1858, Prince Edward County, CirCt, Law Papers, March 1856–August 1858 [mislabeled; should be 1868], box 117, SRC. See also Prince Edward County, CirSupCt OB, 1853–1870/211, Prince Edward County courthouse, Farmville, Virginia. For William's petition, see William ex parte Petition, 15 March 1859, Prince Edward County, CirCt, Law Papers, March 1856–August 1858 [mislabeled; should be 1868], box 117, SRC. See also Prince Edward County, CirSupCt OB, 1853–1870/211, Prince Edward County courthouse, Farmville, Virginia.

133. Emily Howe Dupuy became aware of the voluntary enslavement law at some point, and wrote herself a copy of the law in its entirety. See Law Relating to Free Negroes Becoming Slaves, n.d., Virginia Historical Society, Watkins Family Papers, 1801–1960, section 5, Mss1W3286a24. On Emily Dupuy, see Adams, "New England Teacher."

134. Dupuy to McLain, 25 February 1859, ACS, Incoming Correspondence, Domestic Letters, LOC mss.

135. Prince Edward County Chancery, Dosha etc. vs. Exrs of John Watson, etc., 1873–001/cc, LVA mss.

136. Limus Watson and others to Joseph Dupuy, 7 February 1859, Dupuy Family Papers, 1810–66, Accounts of Joseph Dupuy and Robert J. Smith as Executors of John Watson, Prince Edward County, 1854–66, Memo of James Watson's Will & estate, on Record, 22 December 1824, accession #21781c, LVA mss.

137. Ibid.

138. Dupuy to McLain, 25 February 1859, ACS, Incoming Correspondence, Domestic Letters, LOC mss.

139. Prince Edward County, CirSupCt OB, 1853–1870/226, Prince Edward County courthouse, Farmville, Virginia; see also Prince Edward County CirSupCt MB, 1846–1870/n.p., entry dated 15 Mar 1859, SRC; Dupuy Family Papers, 1810–66, Personal Papers, Dupuy Account Book, 1856–65, accession #21780, p. 171, LVA mss.

140. Emily Howe Dupuy paid $425 to the court, one-half the assessed value of Booker. See Prince Edward County, CirSupCt OB, 1853–1870/246, Prince Edward County courthouse, Farmville, Virginia; see also Prince Edward County CirSupCt MB, 1846–1870/n.p., entry dated 16 August 1859, SRC; Dupuy Family Papers, 1810–66, Personal Papers, Dupuy Account Book, 1856–65, accession #21780, p. 171, LVA mss.

141. George Watson and others to Joseph Dupuy, 27 August 1859, Dupuy Family Papers, 1810–66, Accounts of Joseph Dupuy and Robert J. Smith as Executors of John Watson, Prince Edward County, 1854–66, accession #21781c, LVA mss.

142. Dupuy to R. L. Stryker (unsent), 25 September 1860, Dupuy Family Papers, 1810–66, Accounts of Joseph Dupuy and Robert J. Smith as Executors of John Watson, Prince Edward County, 1854–66, accession #21781c, LVA mss.

143. Dupuy to McLain, 28 September 1860, ACS, Incoming Letters, LOC mss.

144. William McLain to Joseph Dupuy, 1 October 1860, Dupuy Family Papers, 1810–66, Accounts of Joseph Dupuy and Robert J. Smith as Executors of John Watson, Prince Edward County, 1854–66, accession #21781c, LVA mss.

145. Agnes Watson to Joseph Dupuy, 12 February 1861, Dupuy Family Papers, 1810–66, Accounts of Joseph Dupuy and Robert J. Smith as Executors of John Watson, Prince Edward County, 1854–66, accession #21781c, LVA mss.

146. "James Booker" and "Wm. Watson" or "William Watson" lived in Prince Edward County in 1866 and 1867. See Prince Edward County PPTBs 1866 and 1867, LVA microfilm. A seventy-six-year-old "Caesar Watson" lived in Prince Edward County in 1866. See Prince Edward County Cohabitation Register, 1866, LVA mss.

CHAPTER SIX

1. African Americans separated during the Civil War made extraordinary efforts to maintain family connections over great distances. See, for example, Berlin and Rowland, *Families and Freedom*, 21–53. Many newly emancipated men and women used the opportunity of war to reunite themselves with family members from whom they had been separated in slavery. See Litwack, *Been in the Storm So Long*, 229–37. Efforts to locate family members continued for years after the Civil War ended. See Williams, *Help Me to Find My People*, especially 139–88. When possible, the enslaved fled their bondage during the war in family units. See Gutman, *Black Family in Slavery and Freedom*, 267–69; Swint, *Dear Ones at Home*, 88–94.

2. Letter to William H. Payne from R. A. Rector, 21 May 1889, Fauquier County Chancery, 1897-02, Exr of CR Ayres v. W. Kemp Flowerree, LVA online.

3. See Edmonds and Baird, *Journals of Amanda Virginia Edmonds*; Fauquier County CoCt MB, 1859–1865/323, 334, LVA microfilm; McPherson, *Battle Cry of Freedom*, 339–50, especially 341.

4. In September 1861 the assistant quartermaster of the Army of Mississippi petitioned the Fauquier County court to allow him to use the basement of the courthouse as a hospital. See Fauquier County CoCt MB, 1859–1865/343, LVA microfilm.

5. On the reshuffling of the court's priorities and resources, see Fauquier County CoCt MB, 1859–1865/317, 323, 332, 335, 343, 392, LVA microfilm. On 6 June 1861, Amanda Virginia Edmonds noted in her diary, "We are expecting an attack every day at the Junction (Manassas Junction), ordered our hands out to assist in throwing up a breast-work. Jack and our hands with others from the neighborhood start in the morning bright and early." See Edmonds and Baird, *Journals of Amanda Virginia Edmonds*, 50 (quotation). On 23 July 1861, the Fauquier County court echoed a state law that had been passed earlier that month in Richmond that ordered "that the clerk of this Court do enroll the male free Negroes of the County between the ages of Eighteen and fifty years." See Fauquier County CoCt MB, 1859–1865/335, LVA microfilm. On free and enslaved Virginians employed and conscripted by the Confederate military, see Jordan, *Black Confederates and Afro-Yankees*, especially 58–62. For details on Virginia's conscription laws and their effects on free black Virginians, see Brewer, *Confederate Negro*, especially 6–14.

6. On the effects of national politics and the actions of Union forces upon the daily lives of the enslaved and "the circulation of news and rumor" throughout the South more generally, see Hahn, *Nation under Our Feet*, 66 (quotation). For instances of wartime disorder in Virginia, see Bedford County CirCt OB 13, 1859–1866/215–16, 233,

LVA microfilm; Charles City County CirCt OB, 1853–1863/n.p., 19 November 1863, LVA microfilm; Essex County CirCt OB 3, 1856–1864/568–70, LVA microfilm; Greene County CirCt OB 3, 1857–1874/146, LVA microfilm; Albemarle County CirCt OB, 1857–1865/532, 553, LVA microfilm; Rockbridge County CirCt OB, 1852–1867/463, LVA microfilm; Augusta County CirCt OB 7, 1859–1866/280, LVA microfilm; Highland County CirCt OB 2, 1861–1879/37, LVA microfilm; Botetourt County CirCt OB, 1857–1878/177–78, LVA microfilm; Northumberland County CoCt, OB, 1861–1871/68, LVA microfilm.

7. Bill of Wm H. Payne, N.D., Fauquier County Chancery, 1897–02, Exr of CR Ayres v. W. Kemp Flowerree, LVA online.

8. Deposition of Nellie B. Slocum, 29 November 1889, Fauquier County Chancery, 1897–02 ("Betty"), Exr of CR Ayres v. W. Kemp Flowerree, LVA online; Ben and Bill: Deposition of Fanny N.C. Lawrence, 9 October 1871, Fauquier County Chancery, 1897–02, Exr of CR Ayres v. W. Kemp Flowerree, LVA online.

9. At least one of the children whom Ayres fathered with an enslaved woman named Mary Fletcher was called "'Rufus Ayres' on account of her likeness to her father." See deposition of Catherine S. Lawrence, 9 October 1871, Fauquier County Chancery, 1897–02, Exr of CR Ayres v. W. Kemp Floweree, LVA online. On the circumstances of Ayres's death, see Petition of Wm H. Payne, 4 September 1889 ("in a street fight"), Fauquier County Chancery, 1897–02, Exr of CR Ayres v. W. Kemp Flowerree, LVA online; see Deposition of John A. Rumsey, 9 October 1871, Fauquier County Chancery, 1897–02, Exr of CR Ayres v. W. Kemp Flowerree, LVA online.

10. R. A. Rector recollected that "though Viana wrote to one of her friends that it had been said that she and Fannie were not whole sisters she seemed quite indignant and asked her to contradict it, what she of course could not do, but *they remained under the* impression that *they all* had *one father*." See letter to William H. Payne from R. A. Rector, Fauquier County Chancery, 1897–02, Exr of CR Ayres v. W. Kemp Flowerree, LVA online.

11. Fauquier County WB 28, 1858–1860/274, LVA microfilm; Will of C. R. Ayres, 28 July 1857, Fauquier County Chancery, 1897–02, Exr of CR Ayres v. W. Kemp Flowerree, LVA online.

12. Will of C R Ayres, 28 July 1857, Fauquier County Chancery, 1897–02, Exr of CR Ayres v. W. Kemp Flowerree, LVA online.

13. Bill of Wm H. Payne, n.d. Fauquier County Chancery, 1897–02, Exr of CR Ayres v. W. Kemp Flowerree, LVA online.

14. Comth Report, 14 March 1871, Fauquier County Chancery, 1897–02, Exr of CR Ayres v. W. Kemp Flowerree, LVA online.

15. The removal of emancipated slaves from the state frequently proved challenging for executors throughout the nineteenth century, as time and again freedpeople refused to leave their loved ones and their Virginia communities behind. See, for example, Chesterfield County WB 19, 1850–1852/158–59, LVA microfilm; Petition of Elizabeth & Others, 14 April 1856, Watkins, Adr. of Sarah Branch (Decd) Petition, November 1873, Chesterfield County Chancery, 1873–033, box 75, LVA mss; and Report of W. L. Watkins, October 1856, Watkins, Adr. of Sarah Branch (Decd) Petition, November 1873, Chesterfield County Chancery, 1873–033, box 75, LVA mss.

16. Occasionally free blacks were charged with illegally entering Virginia, especially those who had left the commonwealth and had returned from the North. Luther Porter Jackson concluded, "This law, forbidding the return of free Negroes who had left the state to be educated, appears to have been enforced." See Jackson, *Free Negro Labor*, 21 n. 47 (quotation). Less common were charges against whites for "bringing a free negro . . . into this state." See Gloucester County CirCt MB, 1854–1859/n.p. [14 April 1857] (quotation), LVA microfilm.

17. In the 1860 federal census, Fauquier County is listed with a population of 821 "free colored" men and women, who made up nearly 3.8 percent of the county's total population. Though the number of those individuals who had been emancipated or born of parents freed since 1806 is unknown, it is likely that a majority of Fauquier's free black population lived there in violation of the expulsion law of 1806. See Blomberg, "Free Black Adaptive Responses," 37.

18. Cashin, "Landscape and Memory in Antebellum Virginia," 499. See also Calomiris and Schweikart, "The Panic of 1857," 807–34; Ó Gráda and White, "The Panics of 1854 and 1857," 213–40.

19. Ehrlich, "Origins of the Dred Scott Case," 132–42. See also William W. Freehling, *Road to Disunion*, vol. 2, especially 109–11, 271–72, 118–19.

20. Freehling, *Road to Disunion*, 2: 112–13, 154–55, 185–201.

21. *Daily Richmond Enquirer*, "On the Necessity of Removing or Reducing to Slavery the Free Negroes of the Commonwealth [no. II]," p. 2, col. 3 (quotations), 8 August 1857.

22. *Daily Richmond Enquirer*, "Free Negroes, &c," p. 2, col. 2, 10 August 1857.

23. *Daily Richmond Enquirer*, "On the Necessity of Removing or Reducing to Slavery the Free Negroes of the Commonwealth [no. V]," p. 2, col. 3 (quotations), 28 August 1857. Portions of this series of articles in the *Daily Richmond Enquirer* were reprinted in several newspapers throughout the eastern United States in the fall of 1857. For example, see *Liberator* (Boston), "On the Necessity of Removing or Reducing to Slavery the Free Negroes of the Commonwealth," p. 1, col. D, 11 December 1857.

24. *Daily Richmond Enquirer*, "The Free Negro Question," p. 2, col. 5 (quotations), 17 October 1857.

25. *Daily Richmond Enquirer*, "King William County," p. 2, col. 2 (quotation), 22 September 1857. See also ibid., "'Ollin' on the Removal of the Free Negroes of Virginia," p. 2., col. 2, 20 October 1857.

26. "Gov. Henry A. Wise's Address to General Assembly," in *Journal of the House of Delegates*, 1857–58, 151 ("This class," "emancipated either," "by a spirit," "But what"), 152 ("They are," "more humane," "more just," "to take," "We ought"), 152–53 ("that a free negro").

27. *Journal of the House of Delegates*, 1857–58, 29.

28. Ibid., 133 (quotation).

29. *Journal of the Senate*, 1857–58, 296.

30. Ibid., 448 (quotation).

31. *New York Herald*, "Our Virginia Correspondence," p. 8, col. A (quotation), 1 February 1858. See a similar article published as "Free negroes in Virginia," *Mississippian and State Gazette*, p. 1, col. c, 3 March 1858.

32. *Journal of the House of Delegates*, 1857–58, 260 (quotation).

33. *South-Side Democrat*, "Removal of the Free Negro Population," 3 February 1858 (quotations).

34. Ibid., "Free Negro Sympathy!" 6 February 1858 (quotation).

35. Ira Berlin writes that in Virginia in 1858, "The movement for expulsion failed again, but the tone of the debate revealed a much more favorable attitude toward enslavement than before. Many legislators now demanded enslavement of free blacks, not as a last resort, but as the first." See Ira Berlin, *Slaves without Masters*, 371 (quotation). Though extremists were more vocal by 1858 than they had been earlier in the decade, the proportion of Virginia legislators in 1858 who were radicals on removal and re-enslavement appears to have been only slightly higher than in 1853.

36. For specific examples of local enforcement of the expulsion law during a twelve-month period from fall 1857 to fall 1858, see Chapter 5.

37. Archie and Mima failed to appear in court to respond to the allegations made against them. The county clerk concluded, "They have left the Commonwealth of Virginia" and dropped the charges. Their case proved how effective the law could be at removing free blacks from Virginia, even if its enforcement resulted in nonprosecution and dismissal. See Fauquier County CirCt OB F, 1854–1860/262, 306 (quotation), LVA microfilm.

38. Sarah Ann Shepherd's case lasted nearly two years, from indictment to dismissal. See Fauquier County CoCt MB, 1857–1859/107, 163, 312, 344 ("the said Sarah"), LVA microfilm; Fauquier County CoCt MB, 1859–1865/105, LVA microfilm. Shepherd and her eight children (Martha, Frederick, Staunton, Aaron, Susan Frances, Sylva Ann, John Wilson, and Charles William) were eventually permitted to register with the court and to stay in the county, though as illegals. See Fauquier County CoCt MB, 1859–1865/5, 6, LVA microfilm.

39. In contrast to the duration of the case against Sarah Ann Shepherd above, that against Eliza Payne took only three days. See Fauquier County CoCt MB, 1857–1859/210, 222, LVA microfilm. Eliza Payne's children, Richard and Syphax, ages four and six, were ordered to be bound to James W. Holland until they reached the age of twenty-one. See Fauquier County CoCt MB, 1857–1859/240, LVA microfilm.

40. Fauquier County CoCt MB, 1857–1859/306, LVA microfilm.

41. Petition of Annah Gleaves Poters, Fauquier County Chancery, 1861–042, LVA online.

42. Petition of Jane Payne, Fauquier County Chancery, 1861–044, LVA online.

43. Petition of Mary Fletcher, Fauquier County Chancery, 1861–043, LVA online.

44. Sinah Ambers Petition to Become a Slave, Loudoun County Free Black Papers Series, 1857–33, Loudoun County courthouse, Leesburg, Va.

45. Richmond City CirCt OB 6, 1859–1860/103, LVA microfilm.

46. Petition of Lavinia Napper, Fauquier County Chancery, 1859–080, LVA online; Fauquier County CirCt OB F, 1854–1860/398, LVA microfilm.

47. Petition of John Martin, October 1857, Albemarle County, FNSR, 1796–1870 ca., box 2, LVA mss.

48. Petition of Satchel Grayson, Albemarle County FNSR, 1796–1870 ca., box 2, LVA mss. (Note that there is no ended date on petition and petition was removed from court records for filing in the FNSR, so it lacks chronological context).

49. Petition of Dennis Holt, 24 October 1860, Campbell County FNSR, 1791–1867, box 4, LVA mss; "Thomas Hill (fn) Petition," Greensville County Common Law Papers, 1866 to 1867, Judgments Rendered in 1862 on Some of which Executions have not issued, Greensville County courthouse, Emporia, Virginia.

50. Wilkerson Lewis Petition, Amelia County, Various Records, 1857–59, box 10 ("wife now living"), folder "Wills, 1857, 1859," SRC; Rogers, "Daniel Pet. to become slave to Robert C. Mitchell," 25 April 1862, Bedford County FNSR, 1862 ("five children"), Bedford County courthouse, Bedford, Virginia.

51. Throughout the nineteenth century until the Civil War, Virginia lawmakers passed legislation designed to separate the social worlds of free blacks and the enslaved. Though a number of scholars have asserted that freedom in the age of slavery created a division between freedpeople and the enslaved, Tommy L. Bogger, Bernard Powers, and Wilma King, among others, have shown more recently that slaves and free blacks "interacted freely and naturally." See King, "Out of Bounds," 127–44 (quotations, 129). Historian Midori Takagi appears to have correctly described relations in nineteenth-century Virginia: "While these laws may have prevented certain transactions from transpiring between free and slave residents, they could never completely separate the two. Free black and slave residents continued to worship, celebrate, and raise families together in spite of the increasing restrictions against such interaction." Takagi, *Rearing Wolves to Our Own Destruction*," 66. A survey of any of the existing cohabitation registers for Virginia counties made by the Freedmen's Bureau in 1866 shows the extent to which free and enslaved Virginians constructed meaningful lives together, despite the state's prohibition of legal marriage between individuals belonging to the two groups. For example, of the 146 couples listed who had been cohabiting before 1865 in the Richmond County register, 19 were combinations of free and enslaved men and women. By comparison, only slightly more of the couples listed (21) were unions between two free blacks. See Richmond County Register of Colored Persons Co-habitating, FNSR, box 2, LVA mss.

52. Hanover County CirCt OB, 1856–1868/287, Hanover County courthouse, Hanover, Virginia; 1860 federal census; Will of Elizabeth C. Clarke, 11 December 1865, Hanover County Chancery, 1867–005, N.B. Clarke vs. Trst(s) of Elizabeth B. Broil, LVA online; Hanover County CoCt WB 1, 1862–1868/101, 137, 274, 506–508, LVA microfilm.

53. Mary Roland: Rockbridge County CirCt OB, 1852–1867/368, LVA microfilm; Rockbridge County WB 8, 1837–1840/431, LVA microfilm. Joseph Fry, George Kent, Humphrey Kent, James Hughlett, James Cockanill, and Betty Flynt: Northumberland County CirCt OB 2, 1854–1877/256, LVA microfilm.

54. For example, Jerry Glascock of Northumberland County selected James W. Kelly, the nephew of his former owner, as his new master. See Northumberland County CirCt OB 2, 1854–1877/84, LVA microfilm; Northumberland County, Judgments, 1857 April–Petition of Jerry Glascock, LVA mss.. Elizabeth Taylor of Fauquier County chose to enslave herself to Charles B. Tebbs, the grandson of her former owner. See Fauquier County CirCt OB F, 1854–1860/204, LVA microfilm; Elizabeth, alias Betsy Taylor, Petition, Fauquier County Chancery, 1859–074, LVA online. Watkins (Watt) Love of Mecklenburg County asked that he be enslaved to James W. Love, the brother-in-law of his for-

mer owner. See Mecklenburg County CirCt OB 6, 1860–1867/26, LVA microfilm; will of Fleming J. Jeffress, Mecklenburg County WB 19, 1856–1859/465, LVA microfilm.

55. Petition of Lavinia Napper, Fauquier County Chancery, 1859–080, LVA online.

56. Fauquier County CirCt OB F, 1854–1860/398, LVA microfilm.

57. Fauquier County DB 58, 1859–1860/195, LVA microfilm.

58. Ibid.

59. Ibid.

60. See "Mary Philips, Exparte, Petition to go into Voluntary Slavery," 18 June 1866, Frederick County CirCt, Ended Causes, 1866–68, SRC.

61. Orange County CirCt OB, 1853–1867/384, Orange County courthouse, Orange, Virginia.

62. Lewis Wilkerson elected to enslave himself to James W. Ellis, the executor of his former owner's estate in Amelia County, as did Armistead Currie in Lancaster County (to Addison Hall), Araminta Frances in Lunenburg County (to John L. Coleman), and Mary in Culpeper County (to John H. Eggborn). Wilkerson: Amelia County WB 16, 1847–1851/309, LVA microfilm; Amelia County CirCt OB 5, 1853–1872/190, LVA microfilm. Currie: Lancaster County CirCt OB, 1854–1869/52–53, LVA microfilm; Will of James Kelley, Lancaster County Chancery, 1857–011, LVA online. Frances: Lunenburg County CoCt OB 30, 1849–1856/552, LVA microfilm; Lunenburg County WB 13, 1846–1851/432, LVA microfilm. Mary: Culpeper County CoCt MB 24, 1858–1864/225, LVA microfilm; Culpeper County WB U, 1857–1862/74, LVA microfilm.

63. Thomas Hill: Petition, Greensville County, Common Law Papers, 1866 to 1867, Judments Rendered in 1862 on some of which Executions have not issued, Greensville County courthouse, Emporia, Virginia; William Williamson: Campbell County CirCt OB 9, 1855–1867/222, LVA microfilm; Campbell County DB, 1852–1854/449, LVA microfilm. Levin Crippin: Accomack County CirCt OB, 1857–1866/69, LVA microfilm; 1850 federal census; 1860 federal census. Mike Ailstock: Albemarle County CirCt OB, 1857–1865/559, LVA microfilm; 1860 federal census. Thomas Goings: Augusta County CirCt OB 7, 1859–1866/215–16, LVA microfilm; 1860 federal census. Jane Horton: *Journal of the Senate*, Extra Session 1861, 115; 1860 federal census.

64. Celia Hale: Bedford County CirCt OB 11, 1854–1859/514, LVA microfilm; "Hale Celia pet. to become Slave & affdvt," 5 October 1858, Bedford County FNSR, 1850–59, Bedford County courthouse, Bedford, Virginia. Tom Squire: Halifax County CirCt OB 6, 1858–1866/444, LVA microfilm; 1860 federal census.

65. The inventory of Deboux Williamson listed only one enslaved individual: "one Negro Man named Billy," valued at $800. See Campbell County WB 8, 1836–1841/214–15, LVA microfilm.

66. Campbell County WB 8, 1836–1841/202–203 (quotation).

67. VGALP, Campbell County, 17 January 1851, reel 33, box 48, folder 49, LVA microfilm; 1870 federal census.

68. Campbell County PPTBs, 1843–49, LVA microfilm; Campbell County DB 9, 1810–1813/491–92, LVA microfilm. Thomas H. Rosser (along with Pleasant B. Rosser) conducted the inventory of Martha Williamson's estate upon her death. See Campbell County WB 9, 1841–1847/190–91, LVA microfilm.

69. VGALP, Campbell County, 17 January 1851, reel 33, box 48, folder 49, ("prosperous"), LVA microfilm. William Williamson purchased a 100-acre tract on "Gattoway Creek" in Campbell County from Joel and Nancy Rosser, but the purchase seems not to have been formalized for three years after Williamson took possession of it in 1850—perhaps to avoid notice by local tax commissioners. See Campbell County DB 29, 1852-1854/299-300, LVA microfilm; Campbell County CoCt OB, 1853-1858/38, LVA microfilm.

70. Campbell County Register of Free Negroes, 1801-1850/24 LVA microfilm.

71. VGALP, Campbell County, 17 January 1851, reel 33, box 48, folder 49, LVA microfilm.

72. Campbell County PPTB, 1853, LVA microfilm.

73. Order on Petition of William Williamson, Campbell County FNSR, 1791-1867, box 4 ("the information"), LVA mss. The deed that transferred William Williamson's property to Thomas H. Rosser explained Williamson's transfer of his vast property holdings for only five dollars in terms of his "natural love and affection" for Rosser. See Campbell County DB, 1852-1854/449 ("two horses"), LVA microfilm.

74. Bond, Rosser to Comm., Comm. v. Williamson, October 1858 in Campbell County FNSR, 1784-1867, box 1, LVA mss; Campbell County CirCt OB 9, 1855-1867 /311-12, LVA microfilm.

75. Campbell County CirCt OB 9, 1855-1867/301, LVA microfilm; Campbell County DB, 1852-1854/449, LVA microfilm; Campbell County Land Tax Book, 1855, LVA microfilm; Campbell County DB 35, 1868-1872/517-18, LVA microfilm. The circuit court's case against Williamson was dismissed soon after his enslavement to Rosser. See Campbell County CirCt OB 9, 1855-1867/314, LVA microfilm. Other petitioners for self-enslavement maintained lasting connections with their chosen owners. For example, Thomas Grayson of Culpeper County had chosen Charles W. Rixey as his owner in 1856 and still lived or worked on Rixey's plantation in 1869. See Culpeper County CoCt MB 23, 1853-1858/282-83, 313, LVA microfilm; Culpeper County PPTB 1869, LVA microfilm.

76. The three women's expectations of life as self-enslaved individuals are clear from their later rejection of the terms of absolute, unconditional enslavement presented to them during proceedings in the Fauquier Circuit Court. The law directed that once enslaved, "the condition of the petitioner shall in all respects be the same as though such negro had been born a slave," a condition that each woman subsequently rejected. See "An ACT Providing for the Voluntary Enslavement of the Free Negroes of the Commonwealth," *Acts of the General Assembly*, 1855-56, 37 (quotation).

77. By 1860 Virginia law prohibited free blacks from holding public office, voting, serving as jurors, possessing weapons, participating in the Virginia militia, moving freely within the state without registering with the courts, and—along with the enslaved—testifying against whites in court because of their race. Evidence of the second-class status of free blacks in Virginia before and during the Civil War abounds. When analyzing Virginia law directed at free people of color in Virginia at the time, it would be difficult to disagree with those legal scholars who characterize it as anything but "tragic oppression." See Higginbotham and Bosworth, "'Rather than the Free,'" 63 (quotation). Nonetheless, recent scholars of the free black experience in Virginia have found that in the everyday lives of people of color during the nineteenth century,

freedom meant a great deal to those individuals who attained it. Melvin Patrick Ely writes that a free person of color who had experienced both slavery and freedom "knew how much even his imperfect freedom was worth. No one could buy or sell him or separate him from his wife and children. A slave could not buy, sell, bequeath, or inherit property." See Ely, *Israel on the Appomattox*, 10–11 (quotation). On the significance of property to free blacks in Virginia, see Ellen Katz, "African-American Freedom," 933–34; Schwarz, *Migrants against Slavery*, 13–14; Lebsock, *Free Women of Petersburg*, 112–45; Jackson, *Free Negro Labor*.

78. In her examination of self-enslavement cases in Louisiana, Judith Kelleher Schafer concluded, "Even if a prospective owner promised not to treat one as a slave, those who enslaved themselves had no way to enforce such a promise, since slaves could only initiate suits for freedom—an action courts would find specious after self-enslavement." See Schafer, *Becoming Free, Remaining Free*, 153–54. Despite the threat posed by potential enforcement of restrictive laws and their status as women in a male-centered legal system, many free women of color in nineteenth-century Virginia were able to defy the odds as successful property owners by avoiding marriage, which would have transferred control over their interests to their husbands. See Lebsock, *Free Women of Petersburg*, especially 89–100. For an examination into the meaning of freedom to free women of color in towns in the Deep South, see Virginia Meacham Gould, *Chained to the Rock of Adversity*, xix–xxxi.

79. For an example of such indifference expressed by a proposed owner toward one woman's interest in self-enslavement, see "Hale Celia pet. to become Slave & affdvt," 5 October 1858, Bedford County FNSR, 1850–59, Bedford County courthouse, Bedford, Virginia.

80. It is possible, though not likely, that in other instances, prospective owners saw the acquisition of self-enslaved individuals in a different light; the acquisition of additional *real property* might increase one's social standing in the county, and, if times got tough, could generate wealth for a prospective master (through their hires, industry, or, if necessary, sale) on a scale far greater than the initial investment required for self-enslavement. For some slaveholders at the time, the acquisition of slaves "held dreams of transformative possibilities" and allowed them to gain increased prestige in society. See Johnson, *Soul by Soul*, 78 (quotation). I have found no evidence for this attitude from prospective owners in self-enslavement cases, however.

81. Exhibit C, letter from James S. Green to Wm H. Payne, 6 April 1861, Fauquier County Chancery, 1897-02, Exr of CR Ayres v. W. Kemp Flowerree, LVA online.

82. See "An ACT Providing for the Voluntary Enslavement of the Free Negroes of the Commonwealth," *Acts of the General Assembly*, 1855–56, 37. Virginia's circuit court judges respected the law's child protection clause and often went out of their way to protect the legal freedom of and to make arrangements for petitioner's free children. For example, when Adeline Stewart enslaved herself to James J. Tinsley in Pittsylvania County in October 1856, the court clerk noted, "But the above order is not in any manner to affect the rights or liberty of Thomas, Bettie and James three children of the said Adaline the first named being between five and Six years of age the second between four and five and the third one year old the 20th day this month all of whom are black." See Pittsylvania County CirCt OB 8, 1854–59/278 (quotation), LVA microfilm.

83. Lunenburg County OB 30, 1849–1856/553, LVA microfilm.

84. Fauquier County CoCt MB, 1856–1857/297 ("as apprentices"), LVA microfilm; Fauquier County CirCt OB F, 1854–1860/204, 322, LVA microfilm; Elizabeth, alias Betsy Taylor, Petition, Fauquier County Chancery, 1859–074, LVA online.

85. "Hale Celia pet. to become Slave & affdvt," 5 October 1858, Bedford County FNSR, 1850–59, Bedford County courthouse, Bedford, Virginia.

86. It was common for free African Americans in Virginia to bind out or apprentice their children to local whites during the first half of the nineteenth century. See Ellen D. Katz, "African-American Freedom," especially 938–39. Virginia's county courts also initiated such arrangements and thus cannot be assumed to have been voluntary. See, for example, Fauquier County CoCt MB, 1856–1857/111, 162, 227, LVA microfilm; Fauquier County CoCt MB, 1859–1865/94, LVA microfilm; Washington County CoCt MB 12, 1855–1857/187, LVA microfilm. In his exhaustive study of free black life in Goochland County, Virginia, Reginald Dennin Butler concluded that "free black apprenticeship was largely a compulsory institution in Virginia." See Butler, "Evolution of a Rural Black Community," especially 195–96 (quotation).

87. Among the petitions for self-enslavement heard in Richmond after the general law of 1856 had passed was that of "Susan and her children" in Rappahannock County. See *Journal of the House of Delegates*, 1855–56, 448.

88. For the successful petitions of George, Shed, Sam, Sukey of Buckingham County and Thomas Garland (or Gardner) and Mary Anderson of Hanover County, see *Acts of the Virginia General Assembly*, 1861, 251–53.

89. Mary had been manumitted by the will of Nelson Colvin, who instructed that "Mary and all of her decendant" be freed upon his death. See Culpeper County WB U, 1857–1862/74 (quotation), LVA microfilm. Mary's bill for self-enslavement was at first rejected in the Virginia Senate, but eventually passed in February 1860. She enslaved herself and her children to John H. Eggborn in the Culpeper County court on 17 April 1860. See *Journal of the House of Delegates*, 1859–60, 71, 201, 317, 321; *Journal of the Senate*, 1859–60, 139, 143, 147, 159, 253; Culpeper County CoCt MB 24, 1858–1864/222, 225, LVA microfilm. For the names of Mary's children see ibid., 225.

90. A resolution to amend the self-enslavement law of 1856 was introduced on 21 January 1861, the same day that the Committee for Courts and Justice presented Senate Bill 34, with the same objective. *Journal of the House of Delegates*, 1861, 70; *Journal of the Senate*, 1861, 94. See also ibid., Extra Session 1861, 171.

91. For an explanation of the political dynamics present in Richmond during the first few months of 1861, see Link, *Roots of Secession*, especially 223–44.

92. Edmund Ruffin, one of the more articulate pro-slavery propagandists of the era, insisted, "If all the free negroes of Virginia were compelled to choose between emigrating to Liberia, or to be sold to the highest bidder, into perpetual slavery, three-fourths of them, at least, would deliberately choose the latter alternative." See Ruffin, *African Colonization Unveiled*, 14 (quotation). Virginia Senator Robert Mercer Taliaferro Hunter similarly pushed for a system of mandatory enslavement for the state's free blacks, "because their removal from the State would be either impossible, or would be rejected by the persons concerned, and old enough to choose." He added, "In most

of such cases, the mother would greatly prefer enslavement for herself and her children, whom she was unable to support, to exile." See Robert Hunter, "Department of Miscellany," *DeBow's Review and Industrial Resources, Statistics, etc.* 5, no. 1 (January 1861): 114 (quotation).

93. *Daily National Era* (Washington, DC), "Washington Items," p. 22, 11 February 1858.

94. E. C. Burks to Rowland D. Buford, 6 March 1861, in *American Historical Review* 31, no. 1 (October 1925): 92.

95. *Philadelphia Inquirer*, "Free Negroes in Virginia," p. 8, 30 March 1861.

96. *Journal of the House of Delegates*, 1861, 179 (quotation).

97. E. C. Burks to Rowland D. Buford, 6 March 1861, in *American Historical Review* 31, no. 1 (October 1925): 92 (quotation).

98. For the names and approximate birth dates of the children of Payne, Fletcher, and Poters, see deposition of Nellie B. Slocum, Fauquier County Chancery, 1897–02, Exr of CR Ayres v. W. Kemp Flowerree, LVA online (Nellie B. Payne); "Comth Report," 10 April 1880, Fauquier County Chancery, 1897–02, Exr of CR Ayres v. W. Kemp Flowerree, LVA online (Viana Fletcher, Fanny Fletcher, Sally Fletcher); letter from C. Minnigerode to W. H. Payne, 17 March 1875; and deposition of Selina Peters [Poters], 19 October 1889, both in Fauquier County Chancery, 1897–02, Exr of CR Ayres v. W. Kemp Flowerree, LVA online.

99. "An ACT for the Voluntary Enslavement of Free Negroes, without Compensation to the Commonwealth," *Acts of the General Assembly*, 1861, 52–53, especially 52 ("to have").

100. Another addition to the law of 1861 allowed the owner of "any free negro heretofore voluntarily enslaved" under the law of 1856 to have "the same right to the custody, control and services of any infant child or children" on the same terms provided for above. In such a case, masters or mistresses were required to "appear before a court of record, and make claim to such custody, control and services." Children who had been bound out already by the overseers of the poor, however, were exempt from the provision. See *Acts of the General Assembly*, 1861, 53 (quotation).

101. Ibid., 52 (quotation).

102. *Weekly Anglo-African*, "Virginia's Last Crime," (quotation), 6 April 1861.

103. The self-enslavement law of 1861 received only minor mention in Virginia's newspapers at the time of its passage. See, for example, *Daily Richmond Enquirer*, "House of Delegates," p. 3, col. 1, 14 March 1861; ibid., "Senate," p. 3, col. 6, 28 March 1861; *Richmond Whig and Public Advertiser*, "House of Delegates," p. 2, col. 3, 14 March 1861; ibid., "Virginia Legislature," p. 2, col. 3, 28 March 1861; *Richmond Daily Dispatch*, "House of Delegates," p. 1, col. 2, 14 March 1861; ibid., "The Legislature," p. 2, col. 2, 28 March 1861.

104. William Goens applied to the Augusta County Circuit Court for self-enslavement on 1 November 1864. His application was approved, and he was enslaved to Sammuel Kennerly Jr. the same day. See Augusta County CirCt OB 7, 1859–1866/329, LVA microfilm.

105. Richmond County CirCt OB, 1858–1874/233–34, especially 234 ("have and take"), Richmond County courthouse, Warsaw, Virginia. It is clear that the dollar

amounts ascribed to the future service of Eliza Ann, Sarah, and Littleton were negotiated on the spot. See the edited and seemingly improvised numbers written in the bond of A. F. Yerby and A. O. Yerby made at the conclusion of Priscilla Rich's self-enslavement case, Yerby &c. to Commonwealth, Bond, 25 October 1861, Richmond County Loose Papers, 1849, 1853–68, box 19, SRC. Other instances of free women enslaving themselves while binding their children during the Civil War include two self-enslavement cases in Sussex County in April 1864. Coriceda Reid bound her three young children, John (aged three), Mary (aged two), and Grace (only five months old) to James R. Graves, her new owner. The same day, Martha Reid bound her two infant daughters, Elizabeth (aged two) and an unnamed "female child" born that year, to her chosen owner James D. Howle. See Sussex County CirCt OB, 1831–1866/415–16, Sussex County courthouse, Sussex, Virginia.

106. One of Betsy Stevens's sons, Thomas Taylor Stevens, had been bound out to Stephen D. Tucker several months earlier than were the others. Betsy Stevens also had another son, James Stevens, whom she had bound previously to Captain J. P. Barksdale. See Halifax County CoCt MB 20, 1863–1866/97, LVA microfilm. For the record of Stevens and Hancock's self-enslavement in the Halifax County Circuit Court, see Halifax County CirCt OB 6, 1858–1866/474 (quotations), LVA microfilm; see also Halifax County CirCt Wills & Bonds 2–A, 1857–1878/174–75, Halifax County courthouse, Halifax, Virginia. Legal apprenticeship posed its own risks to free children of color who found themselves bound to others. Four years into Laura Taylor's servitude, for example, the Fauquier County court gave Charles B. Tebbs permission "to remove said apprentice Laura Taylor from this County to reside in the County of Augusta Virginia." Such relocations of free and enslaved individuals could occur without warning, frustrating attempts by family members to maintain proximity to one another. See Fauquier County CoCt MB, 1857–1859/294 (quotation), LVA microfilm.

107. Green, *This Business of Relief*, especially 74 ("the poor"), 75 ("Even in").

108. Register in Albemarle County Court, FNSR, 1796–1870 ca., box 2, LVA mss.

109. Albemarle County CoCt MB, 1856–1859/17, LVA microfilm.

110. "A list of the names of persons, and the value of property owed by each, returned delinquent for the nonpayment of taxes, for the year 1863," Albemarle County, Civil War Era, Tax & Fiscal, 1858–70, box 10, p. 4, LVA mss.

111. Albemarle County CirCt OB, 1857–1865/528; Albemarle County Court, FNSR, 1796–1870 ca., box 2, LVA mss. For Benjamin F. Abell's slaveholdings, see 1860 federal census and slave schedule, Albemarle County, Virginia.

112. It is unclear whether or not Ailstock had been the son of a free-born woman. Albemarle County CirCt OB, 1857–1865/559, LVA microfilm. "Mike Ale stock," and seventy-four other free black males appear on a list of those to be notified by the Albemarle County sheriff "to meet at the Court House on the 2nd. Monday in September" 1861 to report for service to the Confederate Army. See Albemarle County Military & Pension, 1785–1919, box 1 (quotations), LVA mss.

113. Shepherd S. Moore agreed to pay the debts and liabilities of Ailstock "existing before his enslavement." See Albemarle County Court, FNSR, 1796–1870 ca., box 2 (quotation), LVA mss; Albemarle County CirCt OB, 1857–1865/559, LVA microfilm. See also 1860 federal census, Albemarle County, Virginia.

114. 1850 federal census, Louisa County, Virginia ("Laborer"). Nicholas Poindexter's register of 1850 stated that he "was born free in the County of Louisa." See Poindexter's register dated 25 December 1850, in Louisa County Free Negro Register, 1837–1865/74–75 (#399), LVA microfilm.

115. Louisa County PPTBs [Commissioner of the Revenue Quarles's list] for 1851, 1852, 1853; "List of Free Negroes, over 12 years of age, within the district of the undersigned Com. Rev. in the year 1852," Louisa County FNSR, 1770–1864, box 1, LVA mss; "A List of free Negroes returned delinquent for the non payment of taxes at August Court," Louisa County FNSR, 1770–1864, box 1, LVA mss. The fact that Poindexter did not pay his taxes in 1851 does not necessarily mean that he was unable to pay. Melvin Patrick Ely shows that in Prince Edward County, at about the same time, "neither white nor black tax delinquents were invariably poor"; that many who could have paid simply did not. See Ely, *Israel on the Appomattox*, 327 (quotation).

116. Nicholas Poindexter appears in Orange County tax lists in 1854, 1859, 1860, and 1861. See Orange County PPTBs, 1854–61, LVA microfilm.

117. Poindexter's second register in the Louisa County court, dated 9 September 1856, reads almost identically to that recorded by the same court in 1850. Louisa County Free Negro Register, 1837–1865/161 (#562), LVA microfilm.

118. Orange County CirCt OB, 1853–1867/384, Orange County courthouse, Orange, Virginia.

119. Coriceda Reid and Martha Reid were the daughters of Fannie Reid (or Read), a granddaughter of Jemima Read, who was a free woman by 1800. Louisa Myrick had inherited her freedom from those emancipated by Howell Myrick before 1798. Billy Barlow and Arthur Barlow were likely the grandsons of Phoebe Barlow, who had been emancipated by her owner before 1800. For this and other critical information provided on nineteenth-century Sussex County residents, I am deeply indebted to Gary M. Williams, Clerk of the Circuit Court of Sussex County, without whom none of this information would have come to light. Gary M. Williams, personal communication, 26 June 2008 ("the poor house"); Gary M. Williams, personal communication, 28 June 2008 ("need of assistance").

120. Sussex County CirCt OB, 1831–1866/402, 409, Sussex County courthouse, Sussex, Virginia. It should be noted that in the case of Billy Barlow, the Sussex County Circuit Court followed the process for self-enslavement outlined in the original 1856 law providing for voluntary enslavement, not the revised law of 1861, which waived the requirement for a formal petition, removed the one-month delay required between application for self-enslavement and court examination, and eliminated the fee for chosen owners that had been priced at one-half the petitioner's assessed value. Thus, not only was Barlow's case delayed significantly longer than other such cases in Virginia at the time (he petitioned in April 1863 and was examined and enslaved in October 1863), but his new owner, William E. Prince, mistakenly paid the court $300 (one-half Barlow's assessed value) that the law no longer required him to do. See also 1860 federal census, Sussex County, Virginia.

121. Sussex County CirCt OB, 1831–1866/414, Sussex County courthouse, Sussex, Virginia. See also 1850 federal census, Sussex County, Virginia.

122. Sussex County CirCt OB, 1831–1866/414–15, Sussex County courthouse, Sussex, Virginia. See also 1850 federal census, Sussex County, Virginia; 1860 federal census, Sussex County, Virginia.

123. Sussex County CirCt OB, 1831–1866/415, Sussex County courthouse, Sussex, Virginia. See also 1850 federal census, Sussex County, Virginia.

124. Sussex County CirCt OB, 1831–1866/415–16, Sussex County courthouse, Sussex, Virginia. See also 1850 federal census, Sussex County, Virginia; 1860 federal census, Sussex County, Virginia.

125. Bedford County Register of Free Negroes, 1820–1860/46, LVA microfilm; "Hale Celia pet. to become Slave & affdvt," 5 October 1858, Bedford County FNSR, 1850–59, Bedford County courthouse, Bedford, Virginia. See also 1860 federal census and slave schedule.

126. "Hale Celia pet. to become Slave & affdvt," 5 October 1858, Bedford County FNSR, 1850–59, Bedford County courthouse, Bedford, Virginia.

127. Ibid.

128. Ibid.

129. Bedford County CirCt OB 12, 1857–1859/355, LVA microfilm.

130. It should be noted that mass manumissions like John Williamson's continued up to the Civil War, long after all whites supposedly espoused the "positive-good" view of slavery.

131. Document 1 and petition, 21 February 1851, Simon et. al vs. Branch et. al, Southampton County Chancery, 1856–57, 1856–016, LVA microfilm. For a list of the names of the twenty-nine others under Summerall's control at the time of his death, see Decree of Southampton CirCt, May 1855, Simon et. al vs. Branch et. al, Southampton County Chancery, 1856–57, 1856–016, LVA microfilm.

132. For example, the administrator of Williamson's estate received only $50.40 for the hires of Lewis, Simon, Martha, Margaret, Judy, and others from December 1850 to July 1855. See Report of Administrator, 8 November 1856, Simon & others vs. Wm. Jones, Exr, 1856–016, Southampton County Chancery, 1856–57, LVA microfilm.

133. "Dep. of William Whitney, Simon & others vs. Wm. Jones, Exr," 1856–016, Southampton County Chancery, 1856–57 ("rumpus"), LVA microfilm; "The Estate of John Williamson deceased," Simon & others vs. Wm. Jones, Exr," 1856–016, Southampton County Chancery, 1856–57 ("the extraordinary"), LVA microfilm.

134. Decree, 20 November 1855, Simon & others vs. Wm. Jones, Exr, 1856–016, Southampton County Chancery, 1856–57 ("all the expenses"), LVA microfilm.

135. Simon, Martha, Margaret, and Judy each marked an "x" to acknowledge their individual receipts for the $45.12 in damages won in the suit. See "Receipts from the negroes," 8 November 1856, Simon & others vs. Wm. Jones, Exr, 1856–016, Southampton County Chancery, 1856–57, LVA microfilm.

136. *Journal of the Senate*, 1855–56, 222, 227, 235, 277, 312, 385, 386, 409.

137. Simon, Martha, Judy, and Margaret never followed through on their self-enslavement in the Southampton County court, to which the law permitted them to apply. See *Acts of the General Assembly*, 1855–56, 278. Southampton County, County Court Free Negroes Register, 1833–64, #1169 (Simon), #1170 (Martha), #1172 (Mar-

garet), and #1171 (Judy) ("a scar," "subject to fits"), LVA microfilm. Note that in an undated chancery court document likely written in or about 1847, Simon was reported to be sixty-five years old, Martha sixty, Margaret twenty-two, and Judith twenty-five. See "John Williamson's Negroes," n.d., Simon & others vs. Wm. Jones, Exr, 1856–016, Southampton County Chancery, 1856–57, LVA microfilm.

138. See Southampton County CirCt OB 6, 1851–1875/160 (quotations). For examples of other such petitions in Southampton County, see ibid./298–99, 346. Similar petitions were fairly common throughout Virginia in the 1850s and 1860s and frequently occurred in counties in which free people applied for self-enslavement. See, for example, Cumberland County CirCt OB, 1860–1884/107, LVA microfilm; Campbell County CirCt OB 9, 1855–1867/478, LVA microfilm; Halifax County CirCt OB 6, 1858–1866/309, 424, LVA microfilm; Northumberland County CirCt OB 2, 1854–1877/107, LVA microfilm; Culpeper County CirCt OB 6, 1856–1866/166, LVA microfilm; Albemarle County CirCt OB, 1857–1865/89, LVA microfilm; Fluvanna County CirCt OB 5, 1856–1860/289, LVA microfilm; Augusta County CirCt OB 6, 1857–1859/324, LVA microfilm; Accomack County CirCt OB, 1850–1857/415, LVA microfilm; Gloucester County CirCt MB, 1854–1859/n.p. [17 December 1857], LVA microfilm; "Judgment: Gracy & children vs. Exr of James Fulton," October 1856, Rockingham County FNSR, box 9, LVA mss; Fairfax County CirCt MB 1, 1852–1859/255, Fairfax County courthouse, Fairfax, Virginia; Lee County CirCt OB 3, 1854–1872/84, LVA microfilm.

139. At least eleven men and women followed Jane Payne, Mary Fletcher, and Annah Gleaves Poters in petitioning the state legislature for special laws permitting them to self-enslave.

140. Petition of Jane Payne Etc., Fauquier County Chancery, 1861–045, LVA online. Interestingly, William H. Payne got it wrong when he later recalled that Payne, Fletcher, and Poters had "filed an application in the Circuit Court of Fauquier County to become the slaves of Alfred Rector." See Bill of Wm H. Payne, n.d., Fauquier County Chancery, 1897–02, Exr of CR Ayres v. W. Kemp Flowerree, LVA online.

141. The enslaved population of Fauquier County in 1860 numbered 10,455, or just over 48 percent of the total population. See 1860 federal census.

142. See Chapter 4.

143. Fauquier County CirCt OB G, 1860–1872/48, LVA microfilm. See also "Comth Report," 14 March 1871, Fauquier County Chancery, 1897–02, Exr of CR Ayres v. W. Kemp Flowerree, LVA online.

144. Petition of Mary Elizabeth, Rockbridge County FNSR, 1848–81, LVA mss; Petition of Mary Elizabeth, Rockbridge County Court Records: Judgments, October–December 1859–October–December 1860, in folder for judgments M–Z, August 1860, SRC; Register of "Mary Elizabeth Roland," 2 April 1860, Rockbridge County Register of Free Negroes, 1831–1860/197, LVA microfilm; Rockbridge County CirCt OB, 1852–1867/287, 316–17, 318, 363, 368, 384–85, LVA microfilm. For William Miller [Jr.]'s relationship to William Miller [Sr.], see will of William Miller in EXRS of William Miller v. Thomas L. Miller etc., Rockbridge Chancery, 1853–009, LVA online.

145. Madison County WB 9, 1849–1855/184–86, LVA microfilm; Madison County DB 21, 1852–1856/624, LVA microfilm; Madison County WB 10, 1850–1858/209, LVA microfilm; Madison County CirCt OB 3, 1850–1860/141–42, 143, 159, LVA microfilm.

146. VGALP, Madison County, 19 April 1857, reel 118, box 152, folder 72, LVA microfilm.

147. *Journal of the House of Delegates*, 1857–58, 38, 223. There had clearly been ill will among the beneficiaries of Isham Tatum's estate over the freeing not only of Jeptha, Thadeus, and Timothy Chapman, but of other enslaved individuals as well. A later court document explained, "Isham Tatum died leaving some thirteen distributies of his Estate and that he left none of them enough of personal property to pay debts &c, and his land to be divided among his descendents free of debt." See Bill, October 1872, Twyman v. Sparks &c, Madison County Chancery, 1873–09, Madison courthouse, Madison, Virginia. See also Madison County WB 9, 1849–1855/184–86, LVA microfilm.

148. Madison County CirCt OB 3, 1850–1860/168–69, (quotation), 177–78, LVA microfilm; Auditor of Public Accounts, Voluntary Enslavement Reports, 1857–60, LVA microfilm. One historian concluded that in the case of Timothy Chapman, "the Court made its decision in consideration of fraud or collusion between the parties," but the court's reasoning was not explained in any of the available documents. See Margaret G. Davis, *Madison County*, 121 (quotation), 120–24, 312–13.

149. See Madison County WB 9, 1849–1855/184–86, LVA microfilm; VGALP, Madison County, 19 April 1857, reel 118, box 152, folder 72, LVA microfilm; Madison County CoCt OB 12, 1856–1863/298, LVA microfilm.

150. Madison County CoCt OB 12, 1856–1863/298, LVA microfilm.

151. Jaime Amanda Martinez has argued that Virginia slaveholders and slave traders maintained "sufficient confidence" in the viability of slave property until the very end of the Civil War. This confidence was reflected in ever-increasing slave prices in the state from May 1861 to January 1865. See Martinez, "Slave Market in Civil War Virginia," especially 117, 129 (quotation).

152. Fauquier County WB 30, 1865–1867/387, LVA microfilm; Judge's Opinion, 22 April 1871, Fauquier County Chancery, 1897–02, Exr of CR Ayres v. W. Kemp Flowerree, LVA online. For one listing of Charles R. Ayres's slaves at his death, see Fauquier County WB 28, 1858–1860/280–81, LVA microfilm.

153. The exact number of slaves who fled from William H. Payne's control is not known. For the flight of enslaved Virginians to Union-controlled areas by mid-May 1861, see Berlin and Miller, *Wartime Genesis*, 2: 85–110, especially 85–87. Steven Hahn argues that the escape of nearly four hundred thousand enslaved individuals from their owners by 1864 amounted to a massive, widespread slave uprising. Hahn writes, "For the slaves' rebellion properly started not with acts of vengeance against their owners, but rather with small-scale and often clandestine departures for Union lines and the freedom they believed they might find there." See Hahn, *Nation under Our Feet*, 69 (quotation), 82.

154. Bill of Wm H. Payne, N.D., Fauquier County Chancery, 1897–02, Exr of CR Ayres v. W. Kemp Flowerree, LVA online.

155. Poters and other free blacks in Fauquier County joined numerous enslaved individuals in leaving their homes for positions behind Union lines. Writing on 19 April 1862, one Fauquier County resident lamented in her diary, "It is thought the *remaining ebonys* will take to themselves the wings of liberty as some have declared as much. The cars are so convenient to carry them off. Let them go, yes, the last one, provided

we never be harassed with the same unfaithful ones again. I hope they may get their freedom, but no nearer than the isle of Cuba, where they may carry them by the ship loads. The very sight of one provokes me and often I am harsh in commanding them, but who can help it when they all seem to be lifted up at the fair prospect before them." See Edmonds and Chappelear, *Journals of Amanda Virginia Edmonds*, 82 (quotation). Indeed, many slaveholders in Fauquier County and throughout the South found themselves in the midst of war "without a cook and in quite a fix," ibid., 121 (quotation).

156. Bill of Wm H. Payne, n.d., Fauquier County Chancery, 1897–02, Exr of CR Ayres v. W. Kemp Flowerree, LVA online; Report, 17 December 1889, Fauquier County Chancery, 1897–02, Exr of CR Ayres v. W. Kemp Flowerree, LVA online; Letter to William H. Payne from R. A. Rector, Fauquier County Chancery, 1897–02, Exr of CR Ayres v. W. Kemp Flowerree, LVA online.

157. Recent works that highlight the African American experience during the Civil War tend to focus on the experiences of the enslaved. See, for example, Blight, *Slave No More*; Jenkins, *Climbing up to Glory*; Hahn, *Nation under Our Feet*; Ira Berlin and Rowland, *Families and Freedom*; Berlin and Miller, *Wartime Genesis*. Exceptions include Ely, *Israel on the Appomattox*, 370–417; Jordan, *Black Confederates*.

158. William H. Payne recalled, "Vianna Fletcher & her sister Sallie only one of whom Vianna had reached the age of 10 fled from the county with the Yankee Army about 1862." See Bill of Wm H. Payne, n.d., Fauquier County Chancery, 1897–02, Exr of CR Ayres v. W. Kemp Flowerree, (quotation), LVA online. In another instance, Payne characterized the departure of free blacks from the area as if it had been against their will, as part of a Union raid. He wrote that some had been "carried off by the Yankees" and not heard from since. See Petition of Wm H. Payne, 4 September 1889, Fauquier County Chancery, 1897–02, Exr of CR Ayres v. W. Kemp Flowerree, LVA online. From neighboring Culpeper County, Jonathan S. Pendleton reported in October 1863 that "the last Yankee raid has swept every description of stock from the country[,] negroes included." See letter from Pendleton to William Campbell Scott dated 12 October 1863, William Campbell Scott Journal, 1842–64, SRC.

159. Deposition of Fanny N. C. Lawrence, 9 October 1871, Fauquier County Chancery, 1897–02, Exr of CR Ayres v. W. Kemp Flowerree, LVA online.

160. Ibid.

161. For an insightful analysis of Virginia's contraband camps and the hardships that African Americans endured as residents there, see Lowe, "Meanings of Freedom," 17–22.

162. Deposition of Catherine S. Lawrence, 9 October 1871, Fauquier County Chancery, 1897–02, Exr of CR Ayres v. W. Kemp Flowerree, LVA online.

163. Ibid. For a sense of the hopes, fears, and motivations of those like Catherine S. Lawrence who volunteered to leave communities in the North to serve the Union Army as nurses in contraband camps in the South, see the various letters in Swint, *Dear Ones at Home*, especially 13–18.

164. Deposition of James Jefferson, 3 December 1889, Fauquier County Chancery, 1897–02, Exr of CR Ayres v. W. Kemp Flowerree, LVA online.

165. Deposition of Nellie B. Slocum, 29 November 1889, Fauquier County Chancery, 1897–02, Exr of CR Ayres v. W. Kemp Flowerree, LVA online.

166. See report dated 25 January 1888, Commissioner's Office, Warrenton, Virginia, in Fauquier County Chancery, 1897–02, Exr of CR Ayres v. W. Kemp Flowerree, LVA online.

CHAPTER SEVEN

1. *Tobacco Plant* (Clarksville, Va.), 2, 12 April 1867 ("mounted," "some twelve," "files of four," "extended," "general jollification," "oratorical powers.") The author is deeply indebted to the work of Harold S. Forsythe, who first brought Watt Love's story to light. See Forsythe, "'But My Friends Are Poor,'" especially 412 ("a freedman cobbler"). See business dealings between John Watson and Love in "Hoggs Book," Watkins Love vs. Wm. A. Homes, Mecklenburg County Chancery, 1871–055, box 145, LVA mss. On the long-standing tradition of commemorating emancipation in African-descended communities, see Kerr-Ritchie, *Rites of August First*, especially 82–117.

2. In his study of Virginia's black political leaders during Reconstruction, Richard Lowe concluded that those who rose to leadership positions "were clearly separated from the average Virginia black man. They were wealthier, more likely to be literate, more likely to be of mixed racial ancestry, more likely to have been free before the war, and more likely to be professionals or skilled workers than the general black male population of the Old Dominion." See Richard Lowe, "Local Black Leaders," especially 206 (quotation).

3. *Tobacco Plant*, 3 August 1860, quoted in Bracey, *Life by the Roaring Roanoke*, 238 ("the barber"). It is likely that Love began his barbering business while enslaved to Fleming J. Jeffress. For a nearly complete record of Watt Love's barbering business from 1859 to 1864, see Wat Love, Barber Book, 1859 in Mecklenburg County Chancery, 1871–055, box 145, LVA mss.

4. See Mills, "'Color-Line' Barbers," 1: 22–55. Martin Ruef and Ben Fletcher place black barbers in the antebellum South in a class of domestic servants "between common field laborers and the elite slave occupations of artisans and overseers." Which enslaved men would become barbers "was subject to ascriptive decisions by masters based on the skin complexions, interpersonal relationships, and personalities of the slaves." See Ruef and Fletcher, "Legacies of American Slavery," especially 452 (quotations). See also *Black Entrepreneurs of the Eighteenth and Nineteenth Centuries*, especially 18; Bristol, *Knights of the Razor*.

5. In 1860 barbers made up 10 percent of black property holders in the South. A number of Virginia's black barbershop owners accumulated vast amounts of property, especially those in urban centers such as Richmond, Petersburg, and Staunton. Quincy Terrell Mills has concluded that "free black barbers capitalized on their near monopoly of the trade and used their earnings to purchase family members from slavery, accumulate property and venture into other business pursuits. They benefitted from paternal relationships with their white patrons." See Mills, "'Color-Line' Barbers," 1: 40 (quotation), 44–45.

6. *Tobacco Plant*, 3 August 1860, quoted in Bracey, *Life by the Roaring Roanoke*, 238.

7. In her study of self-enslavement in New Orleans, Judith Kelleher Schafer suggested, "Perhaps self-enslavement proved a way not only to avoid being forced to leave

Louisiana, but as an informal way for free blacks to protect their property. If indeed self-enslavement was sometimes an arrangement of convenience, the newly chosen owner could hold the property for the newly enslaved person." See Schafer, *Becoming Free, Remaining Free*, 162 (quotation).

8. Love Watkins' Petition, April 1864, Mecklenburg County Judgments, 1859–65, box 53, LVA mss.

9. Mecklenburg County WB 19, 1856–1859/465, LVA microfilm.

10. Wat Love, Barber Book, 1859 in Mecklenburg County Chancery, 1871-055, box 145, LVA mss.

11. Ibid.

12. Luther Porter Jackson and John Hope Franklin both concluded, as Ira Berlin did many years later, that those free blacks who took advantage of voluntary enslavement laws "were paupers decrepit with age," an assertion that seems to apply only to a minority of cases in Virginia from 1854 to 1864. See Ira Berlin, *Slaves without Masters*, 367 (quotation); Jackson, *Free Negro Labor*; Franklin, "Enslavement of Free Negroes."

13. Lebsock, *Free Women of Petersburg*, especially 112 ("persistent personalism"), 143 ("'deserved' their poverty"). See also Green, *This Business of Relief*, especially 52–53. In the minds of would-be benefactors of the poor, a line was drawn between the deserving and undeserving poor. Robert H. Bremner writes, "Public indifference toward the helpless stemmed from the emphasis upon individual self-help which was the religion of the respectable in the vigorous young republic." See Bremner, *From the Depths*, 46 (quotation). See Michael B. Katz, *In the Shadow of the Poorhouse*, 9 ("willing or able"). Watkinson, "'Fit Objects of Charity,'" 55 ("victims of debt").

14. Petition of Fanny Gillison, Fauquier County Chancery, 1860–090, LVA online; Fauquier County CirCt OB G, 1860–1872/17, LVA microfilm.

15. The fear of prosecution under the 1806 expulsion law was credible in Fauquier County by 1859. It is possible that another factor in Fanny Gillison's decision to enslave herself was the memory of two Gillisons who had been indicted by the Fauquier County court for remaining in the state without lawful permission: Frank Gillison, whose case was dismissed in March 1853 and Catharine Gillison, whose case ended with nonprosecution in May 1853. See Peters, *Index to African-American Records*, 88.

16. Petition of Dennis Holt, 24 October 1860, Campbell County FNSR, 1791–1867, box 4, LVA mss. For Dennis Holt's age in 1860, see 1870 federal census, Campbell County, Virginia. See also Campbell County CirCt OB 9, 1855–1867/424, LVA microfilm.

17. In 1849, Dennis Holt's father, Andrew Holt, a free man of considerable means who worked as a baker, had purchased his sons Dennis and Burwell at an auction of property belonging to James Steptoe. At his death in 1858, Andrew Holt left behind a will that immediately "emancipated and set free" Dennis and Burwell. See Will of Andrew Holt, 7 June 1857, Campbell County FNSR, 1791–1867, box 4 (quotation), LVA mss; Campbell County WB 12, 1858–1862/88, LVA microfilm. See also Campbell County DB 27, 1847–1849/148-49, 152–53, LVA microfilm; 1850 federal census. Dennis Holt apparently chose not to pursue his petition, and it was eventually dismissed when the court's docket was cleared after the Civil War. See Campbell County CirCt OB 10, 1867–1879/37, LVA microfilm.

18. Lewis Wilkerson's surname was also frequently spelled "Wilkinson" or "Wilkenson."

19. On Lewis Wilkerson's birth year, see Amelia County Register of Free Negroes, 1835–1855/129, Register #399, LVA microfilm; Amelia County Register of Deaths, 1853–71, LVA microfilm. For Polly Morris's will, see Amelia County WB 16, 1847–1851/309, LVA microfilm; Morris Polly's Will, Amelia County, Various Records, 1857–59, box 10, folder "Wills, 1857, 1859," SRC. For Wilkerson's register see Amelia County Register of Free Negroes, 1835–1855/129, Register #399 ("a free man"), LVA microfilm.

20. Wilkerson's wife was an enslaved woman, which also served as a primary motivation for remaining in Amelia County and for self-enslavement. See Wilkerson Lewis Petition, Amelia County, various records, 1857–59, box 10, folder "Wills, 1857, 1859" ("his wish"), SRC; Amelia County CirCt OB 5, 1853–1872/211, LVA microfilm; Auditor of Public Accounts, Voluntary Enslavement Reports, 1857–60, misc. reel 1322, LVA microfilm. It is likely that Wilkerson was the man identified in the county Register of Deaths as "Lewis," the property of Worsham Foster, who died of "Old Age," at the age of 79 years, 9 months, 14 days. See Amelia County Register of Deaths, 1853–71, LVA microfilm. If so, it is unclear how or when Wilkerson might have been transferred to Foster from James W. Ellis, to whom he had enslaved himself four years earlier.

21. Walker Fitch owned $100 in personal property in 1860, as did Margaret Fitch and Elvira Fitch, who were both listed in his household as washerwomen and ironers. All three had been born in adjacent Nelson County. See 1860 federal census. See also VGALP, Augusta County, 7 January 1861, reel 14, box 19, folder 39, LVA microfilm. In his petition to the Virginia General Assembly, Fitch is referred to both as "Walker Fitch" and as "Walker Fitz." See *Journal of the House of Delegates*, 1861, 20 ("Walker Fitch"), 30 ("Walker Fitz"). It is possible that Fitch had been born free in Nelson County and had only recently moved to Staunton. A "Walker Fitz" was registered in Nelson County in July 1857. See Nelson County Register of Free Negroes, vol. 1, 1853–1865/4 (quotation), LVA microfilm. Note that this "Walker Fitz" was also referred to as "Braxton Fitz" by the Nelson County court clerk. See Nelson County CoCt MB 12, 1855–1861/79, LVA microfilm.

22. For Matthew Feggins's age, see Register #586, Mecklenburg County Register of Free Negroes No. 2, 1841–65, LVA microfilm; note that his register is undated, but falls between registers dated 20 October 1851 and 17 November 1851. For Feggins's petition to the circuit court, see Feggins Matthew's Petition, September 1860, Mecklenburg County Judgments, 1859–65, box #53, LVA mss; Mecklenburg County CirCt, OB 6, 1860–1867/26, LVA microfilm. Feggins was consistently listed in the PPTBs as having no personal property. Interestingly, there is no mention of Watt Love in these same records. See Mecklenburg County PPTBs 1859, 1860, 1861. On Feggins's tribulations in the Mecklenburg County court, see Warrant, Comm. v. Faggins, November 1858, Mecklenburg County CoCt Judgments, 1857–59, box 52, LVA mss; Certificate to Clerk of County Court, ibid.; Mecklenburg County CoCt OB 6, 1853–1858/578 ("thirty nine lashes"), LVA microfilm; [paper wrapper around case documents], Comm. v. Faggins, November 1858, Mecklenburg County CoCt Judgments, 1857–59, box 52, LVA mss. The connection (if any) between Feggins and Love remains unclear.

23. Isaac Burnett's register in the Mecklenburg County court described him as "Isaac a man of bright yellow—Complexion about 30 years of age five feet 7 1/2 inches high has a mole on the back of his neck and a scar on the left thumb." See Register #909, Mecklenburg County, Register of Free Negroes, No. 2, 1841–65, LVA microfilm. All those emancipated by the will of Pleasant Burnett were ordered to be registered by the county court. See Mecklenburg CoCt OB 7, 1859–1865/70, LVA microfilm.

24. Four years after their master's death, Isaac Burnett, along with Robert and Big Peter and others, was still being hired out as property of the estate. In a suit filed in the Mecklenburg Circuit Court of Chancery, Burnett and others expressed that they did "not wish to be kept longer in bondage." The chancery court ruled that they were to be freed and sent to Ohio. See Decree, 19 March 1859, Peter &c vs. Burnett's Administrators, Mecklenburg County Chancery, 1859–009/cc, box 42, LVA mss. Clearly, Isaac Burnett had refused to leave Mecklenburg County for Ohio. The clerk of the Circuit Court, Robert F. Clack, was likely a customer of Watt Love's as well. See entry for "R. Clack cut hair" in Wat Love, Barber Book, 1859 in Mecklenburg County Chancery, 1871–055, box 145, LVA mss. See entry for W. F. Small in "Hoggs Book," ibid.

25. Mecklenburg County CirCt, OB 6, 1860–1867/78, LVA microfilm.

26. Ibid., 121, 141. See entries for C. R. Edmonson in Wat Love, Barber Book, 1859, in Mecklenburg County Chancery, 1871–055, box 145, LVA mss.

27. Charles R. Edmonson would be presented by the Mecklenburg County court in April 1864 for illegally selling brandy by retail in Boydton. See Mecklenburg County CirCt OB 6, 1860–1867/172, LVA microfilm. A number of petitioners for self-enslavement simply allowed their applications to remain inactive on the court's docket for years, as they continued to live their lives as free people in violation of the expulsion law of 1806. Dennis Holt, for example, submitted his petition for self-enslavement in October 1860, two days after nine free blacks had been presented by the Campbell County Circuit Court for remaining in the state illegally. Holt never followed up on his petition, however, and it was dismissed in 1867. See Campbell County CirCt OB 9, 1855–1867/424, LVA microfilm; Petition of Dennis Holt, 24 October 1860, Campbell County FNSR, 1791–1867, box 4, LVA mss; Campbell County CirCt OB 10, 1867–1879/37, LVA microfilm. See also Mecklenburg County CirCt OB 6, 1860–1867/211, LVA microfilm.

28. Mecklenburg County CirCt OB 6, 1860–1867/101, LVA microfilm.

29. Bill, Mar. 1867, Watkins Love vs. Wm. A. Homes, folder A, Mecklenburg County Chancery, 1871–055, box 56, LVA mss. See also Deposition of Edward R. Chambers, 22 February 1871, Watkins Love vs. Wm. A. Homes, folder B, Mecklenburg County Chancery, 1871–055, box 56, LVA mss.

30. Bill, Mar. 1867, Watkins Love vs. Wm. A. Homes, folder A, Mecklenburg County Chancery, 1871–055, box 56, LVA mss. This account is Watt Love's. In an opposing deposition, William A. Homes "emphatically denied that there was any Copartnership between the Comply and the respondent for the purpose of keeping a 'hotel or Bar' in Boydton—The Complainant at his private rooms in Boydton sold at different times several barrels of liquor upon the joint account of himself and the respondent which the complainant was in the habit of doing upon similar terms for other person." See Answer, Mar. 1867, Watkins Love vs. Wm. A. Homes, folder A, Mecklenburg County Chancery, 1871–055, box 56, LVA mss.

31. For example, one customer related, "Either Mr. Homes or Watt Love, one of the two, said to me, if a wagon comes for the corn to let it have it—I dont remember which one told me." See Deposition of E. Binford, 4 September 1871, Watkins Love vs. Wm. A. Homes, Folder A, Mecklenburg County Chancery, 1871–055, box 56, LVA mss.

32. In her study of free black entrepreneurs before the Civil War, Juliet E. K. Walker concludes that "even while confronted with severe racial constraints, which not only suppressed full antebellum black business participation, but also limited the full expression of black entrepreneurial talents, some antebellum blacks did establish enterprises that were neither marginal in profits nor peripheral to mainstream American business activity." Though constrained in his activities and in the extent to which he could transact money publicly, Watt Love succeeded in building a highly profitable and visible business. See Juliet E. K. Walker, "Racism, Slavery, and Free Enterprise," especially 345 (quotation).

33. The same day, William A. Homes purchased his contributions to the business: "2 Mules," "One sot of Harness," and "one waggon," amounting to $616. For Love's and Home's contributions, see Wat Love, Barber Book, 1859 in Mecklenburg County Chancery, 1871–055, box 145, LVA mss. See also "On testimony of Watkins Love," n.d., Mecklenburg County Chancery, 1871–055, box 56, LVA mss.

34. "On testimony of Watkins Love," n.d., Mecklenburg County Chancery, 1871–055, box 56, LVA mss. It should be noted that the $1,090 in profits reaped by Watt Love and William A. Homes was in inflated Confederate money.

35. Deposition of Watkins Love, 4 March 1871, Watkins Love v. Wm. A. Homes, folder B, Mecklenburg County Chancery, 1871–055, box 56, LVA mss. For a copy of Love's exemption certification, see "Richmond June 17th 1863," Watkins Love v. Wm. A. Homes, Exhibit B-1, Mecklenburg County Chancery, 1871–055, box 56, folder A, LVA mss.

36. Mecklenburg County CirCt OB 6, 1860–1867/171, LVA microfilm.

37. See a copy of list of four presentments against Love in Exhibit, Presentments Against Watt Love, Watkins Love vs. Wm. A. Homes, folder A, Mecklenburg County Chancery, 1871–055, box 56, LVA mss.

38. See Report of Division of Land, May 1880, Eliza Bowers vs. Love, Watt & Wife, etc., Mecklenburg County Chancery, 1880–001cc, box 90, LVA mss.

39. Mecklenburg County CirCt OB 6, 1860–1867/174, LVA microfilm. Watt Love's second petition read: "Your petitioner Watkins L. Love respectfully represents that he is a free man of color resident of the county of Mecklenburg Va and over the age of twenty one years that he desires to enslave himself and to select James Bowers as his master or owner—Your petitioner therefore prays that he may be allowed to exercise the privilege . . . conferred upon free persons of color in the act of March 28 1861." See Love Watkins Petition to choose an owner, April 1864, Mecklenburg County Judgments, 1859–65, box 53, LVA mss.

40. Love Watt Petition to choose an owner, April 1864, Mecklenburg County Judgments, 1859–65, box 53, LVA mss.

41. Thomas F. Goode was a prominent Mecklenburg lawyer and long-time associate of Love's who before had agreed to become the owner of another Mecklenburg man, Isaac Burnett, in 1860. See "Burnett Isaacs Petition," April 1861, Mecklenburg County

Judgments, 1859–65, box 53, LVA mss; Mecklenburg County CirCt OB 6, 1860–1867/175, LVA microfilm; see also Exhibit L, Watkins Love vs. Wm. A. Homes, folder C, Mecklenburg County Chancery, 1871–055, box 56, LVA mss; "Love Watt Petition to choose an owner," April 1864, Mecklenburg County Judgments, 1859–65, box 53, LVA mss; Wat Love, Barber Book, 1859 in Mecklenburg County Chancery, 1871–055, box 145, LVA mss. Harold S. Forsythe has written that Love's enslavement to Mason was a ploy to trick Mason into assuming Love's business debts. Though Forsythe's description of Love as "wily beyond belief" is easily agreed with, it is more difficult to accept the fact that Mason (as well as Goode and others present at the proceeding) were unaware of Love's personal wealth and resources. See Forsythe, "'But My Friends Are Poor,'" 422 (quotation).

42. Deposition of Watt Love, 2 March 1871, Watkins Love vs. Wm. A. Homes, folder B, Mecklenburg County Chancery, 1871–055, box 56, LVA mss.

43. Deposition of James Bowers, 6 December 1867, Watkins Love vs. Wm. A. Homes, folder C, Mecklenburg County Chancery, 1871–055, box 56, LVA mss.

44. Deposition of Watkins Love, 4 March 1871, Watkins Love vs. Wm. A. Homes, folder B, Mecklenburg County Chancery, 1871–055, box 56, LVA mss.

45. See, for example, ibid.

46. Forsythe, "'But My Friends Are Poor,'" 422 (quotation); Mecklenburg County CirCt OB 6, 1860–1867/338, 435, 476, LVA microfilm.

47. Deposition of Watkins Love, 27 February 1871, Watkins Love vs. Wm. A. Homes, folder B, Mecklenburg County Chancery, 1871–055, box 56 ("which passed through"), LVA mss.

48. Exhibit A, 27 November 1865, Watkins Love vs. Wm. A. Homes, folder B, Mecklenburg County Chancery, 1871–055, box 56, LVA mss.

49. See, for example, a receipt of James A. Foster, who wrote that "Watt a Free man" had paid him $10 for "Repares to Carrage," in Exhibit G, A/C Watt Freeman to J. A. Foster, 9 April 1864, Watkins Love vs. Wm. A. Homes, folder A, Mecklenburg County Chancery, 1871–055, box 56, LVA mss.

50. Deposition of Lucy Homes, 10 July 1868, Watkins Love vs. Wm. A. Homes, folder C, Mecklenburg County Chancery, 1871–055, box 56, LVA mss.

51. Exhibit 4, Summons, 9 April 1864, Mecklenburg County Chancery, 1871–055, box 56, LVA mss.

52. Deposition of Thomas F. Goode, 24 February 1871, folder B, Mecklenburg County Chancery, 1871–055, box 56, LVA mss.

53. Ibid.

54. Deposition of L. E. Finch, 2 December 1867 ("the only bar"), deposition of Mary Beard, 18 June 1868 ("all the time," "black & white"), all in folder C, Mecklenburg County Chancery, 1871–055, box 56, LVA mss. On occasion Love exchanged large amounts of cash with his suppliers. One receipt in March 1865 reported, "Received of Watt Love Twenty nine hundred and seventy dollars for twenty two gallons of brandy on account of Wm. A. Homes." See Mecklenburg County Chancery, 1871–055, box 56, LVA mss. As for the ownership of the bar business, one customer remembered, "It was always called Wat Loves house—I dont Know who owned it." See deposition of James Wingfield, 10 July 1868, folder C, Mecklenburg County Chancery, 1871–055, box 56, LVA mss.

55. Deposition of Mary Beard, 18 June 1868, folder C, Watkins Love vs. Wm. A. Homes, Mecklenburg County Chancery, 1871–055, box 56, LVA mss.

56. Ibid.

57. See entry for 19 September 1864, Wat Love, Barber Book, 1859 in Mecklenburg County Chancery, 1871–055, box 145, LVA mss.

58. One Mecklenburg County resident, William T. Adkins, remembered, "About June 1865 I was a candidate for the clerkship of this county and did have an account at the bar—some for my own drinking and some for treating my friends." See deposition of Adkins, 20 January 1871, Watkins Love vs. Wm. A. Homes, folder B, Mecklenburg County Chancery, 1871–055, box 56, LVA mss.

59. Forsythe, "'But My Friends Are Poor,'" 430 ("spent many hours").

60. *Tobacco Plant* (Clarksville, Va.), 2, 12 April 1867 ("harangues"). In October 1869 Watt Love was elected "Colonel" for a fundraising barbecue for "the colored True Republicans" of Mecklenburg County, who sought to overcome the "very heavy majority" of the "radicals." *Tobacco Plant* (Boydton, Va.), 2, 20 October 1869 (quotations).

61. Moore, "The Elusive Center," 212.

62. "Statement X," n.d., Mecklenburg County Chancery, 1869–028cc, box 51 ("plantation"), LVA mss. See also Forsythe, "'But My Friends Are Poor,'" 421.

63. Harold S. Forsythe writes that "black political leaders in Virginia would arise most often as spokesmen and presiding officials of the institutionalized social networks that were the infrastructure of freedpeople's communities." See Forsythe, "'But My Friends Are Poor,'" 413 (quotation).

64. Forsythe, "'But My Friends Are Poor,'" 422 ("the Court House clique," "Hamilton's party," "Hamilton's faction"). See also Hahn, *Nation under Our Feet*, 370.

CONCLUSION

1. *Richmond Daily Dispatch*, p. 1, col. 5, 17 November 1856. The story was reprinted in *the Daily Richmond Enquirer* the following day. See *Daily Richmond Enquirer*, p. 2, col. 5, 18 November 1856. See also Kimball, *American City, Southern Place*, 139–40.

Bibliography

PRIMARY SOURCES

Manuscripts and Archives

Library of Congress, Washington, D.C.
   American Colonization Society records
Library of Virginia, Archives Research Services, Richmond
   Auditor of Public Accounts, Voluntary Enslavement Reports, 1857–60
   Robert Alonzo Brock collection
   Dupuy Family papers, 1810–66
   Executive communications, 1830
   William Haynie Hatchett diary
   Local Government Records collection
   Mountain Plain Baptist Church records (Albemarle County, Va.)
   Northumberland County Chancery records
   Prince Edward County cohabitation register
   William Ludwell Sheppard personal papers
   Virginia General Assembly Legislative Petitions, 1776–1862
National Archives and Records Administration
   Federal census, 1790–1890
   Federal census, slave schedules, 1850, 1860
State Records Center, Richmond, Virginia
   William Campbell Scott journal, 1842–64
Virginia Baptist Historical Society, Richmond, Virginia
   Branch's Church Minute Books (Chesterfield County, Va.)
   Gourdvine Church Minute Book (Culpeper County, Va.)
   Hebron Church records (Frederick County, Va.)
   Moratico Church Minute Books (Lancaster County, Va.)
Virginia Historical Society, Richmond, Virginia
   Claiborne Family papers
   Crutchfield Family papers
   Dabney Family papers
   Emily Howe Dupuy papers
   Joseph Dupuy Account Book
   Henry Family papers
   Watkins Family papers

Accomack County
  CirCt OB, 1850–57, LVA microfilm
  CirCt OB, 1857–66, LVA microfilm
  CoCt OB, 1848–51, LVA microfilm
  CoCt MB, 1857–59, LVA microfilm
  Court Loose Papers, Orders for Process, 1860–65 (Various Courts), SRC
  Land Tax Book, 1831b, LVA microfilm
  PPTB 1831b, LVA microfilm
  Register of Free Negroes, LVA microfilm
  SupCt CLOB, 1831–42, LVA microfilm
  SupCt CLOB, 1842–50, LVA microfilm
  WB, 1828–46, LVA microfilm
Albemarle County
  CirCt OB, 1857–65, LVA microfilm
  Civil War Era, Tax and Fiscal Records, 1858–70, LVA mss
  CoCt MB, 1856–59, LVA microfilm
  Commonwealth Causes, 1858–67, LVA mss
  CoCt Judgments, 1858, 1862–64, LVA mss
  Court Records, Tax and Fiscal Records, 1858–70, LVA mss
  FNSR, 1796–1870, LVA mss
  Military and Pension, 1785–1919, LVA mss
  WB 18, 1847–48, LVA microfilm
  WB 21, 1851–52, LVA microfilm
  WB 24, 1856–57, LVA microfilm
Alleghany County
  CirCt OB 5, 1849–59, LVA microfilm
  CirCt OB 3, 1854–72, Alleghany County courthouse, Covington, Va.
Amelia County
  CirCt OB 5, 1853–72, LVA microfilm
  Register of Deaths, 1853–71, LVA microfilm
  Register of Free Negroes, 1835–55, LVA microfilm
  Various Records, 1857–59, SRC
  WB 16, 1847–51, LVA microfilm
Amherst County
  CirCt OB 6, 1855–60, LVA microfilm
Augusta County
  CirCt OB 6, 1857–59, LVA microfilm
  CirCt OB 7, 1859–66, LVA microfilm
  Loose Papers, Augusta County courthouse, Staunton, Va.
Bath County
  CirCt OB 3, 1855–70, LVA microfilm
Bedford County
  Chancery, 1859-036

CirCt OB 11, 1854–59, LVA microfilm
CirCt OB 12, 1857–59, LVA microfilm
CirCt OB 13, 1859–66, LVA microfilm
CoCt OB 33, 1858–61, LVA microfilm
Register of Free Negroes, 1820–60 LVA microfilm
Judgments, 1858, Bedford County courthouse, Bedford, Va.
FNSR, 1850–62, Bedford County courthouse, Bedford, Va.
Criminal Records, 1860–69, Bedford County courthouse, Bedford, Va.
Chancery Causes, Bedford County courthouse, Bedford, Va.
WB 13, 1848–50, Bedford County courthouse, Bedford, Va.
WB 14, 1851–53, Bedford County courthouse, Bedford, Va.
WB 15, 1853–55, Bedford County courthouse, Bedford, Va.
WB 16, 1855–58, Bedford County courthouse, Bedford, Va.
Bland County
CirCt OB 1, 1861–77, LVA microfilm
Botetourt County
CirCt OB, 1850–57, LVA microfilm
CirCt OB, 1857–78, LVA microfilm
Brunswick County
CirCt OB 2, 1843–67, LVA microfilm
CoCt OB 38, 1851–64, LVA microfilm
CoCt OB 39, 1864–68, LVA microfilm
Register of Free Negroes 1, 1803–20, LVA microfilm
Register of Free Negroes 2, 1820–50, LVA microfilm
Register of Free Negroes 3, 1850–64, LVA microfilm
Campbell County
CirCt OB 9, 1855–67, LVA microfilm
CirCt OB 10, 1867–79, LVA microfilm
CoCt OB, 1853–58, LVA microfilm
DB 9, 1810–13, LVA microfilm
DB 27, 1847–49, LVA microfilm
DB 29, 1852–54, LVA microfilm
DB 35, 1868–72, LVA microfilm
Unspecified various court records, SRC
Unspecified Commonwealth Causes, SRC
FNSR, 1784–1867, LVA mss
FNSR, 1791–1867, LVA mss
Land Tax Books, 1850–60, LVA microfilm
PPTBs, 1843–60, LVA microfilm
Register of Free Negroes, 1801–50, LVA microfilm
WB 8, 1836–41, LVA microfilm
WB 9, 1841–47, LVA microfilm
WB 12, 1858–62, LVA microfilm
Caroline County
CirCt OB 1, 1831–36, Fredericksburg Heritage Center, Fredericksburg, Va.

CirCt OB 2, 1836–42, Fredericksburg Heritage Center, Fredericksburg, Va.
CirCt OB 3, 1858–70, Fredericksburg Heritage Center, Fredericksburg, Va.
Chancery OB, 1842–66, LVA microfilm
Charles City County
    CirCt OB, 1853–63, LVA microfilm
    CirCt MB, 1848–68, LVA microfilm
    CirCt OB 2, 1865–94, Charles City County courthouse, Charles City, Va.
Charlotte County
    CirCt OB 5, 1851–63, LVA microfilm
    CirCt OB 6, 1863–73, LVA microfilm
Chesterfield County
    Chancery, 1873–033, LVA mss
    CirCt OB 4, 1856–73, LVA microfilm
    CoCt OB 37, 1852–57, LVA microfilm
    CoCt MB 38, 1857–63, LVA microfilm
    CoCt MB 39, 1863–65, LVA microfilm
    Register of Free Negroes 1, 1804–30, LVA microfilm
    Register of Free Negroes 2, 1830–53, LVA microfilm
    Register of Free Negroes 3, 1853–54, LVA microfilm
    WB 19, 1850–52, LVA microfilm
    WB 20, 1852–55, LVA microfilm
Clarke County
    CirSupCt OB B, 1848–65, LVA microfilm
    CirCt OB C, 1865–75, LVA microfilm
    CoCt OB B, 1845–58, LVA microfilm
    CoCt OB C, 1858–62, LVA microfilm
    CoCt OB D, 1865–68, LVA microfilm
    Ended Causes, 1860–55, Clarke County courthouse, Berryville, Va.
Craig County
    CirCt OB, 1864–89, Craig County courthouse, New Castle, Va.
    CoCt OB 1, 1851–60, LVA microfilm
    CoCt OB 2, 1860–63, LVA microfilm
Culpeper County
    CirCt Judgments, Drawer 3, 1856–58, Culpeper County courthouse,
        Culpeper, Va.
    CirCt Judgments, Drawer 4, 1865–66, Culpeper County courthouse,
        Culpeper, Va.
    CirCt OB 4, 1844–50, LVA microfilm
    CirCt OB 5, 1850–56, LVA microfilm
    CirCt OB 6, 1856–66, LVA microfilm
    CoCt MB 23, 1853–58, LVA microfilm
    CoCt MB 24, 1858–64, LVA microfilm
    DB 13, 1856–58, LVA microfilm
    PPTB 1869, LVA microfilm
    WB N, 1833–36, LVA microfilm

WB P, 1839–43, LVA microfilm
WB R, 1847–57, LVA microfilm
WB S, 1852–54, LVA microfilm
WB T, 1854–57, LVA microfilm
WB U, 1857–62, LVA microfilm
Cumberland County
    CirCt OB, 1849–60, LVA microfilm
    CirCt OB, 1860–84, LVA microfilm
Dinwiddie County
    CirCt OB 1-A, 1855–79, LVA microfilm
    Chancery OB 2, 1852–73, LVA microfilm
    CoCt MB 1, 1855–58, LVA microfilm
    CoCt MB 2, 1858–63, LVA microfilm
    CoCt MB 3, 1863–66, LVA microfilm
    Register of Free Negroes, 1850–64, LVA microfilm
Elizabeth City County
    Process Book, 1837–66, LVA microfilm
Essex County
    CirCt OB 3, 1856–64, LVA microfilm
    CoCt OB 1, 1853–63, LVA microfilm
    FNSR, Essex County courthouse, Tappahannock, Va.
Fairfax County
    CirCt OB 1, 1852–59, LVA microfilm
    CirCt OB 2, 1860–80, LVA microfilm
    CirCt MB 1, 1852–59, Fairfax County courthouse, Fairfax, Va.
    CirCt MB 2, 1860–80, Fairfax County courthouse, Fairfax, Va.
    CoCt MB, 1855–58, Fairfax County courthouse, Fairfax, Va.
    Term Papers, 1857–61, Fairfax County courthouse, Fairfax, Va.
    Black History, Free Negroes [loose papers], Fairfax County courthouse, Fairfax, Va.
Fauquier County
    Chancery, 1859–074, LVA online
    Chancery, 1859–080, LVA online
    Chancery, 1860–090, LVA online
    Chancery, 1861–042, LVA online
    Chancery, 1861–043, LVA online
    Chancery, 1861–044, LVA online
    Chancery, 1861–045, LVA online
    Chancery, 1897–02, LVA online
    CirCt OB F, 1854–60, LVA microfilm
    CirCt OB G, 1860–72, LVA microfilm
    CoCt MB, 1856–57, LVA microfilm
    CoCt MB, 1857–59, LVA microfilm
    CoCt MB, 1859–65, LVA microfilm
    DB 58, 1859–60, LVA microfilm
    WB 24, 1852–53, LVA microfilm

WB 28, 1858–60, LVA microfilm
WB 30, 1865–67, LVA microfilm
Floyd County
    CirCt OB 2, 1853–59, LVA microfilm
    CirCt OB 3, 1859–68, LVA microfilm
Fluvanna County
    CirCt OB 4, 1851–56, LVA microfilm
    CirCt OB 5, 1856–60, LVA microfilm
    CirCt OB 6, 1860–68, LVA microfilm
Franklin County
    CirCt OB 11, 1852–58, Franklin County courthouse, Rocky Mount, Va.
    CirCt OB 12, 1858–64, Franklin County courthouse, Rocky Mount, Va.
    Chancery OB B, 1851–65, LVA microfilm
Frederick County
    CirCt OB 10, 1853–68, LVA microfilm
    CirCt Ended Causes, 1859–68, SRC
    FNSR, 1795–1868, LVA mss
    FNSR, 1795–1871, LVA mss
    Free Negro Registrations and Certificates, LVA mss
    PPTBs, 1855–58, LVA microfilm
    Register of Births, 1853–1912 (A-Ha), LVA microfilm
Fredericksburg City
    DB O, 1845–48, LVA microfilm
    Hustings Court OB H, 1819–27, LVA microfilm
    Hustings Court OB K, 1841–45, LVA microfilm
Giles County
    CirCt OB, 1852–66, Giles County courthouse, Pearisburg, Va.
    CoCt OB, 1856–60, LVA microfilm
    CoCt Judgments, 1860–65, SRC
Gloucester County
    CirCt MB, 1854–59, LVA microfilm
    CirCt MB, 1859–67, LVA microfilm
    Docket Book, 1853–56, LVA microfilm
    Docket Book, 1856–59, LVA microfilm
    Docket Book, 1859–66, LVA microfilm
    Clerk's Process Book, 1842–59, LVA microfilm
Goochland County
    CirSupCt OB, 1847–63, LVA microfilm
    CirCt OB, 1863–83, LVA microfilm
Grayson County
    CirCt Chancery OB 1, 1832–69, LVA microfilm
    CirCt MB, 1835–70, LVA microfilm
Greene County
    CirCt Memorandum Book, 1855–82, LVA microfilm
    CirCt OB 3, 1857–74, LVA microfilm

Greensville County
    CirCt OB, 1843-71, LVA microfilm
    CirCt OB, 1861-78, LVA microfilm
    Chancery OB, 1861-78, LVA microfilm
    CoCt OB 11, 1850-56, LVA microfilm
    CoCt OB 12, 1852-66, LVA microfilm
    CoCt MB 12, 1852-66, LVA microfilm
    Common Law Papers, 1855-63, Greensville County courthouse, Emporia, Va.
    Common Law Papers, 1866-67, Greensville County courthouse, Emporia, Va.
    Dead Papers Decided, 1861-64, Greensville County courthouse, Emporia, Va.
    Judgments Rendered in 1862, Greensville County courthouse, Emporia, Va.
Halifax County
    Chancery Records, Halifax County courthouse, Halifax, Va.
    CirCt OB 5, 1854-58, LVA microfilm
    CirCt OB 6, 1858-66, LVA microfilm
    CirCt Wills and Bonds, 1857-78, Halifax County courthouse, Halifax, Va.
    CoCt MB 17, 1855-57, LVA microfilm
    CoCt MB 18, 1857-59, LVA microfilm
    CoCt MB 19, 1859-62, LVA microfilm
    CoCt MB 20, 1863-66, LVA microfilm
    FNSR, Halifax County courthouse, Halifax, Va.
    Judgments, Halifax County courthouse, Halifax, Va.
    Register of Free Negroes, Halifax County courthouse, Halifax, Va.
    Confederate States of America, Requisitions for Slaves, Halifax County court-
        house, Halifax, Va.
Hanover County
    Chancery, 1867-005, LVA microfilm
    CirCt OB, 1849-56, Hanover County courthouse, Hanover, Va.
    CirCt OB, 1856-68, Hanover County courthouse, Hanover, Va.
    CoCt OB, 1855-57, Hanover County courthouse, Hanover, Va.
    CoCt WB 1, 1862-68, LVA microfilm
    Cohabitation Register, Online, Hanover County courthouse, Hanover, Va.
Henry County
    CirCt OB, 1850-67, Henry County courthouse, Martinsville, Va.
Highland County
    CirCt OB 2, 1848-60, Highland County courthouse, Monterey, Va.
    CirCt OB 2, 1861-79, LVA microfilm
    Ended Papers, 1857-58, Highland County courthouse, Monterey, Va.
    CoCt OB 1, 1847-58, Highland County courthouse, Monterey, Va.
    CoCt OB 2, 1858-70, LVA microfilm
Isle of Wight County
    CirCt OB, 1855-85, LVA microfilm
King and Queen County
    CirCt OB 3, 1854-67, LVA microfilm
    CirSupCt Law and Chancery OB, 1831-58, LVA microfilm

King George County
  CirCt OB 15, 1843–70, LVA microfilm
Lancaster County
  Chancery, 1857–011, LVA online
  CirCt OB, 1854–69, LVA microfilm
  Judgments, 1855–57, LVA mss
Lee County
  CirCt OB 3, 1854–72, LVA microfilm
Loudoun County
  CirCt OB 2, 1853–58, LVA microfilm
  CirCt OB 1, 1858–68, LVA microfilm
  Free Black Papers Series, Loudoun County courthouse,
    Leesburg, Va.
  Loose Papers, Loudoun County courthouse, Leesburg, Va.
  CoCt MB, 1856–58, LVA microfilm
Louisa County
  CirCt OB, 1851–58, Louisa County courthouse, Louisa, Va.
  CoCt MB, 1856–60, LVA microfilm
  FNSR, 1770–1864, LVA mss
  PPTBs, 1851–53, LVA microfilm
  Register of Free Negroes, 1837–65, LVA microfilm
Lunenburg County
  Chancery, 1850-003
  CirCt OB, 1843–51, LVA microfilm
  CirCt OB, 1852–66, LVA microfilm
  CoCt OB 29, 1842–48, LVA microfilm
  CoCt OB 30, 1849–56, LVA microfilm
  CoCt OB 31, 1856–65, LVA microfilm
  CoCt Records, various series, 1700–1924, SRC
  CoCt Judgments 1850–56, LVA mss
  Commonwealth Causes, 1700–1924, SRC
  Fiduciary Book 1, 1851–55, LVA microfilm
  Fiduciary Book 2, 1855–58, LVA microfilm
  Fiduciary Book 3, 1859–63, LVA microfilm
  Fiduciary Book 4, 1863–68, LVA microfilm
  List of Free Negroes, 1818–50, LVA microfilm
  List of Free Negroes and Mulattoes, 1858, LVA microfilm
  Miscellaneous Records, SRC
  PPTBs, 1842–56, LVA microfilm
  Processioners' Returns, 1848–70, LVA microfilm
  Register of Free Negroes, 1850–65, LVA microfilm
  Road and Bridge Papers, LVA mss
  Tax and Fiscal Records, LVA mss
  WB 13, 1846–51, LVA microfilm
  WB 14, 1851-1916, LVA microfilm

Lynchburg City
    Chancery OB 8, 1855-65, LVA microfilm
    CirCt OB 7, 1855-58, LVA microfilm
    CirCt OB 8, 1859-65, LVA microfilm
    Hustings Court, Chancery and Law OB, 1855-57, LVA microfilm
    Hustings Court, Chancery and Law OB, 1858-60, LVA microfilm
    Hustings Court, Chancery and Law OB, 1860-63, LVA microfilm
Madison County
    CirCt OB 3, 1850-60, LVA microfilm
    CirCt OB 4, 1861-87, LVA microfilm
    CoCt OB 12, 1856-63, LVA microfilm
    DB 21, 1852-56, LVA microfilm
    WB 9, 1849-55, LVA microfilm
    WB 10, 1850-58, LVA microfilm
Mathews County
    CirCt OB 3, 1853-63, Mathews County courthouse, Mathews, Va.
    CirSupCt MB, 1850-62, LVA microfilm
    CoCt OB, 1856-66, LVA microfilm
    Common Law Dead Papers, 1863-67, Mathews County courthouse,
        Mathews, Va.
Mecklenburg County
    Chancery, 1859-009, LVA mss
    Chancery, 1869-028cc, LVA mss
    Chancery, 1880-001cc, LVA mss
    Chancery, 1871-055, LVA mss
    Chancery OB 2, 1845-60, LVA microfilm
    CirCt OB 5, 1853-59, LVA microfilm
    CirCt OB 6, 1860-67, LVA microfilm
    CoCt Judgments, 1857-59, LVA mss
    CoCt Judgments, 1859-65, LVA mss
    CoCt OB 6-A, 1853-58, LVA microfilm
    CoCt OB 7, 1859-65, LVA microfilm
    PPTBs, 1859-61, LVA microfilm
    Register of Free Negroes 1, 1809-41, LVA microfilm
    Register of Free Negroes 2, 1841-65, LVA microfilm
    Surveyors' Book, 1857-69, LVA microfilm
    WB 19, 1856-59, LVA microfilm
Middlesex County
    CirCt OB, 1854-69, LVA microfilm
    CirSupCt OB, 1843-57, LVA microfilm
    CirCt MB, 1845-59, LVA microfilm
    CirCt OB, 1857-65, Middlesex County courthouse,
        Saluda, Va.
Montgomery County
    CirCt OB 4, 1855-68, LVA microfilm

Nelson County
    CirCt OB E, 1854–62, LVA microfilm
    CirCt OB F, 1863–70, LVA microfilm
    CoCt MB 12, 1855–61, LVA microfilm
    Register of Free Negroes, vol. 1, 1853–65, LVA microfilm
New Kent County
    SupCt MB, 1836–60, LVA microfilm
    Judgment Docket, 1850–57, LVA microfilm
    Unspecified OB, 1860–67, LVA microfilm
Norfolk County
    CirCt OB 13, 1853–58, LVA microfilm
    CirCt OB 14, 1858–74, LVA microfilm
    CoCt MB 32, 1854–55, LVA microfilm
    CoCt MB 33, 1856–57, LVA microfilm
    CoCt MB 34, 1857–60, LVA microfilm
    CoCt MB 35, 1860–68, LVA microfilm
    Judgments, 1854–58, SRC
Norfolk City
    CirCt Ended Law Causes, 1857–66, Norfolk City courthouse, Norfolk, Va.
    CirCt OB 6, 1856–59, LVA microfilm
    CirCt OB 7, 1859–66, LVA microfilm
    Hustings Court OB 38, 1855–57, LVA microfilm
    Hustings Court OB 39, 1857–59, LVA microfilm
    Hustings Court OB 40, 1859–61, LVA microfilm
    Hustings Court OB 41, 1861–66, LVA microfilm
    Hustings Court Ended Causes, 1859–63, Norfolk City courthouse,
        Norfolk, Va.
Northampton County
    CirCt OB 2, 1852–74, LVA microfilm
    Chancery OB 1, 1831–66, LVA microfilm
Northumberland County
    Chancery, 1856-003, LVA mss
    Chancery, 1857-002, LVA mss
    Chancery, 1867-015, LVA mss
    CirCt OB 2, 1854–77, LVA microfilm
    CoCt OB, 1852–61, LVA microfilm
    CoCt OB, 1861–71, LVA microfilm
    Judgments, 1850–63, LVA mss
    Misc. Old Papers, 1821–34, 1850–1930, LVA mss
    Misc. Old Papers, 1830–39, 1850–1922, LVA mss
Nottoway County
    CirCt OB 2, 1832–63, LVA microfilm
    Chancery Docket, 1835–61, LVA microfilm
    CirCt MB, 1855–60, LVA mss
    CirCt Memorandum Book, 1855–67, LVA microfilm

CoCt MB 3, 1854–60, LVA microfilm
CoCt MB, 1860–64, LVA microfilm
Orange County
    CirCt OB, 1853–67, Orange County courthouse, Orange, Va.
    CoCt MB, 1856–67, LVA microfilm
    PPTBs, 1854–61, LVA microfilm
Page County
    CirCt OB 1, 1831–59, LVA microfilm
    CirCt OB 2, 1860–65, LVA microfilm
    Judgments, Appeals, and Commonwealth Causes, 1863–67, SRC
Patrick County
    CirCt OB, 1855–81, LVA microfilm
    CirCt OB, 1862–81, LVA microfilm
Petersburg City
    CirCt OB, 1846–91, LVA microfilm
    CirCt OB 6, 1853–58, LVA microfilm
    CirCt OB 7, 1858–69, LVA microfilm
    Hustings Court MB, 1853–56, LVA microfilm
    Hustings Court MB, 1856–58, LVA microfilm
    Hustings Court MB, 1858–61, LVA microfilm
    Hustings Court MB, 1861–67, LVA microfilm
    Register of Free Negroes and Mulattoes, 1794–1819, LVA microfilm
    Hustings Court Registry of Free Negroes, 1819–32, LVA microfilm
    Hustings Court Registry of Free Negroes, 1831–39, LVA microfilm
    Hustings Court Registry of Free Negroes, 1839–50, LVA microfilm
    Hustings Court Registry of Free Negroes, 1850–58, LVA microfilm
    Hustings Court Registry of Free Negroes, 1859–65, LVA microfilm
Pittsylvania County
    CirCt OB 8, 1854–59, LVA microfilm
    CirCt OB 9, 1859–69, LVA microfilm
    Judgments, 1849–60, LVA mss
    Final Decrees, 1856–58, Pittsylvania County courthouse, Chatham, Va.
Powhatan County
    Chancery, 1856–010, LVA mss
    CirCt OB 4, 1850–66, LVA microfilm
    CirCt MB, 1853–71, LVA microfilm
    CoCt Commonwealth Causes 1851, LVA mss
    CoCt OB 28, 1848–51, LVA microfilm
    CoCt OB 29, 1851–56, LVA microfilm
    CoCt OB 30, 1857–61, LVA microfilm
    FNSR, box 4, LVA mss
    Marriage Register, 1777–1853, LVA microfilm
    Register of Free Negroes and Mulattoes, 1800–20, LVA microfilm
    Register of Free Negroes and Mulattoes, 1820–65, LVA microfilm
    WB 9, 1831–36, LVA microfilm

Prince Edward County
    Chancery, 1873-001, LVA mss
    CirCt Court Records, August 1854–August 1855, LVA mss
    CirCt Law Papers, March 1856–August 1858, SRC
    CirCt OB, 1847–58, LVA microfilm
    CirCt OB, 1853–70, Prince Edward County courthouse, Farmville, Va.
    CirCt WB, 1833–99, LVA microfilm
    CirSupCt MB, 1846–70, SRC
    CirSupCt OB, 1847–58, LVA microfilm
    CirSupCt OB, 1853–70, Prince Edward County courthouse,
        Farmville, Va.
    Chancery OB, 1853–70, LVA microfilm
    Chancery OB 1, 1859–72, LVA microfilm
    CoCt OB 27, 1853–62, Prince Edward County courthouse, Farmville, Va.
    PPTBs, 1866–67, LVA microfilm
    WB 7, 1828–37, LVA microfilm
Prince George County
    Index to Common Law Orders, LVA microfilm
    Chancery OB 1, 1859–92, LVA microfilm
Prince William County
    CirCt OB 3, 1854–86, Prince William County courthouse, Manassas, Va.
Princess Anne County
    Chancery OB 1, 1831–58, LVA microfilm
    FNSR, 1771–1862, LVA microfilm
Pulaski County
    CirCt OB 1, 1839–57, LVA microfilm
    CirCt OB 2, 1857–76, LVA microfilm
    CoCt OB, 1850–62, LVA microfilm
    DB 2, 1846–56, LVA microfilm
    Loose Papers, 1840–65, Wilderness Road Museum Archives,
        Newbern, Va.
Rappahannock County
    CirCt OB B, 1842–56, Rappahannock County courthouse, Washington, Va.
    CirCt OB C, 1856–74, Rappahannock County courthouse, Washington, Va.
Richmond City
    CirCt OB 6, 1859–60, LVA microfilm
    CirCt OB 7, 1860–61, LVA microfilm
    CirCt Office Judgments, 1855–70, LVA microfilm
    CirCt OB, 1860, SRC
    CirCt OB, 1861, SRC
    CirCt OB 27, 1861–65, SRC
    Hustings Court MB 10, 1828–31, LVA microfilm
    Hustings Court MB 11, 1831–35, LVA microfilm
    Hustings Court MB 12, 1835–37, LVA microfilm
    WB 9, 1841–43, LVA microfilm

Richmond County
    CirSup and CirCt Chancery OB, 1831–61, LVA microfilm
    CirCt Execution Book, 1842–69, LVA microfilm
    CirCt OB, 1858–74, Richmond County courthouse, Warsaw, Va.
    CoCt OB 31, 1858–71, Richmond County courthouse, Warsaw, Va.
    Loose Papers 1849–68, SRC
    Register of Colored Persons Cohabitating, LVA mss
Roanoke County
    CirCt OB 2, 1853–66, Roanoke County courthouse, Salem, Va.
    CoCt OB D, 1848–56, Roanoke County courthouse, Salem, Va.
    CoCt OB E, 1856–64, Roanoke County courthouse, Salem, Va.
Rockbridge County
    Chancery, 1853-009, LVA online
    Chancery, 1860-065, LVA online
    CirCt OB, 1852–67 (continued), LVA microfilm
    CirCt WB 1, 1809–74, LVA microfilm
    CoCt MB, 1854–57, LVA microfilm
    CoCt Judgments, 1859–60, SRC
    FNSR, 1848–81, LVA mss
    Misc. Documents, 1823–1923, LVA mss
    Register of Free Negroes, 1831–60, LVA microfilm
    WB 8, 1837–40, LVA microfilm
Rockingham County
    FNSR, LVA mss
Russell County
    CirCt OB 4, 1850–71, LVA microfilm
Scott County
    CirCt OB 3, 1852–67, LVA microfilm
Shenandoah County
    CirCt OB, 1856–76, LVA microfilm
Smyth County
    CirCt OB 3, 1849–57, LVA microfilm
    CirCt OB 4, 1857–73, LVA microfilm
Southampton County
    Chancery, 1856-016, LVA microfilm
    Chancery Papers, 1856–57, LVA microfilm
    CirCt Judgments, 1858–70, LVA mss
    CirCt OB 6, 1851–75, LVA microfilm
    CoCt Free Negroes Register, LVA microfilm
    CoCt MB, 1848–55, LVA microfilm
    CoCt MB, 1855–61, LVA microfilm
    CoCt MB, 1861–70, LVA microfilm
    CoCt Papers, 1848–61, LVA microfilm
    CoCt Papers, 1861–84, LVA microfilm
    Commonwealth Causes, 1859–1912, LVA microfilm

FNSR, LVA mss
Judgment papers, 1814–64, LVA microfilm
Judgments (misc.), 1829–66, Southampton County courthouse, Courtland, Va.
Misc. Court Records, 1861–1912, LVA microfilm
Misc. Court Records, 1858–1910, LVA microfilm
Surry County
CirCt OB, 1839–67, Surry County courthouse, Surry, Va.
Chancery OB, 1831–74, LVA microfilm
Orders, 1853–61, LVA microfilm
CoCt OB, 1853–61, Surry County courthouse, Surry, Va.
Sussex County
CirCt OB, 1831–66, Sussex County courthouse, Sussex, Va.
CoCt OB, 1843–52, Sussex County courthouse, Sussex, Va.
CoCt OB, 1852–64, Sussex County courthouse, Sussex, Va.
Deed Book W, Sussex County courthouse, Sussex, Va.
Loose Court Papers, 1754–1870, Sussex County courthouse, Sussex, Va.
Tazewell County
CirCt OB, 1844–59, LVA microfilm
CirCt OB, 1859–78, LVA microfilm
Warren County
CirCt OB B, 1856–86, Warren County courthouse, Front Royal, Va.
Washington County
CirCt OB D, 1853–59, LVA microfilm
CirCt OB E, 1859–70, LVA microfilm
CoCt MB 12, 1855–57, LVA microfilm
CoCt MB 13, 1857–58, LVA microfilm
CoCt MB 14, 1858–60, LVA microfilm
CoCt MB 15, 1860–63, LVA microfilm
Westmoreland County
Chancery Orders, 1851–73, LVA microfilm
Wythe County
CirCt Chancery OB 3, 1853–73, LVA microfilm
York County
CirCt OB, 1845–60, LVA microfilm

Newspapers and Periodicals

African Repository and Colonial Journal (Washington, DC)
Baltimore American & Commercial Advertiser
Baltimore Sun
Boston Atlas
Boston Evening Transcript
Charleston (SC) Mercury
Charleston (WV) Free Press
Cleveland Herald
Daily National Era (Washington, DC)
Daily Richmond Enquirer
Debow's Review and Industrial Resources, Statistics, &c. (New Orleans and Washington, DC)
Liberator (Boston)

Lynchburg Daily Virginian
Macon Weekly Telegraph (Macon, Ga.)
Maryland Colonization Journal
   (Baltimore)
Mississippian and State Gazette
   (Jackson, Miss.)
New York Herald
New York Times
Philadelphia Inquirer
Richmond Daily Dispatch

Richmond Daily Whig
Richmond Dispatch
Richmond Times-Dispatch
Richmond Whig and Public Advertiser
South-Side Democrat (Petersburg, Va.)
Spectator
Tobacco Plant (Clarksville, Va.)
Virginia Free Press
Weekly Anglo-African (New York)

Published Works

Acts of the Virginia General Assembly. Richmond, Va.: William F. Ritchie, 1846–64.

Basler, Roy P., ed. Collected Works. The Abraham Lincoln Association, Springfield, Illinois. New Brunswick, N.J.: Rutgers University Press, 1953.

"Bill No. 470. A BILL of Mr. Browne of Stafford and King George, providing for the Removal of Free Negroes and Mulattoes from the Commonwealth." Richmond, Va: n.p., 1852.

Black Entrepreneurs of the Eighteenth and Nineteenth Centuries. Boston: Federal Reserve Bank of Boston and the Museum of African American History, Boston and Nantucket, 2009. Exhibition program.

Berlin, Ira, and Leslie S. Rowland, eds. Families and Freedom: A Documentary History of African-American Kinship in the Civil War Era. New York: New Press, 1997.

Blassingame, John W. ed. Slave Testimony: Two Centuries of Letters, Speeches, Interviews, and Autobiographies. Baton Rouge: Louisiana State University Press, 1977.

Brown, W. S. A Plan of National Colonization, Adequate to the Entire Removal of the Free Blacks, and All That May Hereafter Become Free, in a Manner Harmonizing with the Peace and Well-Being of Both Races, in Josiah Priest, Bible Defence of Slavery; or the Origin, History, and Fortunes of the Negro Race, as Deduced from History, Both Sacred and Profane, Their Natural Relations—Moral, Mental, and Physical—to the Other Races of Mankind, Compared and Illustrated—Their Future Destiny Predicted, etc. Glasgow, Ky.: W. S. Brown, 1853.

Burks, E. C. Letter to Rowland D. Buford, 6 March 1861. In James Elliott Walmsley, "The Change of Secession Sentiment in Virginia in 1861." American Historical Review 31, no. 1 (October 1925).

Chester, Thomas Morris. Thomas Morris Chester, Black Civil War Correspondent: His Dispatches from the Virginian Front. Edited by R. J. M. Blackett. Baton Rouge: Louisiana State University Press, 1989.

Code of 1819. Richmond, Va.: William F. Ritchie, 1819.

Code of Virginia. Richmond, Va.: William F. Ritchie, 1849.

Edmonds, Amanda Virginia. Journals of Amanda Virginia Edmonds: Lass of the Mosby Confederacy, 1859–67. Edited by Nancy Chappelear Baird. Stephens City, Va.: Commercial Press, 1984.

Grandy, Moses. "Narrative of the Life of Moses Grandy, Late a Slave in the United States of America." In *Five Slave Narratives*. Edited by William Loren Katz. New York: Arno Press, 1968.

Grattan, Peachy R. *Reports of Cases Decided in the Supreme Court of Appeals, and in the General Court of Virginia*, 33 vols., Richmond, Va.: Shepherd and Colin, 1845–81.

Guild, June Purcell. *Black Laws of Virginia: A Summary of the Legislative Acts of Virginia Concerning Negroes from the Earliest Times to the Present*. Lovettsville, Va.: Willow Bend Books, 1995.

Harper, William, Thomas Roderick Dew, James Henry Hammond, and Walter Gilmore Simms. *Pro-Slavery Argument, as Maintained by the Most Distinguished Writers of the Southern States*. Orig. pub. 1852; reprint, New York: Negro Universities Press, 1968.

Hatchett, William Haynie. *Diary, 1853 Feb. 27–1855 Aug. 3*, Misc. microfilm reel # 282, Mss Acc.#28643, LVA.

Hening, William W. *The Statutes at Large; Being a Collection of All Laws of Virginia from the First Session of the Legislature, in the year 1619*. 13 vols. New York: R. & W. & G. Bartow, 1809–23

Hunter, Robert. "Department of Miscellany." *DeBow's Review and Industrial Resources, Statistics, etc.*, 5, no. 1 (January 1861): 114.

Hurd, John Codman. *The Law of Freedom and Bondage in the United States*. Boston: Little, Brown, 1858.

Jefferson, Thomas. *Writings*. Edited by Merrill D. Peterson. New York: Literary Classics of the U.S., 1984.

Journal of the House of Delegates of the State of Virginia. Richmond, Va.: William F. Ritchie, 1846–64.

Journal of the Senate of the Commonwealth of Virginia. Richmond, Va.: John Warrock, 1846–64.

Miller, Randall M., ed. *"Dear Master": Letters of a Slave Family*. Ithaca, N.Y.: Cornell University Press, 1978.

New Constitution of Virginia, with the Amended Bill of Rights, as Adopted by the Reform Convention of 1850–51. Richmond, Va.: John Warrock, 1852.

Ruffin, Edmund. *African Colonization Unveiled*. Washington, D.C.: L. Towers, 1859.

Rutherfoord, John C. *Speech of John C. Rutherfoord, of Goochland, in the House of Delegates of Virginia, on the Removal from the Commonwealth of the Free Colored Population*. Richmond, Va.: Ritchies & Dunnavant, 1853.

Smith, Richard H., Jr., trans. and comp. *Accomack County, Virginia, Free Negro Records: Register of Free Negroes, 1807–1863 and List of Free Negroes, 1804*. Woodsboro, Md.: Firewood Treasures, 2007.

Starobin, Robert S. *Blacks in Bondage: Letters of American Slaves*. New York: New Viewpoints, 1974.

Still, William. *Still's Underground Rail Road Records*. Philadelphia: William Still, 1886.

Tables Showing the Number of Emigrants and Recaptured Africans Sent to the Colony of Liberia by the Government of the United States; also, the Number of Emigrants Free Born, Number That Purchased Their Freedom, Number Emancipated, &c.; Together with a Census of the Colony, and a Report of Its Commerce, &c. (Washington, 1845).

Tucker, Saint George. *A Dissertation on Slavery: With a Proposal for the Gradual Abolition of It, in the State of Virginia*. Philadelphia: M. Carey, 1796.

Supplement to the Revised Code of the Laws of Virginia: Being a Collection of All the Acts of the General Assembly, Of a Public and Permanent Nature, Passed Since the Year 1819, With a General Index : to Which are Prefixed, The Acts Organizing a Convention, The Declaration of Rights, And the Amended Constitution of Virginia. Richmond, Va.: Samuel Shepherd, 1833.

Washington, Booker T. *Up from Slavery*. New York: Oxford University Press, 1995.

Wiley, Bell I. ed. *Slaves No More: Letters from Liberia, 1833–1869*. Lexington: University Press of Kentucky, 1980.

Yetman, Norman R. ed. *When I Was a Slave: Memoires from the Slave Narrative Collection*. New York: Dover Publications, 2002.

SECONDARY SOURCES

Adams, Carrol Franklin. "A New England Teacher in Southside Virginia: A Study of Emily Howe [Dupuy], 1812–1883." Master's thesis, University of Virginia, 1954.

Bailyn, Bernard. "Considering the Slave Trade: History and Memory." *William and Mary Quarterly* 58, no. 1 (January 2001): 245–51.

Ballagh, James Curtis. *A History of Slavery in Virginia*. Baltimore: Johns Hopkins Press, 1902.

Balogh, Brian. "The Enduring Legacy of Nineteenth-Century Governance in the United States: The Emergence of the Associative Order." In *State and Citizen: British America and the Early United States*, edited by Peter Thompson and Peter S. Onuf, 271–94. Charlottesville: University of Virginia Press, 2013.

Bell, Landon C. *The Old Free State*. Richmond, Va.: William Byrd Press, 1927. 2 vols.

Berlin, Ira. *Slaves without Masters: The Free Negro in the Antebellum South*. New York: Pantheon, 1974.

———. *Generations of Captivity: A History of African-American Slaves*. Cambridge, Mass.: The Belknap Press of Harvard University Press, 2003.

———. *The Making of African America: The Four Great Migrations*. New York: Viking Press, 2010.

Berlin, Ira, Steven F. Miller, Joseph P. Reidy, and Leslie S. Rowland, eds., *The Wartime Genesis of Free Labor: The Upper South*. Ser. 1, vol. 2 of *Freedom: A Documentary History of Emancipation, 1861–1867*, 85–110. Cambridge: Cambridge University Press, 1993.

Berlin, Isaiah. *Four Essays on Liberty*. London: Oxford University Press, 1969.

———. *Liberty*. Edited by Henry Hardy. Oxford: Oxford University Press, 2002.

Blight, David W. *Frederick Douglass' Civil War: Keeping Faith in Jubilee*. Baton Rouge: Louisiana State University Press, 1989.

———. *A Slave No More: Two Men Who Escaped to Freedom, Including Their Own Narratives of Emancipation*. New York: Random House, 2007.

Blomberg, Belinda. "Free Black Adaptive Responses to the Antebellum Urban Environment: Neighborhood Formation and Socioeconomic Stratification in Alexandria, Virginia, 1790–1850." Ph.D. diss., American University, 1988.

Bogger, Tommy L. *Free Blacks in Norfolk, Virginia, 1790–1860: The Darker Side of Freedom.* Charlottesville: University of Virginia Press, 1997.

Bracey, Susan L. *Life by the Roaring Roanoke: A History of Mecklenburg County, Virginia.* Richmond, Va.: Mecklenburg County Bicentennial Commission, 1978.

Bradburn, Douglas. *The Citizenship Revolution: Politics and the Creation of the American Union, 1774–1804.* Charlottesville: University of Virginia Press, 2009.

———. "'The Great Field of Human Concerns': The States, the Union, and the Problem of Citizenship in the Era of the American Revolution." In *State and Citizen: British America and the Early United States,* edited by Peter Thompson and Peter S. Onuf, 77–112. Charlottesville: University of Virginia Press, 2013.

Breen T. H., and Stephen Innes. *"Myne Owne Ground": Race and Freedom on Virginia's Eastern Shore, 1640–1676.* New York: Oxford University Press, 1980.

Bremner, Robert H. *From the Depths: The Discovery of Poverty in the United States.* New York: New York University Press, 1964.

Brewer, James H. *The Confederate Negro: Virginia's Craftsmen and Military Laborers, 1861–1865.* Durham, N.C.: Duke University Press, 1969.

Bristol, Douglas Wilder, Jr. *Knights of the Razor: Black Barbers in Slavery and Freedom.* Baltimore: Johns Hopkins University Press, 2009.

Bryson, W. Hamilton, ed., *Legal Education in Virginia, 1779–1979.* Charlottesville, Va.: University Press of Virginia, 1982.

Budros, Art. "The Antislavery Movement in Early America: Religion, Social Environment, and Slave Manumissions." *Social Forces* 84, no. 2 (Dec. 2005): 941–66.

Burin, Eric. *Slavery and the Peculiar Solution: A History of the American Colonization Society.* Gainesville: University Press of Florida, 2005.

Butler, Reginald Dennin. "Evolution of a Rural Black Community: Goochland County, Virginia, 1728–1832." Ph.D. diss., Johns Hopkins University, 1989.

Caldwell, Peter C. "When the Complexity of Lived Experience Finds Itself Before a Court of Law." *Law and History Review* 29, no. 2 (May 2011): 567–72.

Calomiris, Charles W., and Larry Schweikart. "The Panic of 1857: Origins, Transmission, and Containment." *Journal of Economic History* 51, no. 4 (December 1991): 807–34.

Campbell, James M. *Slavery on Trial: Race, Class, and Criminal Justice in Antebellum Richmond, Virginia.* Gainesville: University Press of Florida, 2007.

Cashin, Joan E. "Landscape and Memory in Antebellum Virginia." *Virginia Magazine of History and Biography* 102, no. 4 (October 1994): 477–500.

Countryman, Edward. *Enjoy the Same Liberty: Black Americans and the Revolutionary Era.* Lanham, Md.: Rowman and Littlefield, 2012.

Cromwell, John W. "The Aftermath of Nat Turner's Insurrection." *Journal of Negro History* 5, no. 2 (April 1920): 208–34.

Curtis, Christopher Michael. *Jefferson's Freeholders and the Politics of Ownership in the Old Dominion.* New York: Cambridge University Press, 2012.

Daniel, W. Harrison. *Bedford County, Virginia, 1840–1860: The History of an Upper Piedmont County in the Late Antebellum Era*. Bedford, Va.: Print Shop, 1985.

Davis, David Brion. "The Culmination of Racial Polarities and Prejudice." In *Race and the Early Republic: Racial Consciousness and Nation-Building in the Early Republic*, edited by Michael A. Morrison and James Brewer Stewart. Lanham, Md.: Rowman and Littlefield, 2002.

———. *Inhuman Bondage: The Rise and Fall of Slavery in the New World*. New York: Oxford University Press, 2006.

Davis, Margaret G. *Madison County, Virginia: A Revised History*. Ephrata, Pa.: Board of Supervisors of Madison County, 1977.

Delaney, Ted and Phillip Wayne Rhodes. *Free Blacks of Lynchburg, Virginia, 1805–1856*. Lynchburg, Va.: Warwick House Publishing, 2001.

Dew, Charles B. *Bond of Iron: Master and Slave at Buffalo Forge*. New York: Norton, 1994.

———. "Sam Williams, Forgeman: The Life of an Industrial Slave in the Old South." In *Region, Race, and Reconstruction: Essays in Honor of C. Vann Woodward*. Edited by James M. McPherson and J. Morgan Kousser. New York: Oxford University Press, 1982.

Deyle, Steven. *Carry Me Back: The Domestic Slave Trade in American Life*. New York: Oxford University Press, 2005.

Dubois, Laurent. *Avengers of the New World: The Story of the Haitian Revolution*. Cambridge, Mass.: The Belknap Press of Harvard University Press, 2004.

Dunn, Susan. *Dominion of Memories: Jefferson, Madison, and the Decline of Virginia*. New York: Basic Books, 2007.

Edwards, Laura F. *The People and Their Peace: Legal Culture and the Transformation of Inequality in the Post-Revolutionary South*. Chapel Hill: University of North Carolina Press, 2009.

Egerton, Douglas R. *Gabriel's Rebellion: The Virginia Slave Conspiracies of 1800 and 1802*. Chapel Hill: University of North Carolina Press, 1993.

———. *Death or Liberty: African Americans and Revolutionary America*. New York: Oxford University Press, 2009.

Ehrlich, Walter. "The Origins of the Dred Scott Case." *The Journal of Negro History* 59, no. 2 (April 1974): 132–42.

Ely, Melvin Patrick. *Israel on the Appomattox: A Southern Experiment in Black Freedom from the 1790s through the Civil War*. New York: Vintage Books, 2004.

Engerman, Stanley L. "Slavery at Different Times and Places." *American Historical Review* 105, no. 2 (April 2000): 480–84.

Ericson, David F. *Slavery in the American Republic: Developing the Federal Government, 1791–1861*. Lawrence, Kansas: University Press of Kansas, 2011.

Eslinger, Ellen. "Free Black Residency in Two Antebellum Virginia Counties: How the Laws Functioned." *Journal of Southern History* 79 (May 2013): 261–98.

Fehrenbacher, Don E. *The Slaveholding Republic: An Account of the United States Government's Relations to Slavery*. Edited by Ward McAfee. New York: Oxford University Press, 2001.

Ferguson, Stephen, Sid Lapidus, and Sean Wilentz. *Liberty and the American Revolution: Selections from the Collection of Sid Lapidus, Class of 1959.* Princeton, N.J.: Princeton University Library, 2009.

Finkelman, Paul. "Exploring Southern Legal History." *North Carolina Law Review* 64 (November 1985): 77–116.

Foner, Eric. *The Story of American Freedom.* New York: Norton, 1998.

Ford, Lacy K. *Deliver Us from Evil: The Slavery Question in the Old South.* New York: Oxford, 2009.

Forsythe, Harold S. "'But My Friends Are Poor': Ross Hamilton and Freedpeople's Politics in Mecklenburg County, Virginia, 1869–1901." *Virginia Magazine of History and Biography* 105, no. 4 (Autumn 1997): 409–38.

Fox-Genovese, Elizabeth. *Within the Plantation Household: Black and White Women of the Old South.* Chapel Hill: University of North Carolina Press, 1988.

Franklin, John Hope. "The Enslavement of Free Negroes in North Carolina." *The Journal of Negro History* 29, no. 4 (October 1944): 401–28.

———. *The Free Negro in North Carolina, 1790–1860.* Chapel Hill: University of North Carolina Press, 1995.

Freehling, Alison Goodyear. *Drift toward Dissolution: The Virginia Slavery Debate of 1831–32.* Baton Rouge: Louisiana State University Press, 1982.

Freehling, William W. *The Road to Disunion, vol. 1: Secessionists at Bay, 1776–1854.* New York: Oxford University Press, 1990.

———. *The Road to Disunion, vol. 2: Secessionists Triumphant, 1854–1861.* New York: Oxford University Press, 2007.

Frey, Sylvia R. *Water from the Rock: Black Resistance in a Revolutionary Age.* Princeton, N.J.: Princeton University Press, 1991.

Gaines, Francis Pendleton. "The Virginia Constitutional Convention of 1850–51: A Study in Sectionalism." Ph.D. diss., University of Virginia, 1950.

Gaspar, David Barry and Darlene Clark Hine, eds. *Beyond Bondage: Free Women of Color in the Americas.* Chicago: University of Illinois Press, 2004.

Genovese, Eugene D. *Roll, Jordan, Roll: The World the Slaves Made.* New York: Pantheon Books, 1974.

Gerber, David A. *Black Ohio and the Color Line, 1860–1915.* Chicago: University of Illinois Press, 1976.

Gilbert, Alan. *Black Patriots and Loyalists: Fighting for Emancipation in the War for Independence.* Chicago: University of Chicago Press, 2012.

Gordon-Reed, Annette, ed. *Race on Trial: Law and Justice in American History.* New York: Oxford University Press, 2002.

Gould, Eliga H. "The Laws of War and Peace: Legitimating Slavery in the Age of the American Revolution." In *State and Citizen: British America and the Early United States,* edited by Peter Thompson and Peter S. Onuf, 52–76. Charlottesville: University of Virginia Press, 2013.

Gould, Virginia Meacham, ed. *Chained to the Rock of Adversity: To Be Free, Black & Female in the Old South.* Athens: University of Georgia Press, 1998.

Green, Elna C. *This Business of Relief: Confronting Poverty in a Southern City, 1740–1940.* Athens: University of Georgia Press, 2003.

Grivno, Max. *Gleanings of Freedom: Free and Slave Labor along the Mason-Dixon Line, 1790-1860*, Urbana: Illinois University Press, 2011.

Gross, Ariela. *Double Character: Slavery and Mastery in the Antebellum Southern Courtroom*. Princeton: Princeton University Press, 2000.

———. "Beyond Black and White: Cultural Approaches to Race and Slavery." *Columbia Law Review* 101, no. 3 (April 2001): 640-90.

———. *What Blood Won't Tell: A History of Race on Trial in America*. Cambridge, Mass.: Harvard University Press, 2008.

———. "Race, Law, and Comparative History." *Law and History Review* 29, no. 2 (May 2011): 549-65.

Gudmestad, Robert. *A Troublesome Commerce: The Transformation of the Interstate Slave Trade*. Baton Rouge: Louisiana State University Press, 2003.

Gutman, Herbert G. *The Black Family in Slavery and Freedom, 1750-1925*. New York: Pantheon Books, 1976.

Hadden, Sally. "The Fragmented Laws of Slavery in the Colonial and Revolutionary Eras." In *The Cambridge History of Law in America*, vol. 1, edited by Michael Grossberg and Christopher Tomlins. New York: Cambridge University Press, 2008.

Hahn, Steven. *A Nation under Our Feet: Black Political Struggles in the Rural South from Slavery to the Great Migration*. Cambridge, Mass.: The Belknap Press of Harvard University Press, 2003.

Hamilton, Phillip. "Revolutionary Principles and Family Loyalties: Slavery's Transformation in the St. George Tucker Household of Early National Virginia." *William and Mary Quarterly*, 3rd ser., 55, no. 4 (October 1998): 531-56.

Hartog, Hendrik. "Pigs and Positivism." *Wisconsin Law Review* (July–August 1985): 899-934.

Hayward, Jack, ed. *Out of Slavery: Abolition and After*. New York: Frank Cass, 1985.

Heath, Barbara J. "Slavery and Consumerism: A Case Study from Central Virginia." *Newsletter of the African-American Archaeology Network* 19, 1997: 1-8.

———. *Hidden Lives: The Archaeology of Slave Life at Thomas Jefferson's Poplar Forest*. Charlottesville: University of Virginia Press, 1999.

Heinegg, Paul. *Free African Americans of North Carolina, Virginia, and South Carolina*. Baltimore: Clearfield, 2007.

Hickin, Patricia P. "Antislavery in Virginia, 1831-1861." Ph.D. diss., University of Virginia, 1968.

Higginbotham, A. Leon, Jr. and Greer C. Bosworth. "'Rather than the free': Free Blacks in Colonial and Antebellum Virginia." *Harvard Civil Rights–Civil Liberties Law Review* 26 (Winter 1991): 17-66.

Hillman, Nancy A. Moll. "Drawn Together, Drawn Apart: Race and Reform in the Baptist Churches of Southeastern Virginia, 1800-1870," Ph.D. diss., the College of William and Mary, 2013.

Howe, Daniel Walker. *What Hath God Wrought: The Transformation of America, 1815-1848*. New York: Oxford University Press, 2007.

Hunt, Alfred N. *Haiti's Influence on Antebellum America: Slumbering Volcano in the Caribbean*. Baton Rouge: Louisiana State University Press, 1988.

Isaac, Rhys. *The Transformation of Virginia, 1740–1790*. Chapel Hill: University of North Carolina Press, 1999.

Jackson, Luther Porter. *Free Negro Labor and Property Holding in Virginia, 1830–1860*. New York: Atheneum, 1942.

———. "Manumission in Certain Virginia Cities." *Journal of Negro History* 15, no. 3 (1930): 278–314.

Jenkins, Wilbert L. *Climbing up to Glory: A Short History of African Americans during the Civil War and Reconstruction*. Wilmington, Del.: Scholarly Resources, 2002.

Johnson, James Hugo. *Race Relations in Virginia and Miscegenation in the South, 1776–1860*. Amherst: University of Massachusetts Press, 1970.

Johnson, Walter. *Soul by Soul: Life inside the Antebellum Slave Market*. Cambridge, Mass.: Harvard University Press, 1999.

Jordan, Ervin L., Jr. *Black Confederates and Afro-Yankees in Civil War Virginia*. Charlottesville: University of Virginia Press, 1995.

Kantrowitz, Stephen. *More Than Freedom: Fighting for Black Citizenship in a White Republic, 1829–1889*. New York: Penguin Press, 2012.

Karsten, Peter. *Heart Versus Head: Judge-Made Law in Nineteenth-Century America*. Chapel Hill: University of North Carolina Press, 1997.

Katz, Ellen D. "African-American Freedom in Antebellum Cumberland County, Virginia." *Chicago-Kent Law Review* 70 (1994–95): 927–91.

Katz, Michael B. *In the Shadow of the Poorhouse: A Social History of Welfare in America*. New York: Basic Books, 1996.

Kaye, Anthony E. *Joining Places: Slave Neighborhoods in the Old South*. Chapel Hill: University of North Carolina Press, 2007.

Kennington, Kelly Marie. "River of Injustice: St. Louis's Freedom Suits and the Changing Nature of Legal Slavery in Antebellum America." Ph.D. diss., Duke University, 2009.

———. "Law, Geography, and Mobility: Suing for Freedom in Antebellum St. Louis." *Journal of Southern History* 80, no. 3 (August 2014): 575–604.

Kettner, James H. *The Development of American Citizenship, 1608–1870*. Chapel Hill: The University of North Carolina Press, 1978.

Kimball, Gregg D. *American City, Southern Place: A Cultural History of Antebellum Richmond*. Athens: University of Georgia Press, 2000.

King, Wilma. "Out of Bounds: Emancipated and Enslaved Women in Antebellum America." In *Beyond Bondage: Free Women of Color in the Americas*, edited by David Barry Gaspar and Darlene Clark Hine. Chicago: University of Chicago Press, 2004.

Klebaner, Benjamin Joseph. "American Manumission Laws and the Responsibility of Supporting Slaves." *Virginia Magazine of History and Biography* 63, no. 4 (October 1955): 443–53.

Kolchin, Peter. *Unfree Labor: American Slavery and Russian Serfdom*. Cambridge, Mass.: The Belknap Press of Harvard University Press, 1987.

Lebsock, Suzanne. *The Free Women of Petersburg: Status and Culture in a Southern Town, 1784–1860*. New York: Norton, 1984.

Levine, Lawrence W. *Black Culture and Black Consciousness: Afro-American Folk Thought from Slavery to Freedom.* New York: Oxford University Press, 1978.

Link, William A. *Roots of Secession: Slavery and Politics in Antebellum Virginia.* Chapel Hill: University of North Carolina Press, 2003.

Litwack, Leon F. *Been in the Storm So Long: The Aftermath of Slavery.* New York: Vintage, 1979.

Lowe, Richard. "Local Black Leaders during Reconstruction in Virginia." *Virginia Magazine of History and Biography* 103, no. 2, (April 1995): 181–206.

Lowe, Zachary C. "Meanings of Freedom: Virginia Contraband Settlements and Wartime Reconstruction." Master's thesis, College of William and Mary, 2003.

Maris-Wolf, Edward D. "Liberty, Bondage, and the Pursuit of Happiness: The Free Black Expulsion Law and Self-Enslavement in Virginia, 1806–1864." Ph.D. diss., College of William and Mary, 2011.

Martinez, Jaime Amanda. "The Slave Market in Civil War Virginia." In *Crucible of the Civil War: Virginia from Secession to Commemoration,* edited by Edward L. Ayers, Gary W. Gallagher, and Andrew J. Torget. Charlottesville: University of Virginia Press, 2006.

Matison, Sumner Eliot. "Manumission by Purchase." *Journal of Negro History* 33, no. 2 (April, 1948): 146–67.

McCardell, John. *The Idea of a Southern Nation: Southern Nationalists and Southern Nationalism, 1830–1860.* New York: Norton, 1979.

McCurry, Stephanie. *Masters of Small Worlds: Yeoman Households, Gender Relations, and the Political Culture of the Antebellum South Carolina Low Country.* New York: Oxford University Press, 1995.

McDonnell, Michael A. *The Politics of War: Race, Class, and Conflict in Revolutionary Virginia.* Chapel Hill: University of North Carolina Press, 2007.

Tyler-McGraw, Marie. "The American Colonization Society in Virginia, 1816–1832: A Case in Southern Liberalism." Ph.D. diss., University of Michigan, 1980.

———. *An African Republic: Black and White Virginians in the Making of Liberia.* Chapel Hill: University of North Carolina Press, 2007.

McLeRoy, Sherrie S., and William R. McLeRoy. *Strangers in Their Midst: The Free Black Population of Amherst County, Virginia.* Bowie, Md.: Heritage Books, 1993.

McPherson, James M. *Battle Cry of Freedom: The Civil War Era.* New York: Oxford University Press, 1988.

Milewski, Melissa. "From Slave to Litigant: African Americans in Court in the Postwar South, 1865–1920." *Law and History Review* 30, no. 3 (August 2012): 723–69.

Mills, Quincy Terrell. "'Color-Line' Barbers and the Emergence of a Black Public Space: A Social and Political History of Black Barbers and Barber Shops, 1830–1970. Ph.D. diss., University of Chicago, 2006.

Moore, Louis. "The Elusive Center: Virginia Politics and the General Assembly, 1869–1871," *VMHB* 103, no. 2 (April 1995): 207–36.

Morgan, Edmund S. "Slavery and Freedom: The American Paradox." *The Journal of American History* 59, no. 1 (June 1972): 5–29.

Morris, Thomas D. *Southern Slavery and the Law, 1619-1860*. Chapel Hill: University of North Carolina Press, 1996.

Morrison, Toni. *Beloved*. New York: Knopf, 1987.

Nash, Gary B. *Race and Revolution*. New York: Madison House, 2001.

———. *The Forgotten Fifth: African Americans in the Age of Revolution*. Cambridge, Mass.: Harvard University Press, 2006.

Nathans, Sydney. *To Free a Family: The Journey of Mary Walker*. Cambridge, Mass.: Harvard University Press, 2012.

Novak, William J. "The Legal Transformation of Citizenship in Nineteenth-Century America." In *The Democratic Experiment: New Directions in American Political History*, edited by Meg Jacobs, William J. Novak, and Julian E. Zelizer. Princeton, N.J.: Princeton University Press, 2003.

Nicholls, Michael L. *Whispers of Rebellion: Narrating Gabriel's Conspiracy*. Charlottesville: University of Virginia Press, 2012.

Oakes, James. *Slavery and Freedom: An Interpretation of the Old South*. New York: Knopf, 1990.

O'Donovan, Susan Eva. *Becoming Free in the Cotton South*. Cambridge, Mass.: Harvard University Press, 2007.

Ó Gráda, Cormac, and Eugene N. White. "The Panics of 1854 and 1857: A View from the Emigrant Industrial Savings Bank." *Journal of Economic History* 63, no. 1 (March 2003): 213-40.

Parker, Kunal M. "Making Blacks Foreigners: The Legal Construction of Former Slaves in Post-Revolutionary Massachusetts." *Utah Law Review* (2001): 75-124.

Patterson, Orlando. *Freedom in the Making of Western Culture*. Vol. 1 of *Freedom*. New York: Basic Books, 1991.

Peters, Joan W. *Index to African-American Records in the Fauquier County, Virginia, County Court Papers, 1832-1904*. Broad Run, Va.: J. W. Peters, 2002.

Potter, David M. *The Impending Crisis, 1848-1861*. Edited by Don E. Fehrenbacher. New York: Harper and Row, 1963.

Pushkin, Alexandr. "The Queen of Spades." In *The Complete Prose Tales of Alexandr Sergeyevitch Pushkin*. Translated by Gillon R. Aitken. New York: Norton, 1966.

Pybus, Cassandra. *Epic Journeys of Freedom: Runaway Slaves of the American Revolution and Their Global Quest for Liberty*. Beacon Press: Boston, 2006.

Quarles, Benjamin. *The Negro in the American Revolution*. Chapel Hill: University of North Carolina Press, 1996.

Delaney, Ted, and Phillip Wayne Rhodes. *Free Blacks of Lynchburg, Virginia, 1805-1856*. Lynchburg, Va.: Warwick House, 2001.

Ritchie, Jeffrey Kerr. *Rites of August First: Emancipation Day in the Black Atlantic World*. Baton Rouge, La.: Louisiana State University Press, 2011.

Ruef, Martin, and Ben Fletcher. "Legacies of American Slavery: Status Attainment among Southern Blacks after Emancipation." *Social Forces* 82, no. 2 (December 2003): 445-80.

Russell, John H. *The Free Negro in Virginia, 1619-1865*. Baltimore: Johns Hopkins Press, 1913.

Schafer, Judith Kelleher. *Becoming Free, Remaining Free: Manumission and Enslavement in New Orleans, 1846–1862*. Baton Rouge: Louisiana State University Press, 2003.

Schama, Simon. *Rough Crossings: Britain, the Slaves, and the American Revolution*. New York: Ecco, 2006.

Schlotterbeck, John T. "The Internal Economy of Slavery in Rural Piedmont Virginia." In *The Slaves' Economy: Independent Production by Slaves in the Americas*, edited by Ira Berlin and Philip D. Morgan. London: Frank Cass, 1995.

Schmidt, Leigh Eric. "The Fashioning of a Modern Holiday: St. Valentine's Day, 1840–1870." *Winterthur Portfolio* 28, no. 4 (Winter 1993): 209–45.

Schwarz, Philip J. *Migrants against Slavery: Virginians and the Nation*. Charlottesville: University of Virginia Press, 2001.

———. *Gabriel's Conspiracy: A Documentary History*. Charlottesville: University of Virginia Press, 2012.

Schweninger, Loren. "Freedom Suits, African American Women, and the Genealogy of Slavery." *William and Mary Quarterly* 3rd ser., 71, no. 1 (January 2014): 35–62.

Scott, Julius S. "Afro-American Sailors and the International Communication Network: The Case of Newport Bowers," in *Jack Tar in History: Essays in the History of Maritime Life and Labour*, edited by Colin Howell and Richard Twomey. Fredericton, New Brunswick: Acadiensis Press, 1991.

Scott, Rebecca J. "Paper Thin: Freedom and Re-enslavement in the Diaspora of the Haitian Revolution." *Law and History Review* 29, no. 4 (November 2011): 1061–87.

———. "'She . . . Refuses to Deliver Up Herself as the Slave of Your Petitioner'": Émigrés, Enslavement, and the 1808 Louisiana Digest of the Civil Laws." *Tulane European and Civil Law Forum* 24 (2008): 115–36.

Scott, Rebecca J., and Jean M. Hébrard. *Freedom Papers: An Atlantic Odyssey in the Age of Emancipation*. Cambridge, Mass.: Harvard University Press, 2012.

Shade, William G. *Democratizing the Old Dominion: Virginia and the Second Party System, 1824–1861*. Charlottesville: University of Virginia Press, 1996.

Shaw, Robert B. *A Legal History of Slavery in The United States*. Potsdam, N.Y.: Northern Press, 1991.

Shepard, E. Lee. "'This Being Court Day': Courthouses and Community Life in Rural Virginia." *Virginia Magazine of History and Biography* 103, no. 4 (October 1995): 459–70.

Smith, Johanna Lee Davis. "Mulatto Bend: Free People of Color in Rural Louisiana, 1763–1865." Ph.D. diss., Tulane University, 2012.

Smith, Rogers M. *Civic Ideals: Conflicting Visions of Citizenship in U.S. History*. New Haven, Conn.: Yale University Press, 1997.

Sommerville, Diane Miller. *Rape and Race in the Nineteenth-Century South*. Chapel Hill: University of North Carolina Press, 2004.

Stampp, Kenneth M. *The Peculiar Institution: Slavery in the Ante-Bellum South*. New York: Vintage Books, 1956.

Staudenraus, P. J. *The African Colonization Movement, 1816–1865.* New York: Columbia University Press, 1961.

Stevenson, Brenda E. *Life in Black and White: Family and Community in the Slave South.* New York: Oxford University Press, 1996.

Stowe, Harriet Beecher. *Uncle Tom's Cabin, or Life among the Lowly.* Edited by Ann Douglas. New York: Penguin, 1986.

Suggs, Jon-Christian. *Whispered Consolations: Law and Narrative in African American Life.* Ann Arbor: University of Michigan Press, 2000.

Sweet, James H. *Domingos Álvares, African Healing, and the Intellectual History of the Atlantic World.* Chapel Hill: University of North Carolina Press, 2011.

Swint, Henry L. *Dear Ones at Home: Letters from Contraband Camps.* Nashville, Tenn.: Vanderbilt University Press, 1966.

Takagi, Midori. *"Rearing Wolves to Our Own Destruction": Slavery in Richmond, Virginia, 1782–1865.* Charlottesville: University of Virginia Press, 1999.

Taylor, Alan. *The Internal Enemy: Slavery and War in Virginia, 1772–1832.* New York: Norton, 2013.

Tomlins, Christopher L. *Law, Labor, and Ideology in the Early American Republic.* New York: Cambridge University Press, 1993.

Turner, Felicity. "Rights and the Ambiguities of Law: Infanticide in the Nineteenth-Century U.S. South." *Journal of the Civil War Era* 4, no. 3 (September 2014): 350–72.

Twitty, Anne Silverwood. "Slavery and Freedom in the American Confluence, from the Northwest Ordinance to Dred Scott." Ph.D. diss., Princeton University, 2010.

Van Cleve, George William. *A Slaveholder's Union: Slavery, Politics, and the Constitution in the Early American Republic.* Chicago: University of Chicago Press, 2010.

Varon, Elizabeth R. *We Mean To Be Counted: White Women and Politics in Antebellum Virginia.* Chapel Hill: University of North Carolina Press, 1998.

von Daacke, Kirt. *Freedom Has a Face: Race, Identity, and Community in Jefferson's Virginia.* Charlottesville: University of Virginia Press, 2012.

Walker, David. *Walker's Appeal, in Four Articles, together with a Preamble, to the Colored Citizens of the World . . . .* Boston, 1829 (self-published).

———. *David Walker's Appeal to the Coloured Citizens of the World.* Edited by Peter P. Hinks. University Park: Pennsylvania State University Press, 2000.

Walker, Juliet E. K. "Racism, Slavery, and Free Enterprise: Black Entrepreneurship in the United States before the Civil War." *Business History Review* 60, no. 3 (Autumn 1986): 343–82.

Watkinson, James D. "'Fit Objects of Charity': Community, Race, Faith, and Welfare in Antebellum Lancaster County, Virginia, 1817–1860." *Journal of the Early Republic* 21, no. 1 (Spring 2001): 41–70.

Watson, Walter Allen. *Notes on Southside Virginia.* Baltimore: Clearfield, 2003.

Welch, Kimberly M. "People at Law: Subordinate Southerners, Popular Governance, and Local Legal Culture in Antebellum Mississippi and Louisiana," Ph.D. diss., University of Maryland, 2012.

Welke, Barbara Young. *Law and the Borders of Belonging in the Long Nineteenth Century United States*. New York: Cambridge University Press, 2010.

West, Emily. *Family or Freedom: People of Color in the Antebellum South*. Lexington, Ky: University Press of Kentucky, 2012.

——. "'She is dissatisfied with her present condition': Requests for Voluntary Enslavement in the Antebellum American South." *Slavery and Abolition* 28, no. 3 (December 2007): 329–50.

Widmer, Ted. *Ark of the Liberties: Why American Freedom Matters to the World*. New York: Hill and Wang, 2008.

Williams, Heather Andrea. *Help Me to Find My People: The African American Search for Family Lost in Slavery*. Chapel Hill: University of North Carolina Press, 2012.

Williamson, Samuel H. "Seven Ways to Compute the Relative Value of a U.S. Dollar Amount, 1790 to Present." *MeasuringWorth* (2010), http://www.measuringworth.com/uscompare/.

Wills, Gary. *"Negro President": Jefferson and the Slave Power*. Boston: Houghton Mifflin, 2003.

Wolf, Eva Sheppard. *Race and Liberty in the New Nation: Emancipation in Virginia from the Revolution to Nat Turner's Rebellion*. Baton Rouge: Louisiana State University Press, 2006.

——. *Almost Free: A Story about Family and Race in Antebellum Virginia*. Athens: University of Georgia Press, 2012.

Young, Neely. *Ripe for Emancipation: Rockbridge and Southern Antislavery from Revolution to Civil War*. Buena Vista, Va.: Mariner Publishing, 2011.

Zolberg, Aristide R. *A Nation by Design: Immigration Policy in the Fashioning of America*. Cambridge, Mass.: Harvard University Press, 2006.

Acknowledgments

This book would not exist were it not for the guidance, inspiration, and collaborative spirit generously offered by countless students, scholars, archivists, and colleagues at a number of institutions, as well as family and friends, over many years. The shared history written above belongs to us all, though I alone am responsible for its errors, omissions, and shortcomings.

This project was born at the College of William and Mary, and I have Melvin Patrick Ely to blame. Mel introduced me to the mystical worlds of Virginia county courts and their hidden holdings, and his research, writing, and teaching continue to fire my interest in freedom, slavery, and the experiences of everyday people. I am also immensely grateful for the unflagging support of Jim La Fleur, Joseph Miller, and Scott Nelson, masters of their craft who dedicated a great deal of time and energy to conveying the rigors of scholarship and the joys of teaching.

Others also made my time at the College of William and Mary a pleasure, including Berhanu Abegaz, James Axtell, Joanne Braxton, Gail Conner, Andrew Fisher, Cindy Hahamovitch, Lisa Meyer, Terry Meyers, Neil Norman, Rich Price, and Carol Sheriff. Colleagues and friends at the Omohundro Institute of Early American History and Culture always made life in Williamsburg an adventure. I am deeply indebted to Ron Hoffman and Sally Mason—two remarkable historians and storytellers. I will always treasure my time at the Institute, due in large part to the warmth and spirit of Ron and Sally, as well as Erin Bendiner, Kathy Burdette, Kelly Crawford, Kim Foley, Chris Grasso, Shawn Holl, Gil Kelly, Virginia Montijo, Meg Musselwhite, Beverly Smith, Melody Smith, Fredrika Teute, Karin Wulf, and Nadine Zimmerli.

I cannot thank enough my colleagues and mentors who took the time to read or discuss portions of this work informally and in conference proceedings, including L. Diane Barnes, Ira Berlin, Eric Burin, Mina Donkoh, Larissa Smith Ferguson, Jim Gigantino, Sally Hadden, Daniel Hamilton, Nancy Moll Hillman, Sheri Huerta, Kelly Kennington, Deborah Lee, Jennifer Loux, Alex Lovit, Bonnie Martin, Matthew Mason, Robert Murray, Susan O'Donovan, Irene Odotei, Dylan Penningroth, Dwight Pitcaithley, Lydia Plath, Gautham Rao, Angelita Reyes, Calvin Schermerhorn, Rebecca Scott, Ibrahima Seck, Darlene Spitzer-Antezana, Janice Sumler-Edmund, Shirley Thompson, Kirt von Daacke, Andrea Watkins, and Peter Wood.

My colleagues at Randolph-Macon College—Mathias Bergmann, Michael Fischbach, Alphine Jefferson, Joseph Kyle, Mark Malvasi, Tom Porter, Anne Throckmorton, and Pat Watkinson—made Ashland a vibrant intellectual home for four years. I thank too my colleagues at J. Sargeant Reynolds Community College and Virginia Union University, especially Peter Latartara, Joseph Appiah, and Raymond Hylton.

Wonderful colleagues made for a happy, productive two years at the University of Louisiana, Lafayette. I am enormously grateful to Bob Carriker, Christine DeVine, Jo

Davis-McElligatt, Mary Farmer-Kaiser, Jack Ferstel, Rich Frankel, Judy Gentry, Rob Hermann, Jordan Kellman, Mayonna Landry, Mark Lentz, Michael Martin, Derek Mosley, Susan Nicassio, Chad Parker, Chet Rzadkiewicz, Tom Schoonover, Kim Todt, John Troutman, Sara Ritchie, and Stephanie Souter. This project benefited tremendously from a University of Louisiana, Lafayette, faculty summer research award in 2012.

I had the honor of spending an enjoyable year at the C. V. Starr Center for the Study of the American Experience with Michael Buckley, Jenifer Emley, Daniel Mark Epstein, Adam Goodheart, Lois Kitz, and Jean Wortman. Emily Chamlee-Wright, Ken Miller, Bill Schindler, Janet Sorrentino, Kathy Thornton, Carol Wilson, and many others at Washington College were immensely supportive, as were our wonderful neighbors on Mount Vernon Avenue. Sarah Brown, Armond Fletcher, Nivek Johnson, Candy Miles, Joyce B. Moody, Donald Wilkerson, Janet Wilkerson, and the entire Janes UMC family made Chestertown a home like no other.

My colleagues at Colonial Williamsburg, including Harvey Bakari, Joe Beatty, Joey Bowser, Cindy Decker, Ywone Edwards-Ingram, Lisa Fischer, Mark Fluehr, Cille Honig, Peter Inker, Lindsay Keiter, Meredith Poole, Mitchell Reiss, and Susan Wasem, (among many others) have made the colonial capital an engaging place to work and write.

This work has been enriched by the creative energy and excellent questions of my many inquisitive students over the years at Randolph-Macon College, J. Sargeant Reynolds Community College, the College of William and Mary, Virginia Union University, the University of Louisiana, Lafayette, and Washington College.

This book would not have been researched, contemplated, or completed without the expert help of a most impressive Library Reference Services team at the Library of Virginia, to whom I still owe plates of homemade cookies. Chris Kolbe assisted me with illustrations and permissions and believed in the project from the very beginning. For their invaluable assistance, I cannot thank enough Bill Bynum, Tom Crew, Virginia Dunn, Cara Griggs, Derek Gray, Sarah Huggins, Bill Luebke, Amanda Morrell, Tricia Noel, Kelly Sizemore, Dawn Tinnell, Pat Watkinson, Minor Weisiger, and Lisa Wehrmann. I also want to thank the Library of Virginia's Kristen Allen, Sherri Bagley, Vincent Brooks, Paige Buchbinder, John Deal, Joy Demery, Mark Fogerburg, Mary Hennig, Joyce A. January, Tina Miller, Sarah Nerney, Catherine O'Brion, Tanja Rhodes, Annette L. Robinson, Brent Tarter, and Vanessa Weaver for their kindness and assistance over the years.

Fellow researchers at the Library of Virginia Olen Lewis, Frankie Lyles, and Al Tillson shared their humor and discoveries with me, which made the research room much more than a work place. Major Harvey Hilton Burwell Jr. introduced himself early one morning in the library's lobby and became my archival coconspirator for more than three years. Together, we faced and shared discoveries of a painful past that brought us closer to one another, our respective family histories, and the complicated American history that binds our many traditions into one. His wit, humor, and passion for truth will remain with me forever, and I regret that this work was not completed during his lifetime.

A large portion of the research for this project was conducted in more than fifty courthouses in Virginia. Many county clerks and their assistants helped me to scour their repositories for the records I needed. I especially thank Gary Williams (Sussex County); Richard Francis (Southampton County); Karen Glover (Bedford County); Suzanne Derieux (Essex County); Jean Doyle (Augusta County); William K. Ellenburg (Highland County); Florentine Entsminger (Alleghany County); Tara Leatherwood (Prince Edward County); John Fishback (Loudoun County); Robert S. FitzSimmonds (Prince William County); Karen K. Fridley (Augusta County); Lawrence Martin (Halifax and Charlotte County); Pam Quesenberry (Fairfax County); Lois S. Ralston (Highland County); and Ann Roach (Pittsylvania County). Darlene Slater Herod and R. Michael Whitt at the Virginia Baptist Historical Society also offered invaluable advice and assistance, as did Jamison Davis and Frances Pollard at the Virginia Historical Society.

The editorial team at the University of North Carolina Press, along with two wise anonymous readers, vastly improved the project. I am especially grateful to Paul Betz, Lucas Church, Katherine Fisher, Chuck Grench, and Paula Wald, as well as Edward Connor, James Cappio, and Erin Davis, whose close reading and copyediting transformed the manuscript.

Finally, I want to thank my family for their encouragement and interest. My father, Thomas A. Wolf, a scholar and historian, read the entire draft and encouraged key editorial and substantive revision. My mother, Susan Whittlesey Wolf, my sister, Caroline, my brother, Toby, and my stepmother, Libby Wolf, encouraged me every step of the way, as did David and Beula Maris, who supported me and never doubted the eventual completion of this project. Bill Wertenbaker always kept morale high with sage Latin phrases and his sharp wit.

My wife and best friend Rachel, to whom this work is dedicated, is my hero. She is the hardest working person I know and never failed to remind me of my obligation to "do it right," no matter how long it might take. Her interest in the individuals and families detailed on these pages helped me to persevere. For her support, humor, faith, and love, I am forever grateful. And thank you to little Micah, to whom this work is also dedicated. You continue to teach us the meaning of life, love, and family.

Index

313

Doswell, William, 65–67, 92, 95
Doswell, Willis, 62–97 passim, 102–5, 119, 161–62
Douglass, Frederick, 40
Dred Scott, 159, 160
Drew, Payton, 66
Duncan, Thomas, 221 (n. 51)
Dunmore, Mary, 14, 106–7
Dunn, Susan, 228 (n. 5)
Dupuy, Asa, 124
Dupuy, Emily Howe, 124, 149
Dupuy, Joseph, 123–55 passim

Edmonson, Charles R., 198
Edwards, Laura F., 214 (n. 23), 224 (n. 8)
Egerton, Douglas R., 218 (n. 15), 219 (n. 25)
Eggborn, John H., 266 (n. 89)
Eliza (Lunenburg Co., Va.), 68
Elizabeth, Mary, 157–91 passim
Elliott, Leah, 220 (n. 40)
Ely, Melvin Patrick, 218 (n. 21), 243 (n. 41), 252 (n. 87), 265 (n. 77)
Emancipation: proposed, 25, 38; factors affecting, 157–58; celebration of, 192, 274 (n. 1)
Emanuel (Richmond City, Va.), 50
Enslaved people: and Virginia courts, 64; and literacy, 128, 133; with store accounts, 130
Eslinger, Ellen, 219 (n. 30)
Essex County, Va., 34, 35, 51, 212 (n. 4)
Evans, Adah, 110
Evans, George, 110
Ewell family, 31–32, 57, 110
Expulsion: rationale behind, 1; law of 1806, 8, 27, 47, 69, 85; law enforced, 8, 30–31, 69, 107–13, 139, 164, 243 (n. 38); law resulting in sale as slave, 106–7; threat of, 112, 158; and colonization, 138–39

Fairfax County, Va., 21
Fairfax Seminary, 190

Family: separation of, 4–5, 89, 118, 134, 137, 140, 150, 156, 258 (n. 1), 259 (n. 15); as impetus for running away, 89; and colonization, 134, 137, 140–41, 150; and Civil War, 156–91; reunification of, 258 (n. 1)
Farmville, Va., 132
Farmville Journal, 142, 145
Faro, 64, 70, 229 (n. 6)
Farrar, Sam, 200
Fauquier County, Va., 29, 52, 117, 124, 156–91, 211 (n. 2)
Feggins, Matthew, 197–98
Finkelman, Paul, 214 (n. 23)
First Baptist Church of Richmond, 225 (n. 15)
Fisher, Miers W., 41, 223 (n. 79)
Fitch family, 197, 276 (n. 21)
Fletcher, Ben, 274 (n. 4)
Fletcher, Fanny, 177
Fletcher, Mary, 157–91 passim
Fletcher, Sally, 177
Fletcher, Viana, 177
Florida, 175
Floyd, John, 30, 65
Flynt, Betty, 140–41
Ford, Hezekiah, 225 (n. 16)
Ford, Rachel, 148
Forman, Isaac, 4–5
Forsythe, Harold S., 279 (n. 41)
Foster, Josiah W., 67
Foster, Worsham, 274 (n. 1), 276 (n. 20), 280 (n. 63)
Fourteenth Amendment, 62
Fowlkes, William J., 92
Fox, Elisha, 111
Frances, Araminta, 3, 68, 99, 104–5, 119, 162, 169
Frances, Mary, 125, 206, 209, 248 (n. 28)
Francis, John C., 190–91
Francis, Nellie B., 156
Franklin, Joel, 170
Franklin, John Hope, 244 (n. 59)
Franklin County, Va., 53
Frazier, Hannah, 66

Frederick County, Va., 1, 6–12, 21, 39, 114, 169

Fredericksburg, Va., 48, 60

Free blacks: and belonging, 1, 14, 50, 62, 138, 167; and rights, 2, 86; use of legal system, 3, 5, 48–62, 113–14, 118–19; and state law, 5, 64; meanings of freedom to, 7, 20, 95, 119–20, 134, 147–48, 150, 153; conception of home, 28, 51, 119, 134, 136, 137, 150, 151, 157, 165; certificates of good character for, 42, 50–51; and property ownership, 51, 60; ordered to be sold as slaves, 57, 164, 241–42 (n. 34); mobility of, 181

Freedmen's Bureau, 262 (n. 51)

Freedom: meanings of to free blacks, 7, 20, 95, 119–20, 134, 147–48, 150, 153; fragility of, 9; of whites in relation to slavery, 16, 25, 124–25; vs. concept of liberty, 215 (n. 34); expectations of, 249 (n. 45)

Freedom suits, 58–59, 112, 183–84, 221 (n. 40), 271 (n. 138), 277 (n. 24)

Freehling, Alison Goodyear, 221 (n. 45), 253 (n. 91)

Freeman, Adolphus, 184

Freeman, Mason, 184

Freeman, Sam, 184

Free papers. See Registration

Fry, Joseph, 140–41

Fugitive slaves, 4, 32, 126, 242 (n. 36), 248 (n. 28)

Gabriel's Rebellion, 26–27, 58, 219 (n. 23)

Gambling, 64, 67, 70. See also Faro

Gant, Nelson Talbert, 220 (n. 30)

Gardening, 107, 114

Gardner, Thomas, 167

Garms (Richmond City, Va.), 227 (n. 51)

George Jr. (Prince Edward Co., Va.), 131

Georgia, 147, 175

Gettysburg, Pa., 36

Giles County, Va., 21

Gileson, David A., 248 (n. 37)

Gilkerson and McNutt, 127

Gillison, Catharine, 275 (n. 15)

Gillison, Fanny, 195, 216 (n. 48)

Gillison, Frank, 275 (n. 15)

Glascock, Jerry, 142, 216 (n. 48)

Goens, William, 267 (n. 104)

Goff, James, 244 (n. 55)

Goings, Thomas, 169

Goochland County, Va., 83, 84–86

Goode, Lucy, 55

Goode, Thomas F., 195, 198, 200, 203, 204, 278 (n. 41)

Graves, James R., 181

Gray, James, 68

Grayson, Satchell, 108–11, 113, 114, 166

Grayson, Thomas, 78, 102, 110, 264 (n. 75)

Grayson, William, 110

Green, James S., 173

Greensville County, Va., 166

Gregory, Richard, 51, 54

Gross, Ariela, 213 (n. 11), 214 (nn. 23–24)

Gustavus, Alpheus Adolphus, 68

Hadden, Sally, 213 (n. 9)

Hahn, Steven, 272 (n. 153)

Haiti. See Saint-Domingue

Hale, Celia, 170, 174, 181–82

Halifax County, Va., 162, 170, 179, 242 (n. 36)

Ham, Betsy, 55, 227 (n. 49)

Ham, Robinson, 55, 227 (n. 49)

Hamilton, John, 60

Hamilton, Ross, 204–5

Hancock, Morgan, 179

Hanover County, Va., 48, 55, 167

Hardy, George W., 70, 77, 91, 101, 104, 162

Harman, Frank, 102

Harman, Michael G., 197

Harpers Ferry, W.Va., 164

Harris, James, 55

Harris, John, 242 (n. 36)

Harris, Lucy, 60

Harris, Samuel, 51

Harrison, B. E., 75

Sherman, William T., 201
Simon (Southhampton Co., Va.), 102, 183–84
Sindler, William, 108
Skurry, David, 52
Skurry, Mrs., 52
Slavery: centrality to American history, 5; and whites' happiness, 16; argued as essential, 88–90; modernization of, 130–31
Slaves. *See* Enslaved people
Slave trade (U.S.), 122, 246 (n. 5)
Slocum, Nellie B., 190–91
Small, William F., 198
Smith, Charles, 92
Smith, Edwin, 167
Smith, Mary H., 168
Smith, Robert J., 123–55 passim
Smith, William, 33–40, 65, 83, 161, 222 (nn. 57, 60)
Sommerville, Diane M., 230 (n. 18)
Southampton County, Va., 29, 81, 102, 183–84
South Carolina, 25, 175
Spencer, Jesse, 102
Spinning, 29, 68, 121
Squire, Tom, 170
Stafford County, Va., 79, 126
Stanton (Culpeper Co., Va.), 78, 139
Staples, Thomas, 231 (n. 20)
Staudenraus, P. J., 246 (n. 8)
Staunton, Va., 197
Steamship, 4, 133
Steptoe, James, 275 (n. 17)
Stevens, Betsy, 179
Stevens, Nora, 179
Stewart, Adeline, 265 (n. 82)
Stewart, John, 212 (n. 7)
Still, William, 5
St. Louis, Mo., 193
Stokes, Jonathan A., 70, 81, 92
Stores, 127–28, 150
Stowe, Harriet Beecher, 212 (n. 1)
Stratton, William, 55
Stryker, Richard, 138, 146, 152

Stubbs, John S., 60
Suggs, Jon-Christian, 215 (n. 44)
Summerall, John C., 183
Supreme Court (U.S.), 159
Susan (Rockbridge Co., Va.), 127–28
Sussex County, Va., 111–12, 181
Sylla Jane (Rockbridge Co., Va.), 127–29

Takagi, Midori, 262 (n. 51)
Tatum, Isham, 187
Tatum, Nathaniel, 187
Taverns, 4, 67, 70
Taxes: nonpayment of, 6, 25, 242 (n. 36); exemption to, 43. *See also* Capitation tax
Taylor, Creed, 16
Taylor, Laura, 174
Taylor, William, 174
Tebbs, Betsy, 124, 174
Tebbs, Charles B., Jr., 174
Tebbs, Charles B., Sr., 174
Terrell, John, 247 (n. 16)
Texas, 175
Thomas (Richmond City, Va.), 55
Thompson, Lucas Powell, 116
Tinsley, James J., 265 (n. 82)
Tobacco, 63, 105, 131, 172
Tom (Chesterfield Co., Va.), 125
Topping, Nathaniel, 41, 43
Towles, Bettie C., 169, 181
Trans-Alleghany region (Va.), 30–31, 63, 72, 86
True Republicans, 205
Tucker, St. George, 38
Tucker, Stephen D., 179
Turner, Nat, 29, 31, 41, 47
Tyler, John, 64
Tyler-McGraw, Marie, 219 (n. 25), 246 (n. 7), 251 (n. 73)

Underground Railroad, 4, 193
Upshur, Abel P., 31

Vai (Liberia), 133, 144
Valentine's Day, 127, 248 (n. 33)

CPSIA information can be obtained at www.ICGtesting.com
Printed in the USA
LVOW11s1710200916

505434LV00006BA/1272/P